DISCOVER

Israel
& the West Bank

MOON

ISREAL & THE WEST BANK

GENEVIEVE BELMAKER

Contents

Israel and the West Bank are lands of religious pilgrimages and ancient stories, where even the bodies of water whisper of miracles and the faithful of multiple religions carry out their observances. Yet they are also places where modern, secular life thrives and some of the most advanced technology in the world is born.

This deeply significant region to the three largest monotheistic religions in the world—Judaism, Christianity, and Islam—is filled with timeworn stones that have witnessed thousands of years of epic history. That history continues to unfold even today through news headlines that capture the attention of the world.

Many people dream for their entire lives of journeying here, largely for religious reasons. The numerous archaeological and anthropological sites, museums, and more make it a prime destination for students and scholars as well.

The diversity in beliefs and lifestyles can make your trip a journey toward connection and understanding. The crown jewel for most visitors is Jerusalem, a city that is bursting at the seams with incredible historical and religious adventures alongside fine restaurants, excellent shopping choices, and an

Clockwise from top left: stained glass window in a Jerusalem church; local women walking in Petra; the Dome of the Rock; traditional sweets available at the *shuk*; clock tower in Akko; colorful *kippot* for sale.

ever-increasing vast array of entertainment for every taste and age. As much as Jerusalem makes the past feel present, liberal, freewheeling Tel Aviv is intently focused on the future. The fresh scent of sand and sea seems soaked into everything, and marketplaces smell of spices, falafel, and Turkish coffee. It's an assault on the senses, in the best possible way. North along the Mediterranean in sparkling Haifa, Jews and Arabs coexist peacefully in the shadow of the world-famous Baha'i Golden Dome.

The West Bank, with its ancient cities of Bethlehem, Jericho, and Hebron and the more modern city of Ramallah, offers a journey into another world. On a hot summer day with the warm smell of olive trees set against a backdrop of rolling brown hills, you'll almost forget the political tensions that have troubled this area for centuries.

Is it any wonder this region has inspired such passions, such creativity, such devotion, such faith? Beyond the history books and news headlines, it must be experienced firsthand to be truly appreciated.

Clockwise from top left: the beaches and promenade at Tel Aviv; the Baha'i Gardens in Haifa; Christmas in Nazareth; floating in the Dead Sea.

Planning Your Trip

Where to Go

Jerusalem

A city of just over 800,000 people and an important locale to the three major religions of Judaism, Christianity, and Islam, Jerusalem seems older than time itself and is enthralling with its dozens of **archaeological, religious, and historical sites and museums.** When you tire of tours and history lessons, it is just as interesting to stroll through the unique districts of the city, such as the **German Colony,** with its many family entertainment options, lush greenery, unique homes, and numerous shops, and then stop for a **world-class meal** in one of the city's many restaurants. A classic destination for **religious pilgrimage,** Jerusalem also has a **lively arts scene** and some **nightlife** offerings, though it is tame compared to Tel Aviv. A claim to fame is that it is home to more museums than anywhere else in Israel.

Tel Aviv

Tel Aviv isn't called the "center" for nothing, with a dizzying offering of **restaurants, clubs, museums, performing arts venues** of all sizes, **nightlife, music, beaches, surfing,** and **outdoor sports.** The first modern Jewish city, Tel Aviv has earned its reputation as the core of contemporary Israeli life. It is a place known for its openly accepting atmosphere of all kinds of people, a high-powered technical and business sector, and the heart of the country's famed diamond industry. Tel Aviv's **world-class parks** and recreation offerings are at the heart of its many **summer festivals, events, and live concerts.** It is, far and away, the most popular place in Israel to party and just enjoy life.

Haifa and the North Coast

Once you're in Haifa, Israel's third largest city, situated on the coast about an hour north of Tel Aviv, you can easily jump off to other charming coastal towns and nearby historical and religious sites, such as **Akko, Caesarea,** and **Zichron Ya'akov,** with minimal hassle. The life of Haifa, the only city in Israel with any public transportation on the weekend, revolves around the dominating **Baha'i Gardens and Golden Dome.** You can spend days just going between exploring Haifa's **museums, restaurants, and beaches** and then wandering through the serene and pristine grounds of the Baha'i Gardens.

If You Have ...

- **ONE WEEK:** Jerusalem and Tel Aviv
- **10 DAYS:** Add Haifa, the Dead Sea and Bethlehem
- **TWO WEEKS:** Add the Negev, the Sea of Galilee, and Akko
- **ONE MONTH:** Add Jericho, Ramallah, Eilat, and Petra

market in Jerusalem's Old City

the Sea of Galilee with the Golan Heights in the background

The Galilee and the Golan Heights

The north of Israel encompasses the **Upper Galilee,** the **Lower Galilee,** and the **Golan Heights,** home to some of the most **gorgeous parks** and **nature reserves** that include countless **hiking and camping** opportunities. The area is known for its **world-class wineries** and numerous significant **archaeological, religious, and historical sites.** The Golan and the Galilee are also home to some **fascinating people,** like the Druze; important cities, like **Nazareth;** and spiritually moving locales, like the **Sea of Galilee.**

The West Bank

The West Bank is where many important **historic and religious sites,** including the towns of **Bethlehem, Jericho,** and **Hebron,** can be found. The Arab city of **Ramallah,** just a short drive from Jerusalem, is the hub of **Arab arts and culture** in the West Bank and known for the important cultural **festivals** it puts on every year. A complex security situation requires advance planning.

Eilat and the Negev

The bosom of the **Negev Desert,** which makes up more than half of Israel's landmass, the south is considered by many to be **wild and untamed** in many ways, though it is also an up-and-coming tech center. A popular destination for **desert ecotourism,** the Negev is the perfect place to experience **camping out under the stars** and discovering the unique beauty of the desert on **long hikes.** Home to the **Dead Sea,** the lowest point on Earth, the south is sparsely populated, but boasts the thriving tourist hub of **Eilat** at its far south end. Eilat has some of the best **coral diving** in the world, **tax-free shopping,** and it is the gateway to Petra, Jordan.

Petra, Jordan

Nothing can prepare you for the incomparable experience of seeing the **ancient Nabataean city** of Petra. Once the capital city of powerful and wealthy spice route merchants, modern Petra is a **massive archaeological site** that takes several days to explore thoroughly. Replete with **hikes** of varying lengths that end at gorgeous archaeological finds, Petra can be experienced in tandem with the immediately adjacent **Arab village Wadi Musa,** with its many offerings of **Bedouin food and hospitality.**

Know Before You Go

High and Low Seasons

There are distinct high and low seasons in this region. The **high season** is **April-October** (approximately from Passover through Sukkot on the Jewish calendar), and the **low season** is **November-March.** Check the calendar carefully before planning your trip with an eye out for **major Jewish, Christian, and Muslim holidays.** The airfare and cost of hotels will be much higher during those times, and many businesses and tourist sites will be closed or have shorter hours.

The three **most challenging times** to visit are during the Jewish holiday of **Passover week** (approximately the end of March), which ends in the Christian holiday of **Easter Sunday,** and during the week of the Jewish holiday of **Sukkot** (approximately the end of October). The month-long Muslim holiday of **Ramadan,** around **July-August,** puts a bit of a damper on any sightseeing related to sites in the West Bank.

Easter observances draw many pilgrims to Jerusalem.

A generally **good period to visit,** when it is not too hot and not too cold, and there are not too many holidays to affect the opening and closing of sites is any time in **April-June.**

Try to **avoid visiting Jerusalem during August,** when the heat coupled with the chaos of annual vacations and events among local residents make for an overwhelming (not in a good way) experience. Essentially, the city becomes **extremely crowded.**

Passports and Visas

Many countries have a **visa waiver agreement** with Israel, including the United States, Canada, and the United Kingdom, which means you only need to purchase a round-trip ticket to show your impending departure. You will be issued a **visa** upon entering Israel. Your **passport** must be good for at least six months past the date of your departure from the country.

Tel Aviv's Ben Gurion International Airport

Security

Check any travel advisories from foreign governments, such as the U.S. Department of State's travel advisories section on its website, before departing. Sporadic violence might mean that you choose not to visit a certain area.

Transportation

The best and most common way to get to this region is by airplane which will take you to Tel Aviv's **Ben Gurion International Airport.** Entry from Jordan or Egypt is also possible by **car,** and arrival by **cruise ship** over international waters commonly occurs via the **Port of Haifa. Eilat Airport** in the south handles domestic flights if that is your final destination.

Though the geographic area is fairly small (you can drive from the northern to southern border in one day), the complex security situation does require some advance planning. Within most towns and cities—particularly Tel Aviv, Haifa, Jerusalem and Eilat—**public transportation and taxis** make it fairly easy to get around. For travel beyond isolated locales, it is best to get a **rental car.** Long-distance **buses** will also get you around cheaply and efficiently, but they can require a sense of adventure and extra time for potential mishaps. The **Israel Railways train** is also an option, especially for going to and from the airport.

What to Pack

Bringing the right clothing is incredibly important, particularly **comfortable shoes,** as there is a lot of rough terrain and bumpy cobblestones at various tourist sites, parks, and some cities. In some places you will be need to **dress conservatively,** particularly if you're a woman. A few long-sleeve shirts, pants, and long skirts should suffice. At least one cotton scarf to guard against dusty winds, chills, and sweat is a must for men and women. A scarf can be easily purchased once there, too.

Stick to skirts that are either below the knee or more fitted, and lower-heeled or flat shoes, preferably with more support so you won't twist your ankle while walking on the uneven stones.

No matter when you go, take some kind of a **light jacket** (heavier in the winter months), as it can get cool in many areas during the evening. You will also need a **hat, sunglasses, sunscreen,** and a **good water canister** if you have one. Beyond that, you will just need a sense of adventure and a **good guidebook.**

Best of Israel and the West Bank

If you are traveling to Israel and the West Bank with the intention of having a wide variety of experiences, mapping out at least a general strategy is a must. This itinerary describes how to get a taste of the best of the region in two weeks, and includes the major highlights and most popular sites of several cities and regions.

Jerusalem
DAY 1

Have breakfast at your hotel and get an early start to the **Old City** to beat the heat and crowds. Take the most accessible entrance at the Jaffa Gate, and stop by the information center for any current happenings and available tours. From here you can also start to explore with a visit to either the **Rockefeller Archaeological Museum** or the **Tower of David Museum.**

Follow the main road downhill through the tightly packed shops selling all kinds of scarves, food, trinkets, jewelry, and souvenirs and try your hand at the regional custom of negotiating for a deal. Then head for the **Church of the Holy Sepulchre,** built on the spot where many believe Jesus was crucified, buried, and resurrected. From here, head to the **Austrian Hospice** for an incredible view of old and new Jerusalem from the rooftop and a piece of famous apple strudel in the quiet gardens.

After leaving the Austrian Hospice, wander around a bit as you work your way toward the **Western Wall, Al Aqsa Mosque,** and the **Dome of the Rock.** Pass the Western Wall and keep going toward the outer wall of the Old City, toward the **City of David** archaeological site. Here you can take a guided tour and walk through the ancient **Hezekiah's Tunnel,** knee-high in water. Skip the tunnel if you are claustrophobic, but if you're not, bring a flashlight.

Go back toward the Old City and take one of

Jerusalem's Old City

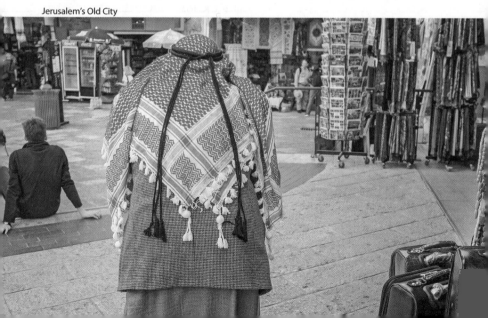

the many waiting taxis to dinner in City Center, preferably somewhere off of King David Street or in the popular pedestrian plaza and historic neighborhood of **Nahalat Shiva.**

DAY 2

Take a taxi to the popular outdoor pedestrian shopping center **Mamilla,** where you can have breakfast alfresco at one of the restaurants with a vista of the new city and the landmark **Montefiore Windmill.** From Mamilla, it is a quick hop to the Old City, where you can check out anything you missed the previous day, such as the popular **Ramparts Walk tour** that circles the Old City along the top of the walls. Alternatively, there is the walk up the belfry tower at the **Church of the Redeemer** for one of the most highly rated and under-visited 360-degree views of the Old City.

Before it gets too late, exit the Old City through the Zion Gate and head up the hillside to **Mount Zion,** where some believe that Jesus held the Last Supper and King David's Tomb can be found. Don't let anybody talk you into making a "donation" here; the site is free. At Mount Zion you will

also find the lovely **Dormition Abbey** and great vistas of the city from multiple vantage points.

Take a taxi to the top of the **Mount of Olives,** where you will see the view of the Old City of Jerusalem that Jesus is said to have shed tears over when telling of its coming destruction. Go by foot into the nearby Arab village and have lunch at one of the many small restaurants serving Arab food before heading back down the hillside by taxi. Ask to be dropped off at the **Church of the Pater Noster,** and then walk downhill to the nearby **Dome and Chapel of the Ascension** and the **Garden of Gethsemane.**

From the Garden of Gethsemane, it is a long walk or a quick taxi ride to a City Center restaurant; try something near Tolerance Square this time.

DAY 3

Enjoy breakfast at your hotel before heading out to see some of Jerusalem's museums. Go by bus or taxi to **The Israel Museum,** about 20 minutes west of the Old City by car. Allow at least a half day to explore the museum and its rich, famed exhibits specializing in Judaica and

Bible Lands Museum in Jerusalem

Tel Aviv's Dizengoff Center

Jewish history as well as regional history. Take advantage of the museum's restaurant for lunch and hop across the street to the **Bible Lands Museum.** Then take a taxi to the nearby and underrated **Monastery of the Cross,** located in the valley where the wood for Jesus's cross is said to have been taken from. From here take another taxi to **Yad Vashem** Holocaust memorial, or walk five minutes to the bus that will take you to the light-rail. The light-rail will deliver you to **Mount Herzl** and the associated Herzl museum, near the shuttle buses that take you down Yad Vashem's long drive. Allow at least four hours and some time for food or a cold drink at the cafeteria where you can meditate on the sweeping view of the Jerusalem forest.

From Yad Vashem, take the light-rail train to City Center and the famous **Machane Yehuda Market** (the *shuk*), where you can wander around and finish with dinner in one of the *shuk*'s many wonderful restaurants or cafés. In the evening, the *shuk*'s nightlife cranks up, and the quiet pubs turn into hopping parties, some with live music.

Tel Aviv
DAY 4
BUS FROM JERUSALEM (1 HOUR)

Go by bus from Jerusalem to **Tel Aviv** in the morning after breakfast (and after rush hour)—it's very easy to go back and forth between these cities by bus. After checking in at your hotel, take a stroll around **Dizengoff Center**'s great shopping district, and stop by the **Bauhaus Center** to pick up maps and information about Tel Aviv's famed **White City** and available tours. Stay near Dizengoff to enjoy one of the area's many outstanding restaurants for lunch.

After lunch, get ready for a late afternoon beach session (in summer months wait until after 2pm at the earliest). Take water and a change of clothes so you can go straight to dinner afterward. Try **Aviv Beach,** just north of Charles Clore Park, or any of the beaches that are north of Charles Clore Park but south of the Marina. From Aviv Beach, take a nice 25-minute stroll to the **HaTachana Train Station Complex** for some shopping and dining; make sure to check out the **Made in TLV** store. Five minutes away, wander through Tel Aviv's historic **Neve Tzedek** neighborhood, the oldest neighborhood in the city, for a European-style dinner. If you can recharge at your hotel, head back out to party when things get started at the clubs around midnight.

DAY 5

Take a rest from the sun and nightlife of Tel Aviv to see the new and extremely popular addition of **Sarona** market for some shopping and cuisine. Self-described as the "heartbeat of Israeli culinary art," it is an assault of regional colors and smells. Stay for a wine-tasting, try some olive oil straight from the press, and enjoy a three-course gourmet meal.

From the market, take a taxi or bus to one of the city's offerings of museums, including the **Tel Aviv Museum of Art.** Take in the best view of the city at the **Azrieli Observatory** just before sunset, and then head back down to city level for dinner in one of the many nearby restaurants. You can take the train back to your hotel from **Azrieli Center** after doing any shopping in the mall there if needed.

DAY 6
DRIVE TO HAIFA (1 HOUR)

Before checking out of your Tel Aviv hotel, head to the north of the city and have a breakfast of *shakshuka* eggs at one of the **Port of Tel Aviv**'s many seaside restaurants. If you time it right, you can catch the weekly **outdoor market.** Swing by **Old Jaffa** for an afternoon of sightseeing at one of the oldest ports in the world.

A good place to start in Old Jaffa is just off Yefet Street. From there you can wander around the center and the nearby promenade for some scenic, wish-you-were-here photographs of the Mediterranean Sea. Look for the **clock tower,** surrounded by galleries and shops for browsing, as an anchoring landmark. Stay in Old Jaffa for lunch at one of their many world-class restaurants that serve up Arabic specialties, often with a European twist.

Pick up a rental car for the short drive to **Haifa,** about an hour north of Tel Aviv. Leave some daylight, because the road to Haifa hugs the scenic shoreline of the Mediterranean most of the way. Once you've settled into one of Haifa's gorgeous boutique hotels in the historic

the fashionable Neve Tzedek neighborhood of Tel Aviv

a section of the Baha'i Gardens in Haifa

A visitor walks along the ruins at Caesarea.

German Colony, have dinner under the twinkling lights of the Baha'i Gardens and Golden Dome at one of the area's many sumptuous restaurants.

Caesarea and Zichron Ya'akov
DAY 7
DRIVE FROM HAIFA (30 MINUTES TO CAESAREA, THEN 20 MINUTES TO ZICHRON YA'AKOV)
After breakfast, set out from Haifa for the Caesarea National Antiquities Park, where you can spend most of the day exploring the gorgeous Roman ruins by the sea that include the aqueduct, an amphitheater, mosaic floors, and bathhouses. There are many great options for lunch at the old Port, which also has some nice shops showing off the work of local artisans.

Just 20 minutes up the coast is the charming Mediterranean village of Zichron Ya'akov with a redesigned town center created to foster sidewalk café culture, with street musicians and all kinds of locally made arts. There are also several places to enjoy regionally produced wine. After dinner, head back to Haifa.

Haifa
DAY 8
Plan to start your day early and spend it exploring Haifa by car or by ample public transportation, including the city's subway—the only subway in Israel.

Start at the top of the Baha'i Gardens and Golden Dome for an incomparable view of the Mediterranean Sea and the Haifa Port. Take the middle entrance if you want to explore more of the gardens, but check visiting hours in advance, as they fluctuate. For more views and strolling, the nearby Louis Promenade off of Yefe Nof Street is fantastic and leads to the small but elegant Mane Katz Museum and the Tikotin Museum of Japanese Art.

At the top of Mount Carmel in Haifa is the Stella Maris Carmelite Monastery, with its small, but extensively painted, domed chapel and peaceful grounds filled with tropical plants and flowers. Just across the street from Stella Maris is the San Francisco Observation Point with a multilingual and comprehensive audio history of the area. Steps away is Haifa's cable car, which will take you down the mountainside to Bat Galim Promenade. Next to the promenade aerial view of Acre Old City and the waterfront

are **Elijah's Cave** and the **National Maritime Museum.**

For dinner, some of the best options in the most idyllic setting are located in the **German Colony,** at the base of the Baha'i Gardens. The area is small, so it's easy to wander through and find a range of options.

Akko (Acre)
DAY 9
DRIVE FROM HAIFA (30 MINUTES TO AKKO, THEN 1 HOUR TO TIBERIAS)

Leave your hotel by car for the 30-minute drive to Akko (also called Acre), where you can spend the day touring the **Acre Old City** and its network of **Crusader walls, fortresses, knights' halls, and tunnels.** Before lunch, take the long walk to the **Templars' Tunnel,** and stop near the *shuk* on the way back for some falafel and hummus. On your way out of Akko, you'll pass by the **Baha'i Gardens,** which are just as serene as their sister site in Haifa, but much smaller. Entrance is free and there is parking, so stop in for a look. Then make the one-hour drive from Akko to **Tiberias,** check into your hotel and have dinner at one of the many restaurants in the town center on the shore of the **Sea of Galilee,** where you can enjoy the sunset and the moonrise over the waters if you time it right.

Tiberias
DAY 10

After breakfast in Tiberias, drive to the nearby grouping of historic and archaeological sites just 15 minutes away. Start at the archaeological site at **Magdala,** a 1st-century synagogue where Jesus is believed to have taught and where the earliest known depiction of the Second Temple in Jerusalem exists. Next head to the **Mount of Beatitudes,** where the Sermon on the Mount was given by Jesus, with its serene gardens and wonderful vista of the Sea of Galilee. Then head to the breathtaking archaeological and religious site of **Capernaum.** From Capernaum, leave your car and follow the footpath that hugs the shore of the Sea of Galilee for about 30 minutes until you reach **Tabgha** and the **Church of the Multiplication,** where bread and fish were multiplied by Jesus to feed thousands. Have dinner in Tiberias or take a short drive to one of the regional, family-run restaurants in the area.

Petra

The Dead Sea
DAY 11
DRIVE FROM TIBERIAS (2.5 HOURS)

Drive from Tiberias straight south to the Dead Sea for some rest and relaxation. It's a 2.5-hour run, so take a break along the way by stopping at the renowned archaeological site of **Beit She'an.** Once you've checked into your Dead Sea hotel, go to one of the many beaches to float on the **salty waters** and slather **therapeutic mud** on your body. Take your time and enjoy a leisurely dinner at an area restaurant before going back to your hotel.

DAY 12
DRIVE TO EILAT (2.5 HOURS)

Start out early before it gets too hot and take the tram to the famed archaeological site of Masada where it is said that a small band of Jews held off the Roman army. The views of the Dead Sea below and Jordan in the distance are incomparable. Take a picnic lunch and stop by the **Ein Gedi Nature Reserve** and its 2,000-year-old **natural spring** that flows down the mountainside and forms multiple **waterfalls and pools** along the way. You can swim in many of the pools, the best of which is about a 15-minute walk from the park

entrance. Drive from Ein Gedi to **Eilat** (2.5 hours) and stay overnight.

Petra, Jordan
DAY 13
DRIVE FROM EILAT (2 HOURS)

Start out early and get to the Eilat-Aqaba border by taxi (about 10 minutes). After crossing the border, go by taxi to one of Aqaba's many car rental offices and pick up a car for the two-hour drive to **Petra.** Once you are in Petra, take an afternoon hike, and a late afternoon lunch in one of the restaurants in the village adjacent to Petra, **Wadi Musa.** Spend the rest of the afternoon exploring Wadi Musa, and do a bit of shopping. After a rest at your hotel, head back by foot to get dinner in town, and try some local Bedouin food.

DAY 14

Start off from your hotel early for a **morning hike** in Petra up one of the paths that leads to a high vantage point so you can see the area. Make sure to stop at the **Petra Nabataean Museum** and see the antiquities that have been found over the years. Go by foot back out to Wadi Musa for an early lunch and head out of town in your rental car for Aqaba and the Israel border.

A Middle East Feast

Certain towns in Israel and the West Bank are known for specializing in a regional cuisine. While there are long-standing debates over where the best of certain dishes originate, some undisputed reigning champions exist.

For **hummus,** the Arab village Abu Ghosh just outside of Jerusalem is high on the list. At **The Lebanese Restaurant** (65 Kvish Ha-Shalom, tel. 02/533-2019, 11am-11pm daily, NIS30), at the entrance to the village, the decor is spartan but the food is divine. Multiple additional options are within easy walking distance. Farther up the coast, Akko's hummus is known far and wide. A renowned favorite is **Hummus Said** (middle of the Old City market area off Salah ad Din St., tel. 04/991-3945, 6am-2:30pm Sun.-Fri., NIS30) for its traditional presentation, cheap prices, and central location.

Ruin yourself on the popular Arab sweet treat *knafe* by trying it first in the West Bank Arab village of Nablus. Go anywhere in the Old City and you will easily find vendors preparing it fresh.

Decent **falafel** can be found almost everywhere in the region, but if you really want to experience it hot and fresh, the *shuk* in almost any town will have offerings. In Jerusalem, a reigning falafel master is **Yemenite Falafel** (48 Hanevi'im St., tel. 02/624-2346, 9:30am-9:30pm Sun.-Thurs., 9:30am-3pm Fri., NIS40). Another extremely popular falafel joint is **Moshiko** (5 Ben Yehuda St., tel. 050/535-6861, 9am-midnight Sun.-Thurs., 9am-2pm Fri., NIS50), with its bright sign that is easy to spot.

No trip to the Middle East would be complete without **pita.** In south Tel Aviv's Jaffa, **Abulafia Bakery** (7 Yefet St., tel. 03/683-0958, 24 hours a day

the Arab sweet treat *knafe* for sale in the Old City of Nablus

Sun.-Sat., NIS20) is renowned for its pita and Arab sweet treats.

Many try to claim the title of the best *shakshuka* ever created, but if you're new to the dish, Jerusalem's **Tmol Shilshom** (5 Solomon St. through the back alley, tel. 02/623-2758, www.tmol-shilshom.co.il, 9am-1am Sun.-Thurs., 9am-3pm Fri., NIS55) has mastered this regional staple dish of eggs, tomatoes, and other vegetables. Tel Aviv's **Dr. Shakshuka** (3 Beit Eshel St., tel. 057/944-4193, http://shakshuka.rest.co.il, 8am-midnight Sun.-Thurs., NIS45) is widely known by reputation and considered a reigning champion of the cuisine. A very inventive and increasingly popular *shakshuka* option in Tel Aviv can be found at **Shakshukia** (94 Ben Yehuda St., tel. 03/522-3433, 10am-10pm Sun.-Thurs., 10am-4pm Fri., NIS60).

Tasty hummus and pita are found throughout Israel and the West Bank.

Mamilla shopping center

Journey into Jerusalem

Though six days is just enough to scratch the surface of what Jerusalem has to offer, this section maps out a travel strategy with an emphasis on archaeological sites alongside new attractions and places to eat and play. Think **ancient archaeological sites** in and around the Old City by day, and **rooftop drinks and food** overlooking the city or live music by night. It also includes a few notable places in the vicinity of Jerusalem. The time frame is divided based on the days of the week, due to Jerusalem's limited access during Shabbat (Fri.-Sat. night).

Day 1: Sunday

After a good night's sleep at your hotel, put on your most comfortable shoes and get ready for some serious walking in the **Old City.** Start from the information center at the Jaffa Gate, and pick a couple of key points in the Old City to explore, but allow for plenty of time to wander, take photos, and bargain for deals.

From the Jaffa Gate, you can easily explore the

Armenian Quarter (mostly residential) and loop back up to the **Jewish Quarter** and the old Roman **Cardo,** which includes some high-end shopping. Keep going north to the **Christian Quarter** and you can see a number of churches, including the **Church of the Holy Sepulchre.** Head back out to the foot of the Jaffa Gate where you can take in the air-conditioned shops and bookstores at modern and upscale **Mamilla,** and have lunch and a coffee.

Walk from Mamilla to **Nahalat Shiva,** where you can spend a couple of leisurely hours exploring the shops full of handmade crafts, before you walk to the **Jerusalem Time Elevator** exhibit for an interactive trip through Jerusalem history. Stay in Nahalat Shiva for dinner to experience one of Jerusalem's most famous and authentically Middle Eastern restaurants, **Tmol Shilshom.**

Day 2: Monday

After a leisurely breakfast, get a picnic lunch and

the Shrine of the Book at the Israel Museum

head to **The Israel Museum** by taxi or bus for a late morning viewing session of antiquities and Jewish and regional history and art, including the Shrine of the Book, which houses the Dead Sea Scrolls. Directly across the way is the **Bible Lands Museum,** with its gorgeous ancient jewelry displays and emphasis on biblical history.

When you've had enough air-conditioning, take a quick taxi ride or a 25-minute walk to a free tour of the **Supreme Court of Israel;** the tour starts at noon and then just hop over to the **Knesset (Israeli Parliament)** for another free tour, starting at 2pm, if you have time. Stop in the **Wohl Rose Garden** with its vast collection of roses on a gently sloping lawn overlooking Jerusalem for your picnic lunch. The roses will stay in full bloom late into the year, and after lunch you can explore the grounds and the approximately 400 varieties of roses.

Head back to your hotel by taxi and rest up before dinner at any one of the City Center restaurants near Tolerance Square. After dinner, take a stroll through **Tolerance Square** with its lively evening atmosphere including street musicians, and get dessert from one of the ice cream shops.

Day 3: Tuesday

Make sure you are conservatively dressed or have something to cover your shoulders and legs, but with pants that can be rolled up, and head back to the **Old City** in the morning (bring a flashlight). Take a taxi to the Damascus Gate in East Jerusalem, and enter the Old City through the gate to explore the **Muslim Quarter** and see some of the stations along the **Via Dolorosa,** where Jesus carried his cross on his way to be crucified. Continue along the Via Dolorosa to the northern side of the **Dome of the Rock, Al Aqsa Mosque,** and the **Western Wall,** holy sites to Christians, Muslims, and Jews. Just before the entrance to the Western Wall there are a number of restaurants where you can get lunch and rest before continuing.

Exit the Old City just past the Western Wall and you'll be in the East Jerusalem neighborhood of **Silwan,** where the **City of David** is located. Make sure you buy a ticket that includes a trip through **Hezekiah's Tunnel** (a good activity when the midday sun is out). After traipsing through the 2,700-year-old tunnel for 580 yards to the **Pool of Siloam** and touring the City of

Station 9 on the Via Dolorosa

David, take a rest back at your hotel and freshen up for the evening.

Before dinner, take in the sunset at the swanky Mamilla Hotel's rooftop terrace bar and restaurant (make reservations in advance). You can stay for dinner after enjoying the view of the old and new cities, or head downstairs to try one of Mamilla's restaurants.

Day 4: Wednesday

Set out early to the **Mount of Olives** for an awe-inspiring sunrise. Get a taxi to take you to the top of the Mount of Olives' highest vista point, above the old Jewish Cemetery, right next to the Seven Arches Hotel. From here, enjoy the incredible view of old and new Jerusalem. Walk down the hill and go through the **Jewish Cemetery,** or just continue downhill to various vista points for photos. Continue downhill toward the Old City, stopping to peek inside the churches along the way. It's a long walk, but frequented by taxis if you get tired.

Take a taxi to **Mount Zion** just outside the Zion Gate at the Old City, and explore **Dormition Abbey** and the area near **King David's Tomb.** If you have time, stop at the small **Holocaust museum.**

For lunch, hop on the light-rail train bound for the **Machane Yehuda Market** (the *shuk*) where you can explore the massive array of stalls with its fresh produce, spices, and regional sweets and snacks. Stop off at one of the *shuk*'s many restaurants for lunch. From here, catch the light-rail train to **Yad Vashem** and **Mount Herzl.** Start with Yad Vashem, which can take several hours (children under the age of 10 are not allowed in the main hall).

Head back out just before dark if you have the energy to the Old City for the **Night Spectacular** light show at the Tower of David Museum citadel at the Jaffa Gate.

Day 5: Thursday

Use Thursday to visit the **Museum on the Seam** for a detailed and clear-eyed look at the juxtaposition of East and West Jerusalem. Go by taxi to looking up at Yad Vashem's Hall of Names

the **L.A. Mayer Museum for Islamic Art** and then take a 15-minute walk downhill to the historic **German Colony** neighborhood either for a guided tour (arranged in advance) of the beautiful, Templar-style buildings and homes or to do some shopping for essentials or souvenirs along popular Emek Refaim Street.

For lunch, walk 10 minutes to the popular **First Station** train station culinary and shopping complex, built from the foundation of Jerusalem's former main train station, which is more than 120 years old. There is more shopping to be had here in a lively atmosphere that often includes musical performances. Follow the adjacent trails in **Train Track Park** north to hilly **Bloomfield Garden** with its beautiful fountain and pathways. Walk through the park until you reach the **Montefiore Windmill** and its sweeping vista point of East Jerusalem and the separation barrier in the distance. Continue on to the **King David Hotel** and the YMCA, both with historic architecture and idyllic outdoor seating for dinner.

Day 6: Friday

Friday in Jerusalem tends to be a bit frenzied as locals take care of last-minute shopping before the city shuts down for 24 hours. It is a good day to go back to the Old City's **Rockefeller Archaeological Museum** to see antiquities or take the **Ramparts Walk** along the top of the wall surrounding the Old City in the morning. A short taxi ride away, at the top of King David Street you will find the Bezalel Art Academy, where the **Bezalel Art Fair** with 150 local vendors selling locally made arts, crafts, and food is held. It is the perfect spot for souvenir shopping. There are numerous restaurants nearby for lunch, but plan to wrap things up by about 2pm.

For a quiet dinner and wine with a rooftop view of the city, go by taxi to the imposing Pontifical Institute Notre Dame's four-star **Roof Top Wine and Cheese Restaurant.**

Have a cup of coffee at the Stars & Bucks Café in Ramallah.

Outward Bound: Excursions from Jerusalem

Using Jerusalem as your base, venture out to explore nearby areas including Tel Aviv, the West Bank, and the Dead Sea.

The West Bank (1-2 days)
GO TO THE WEST BANK BY BUS, SHARE TAXI, TAXI, OR WITH A TOUR GROUP (MAXIMUM OF 1 HOUR TO EACH LOCATION)

Go with a tour guide to **Bethlehem** for the day, where you can explore the various religious and cultural sites, focusing on the area near Manger Square in the town center. Bring your passport, as you'll have to cross through a checkpoint upon entering and exiting the town.

Stay overnight in either Bethlehem or **Ramallah,** and spend the next day exploring Ramallah's shopping and dining offerings in this modern Arab city. Get oriented at the Al Manara roundabout in town center and look for the **Stars & Bucks Café** if you feel lost or want a destination to start from. It's a great place for **window-shopping and dining** at one of the city's many great restaurants, known for their east and west fusion.

Since Ramallah is only a short drive by taxi or bus to Jerusalem, dinner at **Rooftop** is a good choice to round out the day. It has an impressive view of Jerusalem and the Old City in a setting that feels more like Tel Aviv.

Tel Aviv (3 days)
DRIVE (1 HOUR) OR TAKE THE TRAIN (1.5 HOURS) FROM JERUSALEM

A good start in Tel Aviv is always one of the city's many **beaches** for some afternoon fun in the sun and water. The proximity of restaurants and cafés to the beachfront makes it easy to go straight from

Bauhaus buildings in Tel Aviv

the Mediterranean to get a drink or something to eat. Tel Aviv's active and famously late **nightlife** (especially in the summer) means you won't miss much if you take your time at your hotel before going out to dinner at one of the city's many fine restaurants. In fact, the later, the better.

If it's your first time in town, try one of Neve Tzedek's many European-style restaurants for dinner. From here you can easily walk to the lively nightlife and shopping scene at the **HaTachana Train Station Complex,** and you're also not far from **Dizengoff's numerous bars, pubs, and clubs.** For some of the most exciting nightlife in town, the north of the city at the Port of Tel Aviv has tons of seaside clubs, pubs, restaurants, and bars, as well as an enormous promenade right on the water with street performers, huge outdoor bars and restaurants, great stops for dessert, and plenty of strolling space.

Mornings in Tel Aviv are lovely for a stroll or bike ride and a leisurely breakfast on the waterfront, exploring **Old Jaffa** in the south, or getting out to **HaYarkon Park** in the north for a stroll before the heat becomes unbearable. The park has **bicycle and boat rentals,** and plenty of space for a **picnic lunch**. You can also dine in a restaurant by the lake, on the eastern side under the massive trees.

If you're looking for some city tours, you can arrange to see Tel Aviv's famed **White City** with an English-speaking guide at the **Bauhaus Center,** or get a map for a self-guided experience through the area. There are always good shopping, dining, and entertainment options around **Dizengoff Street,** and on certain days of the week the Port of Tel Aviv has an **outdoor farmers market.**

Also worth exploring is the largest nonprofit art gallery in Israel in the **Shalom Mayer Tower** and its **Discover Tel Aviv Center,** with its general history of Tel Aviv. From the Shalom Mayer Tower, it's a short walk back to **Neve Tzedek,** where you'll find the **Rokach House Museum** and the **Nachum Gutman Museum of Art,** with a bit about the history of Neve Tzedek and how Tel Aviv's first neighborhood started.

For more suggestions on Tel Aviv, see page 28.

Hebron (1 day)
DRIVE FROM JERUSALEM WITH TOUR GUIDE OR GROUP (1 HOUR)

With a pre-hired tour guide only due to long-standing security concerns, take the one-hour drive to Hebron to see some of the ancient city's sights, including the **Tomb of the Patriarchs** and **Ibrahimi Mosque.**

One of Hebron's highlights is the **Arabic-style food,** but since it's a bit impractical to go there without a tour guide or group, you'll do whatever the tour group does, which will include a restaurant and shopping. You can also request to see one of Hebron's famed **ceramic or glass shops.**

The Dead Sea (2 days)
DRIVE OR TAKE THE BUS FROM JERUSALEM (1-2 HOURS)

Go from Jerusalem about an hour south to the Dead Sea, where you'll find a number of great **beaches** that offer different Dead Sea experiences. Check in advance for any road closures due to frequently occurring sinkholes in the area. About midway down the western shore of the Dead Sea just 15 minutes past Ein Gedi, you'll find the mountaintop fortress of **Masada.**

Masada is a good stop before hitting the beaches (there won't be much shade and it will be unbearable in the afternoon), where you can take in the vista of the Dead Sea from the vantage point of a high peak. The **Yigael Yadin Masada Museum,** which has a very interesting and easy to digest walk-through exhibit with an audio guide, is included with a full ticket and is a must-see.

Near most of the Dead Sea beaches you can have a light lunch or drink. In the area where hotels are concentrated, there are numerous restaurants to choose from, some of which are on the water.

Once you're in the sea, you can float on the salty waters and rub therapeutic mud onto your body. All of the beaches have outdoor showers where you can rinse off the salty water.

Just at the edge of where the Dead Sea meets the border of the West Bank is **Ein Gedi Nature Reserve,** with its 2,000-year-old spring and relatively steep hike up the mountainside. You can see ibex and hyrax on the way into the park, and take a 30-minute **hike** before reaching one of many **freshwater pools and waterfalls** where you can swim. It's always best to go as early in the day as possible, as the park attracts crowds of people and it gets punishingly hot in the summer after about noon. Do not take food into the reserve; park rangers patrol for and ticket violators.

Adventures in Tel Aviv

The weekend is the perfect time to experience Tel Aviv and all that it has to offer. You can start on Saturday and spend 3 days having fun in the sun and enjoying the nightlife.

Day 1: Saturday

There is no better way to spend Saturday morning in Tel Aviv than at popular and easily accessible **Frishman Beach** where you can float in the water and relax in the sand. Bring some snacks and get a city bike rental to cruise along the **promenade** until you find an appealing place to have brunch. Then head to **Sarona** for some shopping, eating, and an afternoon coffee.

Save some energy for a fun night out at one of Tel Aviv's many clubs. The **TLV Club** is a large DJ and live music hot spot that regularly features Israeli rock and pop stars. It's not a place for a laid-back night—only venture here if you're ready to have some serious fun. There are numerous other options in the area if you decide to shift gears.

Day 2: Sunday

After breakfast at your hotel, start with a visit to the scenic charm of **Old Jaffa** where you can take in the unique **Jaffa Flea Market** and its unique offerings of old and new including Persian tiles

Sarona in Tel Aviv

and rugs. Explore the area and stay for lunch before taking a taxi to the **Azrieli Observatory** where you can capture a view of Tel Aviv from the 49th floor of the tallest building in Israel. Enjoy one of the city's many fine jazz clubs in the evening for a relaxing evening out. **Shablul Jazz Club** is an intimate setting with nice wines that hosts prominent musicians; book in advance.

Day 3: Monday

Have a leisurely breakfast in the morning somewhere in the area of **Dizengoff Center** with its many shops and restaurants before hopping on a train north to the quiet and historic beach town of **Caesarea** for a low-key afternoon at **Aqueduct Beach** and dinner in the town's old center.

Ancient Terrain: Desert Hikes and Magical Waters

With Jerusalem as a base, journey by car to the south on a route that will take you past the Dead Sea, Eilat and the Red Sea, and Petra, Jordan.

many beaches along its western shore. Spend the night in one of the Dead Sea hotels and luxuriate in the area's many offerings.

The Dead Sea
DAY 1
DRIVE TO EIN GEDI (1.5 HOURS)

Leave Jerusalem in the morning and go by rental car south to the Dead Sea, the lowest point on Earth. Stay in either **Ein Gedi**, exploring the ancient spring in Ein Gedi Nature Reserve, hiking, and swimming, or go to one of the **Dead Sea's**

Beer Sheva
DAY 2
DRIVE TO BEER SHEVA (2.5 HOURS); BEER SHEVA TO MITZPE RAMON (1 HOUR); MITZPE RAMON TO EILAT (1.5 HOURS)

Continue southwest toward **Beer Sheva**, the largest city in the south of Israel. Stop just north

Pilgrimage Sites

It isn't known as the Holy Land for nothing. Here is a list of some of the most important religious and spiritual sites.

- **Al Aqsa Mosque next to the Dome of the Rock** is the third holiest site in the Muslim world (Jerusalem, Old City).

- **Basilica of the Annunciation** is believed to be built over the site of the Virgin Mary's original home (Nazareth).

- **Capernaum** is believed to be the location of a village where Jesus and some of his disciples lived for a time on the shore of the Sea of Galilee (near Tiberias).

- **Church of the Holy Sepulchre** is widely recognized as the site of the crucifixion and resurrection of Jesus (Jerusalem, Old City).

- **Church of the Multiplication** is believed to be the location where Jesus turned a few fish and a couple loaves of bread into enough food for thousands (Tiberias).

- **Church of the Nativity** is widely believed to be the location where Jesus was born (Bethlehem).

- **Magdala** is the site of a 1st-century synagogue where Jesus taught (western shore of the Sea of Galilee).

- **Mount of Olives** is the site of many miraculous occurrences and an extremely significant location in Judaism, Christianity, and Islam (Jerusalem, near the Old City).

- **Mount Zion** is one possible site of the Last Supper and the locale of King David's Tomb (Jerusalem).

the Mount of Olives

of Beer Sheva in the Lahav Forest, where you'll find the one-of-a-kind **Museum of Bedouin Culture at the Joe Alon Center.** After experiencing some Bedouin culture and history, drive south to the ancient archaeological site of **Tel Beer Sheba.** From here it is just a short drive to the city of **Beer Sheva,** where you can have lunch at one of the many restaurants in City Center. Also near city center is the **Negev Museum of Art.** From Beer Sheva, take the one-hour drive to the enormous **Ramon Crater,** for a short desert hike and a look at the ancient crater before it starts to get dark. After your tour, drive the remaining approximately 90 minutes to **Eilat,** check into your hotel, and call it a night.

- **Tomb of Rabbi Meir** is significant to Jews all over the world as the tomb of the rabbi who was nicknamed the miracle worker and in whose name charity is often given (near Tiberias).

- **Tomb of the Patriarchs** is widely recognized as the burial place of the patriarchs and matriarchs of the Jewish people, including Abraham. The site is sacred to both Jews and Arabs (Hebron).

- **Western Wall** is a remnant of the western wall of the destroyed Second Temple. It is a popular destination for prayer by Jews and sometimes the site of large-scale religious events (Old City, Jerusalem).

prayer in the women's section of the Western Wall

Eilat

DAY 3

Start off your morning in Eilat by taking breakfast at your hotel, and then go by taxi to the **Dolphin Reef Diving Center** for a guided swim with the dolphins. Take a bus back to Eilat's City Center for lunch and then head to one of the many beaches for a swim, or go diving. If you are new to diving, allow an entire day for it.

After freshening up at your hotel, go by foot or taxi to Eilat's version of Rodeo Drive, **La Boulevard,** for upscale shopping. One of the numerous nearby restaurants will be perfect for dinner.

DAY 4

Go by taxi to the **Coral World Underwater Observatory** to see the many varieties of bright, rare fish. You can easily spend half a day exploring this complex. Have an early dinner in City Center at one of the many beachfront restaurants and then take in an evening performance of **The WOW Show.**

Petra

DAY 5
DRIVE FROM EILAT (2 HOURS)

Start as early in the morning as possible with a prearranged tour guide who can escort you to the Eilat-Aqaba border where you will cross the border (about 10 minutes by taxi) and meet up with another guide. During the two-hour ride to **Petra** take note of all the unusual rock formations with ribbons of mineral deposits in the hills of the famous **Wadi Rum.** Take a short hike into Petra for a few hours after arriving, and have lunch in the modern neighboring village, **Wadi Musa.** Though it is small, Wadi Musa is geared heavily toward tourists, and you can find some interesting shopping in the town's center, especially if you gravitate around the Shaheed roundabout. Take a break from the heat and rehydrate before going out for dinner in town at one of the home-style Bedouin restaurants.

DAY 6

Get an early start to Petra and take a hike up one of the paths that leads to a higher vantage point so that you can see the area from a different perspective. Make sure to stop at the **Petra Nabataean Museum** to see many of the antiquities that have been found over the years.

Go by foot back out to Wadi Musa by late afternoon and rest up at your hotel before dinner. Later in the evening, go back to Petra's **Treasury** for the idyllic **Petra by Night Show** with stories and music.

DAY 7
DRIVE TO EILAT (2 HOURS); EILAT TO JERUSALEM (4 HOURS)

Set out from Petra as early as possible in the morning with a rental car for the two-hour trip back to Aqaba, where you will take a taxi to the border, cross by foot, and then take another taxi back to Eilat. Once in Eilat, pick up another rental car for the four-hour drive back to Jerusalem. Including stops to eat and logistics, the return trip will take an entire day.

swimming with dolphins in the Red Sea

Jerusalem

Look for ★ to find recommended sights, activities, dining, and lodging.

Highlights

★ **Church of the Holy Sepulchre:** One of the most important sites for Christians in Jerusalem, this is where Jesus is believed to have been crucified (page 45).

★ **Austrian Hospice:** Hidden from most tourists by a nondescript outer wall, this oasis in the Old City offers respite and an amazing vista (page 46).

★ **Western Wall:** The most important site in Judaism, the Western Wall, also known as the Kotel, is situated in the southeastern corner of the Old City (page 48).

★ **Mount of Olives:** One of the most dramatic views of Jerusalem exists alongside numerous important religious and historic sites (page 54).

★ **City of David:** Play archaeologist by wading through an ancient aqueduct or sifting through ancient dirt (page 56).

★ **The Israel Museum:** The museum's rich, detailed exhibits on Jewish history, archaeology, and regional treasures are a must-see (page 58).

★ **Yad Vashem:** The largest Holocaust museum in the world is a solemn pilgrimage (page 60).

★ **Machane Yehuda Market (The *Shuk*):** The outdoor market near City Center is frequented by locals of all ages and practically a required experience for visitors (page 69).

The region's religious, historical, and political center, Jerusalem is a heady mix of striking architecture, distinct regional cuisine, and compelling tourist attractions.

Jerusalem is also increasingly a center for entertainment and diversion, entrepreneurship, and innovation.

Most people start their time in Jerusalem by exploring some of the thousands of years of epic history contained within the Ottoman-era walls of the Old City. This is also where great shopping, entertainment, guided tours and cultural activities can be found among the four distinct, but overlapping quarters: Muslim, Jewish, Christian, and Armenian. The massive Western Wall and the Dome of the Rock in the background by day and the Tower of David light show by night are must-sees. Plus, nowhere else in the city is bargaining with vendors for a souvenir trinket or scarf quite as fun.

Within an easy distance of the Old City are numerous important churches, synagogues, and other holy sites, many of which can be found along the walk up the hill to the Mount of Olives with its breathtaking view of the city and the important Jewish cemetery below.

Jerusalem also boasts an outstanding offering of restaurants and entertainment, regionally made goods, and world-class museums, parks, and gardens. Any number of restaurants in City Center won't disappoint, and there is no better way to experience the famous soft evening air of Jerusalem than at a sidewalk café with a rich cappuccino, possibly after a trip through the maze of the famed market (the *shuk*). Of the city's many beautiful parks, Wohl Rose Garden's hundreds of roses and rolling hills make for a serene place for a picnic and stroll. It is also within walking distance of a tour of parliament. Just a taxi ride away is the Israel Museum and the Bible Lands Museum with their rich displays of regional history and of course the world-renowned Yad Vashem Holocaust Memorial.

When too much history and culture start to overwhelm, the light atmosphere of First Station in West Jerusalem with its dining, shopping, and entertainment is a great diversion. There are even nearby movie theaters at Cinema City and the Jerusalem Cinematheque with features in English or foreign-language

Previous: the Dome of the Rock; the Western Wall. **Above:** mosaic in the Church of the Holy Sepulchre.

Jerusalem

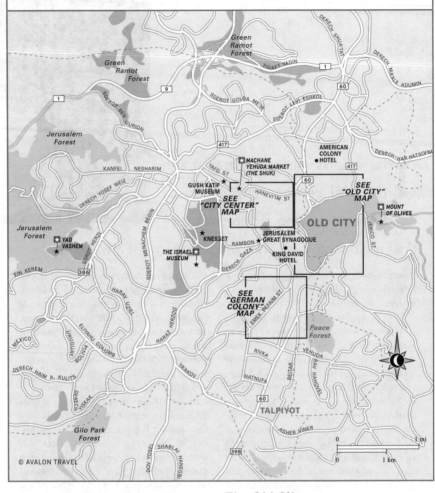

© AVALON TRAVEL

movies with English subtitles. It's all there for the taking.

ORIENTATION

Jerusalem is a very ancient and complex city that has more than 2,000 major and minor archaeological sites. Most visitors explore the city by starting with major tourist spots that include the **Old City, Yad Vashem, Machane Yehuda Market,** the **Western Wall,** and **City Center.**

The Old City

The Old City is an unforgettable experience that is quintessential Jerusalem. You could easily spend days exploring layers of history from thousands of years.

The Old City is divided into four quarters that date back to Roman times: the **Muslim Quarter,** the **Christian Quarter,** the **Armenian Quarter,** and the **Jewish Quarter.** Each quarter has many **free sights** worth a visit, and there are seemingly endless

City Center

© AVALON TRAVEL

0   100 yds
0   100 m

SHILO

MACHANE YEHUDA

CASINO DE PARIS

EZRA RAPHAEL

MACHANE YEHUDA MARKET (THE SHUK)

ETS HAIM

MACHANE YEHUDA

TAVOR

SHOMRON

KI'ACH

AGRIPAS

YAFO ST.

MORDEHAI NARKIS

BEZALEL

MESILAT YESHARIM

BEN YEHUDA

SHMU'EL HANAGID

SHATS

THE BOOK GALLERY

BASHER REST CHEESE BAR

HARAVI'IM ST

ABRAHAM HOSTEL

Meir Shaham Garden

MEIR SHAHAM

HILLEL

MORDEHAI A'LIASH

KING GEORGE V

EZRAT ISRAEL

HAHISTADRUT

BEN HILLEL

BEN YEHUDA

SHAMA

Gan Hatzmaut Garden

RABBI AKIVA

ALICE COFFEE SHOP

LUNZ

ISRAEL

HARAV AGAN

NATHAN ST

ZION SQUARE

HARAVI'IM ST

CITY CENTER

MENASHE BEN ISRAEL

YOEL MOSHE SALOMON

YAFO STREET

HARAV KUK

TICHO HOUSE

Mamilla Cemetery

YOSEF RIVLIN

BELL WOOD BAR

TMOL SHILSHOM

GAYA GAMES

ZUNI

HARAV BRITH

BNEI BRITH

HILLEL

SHIMON BEN SHETACH

DOLPHIN YAM

YOSEF RIVLIN

HATAKLIT

HAHAVATSELET

SHLOMTSYON HAMALKA

KADOSH

KORESH

YAFO ST.

HELENI HAMALKA

SHLOMO HAMELECH

MAMILLA HOTEL

Daniel Garden

CITY HALL

The Old City

© AVALON TRAVEL

The First and Second Temples

No visitor to Jerusalem can escape references to the First Temple and the Second Temple, recalling historical time periods when two different massive Jewish temples stood approximately where Al Aqsa Mosque is now located. Both temples were destroyed, and the main remnant is the outer western wall of the Second Temple courtyard, where people flock from all over the world to pray (known as the Wailing Wall, the Kotel, or the Western Wall).

According to Jewish traditions, both temples were destroyed on the 9th of Av on the Jewish calendar. Every year, those destructions are marked by the day of mourning called Tisha B'av. There are several other tragic disasters in Jewish history associated with Tisha B'av. But, because of its relation to the destruction of the temples, the plaza of the Western Wall is filled with throngs of Jewish mourners every Tisha B'av (in August).

During the **First Temple period** (1200-586 BC), the First Temple was built in 1000 BC by King Solomon after King David had conquered Jerusalem and made it his capital. The Temple was destroyed in 586 BC by Nebuchadnezzar, the king of Babylon, when he conquered Jerusalem. There are scant remains of the temple on the south hill of the City of David. Evidence of the conquering and destruction of the city can be found in the Burnt House and the House of the Bullae.

From the First Temple period there are significant remains of preparations made by King Hezekiah when a siege on the city by the Assyrian king Sennacherib was imminent in 701 BC. Those remains include Hezekiah's Tunnel and the Broad Wall in the Jewish Quarter.

The beginning of the **Second Temple period** (586 BC-AD 70) is marked by the return of Jews to Jerusalem from their exile in Babylon in 538 BC. They were allowed to return under an edict issued by Cyrus, king of Persia. By 515 BC the reinstated Jewish residents had completed building the Second Temple.

The time of the Second Temple and subsequent ages after its destruction are divided into different periods: the **Persian period** (586-332 BC), the **Hellenistic period** (332-63 BC), and the **Roman period** (63 BC-AD 324). In 37 BC, King Herod enlarged the Temple Mount and rebuilt the temple with the consent of the public. During the Roman period, in AD 70, the Second Temple was destroyed, along with all of Jerusalem, by Titus's army. It was also during this period that Jesus was in Jerusalem. He was crucified about 40 years before the destruction of the city.

Significant archaeological remains from the Second Temple period, including the Kidron Valley tombs, the Western Wall, Robinson's Arch, the Herodian residential quarter, numerous other tombs, and walls can be visited today.

BCE (Before Common Era) and CE (Common Era) are used throughout Israel and are numerically equivalent to BC and AD, respectively.

rows of **ancient shops,** selling everything from scarves to antiquities.

Many people follow the **Via Dolorosa,** believed to be the last steps of Jesus on his way to be crucified. The route has 14 stations of historical significance and is rich with additional history that came well after Jesus's time. Following the Via Dolorosa is a good way to learn some of the Old City's story. Free audio guides, pamphlets, and group tours are available.

City Center

Jerusalem's City Center is vibrant, though a bit touristy, and boasts excellent restaurants and sidewalk cafés, shopping, and some entertainment. At the west side of City Center is the renowned **Machane Yehuda Market** (the *shuk*). City Center is bordered on the west by King George Street until it turns into Agripas Street in the north and meets with Agron Street on the south. It is bordered on the east by Shivtet Israel Street and on the north by Hanevi'im Street.

The highlights of Jerusalem **nightlife** are found in City Center, including live music venues, street music, pubs, wine bars, clubs, restaurants, and cafés that stay open into the wee hours. There are also a couple of good **museums,** numerous **hotels,** and some of the best **shopping** in town. It's the most convenient place to go for anything you need during your travels, from electric converters to toiletries to money-changing.

East Jerusalem

Once you cross the (now invisible) line between East and West Jerusalem, there is a palpable sense of stepping into a different culture due to East Jerusalem's largely Arab population.

East Jerusalem has a good selection of affordable **hotels, shopping** options on Salah al-Din Street, and a wide variety of **Arab and Persian food** from Lebanon, Syria, Iraq, Iran, and Turkey.

Because of the Arab cultural and religious stigma against drinking, East Jerusalem is not the best place to have a night out with a few beers and music. Many restaurants do offer the traditional *nargila* (water pipe) that can be smoked with a menu of flavored tobacco after a meal.

West Jerusalem

West Jerusalem consists of several distinctive neighborhoods where visitors tend to spend much time. A popular area for **shopping** and **dining** is the **German Colony** encompassed by the triangle formed by Emek Refaim Street, Yehuda Street, and Hebron Road. The area at the northern tip of the triangle, known as **Yemin Moshe-Mishkenot Sha'ananim,** is surrounded by **parks** and has nearby family-friendly **entertainment.**

Originally settled by German Templars, the German Colony's **Emek Refaim Street** is popular with tourists and locals for its hip and diverse selection of **restaurants,** set against a very distinct backdrop of older homes. The general area also features **museums and theaters** that are within walking distance or a short cab ride of each other. They range from Islamic art to regional historical artifacts to contemporary film and a little bit in between.

West Jerusalem is home to the **Israel Museum,** the **Bible Lands Museum,** the future site of the **National Campus for the Archaeology of Israel,** and several others.

PLANNING YOUR TIME

Jerusalem's terrain and sights are layered and complex. That makes for an interesting visit but presents a challenge in terms of seeing the major highlights of the city in fewer than three days. Six days allow you to comfortably visit all of the best sights as well as enjoy some of the local culture, cuisine, and make a few day trips to nearby spots.

When to Go

There are two major considerations when planning a visit Jerusalem: the weather and the holiday calendar. The climate is inviting. In the summer months, the average temperature typically goes above 80-90°F daily, but when the sun goes down, pleasant, cool, breezy evenings in the mid-70s are the norm.

The best time of year to visit is May-July. August-September is very hot but bearable weather-wise, but could prove very tricky logistically. For three weeks in August, the Jewish orthodox community has a major vacation season, and they flood nearly every corner of the city's museums and parks. At

German Colony

CHOPIN · DAVID MARCUS · DUBNOW · DAVID REMEZ
JERUSALEM THEATRE
EMEK REFAIM STREET · LEV SMADAR
RACHEL IMEINU · LUCIANA · Smuts Garden
EMEK REFAIM ST · HARACKEVAT ST · BEIT LEHEM ST · HEVRON ST
Peace Forest
0   250 yds
0   250 m
TAMAR RESIDENCE
© AVALON TRAVEL

Jerusalem's Conquerors

The list of those who have conquered, occupied, or destroyed Jerusalem is lengthy:

- King David conquers Jerusalem in 1000 BC.

- Nebuchadnezzar, king of Babylon, conquers Jerusalem and destroys the First Temple in 586 BC.

- Alexander the Great conquers Jerusalem in 332 BC.

- Antiochus III conquers Jerusalem in 200 BC.

- Pompeius conquers Jerusalem in 63 BC and Roman rule begins.

- Herod occupies Jerusalem and fortifies significant public buildings.

- Titus's army destroys Jerusalem and the Second Temple in AD 70.

- Transjordan captures East Jerusalem in 1948.

- Israel retakes East Jerusalem and reunifies the city in 1967.

the end of August, the Muslim community of the city finishes their holy month of fasting for Ramadan and come out to enjoy the end of summer in the parks. During August, it is not uncommon to see popular gathering places like Gan Sacher Park overflowing with families cooking out and playing in fountains. Other major Jewish holidays of Yom Kippur and Sukkot usually fall in September (check the Jewish calendar, which changes by the year).

Getting Around

Jerusalem is an ancient city that can be tricky to maneuver in if you take a wrong turn, especially when traveling by car. It's highly recommended to go by foot or take advantage of Jerusalem's efficient bus system, ample taxis, and the light-rail train to get around.

Navigating Jerusalem is fairly easy if you have a clear idea of how much time and money you want to spend. Taxicabs are everywhere but cost 25 percent more on weekends between 9pm and 5am. There is a discounted public transportation ticket for tourists for access to both the light-rail and the public buses. However, the light-rail stops are fairly limited and the bus system, while convenient once you get the hang of it, can be tricky. There is also a double-decker city tour bus that you can hop on and off all day long at major sights with the purchase of a 24- or 48-hour ticket.

HISTORY

Jerusalem's history, like the city itself, is winding, confusing, and full of unexpected twists and turns. For millennia, it has been a religious center for peoples of three major faiths: Jews, Christians, and Muslims. It has endured as a flashpoint of religious, ethnic, and geopolitical tension through to modern times.

In ancient times, Jerusalem was mainly confined to the area now known as the Old City, contained within the walls that offered protection from attackers, invaders, and the elements. The city has been conquered, destroyed, and rebuilt more than once. In fact, it has long been an object of pursuit for ambitious rulers and empires. The first evidence of human life in Jerusalem is around 4500 BC. The first reference to the name Jerusalem (Urushalimum) was in 1500 BC.

In modern times, largely since the return of the Jewish Diaspora to Israel, there have been raging battles and political debates over who controls and has a claim on the holy city.

In 1948, soldiers from Transjordan's Arab Legion (which became the Hashemite Kingdom of Jordan in 1949) tried to capture the entire city during the War of Independence. But Israeli fighters were able to defend significant portions of the western part of the city. After the Arab Legion destroyed the Jewish Quarter of the Old City and expelled the residents, a cease-fire agreement was signed. Outside of the walls was known as the New City and mostly Israeli-controlled.

In April 1949, an armistice agreement was

signed along the 1948 cease-fire line between Israeli and Transjordan forces. The line between east and west was divided by barbed wire, concrete walls, minefields, and bunkers. East Jerusalem, including holy sites, was occupied by Transjordan and West Jerusalem became the capital of Israel.

In 1967, the Israeli Defense Force (or IDF) battled again with Jordan and took control of East Jerusalem. The city was reunified under Israeli control, with a promise that religious sites for all faiths would be protected. For Jews this meant that they gained access to Temple Mount and the Western Wall and could freely visit and pray at these sites.

Today you can still see the dividing line between East and West Jerusalem. If you stand along the route taken by the light-rail train near the Old City, you can imagine a now-invisible line that used to be there. The east side of Jerusalem is a bit more ramshackle, the roads aren't well maintained in many places, and the architecture is more distinctly Arab. The west side of Jerusalem is more upscale and most residents are Jewish.

Tensions between East and West Jerusalem are ongoing but typically take on more subtle and political forms, though sometimes there is violence. The Arab neighborhood of Silwan is a stark example. Under court order, many Arab residents there have been told that their homes do not legally belong to them and have been forced out. Violence between Arabs and Israelis sometimes erupts in the area with Israelis firing rubber bullets and Arabs throwing stones and burning large trash cans.

Sights

You could spend days on end sightseeing in Jerusalem and never run out of interesting things to look at, experience, and learn about. This is especially true for those who have a love of history, archaeology, and spirituality. It is one of the most overwhelming cities in the world; for all the mysteries you discover, there are always a dozen more you have yet to learn.

Many of Jerusalem's major sights are centered on the Old City and the nearby Mount of Olives and Mount Zion. The Old City is the heart of Jerusalem, and includes major sights such as the Western Wall, the Dome of the Rock, the Church of the Holy Sepulchre, the Via Dolorosa, and many, many more. The Mount of Olives is also layered with sights significant to Christians, Muslims, and Jews. Not far from the Old City, the city becomes more residential and moves with the rhythm of its residents, who live in and around important museums, well-known parks, the world-famous Machane Yehuda Market, and the compound of the national government of Israel.

The trick to sightseeing in Jerusalem is to measure how much any particular endeavor might cost in money and energy, especially in the scorching hot summer months. There are no special combination tourism tickets, and the sights that have entrance fees range on average NIS20-50 per person, sometimes more. Some sights that seem fascinating and worth paying the entrance fee for are run by organizations that have a political or religious agenda, and you might be held captive to a monologue about it during your tour.

Many museums have an open late day of the week or windows of limited free admission. In fact, many of the best things to do and see in Jerusalem are free or cost very little.

THE OLD CITY
Via Dolorosa

One of the most revered sites among Christian pilgrims visiting Jerusalem is the Via Dolorosa (Way of Sorrows), the path that Jesus is said to have walked on his way to his crucifixion more than 2,000 years ago. Along the path, fourteen numbered "stations" mark locations of significant moments during Jesus's journey as he bore the cross he was to be crucified upon. The Via Dolorosa begins just inside the Lion's Gate in the Muslim Quarter and ends in the Christian Quarter inside the Church of the Holy Sepulchre, where the last five stations are located. Pilgrims frequently kneel in prayer at the stations, which are points along the street marked with Roman numerals. Much of the Via Dolorosa is accessible 24 hours, and the entire route is free. The Via Dolorosa is part of the living history of the Old City, and the stories connected to it have been passed down through the generations and thus more based in tradition than accurate history.

It is recommended to visit the Via Dolorosa with a guided tour or join the **Via Dolorosa procession** led by Franciscans friars on Fridays from Station 1 (3pm Oct.-Mar., 4pm Apr.-Nov., El Omariye School just inside the Lion's Gate, free). Check with the **Christian Information Centre** in the Old City (Omar Ibn el-Khattab Square at Jaffa Gate, www. cicts.org, 9am-5:30pm Mon.-Fri. and 9am-12:30pm Sat.). As with many other sights, maps, audio tours, and video are available on the **Old City's official website** (www. jerusalem.old-city.org.il). A free MP3 audio file and map of the trail from the Jerusalem Development Authority can be downloaded from the website.

STATION 1
Just inside the Lion's Gate in front of El Omariye School is a round, black seal imprinted with the Roman numeral I on an outer wall. The station is where Pontius Pilate condemned Jesus to death. The station is located at the northwest corner of Temple Mount.

STATION 2
Across the street is the Roman numeral II. Here Jesus was given his cross, whipped, and mockingly dressed in a robe and given a crown of thorns by Roman soldiers. The compound includes the Roman Catholic Church of the Condemnation and the Convent of the Flagellation.

STATION 3
The corner of Via Dolorosa and El Wad (Hagai) Street marks where Jesus fell under the weight of the cross for the first time. The route then traces the western side of the Temple Mount. The Polish Catholic church, the Austrian Hospice, and a 15th-century chapel are nearby.

STATION 4
On El Wad Street is the Roman numeral IV at Our Church of the Lady of the Sun, where Jesus is believed to have encountered his mother, Mary. The Armenian church is home to a 5th-century floor and two sandal footprints said to belong to Mary.

STATION 5
At the corner of El Wad Street is the Roman numeral V and a small Franciscan church built in 1229 to mark the location where Simon bore the cross for Jesus. An old square stone to the right of the door of the church is believed to bear the handprint of Jesus.

STATION 6
Midway down Via Dolorosa just before Souq Khan al-Zeit Street (the market street) is the Roman numeral VI and Our Church of the Holy Face with its restored Crusader arches. This is the station where a woman named Veronica wiped the face of Jesus.

STATION 7
At the intersection of Souq Khan al-Zeit Street and Via Dolorosa is the Roman numeral VII, marking where Jesus fell for the second time. Behind the black doors is a small chapel. Just beyond a massive Roman column is the Chapel of the Seventh Station.

STATION 8
The Roman numeral VIII is at Aqabat al-Khanqah across from the Station VIII

Souvenir bazaar. The station is marked by a stone embedded in the wall of the Monastery of St. Charalampos bearing the engraving IC-XC NI-KA, which means "Jesus Christ conquers." This is where Jesus spoke to the women of Jerusalem and told them not to weep for him, but for themselves and their children.

STATION 9

A zigzag route down Souq Khan al-Zeit Street and up 28 stone steps leads to Station IX with its cross painted on a stone pillar next to an archway where Jesus fell for the third time. Adjacent to the Church of the Holy Sepulchre, the route here winds around the building of the Coptic Patriarchate. Nearby is the Ethiopian Church of St. Michael and a Coptic church with paintings that depict scenes from the Bible.

STATION 10

At the southern end of Souq Khan al-Zeit Street to the right is Souq al-Dabbagha. Cross the courtyard to the entrance of the Church of the Holy Sepulchre, where the last five stations are located. Start at Station X, the Chapel

of the Franks, where Jesus was stripped of his clothes.

STATION 11

Station XI is the interior of the Church of the Holy Sepulchre where Jesus was nailed to the cross.

STATION 12

A Greek Orthodox crucifixion altar inside the church marks Station XII in the Church of the Holy Sepulchre where Jesus was crucified and died on the cross. A silver disk with a central hole under the altar marks where the cross stood. Pilgrims kneel and kiss the spot.

STATION 13

A large stone marks Station XIII in the Church of the Holy Sepulchre where the body of Jesus is said to have been laid and prepared for burial after he died. The station is encased and has an open top for pilgrims to touch.

STATION 14

The tomb of Jesus and the final station of the Via Dolorosa is located in the rotunda inside a small inner chamber past the Chapel of the

the Seventh Station of the Cross on the Via Dolorosa

Angel in the Church of the Holy Sepulchre. A marble lid covers the tomb.

The Christian Quarter
ST. SAVIOR CHURCH (FRANCISCAN MONASTERY OF SAN SALVADOR)

Just inside the New Gate you will find the **Franciscan Monastery of San Salvador**, also known as **St. Savior Church** (1 St. Francis St., tel. 02/626-6595, http://catholic-church-holyland.com, 8am-5pm daily, free). The visit of St. Francis of Assisi to the Holy Land in 1219 marked the beginning of the Franciscan monks following in his footsteps, and to this day the San Salvador Monastery in the Old City is the center of the Franciscan Order in the Holy Land and the Middle East.

The monastery, which visitors cannot enter, does have a church that is free to go into with a magnificent vaulted ceiling and pipe organ. Construction on the church was completed in the 19th century.

You might see members of the Franciscan Order while walking about the Old City. They are distinguishable by their simple, brown robes with a rope belt knotted three times in honor of the vows of their order: obedience, poverty, and chastity.

★ CHURCH OF THE HOLY SEPULCHRE

One of the most popular destinations in the Old City, the **Church of the Holy Sepulchre** (Suq Khan e-Zeit and Christian Quarter Rd., tel. 02/627-3314, www.holysepulchre.com, 5am-8pm daily Apr.-Sept., 5am-7pm daily Oct.-Mar., free) is the most important site for Christians in the world. Also known as the Church of the Resurrection, the dark, cavernous structure houses four stations of the Via Dolorosa and is thus constantly filled with throngs of pilgrims.

Just past the church's massive outdoor courtyard is the end of the Via Dolorosa. At the entrance is the Chapel of the Franks, and the looming interior includes a Greek Orthodox crucifixion altar where Jesus is said to have been crucified. A large stone (stone of unction) to the left is the place where, according to tradition, the body of Jesus was prepared for burial. In the rotunda inside a small inner chamber, past the Chapel of the Angel, is a marble encased tomb said to be

the Church of the Holy Sepulchre

the place where Jesus was buried. A massive vaulted dome rises above the tomb with a center of light that streams downward.

The church was one of many commissioned by Constantine the Great after he converted to Christianity. Work on the church began in AD 326, and some historians believe that Constantine's builders dug around the tomb of Jesus. Since then, it has suffered tremendous neglect, desecration, and damage as the city has changed hands and rulers. The current church is the result of the joint efforts of the Latin, Greek, and Armenian communities who banded together in 1959 for a major restoration project. All that could be preserved in the process was, but the current condition of the church is a mixture of Byzantine, Crusader, medieval, and modern styles. Control of the church is also divided among different denominations of Christians.

CHURCH OF THE REDEEMER
The Lutheran **Church of the Redeemer** (24 Muristan Rd., tel. 02/627-1111, www.elcjhl.org, 9am-1pm and 1:30pm-5pm Mon.-Sat., NIS10) is easy to spot with its distinctive bell tower that can be reached by trekking up almost 200 steps. The church's interior walls are made of simple and relatively unadorned white stone with massive arches. The church was built by Kaiser Wilhelm in the late 1800s, and he later brought his wife with him to personally dedicate it in 1898. He was the first Western ruler to visit Jerusalem and infamously ordered the door of Jaffa Gate to be removed so he could enter the Old City unimpeded while riding his horse wearing a tall, spiked helmet. The gate was never repaired and is the only entrance point in the Old City without full gate.

The church is home to Lutheran congregations that speak Arabic, German, English, and Danish, and it is the site of frequent musical performances.

★ AUSTRIAN HOSPICE
In order to find the **Austrian Hospice** (37 Via Dolorosa, near Damascus Gate, tel.

the outer courtyard at the Austrian Hospice

02/626-5800, www.austrianhospice.com, 24 hours daily, free) you will have to ask merchants for directions because it is extremely well hidden.

You could easily pass by this gem in the Old City without knowing it is here. Behind a very nondescript set of double doors is one of the most serene spots in the Old City. Ring the bell outside and you will be buzzed in to an inner gate. The location was chosen by Austria's first consul general as a place to build (and establish a local presence) in Jerusalem and was opened as a pilgrims' house in 1856. The hospice functions as a high-end hotel, and visitors can wander the hallways filled with photographs of the Holy Land.

There are two points here not to miss: the garden café with its famed apple strudel and the spectacular rooftop view of the Old City and the Dome of the Rock. You can reach the roof by taking the elevator and then the stairs. Once on the roof, you can enjoy the view from a bench, and take your time to absorb the awesome sight of the Old City. You can also take as long as you like at one of the many outdoor tables in the garden near the entrance (which is elevated two stories above street level) for a quiet coffee, beer, or snack.

The Muslim Quarter
CHURCH OF ST. ANNE
Near the beginning of the Via Dolorosa and adjacent to the Pool of Bethesda is the remarkably preserved Crusader-era **Church of St. Anne** (near the Lion's Gate in the Old City off Sha'ar HaArayot St., 8am-noon and 2pm-5pm Mon.-Sat., NIS10). Catholic tradition says this is the birthplace of the Virgin Mary, which is preserved as a cave dwelling located beneath the crypt of the church.

The **Pool of Bethesda** (included with paid entry to the Church of St. Anne) is mentioned in the New Testament as the place where Jesus cured a crippled man. The area is an archaeological site that includes five pools and ruins of Byzantine, Crusader, and medieval churches.

ROCKEFELLER ARCHAEOLOGICAL MUSEUM
The **Rockefeller Archaeological Museum** (27 Sultan Suleiman St., tel. 02/670-8074, www.imj.org.il under Archaeology,

10am-3pm Sun.-Mon. and Wed.-Thurs., 10am-2pm Sat., free) is recommended by most locals and home to thousands of artifacts displayed in chronological order from prehistoric times to the Ottoman period. Among the treasures are a 9,000-year-old statue from Jericho, pieces of gold jewelry from the Bronze Age, and a collection of four dozen photographs of pioneering archaeologists in the region.

LADY TUNSHUQ PALACE
The 14th-century **Lady Tunshuq Palace** (off of Al Wad St. on Aqabat al-Taqiya, 24 hours, free) was built by Muslim Sufi mystics under the direction of Lady Tunshuq. The complex includes large archways with intricate inlaid marble work and also houses a working school.

TEMPLE MOUNT – AL HARAM AL-SHARIF
On the eastern side of the Old City is **Temple Mount—Al Haram al-Sharif** (main access for non-Muslims is between the Western Wall and Dung Gate, tel. 02/622-6250, www.noble-sanctuary.com, 7:30am-11am and 1:30pm-2:30pm Sun.-Thurs. Apr.-Sept., 7:30am-10am and 12:30pm-1:30pm Sun.-Thurs. Oct.-Mar., dress modestly, bring passport, entrance

the Dome of the Rock

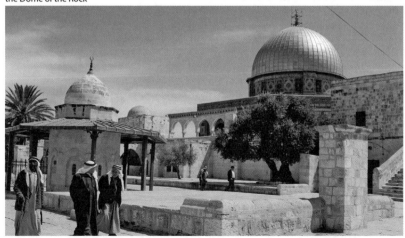

subject to change, free). The complex consists of about 100 buildings known as the Noble Sanctuary and an open plaza with ancient paving stones. The current construction dates back 1,400 years and includes the Dome of the Rock, Mount Moriah, Al Aqsa Mosque, and many other significant religious and cultural sites. It dates back much earlier, though, as it was the site of the first and second Jewish temples, and is one of the most hotly disputed pieces of territory in the world. Exercise caution doing anything resembling praying in the area because of tensions over religious and territorial claims. Guided tours are sometimes available at the information boxes on the plaza, but it is best to hire a guide in advance.

The **Dome of the Rock** is easily recognizable from many points in Jerusalem by its enormous golden dome. Situated atop Temple Mount on the edge of the Old City, the Dome of the Rock is built over the rock where, according to tradition, Prophet Muhammad ascended to heaven and Abraham attempted to sacrifice his son.

Al Aqsa Mosque is the third holiest site in Islam and a popular place for Muslims in Israel and the West Bank to pray, particularly for Friday prayers and major holidays.

The Islamic Museum of Temple Mount (southwest corner of the compound grounds, near the Western Wall, tel. 02/628-3313, 8am-11:30am and 2pm-4pm Mon.-Sat., NIS38 at stone kiosk between Al Aqsa Mosque and the Dome of the Rock) is one of the oldest museums in the country and houses a large collection of Korans, coins, glassware, guns, swords, daggers, and Islamic ceramics. The admission fee will also allow you to enter the mosque depending on the security situation at the time.

The Jewish Quarter
★ WESTERN WALL

Just down from Temple Mount is the most famed religious site in all of Judaism. Named for its position as the outer western wall of the destroyed Second Temple's courtyard, the **Western Wall** (Jewish Quarter of the Old City, tel. 02/627-1333, http://english.thekotel.org, www.jewish-quarter.org.il, 24 hours daily, free, extremely crowded on certain holidays, modest dress required) is also called the Wailing Wall or the Kotel.

The Wall is considered particularly significant to Jews because it is the last remaining piece of the great temple, the most significant site in all of Judaism. The imposing wall is the destination for the faithful who come to pray before it. Modest dress is required at all

The Western Wall draws crowds at all times.

times. Space to pray is divided for men on the left and women on the right, and visitors are permitted to leave small pieces of paper with prayers or messages in the crevices of the wall. You can walk freely about the plaza and take photographs. An upper plaza in the southeastern corner offers an excellent view of the wall and the golden Dome of the Rock behind it.

On the northern end of the Kotel is the **Chain of Generations Center** (near the Western Wall, tel. 02/627-1333, http://english.thekotel.org, visits by reservation in advance Sun.-Thurs. and Fri. morning, NIS20, children NIS10), which tells the story of the Jewish people over 3,500 years and spans history from exile to statehood. The center uses a combination of music, sculpture, archaeology, and light effects and is divided into several rooms. Each room covers a different period and has works of art made from layers of glass lit up by rays of light that shine from dark rooms. There is also a view of the Western Wall from one of portion of the center.

Go south from the Western Wall toward Dung Gate and you will come upon the **Western Wall Excavations** (Western Wall, Jewish Quarter, tel. 02/627-1333, http://english.thekotel.org follow link to Tunnels, www.jewish-quarter.org.il, 7am-11pm Sun.-Thurs., depending on reservations, 7am-noon Fri. and holiday eves, adult NIS25, child NIS15). This 75-minute underground tour of excavations tells the story of ancient Jerusalem and explores hidden layers of the Western Wall. Tours are given only by reservation in advance and with a guide.

HERODIAN QUARTER AND WOHL ARCHAEOLOGICAL MUSEUM

A six-house compound on the slope of the hill facing the Temple Mount makes up the **Herodian Quarter and Wohl Archaeological Museum** (1 Ha-Karaim St., tel. 02/626-5922, www.jewish-quarter.org.il, 9am-5pm Sun.-Thurs., 9am-1pm Fri. and on eve of Jewish holidays, NIS18, combined ticket with the Burnt House NIS35). Here you'll find three main attractions: the Western House, the Middle Complex, and the Palatial Mansion. All thought to be homes of aristocrats and priests during the Herodian period, they are designed in the Hellenistic/Roman style. The 600-square-meter Palatial Mansion is the largest and gives clues to the lifestyle of the wealthy of that time. It includes rich floor mosaics and remarkably preserved wall frescoes. Also unearthed here were utensils, artifacts, decorated plates, and imported wine jugs.

HURVA SYNAGOGUE

The distinctive large, white roof of **Hurva Synagogue** (89 Ha-Yehudim St., tel. 02/626-5922, www.rova-yehudi.org.il, 9am-5pm Sun.-Thurs. and 9am-1pm Fri., NIS30) is home to the world's tallest Holy Ark and boasts a 360-degree view of Jerusalem from the synagogue's roof rampart. The synagogue, which literally means "ruin" in Hebrew, has a long and winding history. Construction began on it in 1700, but 20 years later it was still not complete, and the unfinished building was torched and destroyed for the first time. It was rebuilt in the mid-1800s, only to be blown up by the Transjordan Legion Army just after the War of Independence in 1948. When the Old City was recaptured by Israel in 1967, the site of the ruins was commemorated but nothing was rebuilt there until 40 years later. In 2005, construction on the current Hurva Synagogue began, and it was finished in early 2010. The basement of the synagogue is home to antiquities, and the masterfully renovated building integrates stones from the ruins of the old building with the new. Entry for women is restricted at certain times, but at prayer time it is less restrictive.

BURNT HOUSE MUSEUM

The **Burnt House Museum** (Tiferet Israel St., tel. 02/626-5921, www.rova-yehudi.org.il, 9am-5pm Sun.-Thurs., 9am-1pm Fri. and on eve of Jewish holidays, NIS30, combined ticket with Herodian Quarter NIS35) is the excavated remains of the home of an upper-class priestly Jewish family that burned during the destruction of the Second Temple in 70 BC. The home was later excavated and features unique period archaeological artifacts and a multimedia presentation about the daily life of the people who lived in the house. The movie is screened every 40 minutes starting at 9am.

RACHEL BEN ZVI CENTER

Across from the Israelite Tower is the **Rachel Ben Zvi Center** (7 Bonei ha-Khoma, tel. 02/628-6288, www.ybz.org.il, 9am-4pm Sun.-Thurs., NIS10) is a great place to stop off and see a scale model of the First Temple and educational programming that includes an audio-visual history from 1000 to 586 BC.

RAMBAN SYNAGOGUE

The **Ramban Synagogue** (enter via Jewish Quarter St., tel. 02/627-1422, call in advance to visit, modest dress required) is the second oldest working synagogue in the Old City. It is believed to have been built on Mount Zion and then moved to the Old City in the 14th century. Closed by the Ottomans in 1589, it was reopened in 1967. The synagogue is a small, modest building that many see as a symbol of the enduring power of faith, hope, and tradition.

CARDO

The **Cardo** (HaKardo St., tel. 02/626-5900, ext. 102, www.jewish-quarter.org.il, 8am-6pm Sun.-Thurs., 8am-4pm Fri., closed for Shabbat, free) is the impressive remnants of an ancient Roman double-columned main street (always called a *cardo maximus*) and its shops that were a fixture in many Roman cities. The Old City's Cardo stretched from the Damascus Gate to the Zion Gate.

The southern section of the Cardo was excavated and buildings from later periods were removed to reveal the Byzantine Cardo. Some of the columns from that period were reconstructed and restored, allowing visitors to experience a taste of the 6th-century Cardo.

The covered section of the Cardo, which dates back to the Crusader period, includes shops located in the same place as they were

during ancient times. Most of the Cardo shops sell higher-end items like fine jewelry and Judaica.

Going north along the Cardo toward David Street you will come upon the ruins of five Roman columns, where you'll find the original paving stones of the street, dating to the Byzantine period. Farther on is a reproduction of a section of the Madaba Map, the oldest known map that depicts Jerusalem in the 6th century.

The Armenian Quarter

This section of the Old City is largely residential and makes for a lovely and distinctive place to take a quiet stroll.

ARMENIAN PATRIARCHATE OF ST. JAMES

Just inside Zion Gate and west until the city wall is the **Armenian Patriarchate of St. James** (tel. 02/628-2331, www.armenian-patriarchate.org, nourhan@netvision.net.il, 6:30am-7:30am and 3pm-3:30pm Mon.-Fri., 8:30am-10:30am and 3pm-3:30pm Sat., free), or St. James Cathedral, with its magnificent cathedral built on the tombs of St. James the Apostle and St. James the brother of Jesus. The interior of the cathedral is decorated with ancient hanging oil lamps and includes three chapels and two thrones at the front of the church. The church served as a bomb shelter for residents of the Armenian Quarter during the War of Independence in 1948.

CHRIST CHURCH

Near the intersection of Armenian Patriarchate Road and David Street is **Christ Church** (Omar Ibn Al Hatab St. just inside Jaffa Gate, tel. 02/628-7487, www.jerusalem-oldcity.org.il, www.cmj-israel.org, call in advance before visiting, NIS10), a compound on the right of the street. This is the oldest Protestant church in the Middle East, and it houses a hostel, a heritage center, and a coffee shop. There is a tunnel beneath it dating to the Second Temple period.

A unique aspect of Christ Church is that it

was completed in 1849 in preparation of the return of the Jews to Israel. The believers of the church wanted to establish themselves in Jerusalem in order to be in a position to help the Jews when they returned. Due to its history, there are Hebrew inscriptions inside the church, and modern services have incorporated some Hebrew.

RAMPARTS WALK

For a unique view of Jerusalem, climb up onto the narrow catwalk on the 16th-century wall surrounding the Old City and try the **Ramparts Walk** (Jaffa Gate, tel. 02/627-7550, 9am-4pm Sun.-Thurs., tickets for guided tours at tourist service office, call in advance as tours vary widely by season, self-guided ticket good for two days, NIS16). The southern route starts at the Tower of David and ends at the Dung Gate, the northern route starts at Jaffa Gate and ends at the Lion's Gate. You can also walk around the entire rampart in 3-4 hours or descend at any one of the gates along the way after about 20 minutes. On the ramparts you will see a bird's-eye view of the city, the ancient niches in the wall that used to be used by shooters to defend the city, and many steep steps. There are modern, secure railings along the way but it would be a tiring route for the very young or infirm.

TOWER OF DAVID MUSEUM

Just south of Jaffa Gate is the **Tower of David Museum** (tel. 02/626-5333, www.towerofdavid.org.il, 10am-4pm Sun.-Thurs., 10am-2pm Sat. and holidays Sept.-June, 10am-5pm Sat.-Wed., 10am-7pm Thurs., 10am-2pm Fri. July-Aug., adult NIS30, senior and child NIS15), located in a medieval citadel. The museum tells the story of Jerusalem and includes the archaeological site of the citadel. It is also home to a unique sound and light show, the **Night Spectacular** (9pm and 10:30pm, adult NIS55, senior and child NIS45; museum admission plus show adult NIS70, senior and child NIS55).

Mount Zion

Just outside of **Zion Gate** and a short walk up the hillside is **Mount Zion,** which consists of a series of sites that can be visited in succession. Start with **Dormition Abbey** (Mount Zion, tel. 02/565-5330, www.dormitio.net, 8am-noon and 2pm-6pm daily, free), an active abbey with a distinctive bell tower and lead-covered cupola that can be seen from many points in the city. According to Christian

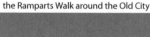
the Ramparts Walk around the Old City

Dormition Abbey on Mount Zion

tradition, Mount Zion is an important place in Jerusalem that was the meeting point for Jesus and his disciples.

You can enter Dormition Abbey, built near the place where Catholic tradition says the Virgin Mary ascended to heaven, and tour the German Benedictine basilica that was finished in 1910. Several mosaics can be seen inside the abbey, including some from a former Byzantine church that was previously at the same location.

Also on Mount Zion is **King David's Tomb** (Mount Zion compound, 8am-6pm and until 2pm on Fri., free) and **St. Mark's Church** (Ararat St., tel. 02/628-3304, 8am-6pm daily, free) or Monastery of St. Mark—the possible site of the Last Supper. King David's Tomb and the Room of the Last Supper can be visited with a short walk from the basement level (the tomb) to a nearby room of stone with enclaves and support pillars. Be wary if you are invited to make a donation to see either site, as there is no fee to enter. There is some dispute about the veracity of claims made about both the tomb and the supposed Room of the Last Supper due to centuries of war and subsequent destruction and rebuilding in the area. Docents will openly tell you

that some theorize that the actual sites are a bit farther downhill.

CITY CENTER
Museum of Italian Jewish Art
Conveniently situated in the midst of City Center, the **Museum of Italian Jewish Art** (25 Hillel St., tel. 02/624-1610, http://ija-museum.com, 10:30am-4:30pm Sun., Tues., Wed., noon-7pm Thurs., 10am-1pm Fri., NIS12) is a renowned as a repository of the history of Italian Jewry. Most famous among its treasures of ritual Jewish objects from the baroque and Renaissance periods is a lavish gold 18th-century synagogue that was transported from Italy to Israel. The museum features permanent and changing exhibitions and is part of the Jerusalemite Star, five boutique museums that are physically connected and form the shape of the Star of David.

Museum of Tolerance
Slated to open at some point in 2017, the **Museum of Tolerance** (Gershon Agron St.) will be part museum and part commercial and residential housing units. The venture is being run under the behest of the Simon Wiesenthal Center and will feature a vast museum. The

controversial project faced criticism during construction due to its location on the site of an old Muslim cemetery.

Jerusalem Time Elevator

The unique trip through Jerusalem's history offered by the **Jerusalem Time Elevator** (37 Hillel St., Agron House, tel. 02/624-8381, www.time-elevator-jerusalem.co.il, 10am-5pm Sun.-Thurs., 10am-2pm Fri., noon-6pm Sat., adult NIS54, senior NIS46, Internet booking NIS46, reservation recommended) is a sensory overload of 3,000 years of history in 2D surround sound, interactive environment. Using crashing ceilings, splashing water, and other special effects, the Time Elevator works well for groups or families whose energy has been spent with long walks in the hot sun from one archaeological site to another.

Ticho House (Israel Museum)

Built by an Arab dignitary in the latter half of the 19th century, the **Ticho House** (9 Harav Kook St., tel. 02/624-5068, www.go-out.com/ticho, 10am-5pm Sun.-Mon. and Wed.-Thurs., 10am-10pm Tues., 10am-2pm Fri., free) was one of the first houses constructed outside of the Old City walls and recently underwent a major renovation. It was home to well-known painter Anna Ticho in the early 20th century. Now part of the Israel Museum, today it has cozy art galleries, a collection of Hanukkah lamps, and a **reference library** (11am-6pm Sun.-Mon. and Thurs., 2pm-6pm Tues., 10am-noon Fri., free) of books about art, literature, and Jerusalem. It is an easy museum stop if you want a change of pace from busy Tolerance Square just outside.

Gush Katif Museum

The small but extremely unique **Gush Katif Museum** (5 Sha'arei Tsedek, tel. 02/625-5456, www.gushkatif.022.co.il, 10am-6pm Sun.-Thurs., 9am-1pm Fri., NIS20) is the only museum in the world that tells the story of the Jewish settlement Gush Katif in the Gaza Strip before it was broken apart in the 2005

unilateral disengagement when Israel pulled out of the region.

Jerusalem Great Synagogue

The unmistakable facade of the **Jerusalem Great Synagogue** (56 King George St., tel. 02/623-0628, www.jerusalemgreatsynagogue.com, tours by appointment only by emailing jgs@zahav.net.il), an imposing structure that was opened in 1982 and dedicated to the memory of the six million Jewish victims of the Holocaust, can be seen easily as you drive by. The synagogue's internationally acclaimed choir is one of the world's chief repositories for Jewish Ashkenazic liturgical music, and massive stained glass windows adorn the main building. The synagogue's annual operating budget of US$1 million comes entirely from donations.

Hechal Shlomo Jewish Heritage Center

A landmark building in the city is the **Hechal Shlomo Jewish Heritage Center** (58 King George St., tel. 02/588-9010, http://eng.hechalshlomo.org.il, 9am-3pm Sun.-Thurs., adult NIS20, senior and child NIS15, family NIS50), which serves as a Jewish spiritual and cultural center. Aside from Hechal Shlomo's cultural events that include live music and its several permanent exhibits, it also houses the 300-year-old **Renanim Synagogue,** which was transported from Italy and features an Italian Ark. The active synagogue is decorated lavishly in 18th-century Italian style and is also home to the **Wolfson Museum of Jewish Art** with its permanent exhibit of Jewish ceremonial art and temporary exhibits of Israeli artists.

Museum on the Seam

On the old border between East and West Jerusalem is the **Museum on the Seam** (4 Chel Handasa St., tel. 02/628-1278, www.mots.org.il, 10am-5pm Sun.-Thurs., 10am-2pm Fri., adult NIS30, senior and student NIS25), a sociopolitical contemporary art museum that focuses on the social situation created by regional conflict. Established in 1999, the museum is not well known among locals, but comes highly recommended by visitors to Jerusalem who are interested in learning more about the regional conflict and artistic interpretations of their effect on the residents of the city.

EAST JERUSALEM
★ Mount of Olives

East from the Lion's Gate of the Old City is the Mount of Olives (www.mountofolives.co.il) which stretches from the Kidron Valley (24 hours daily, free) to the uppermost ridge at the end of E-Sheikh Street. Kidron Valley is where the tombs of Zechariah, Bnei-Hezir, and Absalom can be found, which are actually rather massive ancient structures and not simple gravestones. The tombs are the oldest graves of the ancient Jewish Cemetery (tel. 02/627-5050 for help locating a grave or to arrange a memorial service), which is considered by Jews to be sacred and the future sight of the resurrection. The oldest Jewish cemetery in the world, it covers the entire western and much of the southern slope of the Mount of Olives and is not technically open for public access, although there are no gates to keep people out.

Start or end your journey at the Rehav'am Lookout (turn off from Jericho Rd. and go uphill until the road runs out, follow the signs, free parking), one of the highest points in Jerusalem. From April-September, try to get here before 10am or after 4pm to enjoy the unbelievable view without the heat.

Due to the sacredness of the Mount of Olives to Christianity, Judaism, and Islam, there are several holy sites in the area. If you start from the base of the Mount of Olives, go north along Al-Mansuriya Road and then west along El Monsuriyya toward the Church of the Assumption or the Tomb of the Virgin Mary (intersection of Jericho Rd. and Al-Mansuriya Rd., 6am-noon and 2:30pm-5pm Mon.-Sat., free), an underground tomb thought to be the resting place of the Virgin Mary. The site also includes a place for Muslims to pray, as St. Mary is highly regarded in Muslim tradition. Above the tomb is the 12th-century church. You can enter the tomb area via a set of wide steps that go underground.

Just south of Mary's Tomb on Jericho Road is the Basilica of the Agony or the Church of All Nations (Jericho Rd., tel. 02/628-4371, 8am-noon and 2pm-4:30pm Mon.-Sat., free), with a magnificent mosaic on the front and

olive trees in the Garden of Gethsemane

a row of pillars directly facing the road. The church was completed in 1924 with donations from a dozen different countries. The impressive interior of the church includes massive frescoes painted on vaulted walls and a large rock believed to be the place where Jesus prayed the night he was betrayed. The symbols of the 12 countries that contributed to the building of the church are woven into the 12 inlaid gold cupola ceilings.

Accessible from an alley toward the north side of the church is the Garden of Gethsemane (8am-noon and 2pm-6pm Mon.-Sat., free), where Jesus is said to have been betrayed by Judas. The garden is a grove of ancient olive trees, some of which are over 2,000 years old. It is completely surrounded by a wrought-iron fence, making it impossible to touch the trees or sit or walk among them.

Farther up the hill is the Franciscan Dominus Flevit Church (accessible by a footpath from the base of the Basilica of Agony or from the top of the Mount of Olives, tel. 02/627-4931, 8am-noon and 2pm-5pm Mon.-Sat., free), on a site considered holy as far back as the Bronze Age. The current structure was built in 1954 over the ruins of other buildings that have stood at the location, including a Byzantine period monastery and church whose mosaic floor can still be seen to the left of the entrance. The building, which is adjacent to the Mount of Olives cemetery, has a roof with a tear-shaped dome. This is the site where Jesus is said to have looked over Jerusalem and wept at its future destruction.

Farther up the road is the Church of the Pater Noster (E-Sheikh St., tel. 02/626-4904, 8:30am-noon and 2:30pm-4:30pm Mon.-Sat., NIS7), the traditional place where Jesus taught his disciples the Lord's Prayer. It is famed for the 140 inscriptions of the Lord's Prayer throughout the church in different languages.

Near the Garden of Gethsemane are the golden domes of the Russian Orthodox Church of St. Mary Magdalene (Al-Mansuriya Rd., tel. 02/628-4371, www.jerusalem-mission.org, 10am-11:30am Tues. and Thurs., free), impossible to miss with its

Russian architecture built in the Muscovite style with golden onion domes or cupolas.

Finally, grouped near one another are the Dome and Chapel of the Ascension (al-Tur Village on Rub'a el-Adawiya St., tel. 02/628-4373, www.jerusalem-mission.org, 8am-6pm daily, NIS5), where Jesus is said to have risen to heaven 40 days after his resurrection, and the Greek Orthodox Church of Viri Galilaei (just north of the Chapel of the Ascension, left off Rub'a el-Adawiya St., free), a small Greek Orthodox church that is another of the three places on the Mount of Olives marking Jesus's ascension to heaven. The church is surrounded by an olive grove.

Jerusalem Archaeological Park

The Jerusalem Archaeological Park (Temple Mount Excavations, near the Old City's Dung Gate, tel. 02/627-7550, www.arch-park.org.il, 8am-5pm Sun.-Thurs., 8am-2pm Fri., adult NIS30, senior, student, and child NIS16) covers a vast area near the Old City. The park extends from the north at Temple

Jerusalem Archaeological Park

Mount to the slope of the Mount of Olives and the Kidron Valley on the east, and on the west and south to the Valley of Hinnom.

Considered one of Israel's most significant antiquities site, it includes 5,000 years of history from the Canaanite (Bronze) Age and through the days of the Israelite monarchy in the First Temple period. At the entrance to the park is the **Davidson Center,** a virtual reconstruction and exhibition center that uses state-of-the-art computer technology to give visitors a historical and archaeological orientation.

★ CITY OF DAVID

The **City of David** (off Ophel St. in Silwan, tel. 02/626-8700, www.cityofdavid.org.il, 8am-5pm Sun.-Thurs., 8am-2pm Fri. Nov.-Mar., 8am-7pm Sun.-Thurs., 8am-4pm Fri. Apr.-Oct., closed for Shabbat and holidays, adult NIS29, senior and child NIS15, 3D film add NIS13, guided tour adult NIS45 and senior and child NIS35) is controversial for its location in the Arab neighborhood of Silwan but fascinating for the many historical and archaeological treasures that it encompasses. Part of the controversy over the City of David is the claim that its very existence is a surreptitious attempt to circumvent the law and establish an Israeli presence in East Jerusalem. It is home to numerous important archaeological excavations and historical artifacts that bring the history of Jerusalem and the region to life.

Among the highlights in the City of David is the incredible **Hezekiah's Tunnel,** which is a wonder of ancient engineering. The tunnel starts at Gihon Spring, a major source of water for ancient Jerusalem for 1,000 years. If you are adventurous (and not claustrophobic) you can wade through the 2,700-year-old tunnel for 580 yards to the Pool of Siloam, the source for drawing water during biblical times. Make sure to bring a flashlight with you. The tunnel was built by King Hezekiah in preparation for the Syrian siege and was painstakingly chipped away by hand by two groups of workers. One group started from the

the Pool of Siloam, where Hezekiah's Tunnel ends

top and the other from the bottom, and they met in the middle to join the tunnel and ensure the safety of the city's water supply from impending invaders.

Also in the City of David, the **Temple Mount Sifting Project** (entrance to Emek Tzurim National Park on the ascent to the Mt. of Olives, tel. 02/628-0342, templemount. wordpress.com, 8am-4pm Sun.-Thurs., 8am-1pm Fri. Nov.-Mar., 9am-5pm Sun.-Thurs., 8am-1pm Fri. Apr.-Oct., closed for Shabbat and holidays, adult NIS20, senior and child NIS16, reservation required, free parking) affords a rare experience for the most curious of visitors. The project offers a two-hour participatory archaeological experience. You can sift through rubble that was dug up and dumped during construction and then reclaimed for the purpose of checking for ancient treasures. Any findings during the sifting tour are explained by archaeologists and expert guides at the site.

Garden Tomb

A slightly off-the-beaten-path location not far from the Old City is the **Garden Tomb**

(Conrad Schick St., tel. 02/627-2745, www.gardentomb.com, 8:30am-noon and 2pm-5:30pm Mon.-Sat., free), the only place in Jerusalem other than the Church of the Holy Sepulchre that claims to be the site of the resurrection of Jesus. You can enter the cave in the hillside where it is said that Jesus was buried and inspect clues in the hillside that were said to correlate with historical references to his true burial place.

St. Stephen Basilica

Home to the world-famous Ecole Biblique (French Biblical and Archaeological School) is **St. Stephen Basilica** (6 Nablus Rd., tel. 02/626-4468, www.ebaf.edu, call in advance to visit as there is a locked gate, free). The original church at this location was built at the end of the 5th century as a resting place for the relics of St. Stephen, the first Christian martyr. The massive adjacent monastery was home to an unbelievable 10,000 monks by the end of the 6th century. Destroyed in the 12th century by Crusaders, it was not until 1900 that a new church was rededicated at the site on the base of the ruins. Founded in 1890, the Ecole is the oldest research institute in the Holy Land and has an extensive collection of 20,000 glass photo plates dating from 1890 that are partially on exhibit.

The Separation Barrier

At several points near the Old City and at the border of East and West Jerusalem, you will be able to clearly see the Separation Barrier, also known as the Security Barrier, that separates Israel from the West Bank. The barrier directly abuts neighborhoods and villages along its route, and is not complete. If completed, it would span a distance of about 708 miles from north to south. It is currently about 440 miles long, and the structure varies from fence with barbed wire to concrete walls. Throughout Jerusalem it is mostly concrete.

Tomb of the Kings

The **Tomb of the Kings** (entrance at the corner of Salah a-Din Street and Nablus Road, no formal visiting hours so ring bell, NIS3) is a popular tourist destination as one of the largest and most luxurious tombs in the area. A sign that says "Tombeau des Rois" is situated to left of stairs and a French flag flies above the sight. Enter through a metal gate that leads to a large courtyard dug out of stone to a depth of about 30 feet and the 2,000-year-old family tomb of Queen Helena of the Mesopotamian province of Adiabene. Two channels next to the stairs lead down to ritual baths, and there are about four dozen graves at the site, though grave robbers have long since made off with the contents. The area covers several acres and includes a tunnel that you can crawl through to reach the burial chamber, so bring a flashlight.

WEST JERUSALEM
German Colony

The Templar neighborhood of the **German Colony** (available tours vary, tel. 02/531-4600) is home to numerous historic buildings constructed in the mid-1800s by a group of German Protestants who came to the Holy Land in anticipation of the return of Jesus. There is also a German Colony in Haifa. The buildings in the area, one of Jerusalem's most affluent neighborhoods, are largely residential. It makes the perfect place to start or end a stroll to the nearby shopping and dining on Emek Refaim Street or HaTachana (First Station).

L.A. Mayer Museum for Islamic Art

Home to a small but exquisite collection of Islamic art and antique watches and clocks, the **L.A. Mayer Museum for Islamic Art** (2 HaPalmach St., tel. 02/566-1291, www.islamicart.co.il, 10am-3pm Sun.-Thurs., until 7pm Tues. and Thurs., 10am-2pm Fri. and eves of holidays, 10am-4pm Sat. and holidays, adult NIS40, student NIS30, child NIS20) also features rotating exhibitions.

★ The Israel Museum

The crown jewel of the unofficial museum district of Jerusalem is The Israel Museum (11 Ruppin St., near the intersection with Kaplan St., tel. 02/670-8811, www.imj.org.il, 10am-5pm Sat.-Mon. and Wed.-Thurs. and holidays, 4pm-9pm Tues., 10am-2pm Fri. and holiday eves, adult NIS54, student NIS39, senior, child, and disabled NIS27, NIS27 on repeat visit within 3 months only at box office, paid parking). Even among locals, the Israel Museum is lauded as one of the must-see spots in the city. Home to the Shrine of the Book and the Dead Sea Scrolls, the museum finished a major renovation in 2010 throughout its 20-acre campus to increase exhibition space, expand structures, and add exhibits.

The museum was founded in 1965 and is Israel's largest cultural institution. It also enjoys the renown of being one of the best art and archaeology museums in the world. It is home to artifacts from prehistory to the present time, and has the most extensive biblical and Holy Land archaeology collection in the world.

Among the museum's most spectacular collections are the Dead Sea Scrolls, housed in the unusual-looking building called the Shrine of the Book. You will also want to see the outdoor model of the Second Temple, which covers almost one acre. There is enough here for several hours with a meal at the restaurant along the way, where you can rub shoulders with famous locals.

Jerusalem Biblical Zoo

The Jerusalem Biblical Zoo (1 Aharon Sholov Rd., tel. 02/675-0111, www.jerusalemzoo.org.il, 9am-5pm Sun.-Thurs., 9am-4:30pm Fri. and holiday eves, 10am-5pm Sat. and holidays, adult NIS55, child, senior, and student NIS42) is a remarkably diverse zoo that is also a nonprofit organization owned equally by the Municipality of Jerusalem, the Jerusalem Foundation, and the Jerusalem Development Authority. Opened in 1993, it is home to an incredibly wide array of animals, including monkeys, elephants, lions, lemurs, snakes, flamingos, and more.

National Campus for the Archaeology of Israel

Expected to open sometime in 2017, the National Campus for the Archaeology of Israel (Hamuze'onim St., www.archaeology.org.il) will and act as a center for research,

a model of the Second Temple at the Israel Museum

study, education, and exhibition of the vast collection of Israeli Antiquities Authority materials excavated in Israel. The approximately two million objects in the Archaeological State Treasures will be housed under one roof on the campus for academic and public access.

Bible Lands Museum

The first museum in the world dedicated to the history of the Bible and the ancient Near East is the Bible Lands Museum (25 Avraham Granot St., tel. 02/561-1066, www. blmj.org, 9:30am-5:30pm Sun.-Thurs., closes at 9:30pm Wed., 9:30am-2pm Fri. and holiday eves, 10am-2pm Sat., NIS44, under 18 NIS22). The permanent exhibition, which is made up almost entirely of the former private collection of Dr. Elie Borowski, art collector and academic, spans from earliest civilization to the early Christian era in the lands of the Bible. The classical art collection features Etruscan, Greek, and Roman art from the 7th century BC through the 2nd century AD. A collection of well-preserved frescoes is believed to be from a village near Pompeii.

Bloomfield Museum of Science

The small but ambitious Bloomfield Museum of Science (Hebrew University on Museum Blvd., tel. 02/654-4888, www.mada. org.il, 10am-6pm Mon.-Thurs. and until 8pm in Aug., 10am-2pm Fri., 10am-3pm Sat., NIS45, senior NIS20, children under 5 free) is a very hands-on, interactive museum designed for very young children to about age 12. Consisting of three above-ground levels and two below-ground levels and indoor and outdoor exhibits, the museum is full of science lessons that are built to be played and experimented with. Some of them are a bit worn from excessive play, but it's easy to move on. The museum also hosts rotating exhibits, special events, and has an underground auditorium for shows. A small cafeteria is inside.

National Government Compound

A grouping of significant government buildings, some of which are open for tourists to visit, is known as the National Government Compound.

A visit to The Knesset (Parliament) (intersection of Kaplan St. and Rothschild St. in Givat Ram, tel. 02/675-3337, www.knesset.gov. il, tours@knesset.gov.il, tours 8:30am-2pm Sun.-Thurs., English tours 8:30am, noon, and 2pm Sun.-Thurs., reservations not needed for individuals, just show up 30 minutes before tour starts, free) should include a guided tour, as you will be unable to enter the building unaccompanied. The very general tour touches on the workings of the Knesset, artwork in the Knesset, architecture, and a combined tour with the Supreme Court. The only independent tour is the Knesset Archaeology Park tour, which includes findings from the Second Temple period through the Ottoman period.

Known for its grand architectural design created by the brother-sister team of Ram Karmi and Ada Karmi Melamede from Tel Aviv is the Supreme Court of Israel (intersection of Yitzhak Rabin St. and Rothschild St. in Givat Ram, tel. 02/675-9612, www.court. gov.il, English tours noon Sun.-Thurs., free). Opened in 1992, the building includes a massive restored mosaic, a panoramic window, and the unique library that is an architectural representation of the Second Temple. The overall structure was created to integrate postmodern architectural elements and reflect Jerusalem's rich architectural history. It was also designed to express the values of justice, law, and righteousness.

Monastery of the Cross

Resembling a fort, the Greek Orthodox Monastery of the Cross (enter on Shota Rustaveli St. in Rehavya Valley, tel. 02/679-0961, 10am-4:30pm Mon.-Sat., NIS10) was most recently rebuilt in the 11th century. The monastery is on the site where Christian tradition says the tree grew that was used to make the cross to crucify Jesus.

It was originally built in the 6th century, destroyed in the Persian invasion in 614, and rebuilt again in 1038. An important Christian theological seminary through the 20th century, it has 16th- and 17th-century frescoes and mosaics and includes a courtyard café.

★ Yad Vashem

Nothing can prepare you for the enormous psychological and emotional impact of visiting Yad Vashem. More of an institution than a museum, the **Yad Vashem** complex (enter via the Holland Junction, on the Herzl Route opposite the entrance to Mount Herzl and the descent to Ein Kerem, tel. 02/644-3802, www.yadvashem.org, 9am-5pm Sun.-Wed., 9am-8pm Thurs., 9am-2pm Fri. and holiday eves, closed Sat. and all Jewish holidays, free, no children under 10 years old in Holocaust History Museum and main exhibits, last visitor one hour before closing, paid parking, free shuttle from Mount Herzl stop on the lightrail) is an astounding window on Jewish history and culture. Because of the size of Yad Vashem and the amount of information, it is advisable to plan to spend at least half a day there.

Start with the **Holocaust History Museum**, the building behind the main entrance. You can rent an audio guide (NIS20) and buy a guide map (NIS10) and work your way through the 4,200-square-meter spike-shaped linear structure that stretches mostly underground. The museum includes an overwhelming collection, some of it interactive, of artifacts, firsthand testimonies, and personal possessions from the Holocaust.

As you work your way through the main museum, it ends in a skylight at the uppermost edge and the **Hall of Names**, a circular repository for the names and testimonies of the millions of Holocaust victims. Two million testimonies are included, with room for four million more. The somber and impressive **Hall of Remembrance** features basalt boulders from the Sea of Galilee and the always burning Eternal Flame surrounded by a mosaic of 22 names of the most notorious sites where Nazis committed murder. In front of the flame is a stone crypt with the ashes of Holocaust victims.

the Hall of Names at Yad Vashem

Home to the largest and most wide-ranging collection of Holocaust art in the entire world, the **Holocaust Art Museum** has some of its more than 10,000 pieces of work on display first by artist and then by subject matter. There are plenty of comfortable benches for lingering reflection, and the first computerized archive of Holocaust art and artists is adjacent to the museum's galleries.

Mount Herzl

At the entrance to the Yad Vashem campus, is **Mount Herzl** (Herzl Blvd., Mt. Herzl, tel. 02/632-1515, www.herzl.org, 8:30am-6pm Sun.-Wed. last tour at 5pm, 8:45am-8pm Thurs., 8:30am-1pm Fri. with last tour at 12:15pm, tours must be arranged in advance or on a first-come, first-served basis, NIS25, child NIS20). The museum here, dedicated to the story of famed Zionist Theodor Herzl, gives visitors an audiovisual history through a live action one-hour program. The four rooms of the small museum explore Herzl's path from a European to the modern father

Free Saturday Tours

Saturday is one of the best days of the week to go on a free tour in Jerusalem. Most of the city shuts down and doesn't start opening again until late Saturday evening so there is very little foot and vehicular traffic. It's also a good chance to explore some of Jerusalem's neighborhoods (for detailed tour listings by type, go to the **city's official tourism website** at www.itravelje-rusalem.com).

Several types of three-hour-long Saturday tours depart at 10am from **Safra Square** (24-26 Yafo St., tel. 02/531-4600, call in advance, free).

- **The Explore Ethiopia Tour** explores Eliezer Ben Yehuda's old neighborhood (he was instrumental in reviving the Hebrew language) and also goes through the Russian Compound, The Ticho House, Ethiopia Street, Bnei Brit Library, and Beit Tavor Street.

- **The German Colony Tour** takes you through the neighborhood built by German Templars at the end of the 19th century and includes a route from King David Street down through Emek Refaim Valley.

- **The Hanevi'im Tour** takes visitors through the history of Hanevi'im Street and its ties to the British, Germans, Italians, and Ethiopians. Some of the buildings on the tour help tell the stories of famous leaders, ambassadors, doctors, poets, artists, and hermits.

- **The Kidron Valley Tour** explores the burial grounds of the Second Temple period, the Kidron River and its streams, and the story behind four rock-hewn graves here. The route goes through Jaffa Gate, the Jewish Quarter, Dung Gate, Kidron Valley viewpoint, and Kidron Valley proper.

- **The Muslim Quarter Tour** takes you from Damascus Gate in the Old City to the Western Wall.

- **The Rehavya Walking Tour** includes national institutions in the Rehavya neighborhood, including a monastery and the president of Israel's home.

- **Sandeman's New Jerusalem Tour** meets just inside the Old City's Jaffa Gate by the tourism information stand (11am and 2pm daily) and covers a broad range of sights during this two-hour tour. Look for the guides in the red Sandeman's T-shirts; guides might encourage you to tip them.

of the State of Israel and include artifacts and memorabilia. Mount Herzl is an easy stop on the way to Yad Vashem.

SPECIAL TOURS
Tour Guides

As with any major tourist destination, there are a number of fly-by-night tour guides and companies in Jerusalem selling their services. A good rule of thumb is to work with someone who is a licensed tour guide or get recommendations from the front desk at your hotel.

The **official travel website of Israel** (www.goisrael.com) has a complete listing of tour guides authorized by the Ministry of

Tourism who offer services in a wide range of languages. You can also choose a guide who has a car as part of their services. Check under the "Before You Go" tab on the website, and choose "Tour Guide Search" from the left tab.

Asher Altshul (tel. 052/232-3219, www.asheraltshul.com) is a private licensed tour guide based in Jerusalem who is fluent in English and Hebrew.

Sandeman's New Europe (www.newje-rusalemtours.com) is a large, international company with a good reputation that offers a variety of tours in Jerusalem, including free daily tours of the Old City. They can be contacted online in advance of any special tour you'd like to arrange.

Underground Archaeological Tours

Above the ground, Jerusalem is rich and fascinating. Underground lies another layer of the city that will convince even the most frugal traveler of the value of paying for a tour. These are some of the best underground tours in Jerusalem:

- **Burnt House:** Part of a larger complex under the Old City's Jewish Quarter, the remarkable charred remains date back to AD 70 (www.jewish-quarter.org.il).

- **Herodian Quarter and Wohl Archaeological Museum:** The basement of a Jewish seminary covers the remains of a mansion from the Second Temple period (www.jewish-quarter.org.il).

- **Hezekiah's Tunnel:** You can wade through the water in this 2,700-year-old tunnel, part of the City of David, for 580 yards (www.cityofdavid.org.il).

- **Warren's Shaft:** An underground waterworks system that dates back to the age of the kings of Judea was discovered in 1867 by British engineer Sir Charles Warren (www.cityofdavid.org.il).

Warren's Shaft

- **The Western Wall Tunnels:** This 75-minute tour explores hidden layers of the Western Wall (http://english.thekotel.org).

Nature Tours

The **Society for the Protection of Nature in Israel** (tel. 02/625-2357 or 03/638-8688, www.teva.org.il) gives urban walking tours in English, but not on a fixed schedule. You must call to see if an English tour is available, as they typically only take groups of 10 or more. Their website has a green map that contains useful information about green spaces within the city. They also give ecotours throughout Israel, including relatively cheap places to stay called field schools in remoter regions of the country. They can also be contacted in their U.S., Canadian, French, and British offices.

Archaeological Tours

For tours with an archaeological twist, try **Archaeological Seminars Institute Ltd.** (tel. 02/586-2011, www.archesem.com, US$200 and up, plus VAT and entrance fees) for one of their varied half- and full-day private walking tours for up to 10 people. Some of the tour types include archaeology as it relates to religion, and retracing the footsteps of ancient Jewish residents of the city.

Bus Tours

For those who would rather ride, Egged bus line's **Double-Decker Bus Tour** (tel. 03/920-3992, www.eggedtours.com, from 9am Sun.-Thurs., NIS200-400) can be a great way to see the city if you're independent enough to hop on and off the big red bus at some of the 24 stops that it makes. One- and two-day passes are available, and stops include several major tourist spots in Jerusalem, including Yad Vashem, the Botanical Garden, multiple locations around the Old City, the National Government Compound, and the Israel Museum. It also includes local shopping spots, like Malha Mall. Each seat is equipped with headphone guides in several languages. If you are organized enough and like to stay on a schedule, this could be an efficient way to hit several major sites with less transportation hassle and cost.

Entertainment and Events

Jerusalem, with its emphasis on ancient tradition and spiritual and family life, isn't typically known for its nightlife scene. But new initiatives by the city municipality and new ventures by industrious business owners have been slowly changing that in recent years. If you are looking for evening entertainment, you can find a select variety of bars, pubs, and live music clubs as well as performing arts venues. If you are looking for a club, be prepared to ask around to a lot of locals.

LIVE MUSIC BARS AND CLUBS
City Center

Not quite as lively at night as it is during the day, Machane Yehuda (the *shuk*) has varied entertainment tucked into its nooks and crannies. After the market closes for shopping, it keeps going for dining, drinks, and music. Start with **Casino de Paris** (Machane Yehuda 3, Machane Yehuda Market, tel. 02/650-4235, noon-2am, Sun.-Thurs., closed for Shabbat and opens again after 9pm on Sat., no cover), which was once the gathering place for British officers during the British Mandate period. Now revived to cater to the bar scene, it features a unique menu of cocktails and a limited fish and vegetable menu.

A restaurant-bar with a nightly offering of jazz music by local musicians, **Birman Musical Bistro** (8 Dorot Rishonim St., tel. 02/623-6115, 2pm-3am Sun.-Thurs., no cover) has a cozy atmosphere that includes a loft and couches. The menu features a selection of nonkosher Middle Eastern meat dishes.

Blaze Sport 'N' Rock Bar (23 Hillel St., tel. 054/816-5488, http://blazebar.co.il, 4pm-2am daily, no cover), just south of Ben Yehuda Street, is considered to be the closest thing to a biker bar in the city and owned by one of Jerusalem's leading thrash-metal musicians, Shworchtse Chaye's lead vocalist. Every night of the week the bar features live rock music and alternative bands, and the menu includes over 30 draught and bottled beers. They have live big-screen sports broadcasts.

The trendy **HaTaklit** (7 Heleni HaMalka St., tel. 02/624-4073, 8pm-last customer, no cover) was founded by three music industry Jerusalemites who adorned the walls with vinyl record sleeves. The full bar serves cocktails, and there is beer on tap, English football screenings, live music, DJs, and independent performers. The happy hour (4:30pm-9pm daily) includes buy one tap beer, get one free.

The **Bass Club** (1 Hahistadrut St., tel. 050/477-7791, http://bassclub.wordpress.com, daily 8pm until last customer, cover varies from about NIS30, call in advance) is known for its variety of music, featuring bass music as well as reggae and dancehall music nights.

Oliver Twist (59 Haneviim St., tel. 054/521-2044, 10pm-4:30am Thurs.-Sat., no cover) is a popular DJ club housed in a 150-year-old building that also serves food and has outdoor seating.

West Jerusalem

The bustling, warehouse-size club **17** (17 Haoman St., tel. 02/678-1658, 9pm-3am Tues., 9:30pm-5am Thurs., 9:30pm-3am Sat., NIS80) is known by its former name to locals (Haoman 17) and features Israeli music on Tuesdays, house music on Thursdays, and funk music on Saturdays. They regularly host international DJs.

The **Yellow Submarine** (13 Herkevim St., tel. 02/679-4040, http://yellowsubmarine. org.il, shows daily from around 8pm or later, entrance NIS30 and up depending on show) is a multidisciplinary music center and has a varied offering of live musical performances. It also houses rehearsal rooms, recording studios, and hosts an annual international music showcase.

The stylish and upscale **Zappa** (28 Derech Hevron, tel. 03/762-6666, www.zappa-club.

co.il, price varies by show but generally NIS50 and up) is the Jerusalem branch of a chain of live music venues with locations in Tel Aviv, Herzliya, and Binyamina. It features high-quality local and international music, light food and drinks, and a sizable stage for performers situated within a close distance to the audience, as well as some major names in jazz, rock, and reggae.

BARS, PUBS, AND WINE BARS
City Center
The Mamilla Hotel has a few nice spots for drinks and mingling. **Winery** (11 King Solomon St., 2nd Fl., tel. 02/548-2222, 3pm-8pm Sun.-Thurs., 2pm-6pm Fri., NIS40) has a selection of 300 Israeli wines that gives a nice introduction to the region's vines, and it sells kosher wines. The **Rooftop** (11 King Solomon St., 8th Fl., tel. 02/548-2222, 6pm-midnight Sun.-Thurs., noon-11pm Fri.-Sat. with a cold Shabbat menu, NIS85) offers a commanding view of Jerusalem and the Old City and caters to the wealthy and elite set. A long bar is complemented by a wooden deck and a row of small bar tables and stools near the front, while the back area (with the better view) has a larger area with seating for dinner. The posh **Mirror Bar** (11 King Solomon St., 2nd Fl., tel. 02/548-2230, www.mamillahotel. com, 8pm-last customer Sun.-Thurs., 9pm-last customer Sat., no cover), features a stylish, modern interior and a selection of cigars that can be enjoyed in a glassed-in smoking room.

Part of an Israeli chain but still a great time, **Dublin Irish Pub** (4 Shamai St., tel. 053/944-3740, http://dub.rest-e.co.il, 5pm-3am Sat.-Thurs., 5pm-5am Fri., no cover) features Gothic and Irish design elements with heavy wooden furniture from Ireland and serves 300 drinks and 70 different beers (18 on tap). The popular hangout has several flat-screen sports TVs, a happy hour (5pm-8pm daily), and a menu of nonkosher food.

Easily accessible from central Jaffa Road, **Heder Vehetsi** (31 Yafo St., tel. 054/642-4242, 6pm until late daily, no cover) is a popular hangout for university students and other 20-something patrons. They are known as one of few bars in town open on Friday night and for their inexpensive selection of alcohol.

The distinctly North American flavor of the crowd at **Mike's Place** (33 Yafo St., tel. 02/502-3439, www.mikesplacebars.com, 11am-last customer Sun.-Thurs. and until 3pm on Fri. and opens after 8pm on Sat., no cover) is part of the draw. This sports bar features booths and wood paneling, big-screen TVs, a kosher food menu, a global selection of beers, and a daily happy hour.

Inspired by traditional English pubs and decorated with a rich, cozy atmosphere of wood, **Bellwood Bar** (Yosef Rivlin and Hasorag St. 5, tel. 050/486-3333, www.bellwood.co.il, 5pm-midnight daily, no cover) features over 100 varieties of whiskey and 15 international beers on tap, as well as a robust food menu of classic pub items like fish-and-chips and hamburgers.

PERFORMING ARTS
Cultural Centers
If you're in the mood for something with an ethnic cultural flavor, **Beit Avi Chai** (44 King George St., tel. 02/621-5300, www.bac. org.il, 1pm-9:30pm Sun.-Thurs., 9:30am-noon Fri.) features speakers and artists, including Israeli musicians every Monday, a summer music concert series of Israeli musicians in the courtyard, and evening concerts by Jerusalem and Israeli musical favorites.

The **Gerard Behar Center** (11 Bezalel St., tel. 02/545-6868, http://gerard-behar.jerusalem.muni.il) is home to two acclaimed dance troupes, Kolben Dance Co. and Vertigo, and also plays host to independent productions and collaborations including their hot jazz series.

Extremely well done performances in English are hosted by the World Union for Progressive Judaism at **Beit Shmuel** (6 Eliyahu Shama St., tel. 02/620-3455, www.beitshmuel.com). They play host to a wide variety of staged performances including plays, musicals, ethnic music, and educational and cultural activities.

One of Jerusalem's finest centers for cultural activities is Mishkenot Sha'ananim (9 Yemin Moshe St., tel. 02/629-2220, www.mishkenot.org.il), which hosts a wide variety of festivals, screenings, and lectures, and is home to the INFO Press Club for foreign journalists.

The hot spot for families and those in the mood for some indoor/outdoor dining, shopping, and live music is the First Station, in Hebrew HaTachana (4 David Remez St., tel. 02/653-5239, http://firststation.co.il, open daily), centered around an outdoor stage under a tent where bands perform year-round for no charge. Free entry to the children's Gymboree tent on Thursdays also includes evening performances.

Theaters and Cinemas

The Jerusalem International Convention Center (1 Shazar Blvd., tel. 02/655-8558, www.iccjer.co.il) has the largest auditorium in Israel with 3,000 seats and is the home of the Israel Philharmonic Orchestra when they are in Jerusalem. It is part of a larger complex called Binyanei Ha'uma that also houses the Globus Movie Theater (tel. 02/622-3685).

The Jerusalem Centre for the Performing Arts (20 David Marcus, tel. 02/560-5757, www.jerusalem-theatre.co.il), with its five halls, hosts everything from musical performances to dance, festivals, plays, and films, and is home to the Jerusalem Symphony Orchestra. It is the largest center for performing arts and cultural performances in Israel.

For stage performances of plays and musicals, The Khan Theatre (2 David Remez Sq., tel. 02/630-3600 www.khan.co.il) offers a variety of performances in a quaint and intimate setting, including special children's performances by its company of permanent actors.

The Jerusalem Cinematheque (11 Derech Hevron, tel. 02/565-4356, www.jercin.org.il, NIS38) is an upper-crust movie theater that shows films both old and new from Europe and North America, as well as some television episodes, independent films, and live in HD performances. There is a concessions area, but no food is allowed in the theaters. Many moviegoers tend to eat at the Cinematheque's adjacent Lavan restaurant before or after a film.

The Globus Movie Theater (1 Shazar Blvd., tel. 02/622-3685) and Rav Hen (19 Haoman, tel. 02/679-2799) both offer more

There's fun for the whole family at the First Station.

standard-style theaters with multiplex settings and more mainstream American movies.

New addition **Cinema City** (10 Yitzhak Rabin Blvd., tel. 074/752-6700, www.cinemacity.co.il) is a massive complex that includes shopping, dining, and specialized theaters that are designed for children. It also features live stage performances, live high-definition broadcasting, and 3D movies.

FESTIVALS AND EVENTS

In the past few years, the number and types of festivals and music events taking place in the city have increased dramatically.

Ongoing

The Tower of David Museum hosts a **Night Spectacular** (south of the Old City's Jaffa Gate, tel. 02/626-5333, www.towerofdavid.org.il, 9pm and 10:30pm, adult NIS55, senior and child NIS45, or museum admission plus show adult NIS70, senior and child NIS55), where the outer walls of the Old City are used for an historic program using lights and images, accompanied by music.

Spring

The annual **International Writer's Festival** (writersfestival.co.il) is relatively new to Jerusalem, but its scope and scale are huge. The festival is held in late spring at Mishkenot Sha'ananim and features a week's worth of events, including talks with famous authors, film screenings, and events for kids. Many of the events are in English.

Summer

The **Jerusalem International Film Festival** (Jerusalem Cinematheque, www.jff.org.il) has been running for almost 30 years and is primarily focused on Israeli film.

Just as much fun as it sounds, the **Jerusalem Beer Festival** (Independence Park, tel. 050/594-8844, www.jerusalembeer.com/en) has been in action for over a decade and is staged in a central park on the grounds of the Old Train Station. Featuring about 30 different types of beers, both international and local, the festival lasts two days and includes live music.

The Old City comes alive every summer with **Balabasta** (www.gojerusalem.com, July) when the ancient streets are filled with live performances, art installations, eating contests, puppets, and DJs.

The **Jerusalem Woodstock Revival** (Kraft Stadium, tel. 03/613-3556, www.woodstockrevival.com, NIS85-140) features musical acts performing covers from Pink Floyd, Neil Young, Bob Dylan, and others who were at Woodstock.

The **Zion Reggae Festival** (Gan Sacher, tel. 03/602-3619) features major reggae performers including Ziggy Marley, Alpha Blondy, and Barrington Levy.

A bit more refined crowd can be found at the **Jerusalem Wine Festival** (Billy Rose Garden of the Israel Museum, tel. 02/625-9703, 8:30pm-11pm, NIS80/evening pp, includes a wineglass, unlimited tasting, and admission to the museum galleries until 9pm on Tues.), which takes place over three days at the end of July. The festival brings together some of the best wines from Israel's varied collection of local wineries.

The **End of the Summer Festival** (20 David Marcus, tel. 02/560-5755, www.jerusalem-theatre.co.il) is three days at the end of August of Israeli and foreign artists and performers. The festival consists of some of the latest work in performance art and film. It's hugely popular amongst locals.

Highly energetic and fascinating, **Contact Point** (Israel Museum, www.jerusalemseason.com/en, August) connects artists and audiences through a night of interactions that start at dusk and end at 3am. All contained within the campus of the Israel Museum, Contact Point features interactive art experiences, live music, dance, and access to the museum's permanent exhibitions.

Fall

The **Jerusalem International Chamber Music Festival** (YMCA Mary Nathaniel Hall, tel. 02/625-0444, www.jcmf.org.il, Sept.,

NIS80-150) is a several days-long concert series that highlights a different area of classical music every year.

For an interesting peek at Israeli culture, head to the **President's Open House** (Presidential residence, Hanasi St. in Talbiyeh, Sukkot week) for the traditional Sukkah, photo taking, and live music.

A series of other events take place during Sukkot week, check with the official tourism site of the **Jerusalem Municipality** (www. itraveljerusalem.com) for details and listings of events.

The **Abu Ghosh Vocal Music Festival** (www.agfestival.co.il/en) takes place every year in the Arab village of Abu Ghosh just outside of Jerusalem. Concerts are performed in the 12th-century Crusader-Benedictine Church in the heart of the village, and at the Kiryat Ye'arim Church.

Winter

Taking place for three decades, **The Jerusalem International Book Fair** (Central locations throughout Jerusalem, www.jbookfair.com, free) brings together agents, authors, and exhibitors of all kinds. The festival's Jerusalem Prize is awarded to a writer who exhibits the principles of individual freedom in society.

Shopping

Jerusalem has a wide variety of shops, with an emphasis on religious ornaments and objects, clothing, and locally handmade ceramics. Types of shopping can be divided mainly into Judaica, antiques, jewelry, gifts and souvenirs, regionally designed and manufactured clothing, and outdoor markets. Home decor and houseware shops, shopping malls, and furniture stores are largely concentrated in the neighborhood of Talpiyot. When buying anything of value, do not leave the shop without the proper paperwork for customs, and also make sure to ask for the **tax rebate** calculation on your receipt.

THE OLD CITY
Jaffa Gate

If you enter through Jaffa Gate, follow the flow of foot traffic as it goes past the **Ministry of Tourism Information Center** (1 Jaffa St., tel. 02/627-1422, 8:30am-5pm Sun.-Thurs., 8:30am-noon Fri.) to HaNotsrim Street, a narrow pedestrian street in the Christian Quarter where you can find **religious items, souvenirs, clothing, and jewelry** that should satisfy any urge you have for doing minor shopping and bargaining. If you stay on the main road from Jaffa Gate (David St.)

until you reach the second to last right turn, you'll get to **HaKardo** or the **Cardo** (tel. 02/626-5900, ext. 102, business area and shops 8am-6pm Sun.-Thurs., 8am-4pm Fri.) with its numerous high-end gift shops and galleries for Judaica. This is the border between the Jewish and Armenian Quarters, the latter of which has some interesting shops that sell jewelry, antiques, and textiles.

Damascus Gate

For a vibrant shopping experience (as in, loud and extremely physical), just inside of Damascus Gate at the intersection of Beit Habad Street and El Wad Hagai Street is the gateway to the **Arab Souk,** where you can find trinkets, clothes, spices, sweets, jewelry, raw meat, and other food. Watch out for people running through with carts!

Mamilla

Though not technically connected, the Old City and Mamilla feed off of each other like a mountain and a river. Go down the stairs from the Old City's Jaffa Gate plaza and you'll reach the mellow atmosphere of **Mamilla** (street entrance is at the intersection of Shlomtsiyon HaMalka and Shlomo HaMelech, just across the entrance to the Old City's Jaffa Gate

the street from the David Citadel Hotel, shop hours are generally 9am-10pm Sun.-Thurs., 9am-3pm Fri.). Many shops here are Israeli or international chain stores for clothing, jewelry, and makeup, which makes it a convenient place. There is also a chain pharmacy for SuperPharm. Brands represented include Rolex, MAC, H. Stern, Nike, Polo Ralph Lauren, Gap, Nautica, bebe, and Tommy Hilfiger, as well as local brands like Fox, Castro, Ronen Chen, and Steimatzky Books. You can also come across musical street performers here, which makes it a fun place to wander and window-shop, and it stays active late into the evening.

Take a look inside **Eden Fine Art** (Alrov Mamilla Ave., tel. 02/624-2506, www.eden-gallery.com) for a glimpse at this international art representative. The shop sponsors artwork, sculptures, and photographs from select leading Israeli and international artists. The bright, small venue caters to upper-crust clients and art collectors, and has some interesting pieces from Israeli artists.

The **Stern House** is a charming and interesting preserved and reconstructed building

Mamilla's Numbered Stones

Throughout Jerusalem you will see stone buildings with the curious characteristic of sequential numbers scrolled by hand on each stone. These are historically significant buildings that have been disassembled, preserved, and reassembled. The numbers have been left to indicate the act of preservation and to distinguish the building among its neighbors as having special historic value. It is also a way to honor the authenticity of Jerusalem as an ancient city.

Stroll through Mamilla Alrov Quarter, and you will see five such examples of buildings preserved in this way, either in their entirety or by being incorporated into new buildings. The preservation was done under the guidance of the Israel Antiquities Authority.

Two buildings in Mamilla that have been left in place are particularly notable. The Stern House, situated at about the center of Mamilla's pedestrian promenade, was built in 1877 and hosted Zionist Theodor Herzl on his only trip to Israel. The Clark House was constructed by American evangelicals in the late 19th century.

that played host to Theodor Herzl during his visit to Jerusalem in 1898, and now houses one of the **Steimatzky Books** chain store (tel. 02/625-7268), which has a good selection of English books and magazines, and a **Café Café** (tel. 02/624-4773) chain coffee shop, a place to get a bite to eat or coffee.

One of the leading jewelry chains in Israel, **Miller Jewelry** (tel. 02/622-3414) has a store on the smaller end in Mamilla with a highly selective number of their finest pieces.

CITY CENTER
Yafo Street (Jaffa Street)
Busy **Yafo Street** (also known as Jaffa Street) is the main artery of the city's center and home to the light-rail train. Only pedestrian and train traffic are allowed to go through the length of the street that runs through the heart of town, passing always-happening **Tolerance Square** (formerly known as **Zion Square**) near where Yafo intersects with Shamai Street, which is full of tourists, souvenir shops, ice cream shops, juice bars, and several sidewalk cafés.

Ben Yehuda Street (Pedestrian Mall)
A main pedestrian artery that leads to

Tolerance Square, **Ben Yehuda Street** is full of shops that tend to cater to tourists and sell items such as souvenirs and Judaica. In the past, the highly trafficked area made it a target for terrorist bombings—look for silver plaques on the ground and sides of buildings marking spots where bombings took place. The triangle formed by Ben Yehuda, King George, and Yafo Streets is partially inhabited by shops founded after attacks on the Mamilla commercial center just days after the UN vote on the partition of Palestine in 1947.

★ Machane Yehuda Market (The *Shuk*)
Also accessible by Yafo Street is the open-air market world-famous for its colorful produce stands, restaurants, and characters, and known to locals as the *shuk*. **Machane Yehuda Market** (between Yafo St. and Agripas St. at Beit Ya'acov and Eitz HaChaim, www.machne.co.il/en, 8am-7pm Sun.-Thurs., 8am-3pm Fri.) is overwhelming in its sights, sounds, and tastes. No matter which entrance you take (and there are about a half a dozen ways to go in), you will find yourself in a seemingly endless maze of bins overflowing with fruits and vegetables, sweets and olives, and all kinds of spices and teas. You can enjoy

Shopping options abound in City Center.

sausage for sale in Machane Yehuda Market

one of the market's many restaurants, shop for produce, spices, or sweets, or just browse the ordered chaos of the place.

One of the most interesting things about the *shuk* in Jerusalem is the mixture of people, ranging from the locals who eagerly elbow their way to the vendors and the tourists who wander around taking photographs.

The secret to enjoying the *shuk* is deciding what type of experience you want. The most intense time and day of the week is 11am-3pm on Friday. The level of activity reaches a fever pitch as closing time gets closer and vendors want to sell more goods and shoppers want to buy their last items before the weekend.

The most low-key time to visit is generally any weekday before about 10:30am. You will have plenty of space to move about and enjoy the market without worrying about battling the crowds. You won't get many deals, though. The best deals are cut closest to closing time.

Later in the day, especially on Thursdays and Fridays, you can find all kinds of interesting characters in the main alley that runs through the market and is outdoors. You will likely see some characters here that are fixtures, including the man who takes photographs and sells them, and college kids or tourists who sit down in the middle of the pathway to drink beer and hang out. There is also often live music. It's just lovely, colorful chaos.

King George Street

A main street leading into Jerusalem's heart is **King George Street,** significant for orienting yourself toward the Old City, City Center, West Jerusalem and East Jerusalem. The street is filled with shops of all kinds from electronics to clothing to food, and nearly every side street has additional shopping, hair salons, and restaurants.

Tolerance (Zion) Square

Shopping in City Center rotates on the axis of **Tolerance Square,** which runs between **King George Street** and **Yafo Street** and is at the foot of both **Ben Yehuda Street** and **Yoel Moshe Salomon** pedestrian malls. The square's name was changed in 2016 to honor the victim of a stabbing attack at Tel Aviv's annual gay pride parade. All of these shopping areas are mostly shut down for Shabbat and Jewish holidays, with the exception of a

Shopping in the Old City

Shopping in the Old City can be exciting or intimidating. In many cases, aggressive shop owners won't allow you more than two seconds to glance at their products before pushing you to make a purchase. It is also a notoriously expensive place for English-speaking customers, particularly Americans. Despite that, it's tremendously fun and great exercise.

Be prepared in advance to do the dance of bargaining if you plan to buy something, which might include literally walking away to get the best price. You can bargain if you are confident, but the best bet for avoiding some serious unplanned spending is to decide in advance on your limit.

There are seemingly endless streets of shops and cavernous stalls that are open seven days a week, and they have very similar items. The stores fall mainly into the categories of jewelry, religious items, souvenirs, clothing, antiques, and food. Most visitors enter the Old City area from Jaffa Gate and turn down HaNotsrim Street, a narrow pedestrian street in the Christian Quarter.

a shop in the Old City

A good approach to shopping in this area is to walk past vendors and stores, and only slow down if you are seriously interested in buying something. Otherwise you will spend a great deal of time extricating yourself from negotiations with shop owners.

Shops selling antiques and artifacts, including Roman-glass inlaid jewelry and other locally handmade items, can be found mainly in the Christian and Jewish Quarters, although such stores are scattered throughout all four quarters. Be very cautious when purchasing antiques. You will need the appropriate legal certificate to take the item out of the country, largely due to problems with grave robbers and theft of antiques from archaeological sites. Check with the information center about the proper documentation necessary or visit the Israeli Antiquities Authority website.

Most vendors are more than willing to take American dollars, and you can find nice scarves, sweets, and cute trinkets. One of the great advantages to shopping in this area is that almost everything is open on the weekend.

couple of restaurants. Much of the shopping in the area is limited to a few types of stores that sell souvenirs and Judaica, embroidered *kippot* and T-shirts, camera equipment, electronics and housewares, and local brands of clothing and shoes.

At the top of Tolerance Square, check out **The Book Gallery** (6 Schatz St. at corner of 26 King George St., tel. 02/623-1087, www. bookgallery.co.il, 9am-7pm Sun.-Thurs., 9am-2pm Fri.), the largest secondhand bookstore in Israel. It includes two floors with a separate section for old and rare books and a large basement.

Nahalat Shiva

Small and mostly stocked with books and materials in French, **Vice-Versa** (1 Shim'on Ben Shetach St., tel. 02/624-4412, www.viceversalib.com, 9am-6pm Sun.-Thurs., 9am-1:30pm Fri.) is a sweet shop with a warm atmosphere that highlights the fact that Jerusalem has a subculture of French residents. Mostly fun for browsing, the shop does sell some gift-related items like wrapping paper and cards and also interesting items for children.

For a truly unique souvenir, **Gaya Games** (7 Yoel Moshe Solomon St. at the end of Shamai St., tel. 054/392-0115, www.

gaya-game.com, 10am-10pm Sun.-Thurs., 9am-3pm Fri., 7pm-11pm Sat.) has dozens of unique wooden games and brain teaser toys. The cavernous feel of their Jerusalem store, one of numerous locations throughout Israel, caters to adult customers who are interested in challenging play. Their **Creative Thinking Seminars** (contact Galit, tel. 03/903-3122, galit@gaya-game.com) allow you to play with some of their games and engage in challenging your brain.

The Cadim Ceramic Art Gallery and Collective (4 Yoel Moshe Solomon St., tel. 02/623-4869, 10am-10pm Sun.-Thurs., 9am-3pm Fri.) is a small, charming gallery and shop that serves as the storefront for a cooperative of 15 Israeli ceramists, who also run and staff it. Objects are displayed in groups by artist and every purchase includes the story of the artist. Prices start on the affordable end and go up, and objects include functional pottery, decorative objects, sculptural pieces, Judaica, and jewelry.

A relatively well-kept secret, **The Eighth Note** (12 Ze'ev Raban St., tel. 08/919-9555, www.tav8.co.il, 10am-6pm Sun.-Thurs.) is visible by the small, black-and-white sign on its storefront. This side-street basement store has a nice collection of Arabic, Greek, Turkish, and other Middle Eastern CDs and DVDs. The friendly and knowledgeable sales staff will help you to listen to selections that you're interested in buying and will do their best to make sure you don't leave empty-handed.

EAST JERUSALEM

Renowned as an oasis of books in English on a wide range of subjects about Israel, the West Bank, and the conflict in the region, **Educational Bookshop** (19 and 22 Salah Eddin St., tel. 02/627-5858, www.educationalbookshop.com, 8am-8pm daily) is a combination of two bookshops, a small coffee shop, and a space for events in English. The friendly, knowledgeable staff can help you find a book on nearly any subject, and it makes the perfect place to have a coffee and watch the bustle of East Jerusalem go by.

OUTDOOR MARKETS

Every Friday you can find vendors at the outdoor **Bezalel Art Fair** (Schatz St. and Bor Shiber Garden by the Mashbir, www.bezalelfair.co.il, 10am-4pm Fri.) selling paintings, wood crafts, textiles, jewelry, glasswork, special and unique handicrafts, and food. The lively fair consists of carefully chosen vendors to maintain an overall atmosphere and a varied selection of art and artistic displays. Staged next door to the historic campus of The Bezalel Art Academy, the outdoor fair also includes a tour at noon from Bezalel to City Center.

A popular stop before the weekend is the **Farmers' and Artists' Street Market** (12 Emek Refaim St., 10am-2pm Fri.) that includes vendors selling jewelry, ceramics, toys, food, and a wide variety of other items for very affordable prices.

SHOPPING MALLS
Jerusalem (Malha) Mall

The massive **Jerusalem (Malha) Mall** (Agudat Sport Beitar 1 across from Teddy Stadium, tel. 02/679-1333, www.jerusalem.azrieli.com, 9am-10pm Sun.-Thurs. and 9am-3pm Fri.) is reminiscent of a southern California shopping mall in its size, parking, range of stores, and dining options. With 215 stores, it is Jerusalem's largest and nicest mall.

Hadar Mall

Very easy to reach by bus or taxi, **Hadar Mall** (26 Pierre Koenig St., http://hadar-mall.co.il, 9am-11pm Sun.-Thurs. and 9am-3pm Fri.) is extremely convenient and sells everything from basic necessities to doctor services.

Sports and Recreation

Jerusalem's location in the mountains at about 2,500 feet means that even in the hot summer months it boasts a cool, soothing breeze in the mornings and evenings. This makes outdoor activities a common pastime, including visiting natural springs, hiking, biking, swimming, camping, and cooking out (which is practically a national sport). Many Jerusalemites enjoy taking long walks through the city's scenic (and often hilly) terrain. Playing soccer, having a picnic, or simply sitting and relaxing are common.

PARKS AND GARDENS
Sherover-Haas Promenade
A paved walking trail with fantastic vistas, the **Sherover-Haas Promenade** (enter off of Daniel Yanovski St. at Olei HaGardom St., tel. 02/626-5900, ext. 102, www.s-aronson. co.il, 24 hours daily, free, free parking) boasts fantastic views of East Jerusalem, the Old City walls, and the Judean Desert. The winding walk down the promenade is nearly one mile (there are stairs at different points) and full of native plant and flower gardens, quiet places to sit, and viewing pergolas. The bottom of the promenade is the edge of the Judean Desert.

Orson Hyde Memorial Park
The two-acre wooded **Orson Hyde Memorial Park** (Brigham Young University Mormonic Jerusalem Campus on Hadassa Lampel Rd., free) is known for its views of the Kidron Valley and the Old City. The park is named in honor of Orson Hyde, a prominent member of the Mormon Church who traveled in the Holy Land in the late 19th century.

Gan Sacher
At little over half a mile long, **Gan Sacher** (between Ben Zvi Blvd. and the Knesset, 24 hours daily, free) is easily the park with the largest expanse of open green space in Jerusalem. As a result, it is a staging ground

for major outdoor concerts during the summer, and on national holidays it is covered with a haze of smoke from families cooking out. It is home to two play areas for children, basketball and tennis courts, soccer fields, a skateboarding park, a jogging path, and a set of tunnels that run under Ben Zvi Boulevard and have been used in recent years for graffiti by local artists.

Follow the woodland paths near the center of Gan Sacher uphill toward the Knesset and you'll come upon the one-acre **Bird Observatory** (tel. 02/653-7374, http://natureinisrael.org/jbo, 24 hours daily, free), run by the Society for the Protection of Nature in Israel. The observatory is home to the Israel national bird-ringing center (schedule online) and features a wildlife blind to watch the myriad wild animals that spend time in this richly preserved and fortified natural habitat. Try going at night to see nocturnal animals by moonlight.

Liberty Bell Park
A stunning canopy of purple wisteria can be found in the spring in **Liberty Bell Park** (crossroads of Keren HaYesod and King David St. down to the beginning of Emek Refaim St., 24 hours daily, free) at the eastern end. The western end of the park is home to a very accurate reproduction of the Liberty Bell (hence the name), and there are several different playgrounds, walking paths, basketball courts, and picnic areas. It also hosts festivals, performances, and fairs, and is home to the Train Theater.

Train Track Park
The nearly 4-mile-long linear **Train Track Park** (also known as Railroad Park, 24 hours daily, free entry, paid neighborhood parking) following the old Turkish railway train tracks from the cultural and entertainment center at the First Station to near Malha Mall

is a singular glimpse into local life and architecture. The paved jogging and bike path is always busy, while a boarded walkway covering the old railroad tracks allows for more leisurely strolling. The park is filled with plants, flowers, and benches to stop off for a rest along the route. It also has easy access to numerous dining and shopping venues along the entire route.

Bloomfield Garden

Full of character and history, **Bloomfield Garden** (runs along King David St. from the base of Keren HaYesod St. to Elimelech Admoni St. and west to Mishkenot Sha'ananim St., 24 hours daily, free) features massive agave plants, the family tomb of King Herod, and the remains of an ancient aqueduct. A unique landmark on the southern end of the 17-acre park is a fountain with distinct bronze lions encircling it (the symbol of Jerusalem). At the north end of the park is the venerable artist colony and cultural center Mishkenot Sha'ananim and the little-known **Gozlan Garden,** a beautiful, small park with fountains behind the world-famous King David Hotel.

Wohl Rose Garden

Magical **Wohl Rose Garden** (Government Center opposite the Knesset, tel. 02/563-7233, www.jerusalem.muni.il, 24 hours daily, free, paid parking) covers an area of almost 20 acres and is home to about 400 varieties of roses on 15,000 bushes. The park also has a variety of charming nooks and crannies, including an observation point and an ornamental pool. It is adjacent to other major tourist spots, including the Supreme Court and the Israeli Parliament.

Independence Park

Just on the edge of City Center, you will find the sprawling **Independence Park** (bordered by Gershon Agron St. and King George St., 24 hours daily, free), with some good places to sit and enjoy a picnic if you've been exploring nearby City Center. Its terraced landscaping is dotted with a waterway system of an artificial creek and pools and frequented by families, but is rarely crowded except for the rare outdoor concert or event. The American Consulate is just across Gershon Agron Street.

Train Track Park is full of interesting things to do and see.

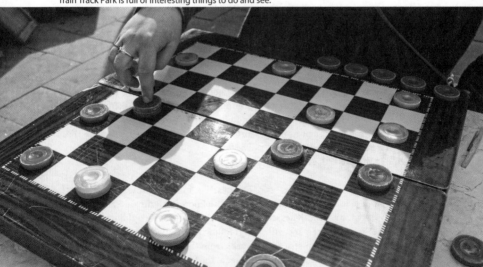

Jerusalem Botanical Garden

A trip to the **Jerusalem Botanical Garden** (1 Yehuda Burla St., tel. 073/243-8914, http://en.botanic.co.il, 9am-5pm Sun.-Thurs., 9am-3pm Fri. and holiday eves, 9am-5pm Sat. and holidays, hours and price subject to change for special events, adult NIS30, senior and child NIS20) includes exploring 30 acres of landscaped grounds that include a renowned bonsai collection and about 10,000 varieties of plants from Europe and North America. Inside the grounds of the garden you can ride the Flower Train or walk along leafy paths. It also includes an indoor tropical conservatory, plants of the Bible trail, an herb and medicinal plant garden, and an African savanna grass maze.

BICYCLING AND SEGWAY RIDING

A tour on wheels is a great way to see and experience Jerusalem, especially at night without the hot Middle Eastern sun beating down on you. Biking and Segway tours also allow you to cover more ground in a shorter time.

For those already comfortable on a bike, the **Jerusalem Midnight Biking** tour (departs from the Karta parking lot, tel. 02/566-1441, http://jerusalembiking.com, call for upcoming rides, NIS115, NIS230 with bike and helmet) offers exercise and a chance to socialize. The three-hour tour covers an approximately a five-mile circular route and passes through the neighborhoods of Abu-Tor, Yemin Moshe, and parts of the Old City.

Gordon Active provides a variety of bicycle tours, including **Bike and Eat Jerusalem** (departs from Abraham Hostel at 67 Nevi'im St., tel. 03/765-9018, www.gordonactive.com, 10am Tues. and Sat., NIS220). The seven-hour tour goes on a fairly exhaustive route and includes passing through the historic center of the city, the Calatrava Bridge, the Knesset and Supreme Court, Valley of the Cross, Rehavya, Talbiyeh, the German Colony, the Sherover-Haas Promenade, Mishkenot Sha'ananim, Jaffa Gate, and the Russian Compound.

A popular way to experience Jerusalem for those who aren't accustomed to the hills, **SmartTours** (tel. 02/561-8056, www.segwayz.co.il, tours daily, NIS180-330 pp) offers a variety of tours that allow you to see much of the city without getting worn out or stuck in traffic.

A new **bike share rental** program

Bloomfield Garden gives access to East and West Jerusalem.

sponsored by the city set to launch in 2016 will initially include about 500 bicycles at 15 stations, largely in and around City Center.

HIKING AND WALKING

For very serious walkers, the Jerusalem Trail (www.jerusalemtrail.com) forms a circular route about 26 miles long through the city. It is part of the larger Israel National Trail that runs from the north to the south of the country. The trail should be marked with blue and white or blue and gold signs along the route, but it is highly recommended to download a GPS map from the trail's website. Between Mount Scopus and Yad Vashem there are occasional markings.

Rehavya Park (off of Ben Tsvi St., 24 hours daily, free) has extensive trails that are easy to navigate with sturdy shoes as the trails are a bit rocky. The views of the Valley of the Cross and its monastery below are magnificent. Walking in this area is better suited for cloudy days or early evening.

The Jerusalem Forest (off Highway 1 just past Yad Vashem, 24 hours daily, free) affords several good places to take relatively easy hikes if you have a reliable, sturdy car that can handle the sometimes extremely rough and rocky roads that lead to the hiking trails in the forest. If you are persistent, you can even find a spring or cistern to swim in along the way.

TENNIS

The Hebrew University maintains 10 outdoor, flood-lit tennis courts and two multipurpose courts (1 Churchill St., Mt. Scopus, tel. 02/588-2796, http://overseas.huji.ac.il, www.cosell.co.il, 3pm-10pm Sun., 8am-10pm Mon.-Thurs., 7am-5pm Fri., 8am-4pm Sat., daytime court rental NIS20/hour, evening court rental NIS25/hour, racket rental NIS20, purchase three balls NIS30) as part of its Lerner Center at its Mount Scopus campus.

The Jerusalem Tennis Center (1 Elmali'akh St. near Teddy Stadium and Malha Mall, tel. 02/679-1439, http://israeltenniscenters.com, court rental NIS40/hour) boasts 19 courts, a practice wall, dressing rooms, a

sporting goods store, and a snack bar. Part of the Israel Tennis Center network, the center has a special purpose and mission to help underprivileged and disadvantaged youth.

SWIMMING

There are several public and private pools in the city that can be accessed, but some have a rather high fee. Check the hours beforehand because of different hours for men and women. The Jerusalem Pool (43 Emek Refaim St., tel. 02/563-2092, www.jerusalem-pool.co.il, 5:30am-8:45pm Sun.-Thurs. with varying hours depending on the day, weekdays adult NIS55, child NIS45, weekends adult NIS60, child NIS50) is an Olympic-size covered pool with five lanes, a large outdoor kiddie pool, and a waterslide. The grassy area near the outdoor pool and the locker room are both a bit run down, but the location is extremely convenient.

The seasonal outdoor half-Olympic-size pool at Beit Yehudah Guest House (Haim Kulitz Rd. 1, Givat Massuah, tel. 02/632-2777, www.byh.co.il, 10am-6pm Sun.-Thurs. summer, NIS70) is in the hills of Jerusalem right near the Biblical Zoo.

The Leonardo Plaza Hotel Jerusalem (47 King George St., tel. 02/629-8666, www.leonardo-hotels.com, 10am-7pm daily, weekdays adult NIS55, child NIS40, Sat. adult NIS70, child NIS60) doesn't include a kids' pool, but there are lounge chairs and the pool is situated in a calming garden.

GYMS AND SPAS

The Dan Jerusalem Hotel (32 Lehi St., Mt. Scopus, tel. 02/533-1234, 6:15am-9pm Sun.-Fri. and 8:45am-9pm Sat., NIS80) has a range of facilities including a gym, Turkish bath, whirlpool bath, saunas, and indoor and outdoor pools (in season).

The Akasha Wellbeing Center (11 King Solomon St., tel. 02/548-2222, www.mamillahotel.com, call for hours and entry fees) is inside the Mamilla Hotel and includes a state-of-the-art gym, luxurious lap pool, spa, health bar, sundeck, and holistic classes.

Food

Restaurants, coffee shops, and other places to eat and drink in Jerusalem tend to be grouped together. In some cases, the distance between these groupings is significant, so it's best to always carry some water and a snack to tide you over if you're out sightseeing. In places like City Center, there are food-related establishments every five feet.

Although it seems as though the city completely shuts down from late Friday afternoon to late Saturday evening for Shabbat, there is still a choice selection of places to eat and drink if you know where to look.

CITY CENTER
Middle Eastern
Yemenite Falafel (48 Hanevi'im St., tel. 02/624-2346, 9:30am-9:30pm Sun.-Thurs., 9:30am-3pm Fri., NIS40) is a reigning falafel master, run by a second-generation cook who learned the tricks of the trade from his father.

Another extremely popular falafel joint in a very touristy area is **Moshiko** (5 Ben Yehuda St., tel. 050/535-6861, 9am-midnight Sun.-Thurs., 9am-2pm Fri., NIS50). Its bright sign with large lettering is easy to spot, and it is en route to numerous other tourist activities in City Center.

Contemporary
A charming and conveniently located Jerusalem institution, **Kadosh** (6 Shlomtsiyon HaMalka, tel. 053/809-1548, www.2eat.co.il/eng/kadosh, 7am-midnight Sun.-Thurs., 7am-4pm Fri., 1 hour after Shabbat-Midnight Sat., NIS50) is known among locals as a good first-date restaurant. Kadosh's floor plan is smallish, but its atmosphere exudes the charm of classic Jerusalem. Kadosh serves an excellent, hearty, Mediterranean, prix fixe breakfast that includes a variety of salads, omelets and eggs, fresh bread, juice, and coffee. They also have a good selection of tasty patisserie and *burekasim*. They can get very crowded, so service is

sometimes slow, but the food and coffee are consistently delicious.

One of the few restaurants in the city that is open 24 hours a day and serves bacon, ★ **Zuni** (15 Yoel Moshe Solomon St., 2nd Fl., tel. 053/934-5582, http://zuni.rest-e.co.il, 24 hours daily, NIS60) is centrally located, has incredibly friendly waitstaff, and an excellent breakfast menu. Housed on the second floor, Zuni is decorated in rich, dark wood with an enclosed bar for smokers away from the main dining room. The restaurant offers breakfast, evening, and late-night menus with fare to accommodate the mood of the time of day. The late-night menu features several desserts familiar to a North American palate, as well as a good selection of seafood and pasta. The morning menu offers various combination breakfasts with coffee and juice included. The evening menu features items like

Zuni is Jerusalem's only restaurant open 24/7.

Restaurants and Cafés Open on Shabbat

From late Friday afternoon to late Saturday evening, if you don't have some insider information, you'll find it difficult to go out for a meal because most places are closed. Scattered throughout the city are some outstanding nonkosher establishments that do stay open. You just have to know where to look.

CITY CENTER AND VICINITY OF THE OLD CITY

This is where most of the open places are concentrated. The Old City is always open, so restaurants are always available.

- **Austrian Hospice Café** (Old City near Damascus Gate, 37 Via Dolorosa, tel. 02/626-5800, www.austrianhospice.com)
- **Barood** (31 Jaffa St. in Feingold Courtyard, tel. 02/625-9081)
- **Blue Dolphin** (7 Shim'on Ha'tsadik St., tel. 02/532-2001)
- **Chakra** (41 King George St., tel. 02/625-2733, www.chakra-rest.com/en)
- **Dublin Irish Pub** (4 Shamai St., tel. 057/944-3740, http://dub.rest-e.co.il)
- **Focaccia Bar** (4 Rabi Akiva St., tel. 057/944-3123, bar.focaccia.co)
- **Lavan at the Cinematheque** (11 Hebron Rd., tel. 02/673-7393)
- **Link** (3 Hama'alot St., tel. 053/809-4510, www.2eat.co.il/eng/link)
- **Meatburger Iwo** (28 Hillel St., tel. 02/622-2513, http://iwos.co.il)
- **Notre Dame Roof Top Wine and Cheese Restaurant** (3 Paratroopers Rd., tel. 02/627-9111, www.notredamecenter.org)
- **YMCA Three Arches** (26 King David St., tel. 02/569-2692, http://ymca.org.il)
- **Zuni** (15 Yoel Moshe Solomon, 2nd Fl., tel. 053/934-5582, http://zuni.rest-e.co.il)

EAST JERUSALEM

Most places in East Jerusalem are open, but it can be a bit trickier to navigate than West Jerusalem. The following are a couple of recommendations on the seam between east and west.

- **American Colony** (1 Louis Vincent St., tel. 02/627-9777, www.americancolony.com)
- **Askadinya Restaurant Bar** (11 Shim'on Ha'tsadik St., tel. 02/532-4590)
- **Pasha's Restaurant** (13 Shimon Siddiq in Sheikh Jarrah, tel. 02/582-5162, www.pashasofjerusalem.com)

WEST JERUSALEM

This area has slim, but quality, pickings.

- **Café Paradiso** (36 Keren HaYesod St., tel. 02/563-4805, http://cafparadiso.rest-e.co.il)
- **The Culinary Workshop** (28 Hebron Rd. in the JVP Media Quarter, tel. 053/934-4990, http://hasadna.rest-e.co.il)
- **Landwer Café** (4 David Remez St., tel. 02/587-7988, www.landwercafe.co.il)
- **P2 Pizzeria** (36 Keren HaYesod St., tel. 02/563-5555)
- **Scottish Guesthouse Restaurant** (1 David Remez St., tel. 02/673-2401, www.scotsguesthouse.com)

mussels, grilled eggplant, risotto, and quiche. Every menu has the option to add—yes, you guessed it—bacon.

Meatburger Iwo (28 Hillel St., tel. 02/622-2513, http://iwos.co.il, 10am-3am Sun.-Thurs., 10am-7pm Fri., 10am-4pm Sat., NIS40) serves up hefty hamburgers, wraps, and grilled chicken sandwiches that are big enough to satisfy the hungriest of customers. They are also English-speaking, deliver, and have a convenient online ordering system. It's better for takeout or delivery, as the atmosphere is more fast food than restaurant.

Nestled discreetly behind a row of buildings and up several staircases in the popular tourist neighborhood of Nahalat Shiva, ★ **Tmol Shilshom** (5 Solomon St. through the back alley, tel. 02/623-2758, www.tmolshilshom.co.il, 9am-1am Sun.-Thurs., 9am-3pm Fri., NIS55) is one of the best ways for visitors to Jerusalem to experience local culture. Housed in a 150-year-old building and famous as a gathering place for well-known authors to read their works in English and Hebrew, Tmol Shilshom has hosted famous writers including Amos Oz, Yehuda Amichai, David Grossman, and others. An interesting and unique feature is the café's completely separate rooms, with a small outdoor patio in between. Among favorite menu items is their Amanda salad, salmon filet in fig sauce, and cheesecake. Their coffee is also excellent, and the cool, cave-like atmosphere makes it the perfect place for a late-night powwow with friends or as a temporary escape from the midday sun.

If you know in advance that you are going to eat out while in Jerusalem and want to experience something that is seriously hyped by Jerusalemites, call in advance for a reservation at **Machane Yehuda Restaurant** (Beit Yaakov 10, tel. 02/533-3442, 12:30pm-4:30pm and 6:30pm-midnight Sun.-Thurs., noon-4pm Fri., 8:30pm-midnight Sat., NIS100). Run by three Jerusalem chefs, Assaf Granit, Yossi Elad, and Uri Avon, the food is prepared with ingredients brought in fresh daily from the *shuk,* and the dishes are designed to reflect the character of each chef. The menu changes on a daily basis, and the kitchen is open for viewing. The general atmosphere of the place is rustic nouveau, which means your food might be served in a jar or on a cutting board, but the dishes are seriously delicious. In the evening, the small place is packed with tables and gets progressively louder and rowdier until you feel like you're in a club. It's not the place to go for a quiet, intimate dinner.

Tmol Shilshom restaurant and café

French

The lovely Shim'on Ben Shetach Street is home to cluster of upper-crust bistros with sidewalk dining, including ★ **Dolphin Yam** (9 Shim'on Ben Shetach St., tel. 02/623-2272, 11am-midnight daily, NIS60-100), one of the best known seafood restaurants in the city. It emphasizes serving moderately priced nonkosher seafood ranging from Israeli favorites to more commonly known items like bass. The menu also includes an array of meat and pasta dishes prepared in the style of French cuisine. Seafood soup, appetizers, and entrées make for seafood dishes for every taste. There are also some vegetarian options.

A refined fine dining atmosphere with indoor and outdoor seating can be found at **Gabriel's** (7 Shim'on Ben Shetach St., tel. 02/624-6444, www.gabriel-jerusalem.co.il, noon-5pm and 7pm-midnight Sun.-Thurs., noon-3pm Fri., NIS130), home to a nice selection of delicate, artistic dishes of meat and fish at this kosher restaurant. Some more unique menu items include the Chinese five spice duck breast and confit and a lamb slider bruschetta.

Although the Pontifical Institute Notre Dame of Jerusalem Center is a massive building in the center of the city, you could easily pass the outer walls without noticing it. Set back from the road behind a security gate, the institute is home to the **Roof Top Wine and Cheese Restaurant** (3 Paratroopers Rd., tel. 02/627-9111, www.notredamecenter. org, 5pm-midnight Mon.-Thurs., noon-midnight Fri.-Sun., reservations recommended, NIS70), which offers outdoor dining on a beautiful rooftop terrace overlooking the city. The menu features 40 types of imported cheese and a large selection of wines from all over the world, including Notre Dame's private label wine. For something beyond cheese and drinks, the dinner menu offers a range of meat and potato dishes with salads.

Italian

For some authentic Italian fare, try **Topoleone** (62 Agripas St., tel. 02/622-3466, www.topolino.biz, 8am-11pm Sun.-Thurs., 8am-2:30pm Fri., NIS60), known for its superior service (waitstaff will bend over backward to accommodate you) and its variety of world-class pasta dishes. A note for those seeking a kosher establishment: the owners do not have a kosher certificate but claim that they serve strictly kosher food.

Headed by world-class chef Michael Katz, **Trattoria Haba** (119 Yafo Street, tel. 02/623-3379, www.haba.co.il, 7am-midnight Sun.-Thurs., 7am-3pm Fri., NIS60) occupies prime territory on the edge of the *shuk* facing busy Yafo Street. The kosher milk establishment serves a huge array of wonderful breads, pasta, meat, and vegetable dishes. Cheese plays a supporting role in many of Haba's entrées, including for cuts of meat. The atmosphere is bright and sunny with counter space facing Yafo Street in the front and outdoor garden seating facing the *shuk* in the back.

Pub Fare and Burgers

Part of a chain of pubs across Israel, **Mike's Place** (33 Yafo St., tel. 02/502-3439, www. mikesplacebars.com, 11am-last customer Sun.-Thurs., 11am-3pm Fri., NIS55) has a sports bar atmosphere. Unique on the menu is an offering of a variety of Mexican food favorites, which is next to impossible to find in Jerusalem. They also serve a wide variety of hamburgers, sandwiches, barbecue items, pizza, and salad.

Beyond popular for its hamburgers, **Josef** (123 Agripas St., tel. 053/936-7983, 11am-1am Sun.-Thurs., 11am-3pm Fri., 7pm-2am Sat., NIS45) serves up a selection of generous burgers prepared in a style that will satisfy the North American stomach. The interior has a warm pub atmosphere and is inviting and well lit. In addition to the standard burger and fries options, the menu also features modern touches such as gluten-free buns and vegan and veggie burgers. A modest selection of beer, liquor, and wine is also available.

More on the refined end for a pub, **O'Connell's** (3 Shim'on Ben Shetach St.,

Jerusalem's Restaurant Culture

Dining out in Jerusalem is a fun diversion and there are some genuinely wonderful gastronomic experiences to be had, but deciphering the unique rules of Jerusalem restaurants is a challenge. Here is a basic primer.

- **Closed for Shabbat:** This means several things, chief among them that they are likely kosher and close sometime on Friday afternoon anywhere between 3pm-5pm depending on the time of year. This type of restaurant often reopens on Saturday evening about 1-2 hours after Shabbat is over (when it is dark enough to see a few stars). The times vary a bit by season, but Shabbat is from sundown on Friday evening until Saturday evening; precise time calculators are available online.

- **Check:** You will never, ever get your bill in a restaurant in Jerusalem, or Israel for that matter, until you ask for it.

- **Coffee Shops:** Due to the strength of several national chain cafés that also serve as coffee shops, the presence of simple coffee shops or espresso stands is nonexistent. You can get a good latte (or cappuccino as locals call them) almost anywhere, though. Ironically, the best coffee is not served in the chain cafés.

- **Business Hours:** Security complications in this region have impacted business hours of establishments with the related decline in customers. Advertised business hours can sometimes be inaccurate; it is best to call in advance to confirm.

- **Kosher:** The kosher system dictates keeping dairy and meat separate, and kosher restaurants serve either milk or meat (meat includes fish). Kosher certification is officially issued by a governing Rabbinate and has degrees of strictness. In laymen's terms, it means you cannot get a cappuccino or real ice cream in a kosher meat restaurant.

- **Restrooms:** A cup with handles next to the restaurant's bathroom sink is for religious hand washing (not drinking) and means you are in a kosher establishment. Some places will have a special sink with a cup in the main dining area of the restaurant.

- **Security:** Watch out for the security fee that some places tack onto your bill. The practice has largely gone out of practice in recent years and it is only a few shekels when used, but you can ask to have it removed if you do spot a strange charge on your bill.

- **Service:** It is not unusual to have no specified waiter or waitress, especially if you are in a busy place. Feel free call on any staff member you see.

- **Tipping:** The tip is almost never included in the bill, and there will be a large note in English on the bottom of your bill indicating "service is not included." A standard tip is about 15 percent.

- **Water:** There is a major shortage of water in this part of the world, so you have to request tap water and usually you have to request refills as well. A bottle of tap water is always free.

- **Wi-Fi:** Almost every single restaurant and coffee shop in Jerusalem has free wireless Internet. Just ask for the code if you need it.

tel. 02/623-2232, 6pm-last customer Sun.-Thurs., NIS50) Irish pub and restaurant has 12 beers on tap including Guinness, over 40 types of whiskey, and menu selections that include hamburger sliders, salad, wraps, and a lamb burger. The house specialty is fish-and-chips.

Dublin Irish Pub (4 Shamai St., tel. 057/944-3740, http://dub.rest-e.co.il, 5pm-3am Sat.-Thurs., 5pm-5am Fri., NIS50) is impossible to miss if you find yourself wandering in the vicinity of Tolerance Square. With its huge trademark painting of a toucan drinking a Guinness beer on a black background,

Dublin is very bold about its presence. Inside there is a similar vibe, with a spacious floor plan that features solid wooden chairs and booths, a huge bar, and TVs for sports games. The menu features stock pub items like hamburgers, pizza, sandwiches, desserts, and a large snack menu to go with their huge bottled and draft beer list. Cocktails and every kind of hard liquor you could want are also available.

In a setting that is just right for a quiet lunch in a serene atmosphere seven days a week, **Link** (3 Hama'alot St., tel. 053/809-4510, www.2eat.co.il/eng/link, 11am-midnight Sun.-Thurs., 10am-midnight Fri.-Sat., NIS60) is fronted by a spacious wooden deck for outdoor seating and a lovely greenhouse-like interior with trees growing through the roof. The hamburger is one of the tastiest and most affordable options on the menu, but Link also serves a nice selection of fish and chicken dishes, calamari rings, fish-and-chips, and some Middle Eastern-style dishes.

South American

El Gaucho (22 Yosef Rivlin St., down the alley, tel. 02/624-2227, www.elgaucho.co.il, noon-midnight Sun.-Thurs., 12:30pm-3:30pm Fri., NIS110) is an upscale restaurant hidden in a back alley that serves an array of cuts of South American beef and a variety of wines. One of seven other El Gaucho restaurants throughout Israel, the interior of the Jerusalem location feels like a calm and inviting cave. The menu features items like *asado* (grilled steak), prime rib, baked potatoes, and meat skewers. They also have a dessert of the day and a children's menu.

To satisfy a meat craving, try **La Boca** (8 Shlomzion Hamalka St., tel. 053/944-2798, http://laboca.rest-e.co.il, noon-last customer Sun.-Thurs., 11:30am-6pm Fri., 8:30pm-last customer Sat., NIS90) for a menu featuring anything to do with meat, including rump steak, chili con carne, as well as some chicken and liver dishes. Self-described as Latin fusion, La Boca presents surprising takes on a wide variety of meat dishes prepared in the South American style.

Cafés and Coffee Shops

Café de Paris (1 Ben Maimon St., tel. 02/566-5126, www.joe.co.il, 8am-11:30pm Sun.-Thurs., 8am-4pm Fri., NIS55) is a relative newcomer to the Jerusalem restaurant scene. Situated just off a main road and easy to reach by a short bus or taxi ride from City Center, Café de Paris is popular for its breakfast menu and regional egg and tomato *shakshuka* dish. It is also favored for its relaxed, casual atmosphere and delicious European dishes cooked with a Mediterranean flair.

Café Mizrachi (12 Hashezif St. in Machane Yehuda, tel. 02/624-2105, 7am-10pm Sun.-Thurs., 7am-2pm Fri., NIS40), whose full name in Hebrew translates to "everything for the baker and coffee too," is a small café tucked into the *shuk*. The inviting shop has indoor and outdoor (under cover) seating, and in addition to food and coffee, it sells items for the home baker. The dairy menu includes sandwiches, salads, soup, and baked goods. It is popular and usually crowded.

The perfect place to stop off for dessert, **Babette Café** (16 Shamai St. at Yoel Moshe Solomon St., tel. 02/625-7004, 4pm-2:30am Sun.-Thurs., 11am-3pm Fri., NIS30) is one of the coolest little hangouts in City Center; little being the operative word. It's easy to overlook their cramped seating arrangements when you get your hands on one of their famous waffle dessert combinations with chocolate and whipped cream.

The draw to the **YMCA Three Arches** (26 King David St., tel. 02/569-2692, http://ymca.org.il, 7am-11pm daily, NIS50) restaurant is largely about the setting. It is the perfect place to enjoy a peaceful, shaded afternoon coffee on the YMCA building's massive veranda. The large front lawn and trees face the splendid King David Hotel, and you're a good distance the street. The menu is limited to a few pasta and egg items later in the day, but there is a daily breakfast buffet (7am-10am).

THE OLD CITY
Near Zion Gate

At the juncture of the old Roman city's center

and the current end of the partially reno-vated Cardo is a cavernous Arab restaurant with multiple names, but most easily located by its large sign outside the southern en-trance that says **Heart of the Old City** (end of Cardo, tel. 02/627-3408, 8am-8pm daily, NIS35). The restaurant staff is friendly and serves up basic dishes of falafel, hummus, shwarma, and the like. It is also known as Afandi Restaurant.

Montefiore (Yemin Moshe St., below the windmill, tel. 02/623-2928 or 057/943-8439, http://montefiore.rest-e.co.il, 8am-midnight Sun.-Thurs., 8am-3pm Fri., 7pm-midnight Sat., NIS90) is a fine dining Italian restau-rant with a menu that includes seafood such as salmon and also offers pasta and pizza. The establishment's main draw is its proxim-ity to both the Old City and to the Jerusalem Cinematheque in the adjacent Mishkenot Sha'ananim complex. Outdoor balcony seat-ing overlooks the Valley of Hinnom and has a nice view of the Old City.

Near Jaffa Gate

Inside Jaffa Gate's David Street, just east of the Church of St. John the Baptist, is Muristan Street, which has a row of sev-eral cafés and small eateries, many of which specialize in freshly squeezed juice drinks. Their hours vary depending on how many customers they have, but the general hours of these eateries are 9am-8pm daily. **Geo's Espresso Bar** (Muristan St. row of sidewalk cafés near the Church of the Holy Sepulchre, NIS20-75) serves chicken dishes, hummus plates, sandwiches, salads, falafel, and kebabs.

Jerusalem Pizza (end of Muristan St., 8am-8pm daily, NIS30) serves pizza at a store-front reminiscent of New York City, with a few guys behind a counter dishing up slices.

Na'aman Old City Coffee Shop (Muristan St., NIS55) looks pleasant as you pass by, and the menu includes *labaneh* (strained yogurt) plates, hot and cold drinks, sandwiches, and salads, but they encourage customers to pay rather high prices in U.S.

dollars and the quality of the food leaves quite a lot to be desired.

The Armenian Tavern (79 Armenian Orthodox Patriarchate Rd., turn right at the Tower of David and restaurant is downstairs, Armenian Quarter, tel. 02/627-3854, 11am-10:30pm Tues.-Sun., NIS50) serves meat dishes with special touches like mint and grape leaves. The interior is what charms most customers the most, though, with its arched ceilings dating to the Crusader period and an indoor fountain.

If you exit from Jaffa Gate and take the stairs down to Mamilla, you will find a vari-ety of places to eat, most of which are domestic chains and are often extremely crowded, par-ticularly on Fridays. But **Roladin** (Mamilla Ave., tel. 02/623-1553, www.roladin.co.il, 7:30am-11pm Sun.-Thurs., 7:30am-3pm Fri., NIS40) bakery and café is always hopping, and for good reason. Its selection of sweet treats are prepackaged to be easily taken out, and they are the main draw for customers, even though a typical selection of egg dishes, sandwiches, and pasta can also be had. During Hanukkah, Roladin customers flock to buy their doughnuts (a traditional Hanukkah treat), which have earned a reputation for being the best in the city. The view of the city with both indoor and outdoor seating is fantastic.

Near Damascus Gate

The **Wiener Kaffe Haus** (37 Via Dolorosa, tel. 02/626-5800, www.austrianhospice.com, 10am-10pm daily, NIS40) is a well-kept secret housed on the ground floor of the Austrian Hospice, one story above the Old City streets. The café has ample indoor seating and an ex-pansive outdoor terrace under a canopy of trees. Wrapped around the building is a ve-randa with more seating, and there are several additional tables and chairs on more secluded vestibules raised above the patio. The limited menu includes a selection of items for a light meal including soups, salads, and toast. Tea in a pot, wine, and beer are also available and the Viennese apple strudel is a nice finish.

Near the Western Wall

Just before the security gate to enter the plaza for the Western Wall is a relatively good find for dining inside the Old City. **Between the Arches** (174 HaGay St., HaKotel HaMaaravi St., tel. 053/809-4584, www.2eat.co.il/eng/bta, 9am-6pm Sun.-Thurs., NIS65) serves a fairly standard fare of sandwiches, salads, fish, and pasta dishes but is extremely easy to find. The restaurant is located in an area that is part of a system of 13th-century tunnels, and you go rather deep underground to reach the dining room. The interior features an array of fish tanks and nice touches of decoration contribute to a relaxed atmosphere for a leisurely lunch.

EAST JERUSALEM
Middle Eastern

For a taste of home-cooked Arab food, **Pasha's Restaurant** (13 Shimon Siddiq in Sheikh Jarrah, tel. 02/582-5162, www.pashasofjerusalem.com, noon-11pm daily, NIS70) will pick you up from any Jerusalem hotel within 15 minutes of you calling them. Their sister establishment, **Borderline,** stays open until about 1:30am and offers a menu of *nargila* water pipes to smoke from for after-dinner relaxation. Pasha's menu includes traditional Arab fare of lentil and other soups, hot and cold appetizers, lamb dishes with mint, and a variety of international dishes such as beef Stroganoff.

Contemporary

The American Colony (1 Louis Vincent St., tel. 02/627-9777, www.americancolony.com, call for hours, open daily, NIS80) has several dining options for every day of the week in a beautiful five-star setting. Even if you're not a guest at the hotel, it's worth enjoying if you're willing to spend a bit more. Their Saturday brunch is extensive, delicious, and includes hard to find items like bacon. Options for dining include the Arabesque Restaurant, The Courtyard, Val's Brasserie,

The Cellar Bar, The Summer Bar, and The Terrace Café.

For a nice gastropub with courtyard dining, **Askadinya Restaurant Bar** (11 Shim'on Ha'tsadik St., tel. 02/532-4590, noon-midnight daily, NIS80) has created a blend of east meets west with meat dishes served with an Asian flair in addition to more common pasta and salad dishes. A specialty is the steak with a raisin and caramel sauce.

WEST JERUSALEM
Middle Eastern

Marvad Haksamim (Magic Carpet) (42 Emek Refaim St., tel. 053/934-5559, http://marvad.mapme.co.il or http://marvad-haksamim.rest-e.co.il, noon-11:30pm Sun.-Thurs., 9am-3:30pm Fri., NIS55), considered a Jerusalem institution, has been in business since 1948, on the eve of the founding of the country. Known for its Yemenite food and convenient catering services, the interior has the look of a diner with Middle Eastern touches, and takeout service is emphasized. The menu includes a variety of hummus dishes, Middle Eastern soups and salads (try the Moroccan carrot salad), as well as meat skewers and stuffed grape leaves.

Café Paradiso (36 Keren HaYesod St., tel. 02/563-4805, http://cafparadiso.rest-e.co.il, noon-1am Mon.-Thurs., 10am-1am Fri., 11am-1am Sat., NIS80) is an understated restaurant serving up creative Mediterranean and Middle Eastern dishes, including items such as grilled baby octopus, Thai lamb patties, and chicken livers on lentils. There's plenty of indoor and outdoor seating, and it is conveniently located midway between different tourism sites and parks, making it a great place to stop on the way to or from somewhere.

Contemporary

Nestled inside of the Jerusalem Cinematheque is **Lavan at the Cinematheque** (11 Hebron Rd., tel. 02/673-7393, 10am-midnight daily,

NIS60), an ideal place for a quiet meal with a scenic view of the Valley of Hinnom and the walls of the Old City. Lavan is all about the atmosphere and the menu is a fairly generic version of what you can find all over Jerusalem, including pasta, egg breakfasts with cheeses, bread, and salad, and good cappuccino.

The Culinary Workshop (28 Hebron Rd. in the JVP Media Quarter, tel. 053/934-4990, http://hasadna.rest-e.co.il, 7:30pm-1am daily, NIS80) is very easy to miss during a trip to Jerusalem, which would be a shame. Tucked into the JVP Media Quarter, The Culinary Workshop has an enormous open kitchen, a multilayered floor plan with soft lighting and outdoor deck seating, and a limited, but extremely inventive menu. Dishes are prepared to give just the right balance of flavors, as with the artichoke à la Romana salad, which will win over anyone who isn't already a fan of artichoke. There is also a nice selection of steak cuts at reasonable prices, a rare find in Jerusalem.

Now in its new home at the First Station complex, local favorite **Adom** (4 David Remez St., tel. 02/624-6242, 12:30pm-2am daily, NIS80) has upped the class factor on their menu and decor to appeal to those who want something just on the verge of fine dining. Adom specializes in wine and international cuisine with French and Italian influences and features their take on a variety of lamb and filet mignon dishes.

Tucked away from view is **Colony** (7 Beit Lechem Rd., tel. 053/938-3942, http://colony. rest.co.il, 8am-midnight Sun.-Thurs. 8am-3pm Fri., 7pm-midnight Saturday, NIS70), known for its expansive indoor and outdoor floor plan and massive selection of wine, beer, and alcohol. The Colony is a favorite gathering place for foreign journalists and offers some fairly standard menu items, including schnitzel and hamburgers, but it also offers delectable crème brûlée and cappuccino. Housed in an old warehouse, Colony has tons of outdoor patio seating with a varied atmosphere that ranges from plush living room to tropical cabana. The waitstaff have a lot of ground to cover so need to be flagged down, but they are always accommodating and friendly.

A fantastic choice in combination with a visit to the Israel Museum is **Modern** (Ruppin through 11 of the Israel Museum, tel. 02/648-0862, www.modern.co.il, 11am-5pm Sun.-Thurs., 6pm-midnight Tues.-Wed., NIS85). The restaurant includes a huge patio area that is mostly used for private events, and a rather small but elegant interior. Known as a spot for frequent VIP sightings, including the president of Israel, Modern has a menu with a fairly standard selection of fish and pasta dishes. Their claim to fame is their Thursday night live jazz music and wine-tasting that starts at 7pm.

Halvrit Café at Cossell Jerusalem Sports Center (The Hebrew University at Givat Ram, across from the Bloomfield Museum of Science, 8am-10pm Sun.-Thurs., 8am-2:30pm Fri., NIS45) is one of the few places to have a light lunch if you are in the vicinity of Museum Row. Directly across the street from the Bloomfield Museum of Science, Halvrit offers health-conscious food to complement the large number of customers coming and going from its sports center. Many of the choices on the menu are light salads and the like. There is nice, shady outdoor seating with a grassy area where kids can run around.

Asian

The flagship location of the popular **Sushi Rehavia** (31 Azza St., tel. 02/567-1971, www.sushirehavia.co.il, noon-11pm Sun.-Thurs., 11am-3pm Fri., NIS80) is one of several branches throughout Jerusalem. In addition to sushi, the restaurant also features delectable noodle dishes, Japanese-style grilled chicken, *gyoza*, and stir-fried dishes. The modern, Asian-style interior and atmosphere caters to the trendy set of Jerusalemites who are into a variety of gastronomic experiences.

Italian

P2 Pizzeria (36 Keren HaYesod St., tel. 02/563-5555, noon-midnight daily, NIS40) is a small, mostly pizza and some pasta restaurant that is open daily. The pasta is made on the premises in a large pasta machine at the front of the restaurant. The thin crust pizza is served up with high-quality ingredients and expert care. There's limited seating, including bar stools and outdoor chairs.

Seafood

Olive and Fish (2 Jabotinsky St., tel. 02/566-5020, noon-11pm Sun.-Thurs., NIS80) is conveniently located and features special seafood dishes as well as salads, chicken, and kebabs. Try the hot salmon salad or the St. Peter's fish filet. The interior of the restaurant is decorated with antique photographs of Jerusalemites through the generations, and is spacious and classy, with an indoor veranda.

Cafés and Coffee Shops

There is a lot of hype surrounding **The Coffee Mill** (23 Emek Refaim St., tel. 02/566-1665, www.thecoffeemill.co, 7:30am-11pm Sun.-Thurs., 7:30am-3pm Fri., 7pm-midnight Sat., NIS30) and some of it is deserved. The very small shop's walls are plastered with old *New Yorker* magazine covers, and the menu is bright and creative with pictures of most of the drinks and food, largely pastries. The late weekday hours make it a great place to stop in for a coffee after dinner nearby.

One of the most consistently excellent dining experiences in Jerusalem can be found at the ★ **Grand Café** (70 Beit Lechem Rd., tel. 02/570-2702, www.rol.co.il/sites/grand-cafe, 7:30am-11pm Sun.-Thurs., 7:30am-3pm Fri., 7pm-11pm Sat., NIS50) with its lovely selection of Middle Eastern-style food prepared in a style that appeals to the western palate. They serve generously portioned, mouthwatering salads and egg dishes, and beautifully done coffee and French-style desserts and pastries. The modern, warm decor includes plenty of outdoor seating year-round (in good and bad weather), and the waitstaff is unfailingly friendly, efficient, and welcoming. It is the perfect place to make the most road-weary of travelers feel at home and well-fed.

Grand Café

Accommodations

Most hotels, motels, and hostels in Jerusalem will accept payment in U.S. dollars, and they will often list their rates in dollars, rather than shekels for tourists. In general, Jerusalem hotels are on the expensive side. Many will offer a 5 percent discount for booking through their website.

Jerusalem has two main types of accommodations: those that are situated conveniently based on overall general location (such as City Center) and those that are situated as close to major tourist sites as possible (such as the Seven Arches Hotel at the top of the Mount of Olives). Beyond that, there are a wide variety of types of accommodations, including hostels, hospices, guesthouses, *zimmers* (bed-and-breakfasts), and kibbutz hotels.

CITY CENTER
Under US$100

Highly recommended by locals, ★ **Abraham Hostel** (67 Hanevi'im St., tel. 02/650-2200, www.abraham-hostel-jerusalem.com, US$29 d) is a medium-size hostel in the heart of Jerusalem that offers a range of rooms from single private rooms to a 10-bed dorm room, though private rooms are almost impossible to come by. The hostel was founded by backpackers and caters to independent travelers by aiming to be a one-stop location. The rooms are austere and sparsely furnished, but the hostel, which is the first in what is now a national chain, includes a wireless Internet lounge, common lounge area, dining hall, kitchen, laundry facilities, rooftop terrace, and a TV lecture room. All common areas are open 24 hours a day. The hostel also offers tours and activities.

US$100-150

If you're looking for luxury at an amazing price, check the **City Center Suites** (2 Hahistadrut St. on the corner of 13 King George St., tel. 02/650-9494, www.citycentervacation.com, US$136 d). It has elegant and modern apartments for short stays and long-term visits. Just at the base of Ben Yehuda Street, City Center Suites' rooms include studio, deluxe studio, and suite, and feature kitchenettes or kitchens, balconies, closet space, toiletries, and housekeeping service. The apartments have clean, modern lines and enough space for a comfortable stay.

The **Caesar Premier Jerusalem** (208 Yafo St., tel. 02/500-5656, www.caesarhotels.co.il, US$139 d) is a three-star hotel with 150 rooms and an intimate atmosphere. A standard room includes a mini-refrigerator, cable TV, breakfast, and wireless Internet.

US$150-200

The **Jerusalem Tower Hotel** (23 Hillel St., tel. 02/620-9209, www.jerusalemtowerhotel.com, US$155 d) is right in the middle of City Center, making it an ideal place to stay if you want easy access to the nightlife and a wide array of restaurants. The rooms are decorated in a very stark, clean modern feel with large, bright paintings on very white walls. Of the 120 rooms in the hotel, the rooms on the higher floors have views of the Old City. Amenities are very basic, such as wireless Internet in the lobby only.

Over US$200

The **YMCA Three Arches Hotel** (26 King David St., tel. 02/569-2692, http://ymca.org.il, US$229 d) is distinguished by a broad and picturesque veranda that wraps around the front of the historic building and a massive lobby with an arched and tiled ceiling that is classic Middle Eastern style. The hotel is part of a larger complex that includes a pool, gym and a restaurant with incredible outdoor seating. The rather austere rooms include free wireless Internet, garden views, and cable television. You can't beat the location on King George

Street just a few blocks from both City Center and the Old City.

Popular, trendy, and smack in the middle of the city's action in Nahalat Shiva is Harmony Hotel (6 Yoel Moshe Solomon St., tel. 03/542-5555, www.atlas.co.il, US$338 d). One of the more popular downtown hotels for its blend of modern urban style in an ancient location, Harmony offers a happy hour in the hotel's English club business lounge with a billiards table, free computer for Internet use, free wireless access, a rooftop lounge area, and rooms with a mini-fridge, safe, and multi-channel LCD TV. Part of the Israeli Atlas boutique hotel group, Harmony's 50 rooms are decked out with bright, modern bedding, rugs, and furniture.

The Notre Dame of Jerusalem Center hotel (3 Paratroopers Rd., tel. 02/627-9111, www.notredamecenter.org, US$330 d) is part of the massive, towering Pontifical Institute Notre Dame of Jerusalem that is situated just behind a hill from the Damascus Gate entrance to the Old City. There are 150 rooms, and the hotel caters to Christian guests making a pilgrimage to the Holy Land, though it welcomes guests of any faith. Amenities and facilities include a cafeteria, fine dining on the rooftop terrace, a chapel, and wireless Internet

for an extra fee. The rooms are decorated in a somewhat plain manner, but are spacious and full of light and the room price includes breakfast.

Without a doubt, the ★ King David Hotel (23 King David St., tel. 02/620-8888, www.danhotels.com, US$600 d, includes large breakfast) is one of the most beautiful and elegant places in the city. Look for the massive table in the rich, lavish lobby where Israeli prime minister Yitzhak Rabin and Jordan's King Hussein signed their historic peace agreement in 1994. The patio and pool area behind the hotel make for a charming (and surprisingly affordable) place to have an elegant outdoor lunch. Some of the rooms include views of the Old and New City and balconies. All are richly appointed with sitting areas, modern furniture, and large-screen televisions. If you wander far enough behind the hotel, you will find the hidden gem, Gozlan Garden. The staff is exceptionally classy and accustomed to dealing with high-profile guests such as heads of state, but equally gracious to the common visitor.

The Jerusalem Gold Hotel (234 Yafo St., tel. 02/501-3333, www.jerusalemgold.com, US$240 d) is a classy, medium-size hotel with a bit of European sass. The rooms are

King David Hotel, behind the landmark Montefiore Windmill

decorated with heavy drapes and rich tapestries, and have extra-long beds, blackout curtains, and double-glazed windows for extra quiet. Guests can select their pillow from a menu, and video games and a laptop-size safe are available. The hotel is also close to several restaurants, shops, and entertainment venues.

Leonardo Plaza Hotel Jerusalem (47 King George St., tel. 02/629-8666, www.leonardo-hotels.com, US$450 d) is one of the easiest hotels to spot if you are in the middle of City Center. The hotel's tower overlooks the rolling green lawns of Independence Park. The 270 rooms are decorated in rich, bright colors, and there is an Italian restaurant on the premises. Guests have access to the new spa, seasonal pool, fitness room, and whirlpool tub.

Designed by renowned architect Moshe Safdie, the **Beit Shmuel Hotel and Hostel** (6 Shamai St., at the corner of 13 King David St., tel. 02/620-3455, www.bshmuel-hotel. com/en, US$205 d) has a distinctive glass dome covering the building's main dining area can be seen from Jaffa Gate and Mamilla. The modern, clean, bright interior of Beit Shmuel makes for a welcoming atmosphere, and the location is central to sights, food, and entertainment in both the Old City and New City. Small overall, but with a variety of accommodations, the guesthouse has 28 rooms for up to six people each, there are 12 hotel rooms for up to four guests each, and one apartment for a family or group visiting for a long-term stay.

The recently opened **Waldorf Astoria Jerusalem** (26-28 Agron St., tel. 02/542-3333, www.waldorfastoriajerusalem.com, US$450 d) is the height of luxury in the center of the city and a Conde Nast Best Hotel in the Middle East pick. The hotel's 223 rooms for guests exists alongside 30 luxury private homes built to specific tastes and needs of residents. Rooms feature Italian marble bathrooms, 46-inch flat-screen televisions, a private wet bar, an espresso coffee machine, free wireless Internet, and crystal chandeliers. In addition to every possible amenity imaginable, the elements of each room can be controlled by the guest.

THE OLD CITY
Under US$100

The **Hashimi Hotel** (73 Khan El Zeit St., tel. 054/547-4189, www.hashimihotel.com, US$90 d) is situated in a building that is over 400 years old and at the center of the Old City. The modern interior features marble throughout

a room in the Waldorf Astoria Jerusalem

and a rooftop terrace. The rooms in this medium-size hotel are quite bare, including bed frames made of wrought iron and rather thin mattresses. Wireless Internet, cable TV, and air-conditioning are included.

Just inside Jaffa Gate is **New Petra Hostel** (1 David St., tel. 02/628-6618, http://newpetrahostel.com, US$80 d), which offers free parking, a communal kitchen, and a rooftop terrace with panoramic views across Jerusalem. This small hostel has 42 private and dormitory rooms, a TV lounge, Internet, and free safety deposit boxes, as well as laundry service. The amenities and rooms are very bare-bones, so you are mostly paying for location.

Jaffa Gate Hostel (Jaffa Gate in front of David's Tower, tel. 02/627-6402, www.jaffagate.hostel.com, US$78 d) includes linens in the price, towels and hair dryers for rent, a place to park bicycles, a tour desk, luggage storage, currency exchange, and a postal and fax service. Dormitories and private rooms are available and are as simple and tiny as you can get, but they have a certain Middle Eastern atmosphere and charm. The hostel has evening movie screenings, free wireless Internet, *nargilot* (hookahs), a terrace area, and space for barbecues.

Although the accommodations are plain, the **Austrian Hospice** (37 Via Dolorosa, near Damascus Gate, tel. 02/626-5800, www.austrianhospice.com, US$85 d) is on one of the best locations in the Old City, and the hotel itself is lovely, clean, and very secure. The rooms and dormitories with bunk beds have only the bare minimum of amenities, and the small lobby is abutted by private, outdoor garden seating for guests and customers of the Austrian Hospice Café. Some of the staff are Austrian and efficient and helpful. The rooftop view is one of the best in the area and a secret favorite spot among locals and those in the know.

Over US$200
Easy to miss in the hustle and bustle immediately after exiting the Old City by the Jaffa Gate and continuing to the end of the Mamilla shopping center, ★ **Mamilla Hotel** (11 King Solomon St., tel. 02/548-2222, www.mamillahotel.com, US$430 d) affords an incredible number of subtle charms for hotel guests and passersby alike. From its rooftop bar and restaurant to its wine bar, Saturday disco, live weekly jazz music in the lobby, and other varied offerings, the Mamilla is a bit like a world unto itself. The rooms are designed with sleek, efficient lines and accented with international touches such as Asian-influenced bathrooms and showers, and movable walls. Subtle touches of art throughout the hotel invite you to interact with your surroundings. Rooms have modern, clean furnishings, free wireless Internet, large screen televisions, and guests can use the Wellbeing Center and gym, swim in the luxurious indoor hotel pool or access the nearby outdoor David Citadel Pool. There is also a business center.

Connected to the Mamilla shopping center physically and historically, the Mamilla Hotel's owner had a direct hand in helping to revitalize the once-blighted area. There are some spots within the hotel that offer quiet places to sit and have a coffee. Try the outdoor patio adjacent to the massive dining room for a swing in a hammock seat and a view of the stars. The Espresso Bar, with a very calm, European vibe, is a lovely place to sit and work.

EAST JERUSALEM
Under US$100
Opposite the Old City's Damascus Gate, **New Palm Guesthouse** (4 Hanevi'im St., tel. 02/627-3189, www.newpalmguesthouse. hostel.com, US$70 d) offers package deals that include airport transportation. Private rooms are available, and there is free wireless Internet. Breakfast is available for an additional cost. The very simple accommodations at this small hostel also include free luggage storage, a common area TV, and a fully equipped kitchen. They also offer tours of Masada and the Dead Sea.

Close to numerous convenient amenities and the Old City, **Victoria Hotel** (8 Al

Masoudi St., tel. 02/627-4466, http://4victoria-hotel.com, US$90 d) is a stone's throw from the central bus station, shops, and banks. The hotel has 49 recently renovated rooms, most with a balcony. Breakfast is included with the room, and there is free wireless Internet, 24-hour room service, cable TV, and hair dryers in the rooms.

Located on the famous and central Salah al-Din Street, **Capitol Hotel** (17 Salah al-Din St., tel. 02/628-2561, www.jrscapitol.com, US$99 d) has 54 rooms that include 24-hour room service, satellite TV, air-conditioning, a minibar, and laundry service. The interior of the hotel is very simple. The ground floor of the hotel features an idyllic garden dining area with a fountain and a large interior dining room.

US$150-200

The family-run boutique **Addar Hotel** (53 Nablus Rd., tel. 02/626-3111, www.addar-hotel.com, US$167 d) was rebuilt from a 19th-century building and features a plush, richly appointed interior. VIPs have been known to stay in this medium-size hotel that features a marble lobby as it is five minutes by foot to the Old City and near the British consulate. Rooms are equipped with marble whirlpool tubs, a balcony, French windows, a sitting area, free wireless Internet, and a safe. Some rooms include a kitchenette. The hotel restaurant has outdoor garden seating.

Well-equipped with an array of comforts and in a central location, **Legacy Hotel** (29 Nablus Rd., tel. 02/627-0800, www.jerusalem-legacy.com, US$170 d) has 49 rooms with sitting areas and hair dryers, a fitness center, and a restaurant with Middle Eastern food and an outdoor panoramic view of the city. There are also a bar, buffet, sushi bar, coffee shop, and garden restaurant.

A boutique hotel with simple modern luxury and design, **National Hotel** (4 Al Zahra St., tel. 02/627-8880, www.nationalhotel-jerusalem.com, US$199 d) is also close to East Jerusalem's shopping district of Salah al-Din Street. The generous-size rooms features large

beds, and guests have access to free newspapers, hotel shops, a gym, and free parking.

The **Ritz Hotel** (8 Ibn Khaldoun St., tel. 02/626-9900, www.jerusalemritz.com, US$175 d) is a recently renovated 104-room hotel that boasts a lovely rooftop terrace dining area, a bar, 24-hour reception service, and satellite TV and free wireless Internet in the rooms. Each room has a personal safe, and the hotel is within easy walking distance to the Old City.

Over US$200

Known for its rooftop pool and outdoor restaurant with a panoramic view of the city, the **St. George Landmark** (6 Omar Ibn Al Aas St., tel. 02/627-7232, www.stgeorgehoteljerusalem.com, US$270 d) features 130 rooms and a Lebanese restaurant. Every room has free wireless Internet, an espresso machine, and tea and coffee machines. Many rooms also include balconies and views of the city.

The **Grand Court Hotel** (15 St. George St., tel. 02/591-7777, www.grandhotels-israel.com, US$216 d) has 446 rooms, including family rooms and rooms that are equipped for people with physical disabilities. There is free wireless Internet and a pool and sundeck that overlook the Old City. There is also a dining room, garden terrace, and lounge bar in the hotel.

The **Olive Tree Hotel** (23 St. George St., tel. 02/541-0410, www.olivetreehotel.co.il, US$300 d) is built around an ancient olive tree, which, according to legend, shaded pilgrims on their way to Jerusalem in ancient times. This large hotel has 304 rooms throughout eight floors and has been recently renovated. Rooms have over 50 international channels on the televisions, capability to dock laptops using the TV screen, and bathtubs. There is also a business center, babysitting service, and a large, inviting lobby with accents of Jerusalem stone.

Known as a gathering place for foreign dignitaries, high-powered business executives, and Jerusalem's foreign press, ★ **The American Colony** (1 Louis Vincent St., tel. 02/627-9777, www.americancolony.com, US$400 d) is still a posh meeting place and a world unto itself in the somewhat desolate surroundings of its East Jerusalem neighborhood. Full of quiet corners and lushly landscaped grounds, it is the perfect place for escaping from the heat and chaos of Jerusalem. Boasting three gardens, this five-star hotel includes an outdoor pool and sauna, fitness and business centers, a wine cellar restaurant, and a shop that sells antiques. The 93 rooms in four buildings offer a variety of luxurious accommodations with rich wood furnishing, arched ceilings, satellite TV, wake-up service, free toiletries, and some with sitting areas and balconies. The hotel has a decidedly Middle Eastern feel throughout the premises, from the beautiful tile flooring to the stone walls and overall decor. All of the staff are highly professional and speak excellent English, and the clientele tends to be seriously upper-crust.

WEST JERUSALEM
Under US$100

Hidden behind a stone wall in the heart of the historic German Colony is **St. Charles Hospice** (12 Lloyd George St., tel. 02/563-7737, pilgerhaus@netvision.net.il, US$90 d), a Christian guesthouse that caters to German-speaking pilgrims and features limited amenities. This small guesthouse offers rooms at a very low rate for the high-demand area it is situated in, and is just around the corner from some outstanding restaurants on nearby Emek Refaim Street. Also nearby is the Railway Park that stretches for miles, and the popular shopping and entertainment center at First Station.

The **Agron Youth Hostel and Guest House** (6 Agron St., tel. 02/594-5522, ext. 3, agron@iyha.org.il, US$98 d) is a 55-room hostel with air-conditioning, showers and bathrooms, TV and Internet, and even a minibar in some rooms. It caters to students and younger travelers and features basic, clean accommodations and the price of the room includes breakfast. The reception desk is closed for Shabbat, and cultural activities are offered on Sundays and Thursdays. The front desk

sells discount tickets to some of the major sites in the city.

US$100-150

Tucked away in a neighborhood heavily populated with North Americans is the ★ **Tamar Residence** (70 Beit Lechem Rd., tel. 077/270-5555, www.tamarresidencejerusalem.com, US$144 d). Just far enough off the beaten path to be more affordable, but not too far to be inconvenient, part of Tamar is situated above the popular Grand Café. Long-term stays are also available, but book as far in advance as possible, especially for stays during the Jewish holidays. Each of the modern, bright rooms comes equipped with a kitchenette and plush furniture, and several also have an outdoor terrace. Most rooms have a separate living room area.

In keeping with the overall trend of guesthouses in the historic German Colony, **Darna Guest House** (12 Hanania St., tel. 054/565-7001 or 054/227-2370, http://bnb.co.il/darna, US$105 d) offers three different locations with furnished apartments in central locations around the neighborhood. A member of the Home Accommodation Association of Jerusalem, Darna offers flexible rates for long stays with advance inquiries. The nicely furnished apartments include all the amenities of home and some include bonus features like outdoor patios.

Just at the entrance to the city is the **Jerusalem Gate Hotel** (43 Yirmiyahu St., tel. 02/500-8500, www.jerusalemgatehotel. com, US$150 d), in close proximity to the convention center and the central bus station, from which you can travel cheaply all over Israel. This large hotel has 298 rooms and caters to business travelers with its understated interior and proximity to the convention center. The rooms are a good size and simply decorated. Every room has wireless Internet, a safe, and hair dryers.

US$150-200

Avissar House (12 Hamevasser St., Yemin Moshe, near the Windmill, tel. 02/625-5447, www.jeru-avisar-house.co.il, US$180 d) has a small, but very nice selection of four do-it-yourself vacation suites. Though this type of suite is a specialty of the Jerusalem hospitality industry, Avissar House has something truly unique to offer: its location. Situated in the Yemin Moshe Artists' Quarter, Avissar is perfect for writers and artists, or those with artistic souls who like to be surrounded by beautiful flowers and the city's ancient stone. Each suite can accommodate several people, and features balconies and free wireless Internet, lush green plants, and comfortable furnishings. You can see the walls of the Old City, the Valley of Hinnom, and surrounding villages from the suites and it's a short, easy walk to the entertainment of City Center.

Part of the Little Houses in Jerusalem group, the boutique **Little House in the Colony** (4a Lloyd George St., tel. 02/566-2424, www.jerusalem-hotel.co.il, US$179) offers 22 rooms, and includes full amenities such as wireless Internet, shuttle service to and from the airport, 24-hour concierge service, and included breakfast.

The **Leonardo Inn Hotel Jerusalem** (4 Vilnay St., tel. 02/655-8811, www.leonardo-hotels.com, US$156 d) is a 200-room hotel situated at the entrance to Jerusalem near the Knesset. Some of the amenities include a spa and health club with sauna, whirlpool tub, and outdoor and indoor swimming pools. The light-rail has a stop in front of the hotel, which seriously ups its level of convenience even though it is not situated in the heart of town. The decor of the rooms is plain and simple, and the hotel caters to practical guests who are also looking for a certain level of comfort, but nothing ostentatious.

Hotel Yehudah (Haim Kulitz Rd. 1, Givat Massuah, tel. 02/632-2777, www.byh.co.il, US$200 d) is in the hills of Jerusalem, close to the zoo, Yad Vashem, and Malha shopping mall. The 129 rooms offered by the hotel include satellite TV, minibars, and many have a view of the gardens and the Jerusalem hills. A swimming pool and café are also on-site. It is the perfect setting if you want to visit Jerusalem in style, but prefer to be a bit removed from the hustle and bustle of the city.

Over US$200

If you're looking for a more customized experience, **Jerusalem Harmony** (various locations, tel. 054/420-2198, http://jerusalemharmonystudio.com, Skype revamann, reva@jerusalemharmonyapartments.com, rates $200 and up) presents some interesting options. Accommodations have chic furnishings and include an array of deluxe guesthouses and vacation apartments fully equipped for longer vacations in prime spots throughout the German Colony; sizes vary from small to very large and can accommodate up to eight people. With writer Reva Mann as the property owner, the emphasis is on spaces that are conducive to fostering creativity.

Conveniently located **Prima Kings** (60 King George St., tel. 02/620-1201, www.prima-hotels-israel.com, US$217 d) is in an ideal location for visitors who plan on extensive sightseeing. The lobby feels a bit dark and small, but the 217 units in the hotel range in size from rooms to suites, some with balconies. There is a large and very useful information rack near the front door with a variety of tourist booklets and restaurant coupons for free. The hotel caters to observant Jewish guests with a synagogue on the premises and a Shabbat elevator. There is also a dining room, coffee shop, and business center, all of which are kosher.

The lovely **Ramat Rachel Kibbutz Hotel** (Kibbutz Ramat Rachel, Tzfon Yehuda, tel. 02/670-2555, www.ramatrachel.co.il, US$220 d) feels like a getaway in the city. The 165-room, four-star hotel is situated on the grounds of one of the oldest settlements outside the Old City walls in Jerusalem. Hotel amenities include an outdoor swimming pool, variety of room types, country club, kosher restaurant, money-changing services, and an active synagogue.

Information and Services

INFORMATION

Tourist and Travel Information

The hotline of the Jerusalem municipality is **106** (from out of the city call tel. 02/531-4600). It covers advisories and basic information for tourists. There are several places throughout Jerusalem that act as information centers. Some are better than others. In the Old City, the **Jaffa Gate Tourist Information Center** (1 Jaffa Gate, tel. 02/627-1422, 8:30am-5pm Sun.-Thurs., 8:30am-noon Fri.) is in a convenient location but has limited information and resources. The **Christian Information Center** (Jaffa Gate, tel. 02/627-2692, www. cicts.org, 9am-5:30pm Mon.-Fri. and 9am-12:30pm Sat.) is nearby and can also offer some help.

Outside of the Old City, near the City Center, the **Abraham Hostel Information Center** (67 Hanevi'im St., tel. 02/650-2200, www.abraham-hostel-jerusalem.com) has a 24-hour front desk and an information center that caters to independent travelers. The **Prima Royale Hotel** (3 Mendele Mocher Sfarim St.) has an extensive and very helpful tourist information rack just inside its front doors. Many of the tourism booklets include coupons for discounts on food and drinks.

Tourist Visas

Most visitors to Israel automatically get a three-month tourist visa at Passport Control depending on the country of the passport holder, which can be renewed at the **Jerusalem Ministry of Interior** (1 Shlomtsiyon HaMalka St., tel. 02/629-0231). A tourist visa can usually be extended for up to 24-27 months, but only in increments of 3-6 months and there is a fee of about NIS400 every time you extend your visa.

Media and Internet Resources

The **Jerusalem Development Authority** (www.jda.gov.il) recently partnered with the **City of Jerusalem** (www.jerusalem.muni. il) to create the **Official Tourism Website of Jerusalem** (www.itraveljerusalem.com). All three websites have useful information for tourism in the city, but the City of Jerusalem site has very relevant information on basics under its "visitors" section. Another helpful site is **Go Jerusalem** (www.gojerusalem. com) with its listings of everything from restaurants to tourist sites.

There are several locally broadcast radio stations, including 101.3FM and 88.2FM (not 88.0FM, which is a different Kol Israel network). A relay of the international broadcast Reshet Hey to shortwave overseas listeners can be had on an additional 10pm broadcast on 88.2FM. **IBA World Service Israel International Radio and TV** (www.iba. org.il/world/#) has an English news radio broadcast online and a TV broadcast at 5pm Sunday-Thursday on Israel Channel 3 (33 on cable) and 6pm Friday-Saturday. On Israel Channel 1, a 9-minute version broadcasts at 4:50pm Sunday-Thursday.

The official tourism website of Israel is **www.goisrael.com.**

Maps

The best place to find tourist maps in Jerusalem is through information centers or from the information racks that some hotels have in their lobbies. No matter which map you use, you will find many differences in street names and the names of sights. These are not errors of the mapmakers, but are due to the city's long history of places and streets being named by different groups, inconsistencies in translating words and names from Arabic and Hebrew to English, and sometimes there are political factors at play.

Holidays

There are several major holidays during the calendar year that draw visitors to Jerusalem from all over the world or greatly impact services and access if you are already in the city. The most impactful are Jewish holidays, and their dates vary slightly from year to year because they are based on the Jewish calendar. It's necessary to check a calendar to see when the holidays will occur.

The most major holidays are Sukkot (Oct.), Yom Kippur (Sept.), Passover (late Mar. or early Apr.), Easter (late March or early April), and Ramadan (one month around June-July).

Hospitals
There are several hospitals in Jerusalem: **Bikur Holim Hospital** (tel. 02/646-4111, www.szmc.org.il); **Hadassah Hospital** (tel. 02/584-4111, www.hadassah.org.il/Hadassa) at Mount Scopus; and **Herzog Hospital** (tel. 02/531-6875, www.herzoghospital.org).

Emergency Services
You can dial for emergency services from any phone by calling **Police,** 100; **Ambulance,** 101; **Fire Department,** 102; **Electric Company Hotline,** 103; and **Municipal Emergency Situation Room,** tel. 02/625-6202 (for information during emergencies).

SERVICES
Currency Services and Money Exchange
There are several "Change" stands located throughout the city that will change foreign currency into New Israel Shekels (shekels for short) and vice versa. Change offices are concentrated in and around Tolerance Square and in the German Colony and Bak'a. If you are in the Old City, a trustworthy and very easy to find money exchange office is **Abu Ghazeleh Money Exchange** (Old City at Damascus Gate, tel. 02/628-2479, 9am-6pm daily) just inside Damascus Gate to the right. The owner speaks perfect English and has been in business at the same location for 40 years.

Post offices (www.israelpost.co.il) cash foreign currency checks and traveler's checks. The official symbol of the post office is a red

sign with white writing and an ibex leaping with its horns above the title of the post office. A complete listing of the post office branches in Jerusalem can be found on the post office website.

Banks are open 8:30am-12:30pm Sunday-Friday (closed for Shabbat and holidays), and some also open from late afternoon until evening. There are several bank branches in Jerusalem that change money, including the **Jerusalem Center Branch** (33 Jaffa St.), the **City Center Shamai Branch** (6 Shamai St.), and the **Old City Jewish Quarter Branch** (69 Hayehudy St.). Near Nahalat Shiva and directly next door to the Ministry of Interior is **Hillel Change** (1 Shlomtsiyon HaMalka St., tel. 02/623-0656), which operates under the supervision of the Bank of Israel.

ATMs
There are ATMs outside of most banks, and they take foreign bank cards. There is a fee of US$3-9 charged by most banks for using their card at a foreign ATM.

Tolerance Square has two conveniently located banks with outdoor ATMs that take foreign cards. **Bank Hapoalim** (www.bankhapoalim.co.il) has red, blue, and white colors on its sign, and other branches can be found throughout Jerusalem, including in Emek Refaim across the street from Masaryk restaurant, in Bak'a downhill from the Sherover-Haas Promenade, and at the base of Tolerance Square where it meets with Yafo Street. The **Israel Discount Bank** (www.discountbank.co.il) has green and white colors and branches throughout Jerusalem.

Internet
Free wireless Internet (often without a password) is available almost everywhere in the city, particularly in restaurants and cafés. City Center has free Wi-Fi provided by the municipality.

There are also about 100 Wi-Fi hotspots in convenience stores adjacent to gas stations, and other spots are available at universities, colleges, museums, visitors centers, convention halls, marinas, tourism sites, and shopping malls.

Postal Service

There are more than 20 branch **post offices**

(main branch at 23 Yafo Street opposite Safra Square, tel. 02/629-0676, www.israelpost.co.il, most operate 9am-3pm Sun.-Thurs., 9am-2pm Fri.) throughout Jerusalem. Check the branch for hours.

Transportation

GETTING THERE
Air

The airport closest to Jerusalem is the **Ben Gurion International Airport** (tel. 03/975-2386, www.iaa.gov.il) outside Tel Aviv.

Known as the de facto national airline, **El Al Airlines** (www.elal.co.il) has frequent flights to Tel Aviv from all over the world and provides kosher meals. Most major international airlines offer at least one flight a day to Tel Aviv.

There are several ways to reach Jerusalem from the airport if you are not staying at a hotel with a shuttle service. Jerusalem is about one hour by car from the airport, about two hours by train, and a little over one hour on the many frequent, convenient, and comfortable buses. Public transportation does not run during Shabbat (from Fri. afternoon through 8pm or 9pm Sat.), but it is possible to get a service taxi from certain locations during that time.

SHABBAT AND HOLIDAYS

Be careful when planning a flight around Shabbat or on a major Jewish holiday. You will have a more difficult time reaching your final destination if you plan to arrive or depart during these times.

SECURITY CHECKPOINTS AND VEHICLE SEARCHES

Jerusalem is under ongoing threats from terrorist attacks, and it is not unusual to be stopped and questioned coming and going from a public place or to have your bag searched before entering a building. Metal detectors at building entrances are common. If

you are in a car, the trunk might be searched, you might be asked for your ID, and you might be questioned. Refrain from joking with security personnel or saying you have a package given to you by someone else.

Train

Israel Railways (www.rail.co.il, NIS22.5) has a train that takes at least two hours from the airport to Jerusalem, and stops for at least 30 minutes between at a train change location. Once in Jerusalem, you will be a good 15 minutes from City Center and will need to go by car or bus to your final destination.

Share Taxi

Just north of Tolerance Square on Harav Kook Street is an unofficial way station for share taxis going to and from Tel Aviv and other locations. The cost is about NIS30, and the vans will not leave until they are full, so you might have to wait for a while. Check with the driver before getting in that they are going to your destination.

GETTING AROUND

Jerusalem can be tricky to maneuver if you take a wrong turn, particularly if you're traveling by car. It's highly recommended to go by foot or take advantage of Jerusalem's efficient bus system, ample taxis, and the light-rail train to get around.

Car Rental and Driving

Visitors to Israel are allowed to drive with their foreign license for up to one year from arrival in the country. As most street signs are in English, it is relatively easy for someone who doesn't speak Hebrew to drive in Jerusalem.

With three locations in Jerusalem, **Hertz** offices can be found in Givat Shaul, King David, and Romema. The King David branch (19 King David St., tel. 02/623-1351, www. hertz.co.il) is centrally located in the city, and you can get compact Suzukis and Hyundais starting at US$37 a day.

Budget (23 King David St., tel. 03/935-0015, www.budget.co.il) has a wide variety of car models, from compact cars to SUVs, and two locations in Jerusalem. Their main Jerusalem office is on centrally located King David Street.

The parking system in Jerusalem has some strict rules and some that you can break. For instance, you might see cars parked on the sidewalk or facing the wrong direction especially during the weekend or when spots are at a premium due to a crowd. One rule you break at your peril, though, is not feeding the meter. Red and white stripes mean no parking, blue and white stripes mean paid parking by a street meter, and gray is free parking. Other paid parking in certain neighborhoods or small lots will have a yellow and black sign with hours of paid parking; for these, you must buy a ticket and leave it in your car dash with the date stamp showing. These machines often take nothing but coins.

If you are going to be in Jerusalem and driving on a daily basis, Yellow gas stations sell an automatic pay-in-advance meter that you leave on the side of your vehicle. The meter costs NIS100 and you can pay for time on it as you go.

Taxis

Taxis in Jerusalem are white cars with a yellow light on the roof and are often BMWs. You can get almost anywhere in the city (without heavy traffic) for NIS50 or less. Drivers might offer you a fixed rate or simply not turn their meter on, but you can rarely beat the meter with a set rate. There is a NIS10 (about US$1.25) drop charge at the start of every ride, and an additional NIS5 charge for summoning a taxi to a hotel. There can be an additional charge for luggage, and some drivers might try to charge more for two or more passengers.

The legal fare system is 25 percent higher during Shabbat and holidays (sundown on Fri. until it is dark on Sat. night, usually about 8pm). Fares are also 25 percent higher at night, 9:01pm-5:29am.

Tips are not generally expected, but are always appreciated. If you need a taxi for a

The Light-Rail Train provides convenient and fast transportation.

long distance, it is better to call and order a cab.

Two reputable taxi companies in Jerusalem are **Rehavia Taxi** (3 Agron St., tel. 02/622-2444) and **HaPisga Taxi** (2 HaPisga St., tel. 02/642-1111).

Public Transportation

Jerusalem's city bus line, **Egged** (tel. 03/694-8888 or *2800 from any local phone, www. egged.co.il), provides service throughout the city and country. Within the city, it costs about NIS7 for a one-way trip. The Rav Kav ticket can be purchased and filled for multiple trips and works in both Tel Aviv and Jerusalem. Egged's bus 99 offers a panoramic tour of Jerusalem aboard a red double-decker tour bus with stops that you can hop on and off with a one- or two-day pass (NIS39). Bus stops throughout the city have a timed arrival chart for every impending arrival, but the bus line explanations are only posted in Hebrew.

The **Central Bus Station** (218 Yafo St., tel. 054/797-1147) is a typical transportation hub

with several levels that also support shops and places to eat or get a snack. Bus tickets can be purchased at the information window on the second level or directly from your driver if you are paying cash. Bus seats are on a first-come, first-served basis, and people stand and sit in the aisles if the seats run out.

Overseas visitors can buy Israbus tickets, valid on all Egged bus lines and on the Light-Rail Train. They are available at all branches of Egged Tours.

The **Light-Rail Train** (tel. 073/210-0601 or *3686 from any local phone, www.citypass. co.il, NIS6.90) is a fast and convenient way to get around in certain parts of the city. It is the most convenient way, for example, to get from City Center to Yad Vashem. But the route is rather limited and does not include many major tourist sites. As it runs roughly along the old border between East and West Jerusalem, it is very convenient if you want to get somewhere in East Jerusalem. The ticket purchasing system is tricky, so leave extra time to get it right the first time.

Vicinity of Jerusalem

Not far from Jerusalem there are several enchanting and interesting places for a different perspective on the region. Visitors with an interest in history, archaeology, spirituality, and nature will find something to pique their interest. It is particularly recommended to visit areas outside of Jerusalem during Shabbat, as the majority of restaurants and sights remain open.

You can take a **taxi** to any of the locations outside of Jerusalem, but the fare will be very costly. A 20-minute ride will cost about NIS120 or more. A **rental car** is a good option, as all of the signs are posted in English.

HADASSAH EIN KEREM

If you're a serious art lover, it might be worth your while to take a major detour to

Hadassah Ein Kerem, one of the leading research hospitals in the world, which is also home to the famous **Marc Chagall Stained Glass Windows** (off of Route 396 near Ein Kerem, tel. 02/677-7111, www.hadassah.org. il), a series of 12 arched, stained glass windows surrounding the hospital's synagogue. They can be viewed for free just after entering the hospital lobby. Chagall called the windows his "modest gift to the Jewish people," and they were recently renovated. The drive to Hadassah through the Jerusalem forest is very scenic, and there are numerous other works of art throughout the hospital donated by the artists themselves or supporters. Nearby Ein Kerem offers several interesting sights as well as a variety of good dining and drinking options.

Getting There

To get to Hadassah Hospital, take **Egged** bus (www.egged.co.il) number 19 from Jerusalem's Central Bus Station.

EIN KEREM

About 20 minutes northwest of Jerusalem is the scenic valley village of **Ein Kerem**, believed to be the birthplace of John the Baptist, whose mother was the Virgin Mary's cousin.

Sights

One of the most popular tourist and pilgrim draws in Ein Kerem is **Mary's Well** (southern end of HaMa'ayan St., 24 hours, free), which Christian tradition says was a site visited by the Virgin Mary when she stopped here to drink from the spring. A 19th-century mosque can be seen above the spring.

The **Shrine of the Visitation** (southern hill facing the village at the top of the pedestrian extension of HaMa'ayan St., tel. 02/641-7291, www.custodia.org, 8am-noon and 2:30pm-6pm Mon.-Sat., NIS5) is a church with a facade on the front with a series of arches, a bell tower, and a painting of the Virgin Mary riding a donkey and accompanied by angels on the front outer wall. The two-story church has large color paintings throughout depicting biblical scenes. It is also home to a guesthouse run by nuns.

The iconic **Gorny Monastery,** also known as Moscavia for its distinctive gold onion domes that are clearly visible from the village, can be reached by taking a short hike up a steep, winding footpath. The 19th-century Russian Orthodox church is also home to a convent. The compound's buildings are closed to the public, but you can get an excellent view from the parking lot on HaOren Street next to Shibboleth Lane.

The **Sisters of Zion Convent** (1/2 HaOren St., tel. 02/641-5738, 9am-noon and 2pm-5pm Mon.-Fri., 9am-5pm Sat., ring for entrance, NIS2) is home to an archaeological garden and chapel.

The **Church of St. John** (Mevo Hasha'ar, tel. 02/632-3000, 6am-noon and 2pm-5pm daily, free) is built at the location where John the Baptist was believed to have been born. The church has a grotto beneath it with the remains of a Byzantine mosaic.

Food

Ein Kerem is a fun place to go during the weekend when not much is happening in Jerusalem. You can do a little sightseeing, take a stroll, get a drink, or have dinner and enjoy a

a section of the Marc Chagall Stained Glass Windows at Hadassah Hospital leisurely coffee and dessert. The main concentration of places to get food and drinks is on two roads: to the end of HaMa'ayan Street and along the part of Ein Kerem Road 74 where it passes through the village.

Offering a nice array of chicken and beef dishes, **Charlotte** (25 Ein Kerem Rd., tel. 02/643-4545, noon-11pm Sun.-Thurs., NIS70) is perfect if you're in the mood for something grilled. Though they are one of the few places not open on the weekend, Charlotte has the unusual offering of goose breast skewers. All of their entrées are served with salad, and their interior is large and spacious with wood paneling and huge windows that give it the feeling of a cabin.

Brasserie (15 HaMa'ayan St., tel. 02/566-5000, www.2eat.co.il/eng/brasseriejer, noon-last customer Sun.-Wed., 10am-last customer Thurs., 9:30am-last customer Sat., NIS60) has a large patio on its second level for outdoor seating in good weather. The patio affords a nice view of the scenic setting. Serving seafood, including mussels and shrimp, the restaurant also has a good selection of steak, chicken, and French-inspired dishes (try the camembert croissant). Brasserie also has a nice liquor and wine selection, and customers can arrange a menu for wine-tasting. Four beers on tap are served, as well as an array of signature cocktails.

Karma (74 Ein Kerem Rd., tel. 02/643-6643, www.karma-rest.co.il, 10am-midnight Sun.-Wed., Thurs.-Sat. 10am-1am, NIS70) has a nice layout and very accommodating waitstaff. The menu is a fairly typical blend of pasta, salad, and meat selections with some delightful surprises. Try the taboon-baked flatbread covered with vegetables and eggs or the Druze-inspired appetizer platter, which consists of a thin pita overstuffed with lamb cuts, pine nuts, red sauce, tahini, and roasted eggplant. Karma also has enclosed veranda seating on the first floor and tons of balcony seating on the second floor.

Accommodations

The **Rosary Sisters Ein Kerem Guest House** (3 HaMa'ayan HaBikur St., tel. 02/641-3755, www.rosary-einkarem.com, US$90 d) is a small guesthouse run by nuns in the hills of Ein Kerem at the site of Sisters of Zion Convent. The rooms are small and simply furnished, and facilities include a reception area and a small dining room.

The **Sister of Sion Guest House** (23 HaOren St., Ein-Kerem D, tel. 02/641-5738, http://sion-ein-karem.org, US$80 d) offers a small selection of simple rooms with free wireless Internet for singles, couples, and families. All rooms have heating, but only some have air-conditioning.

Getting There and Around

To get to Ein Kerem, take **Egged** bus (www.egged.co.il) number 17 from City Center; it takes about 25 minutes (NIS12). Once there, the village is easy to navigate by foot and there is no need for a vehicle.

If you're driving, note that parking is extremely limited on the weekend.

HERODIUM

About eight miles south of Jerusalem is King Herod's palace-fortress, **Herodium** (south of Jerusalem and east of Bethlehem on edge of Judean Desert, tel. 050/623-5821, www.parks.org.il, 8am-5pm daily Apr.-Sept., 8am-4pm daily Oct.-Mar., NIS27). According to one historical account, he built it after winning a victory over the Hasmoneans and Parthians. The palace is 758 meters above sea level. The site contains extensive palatial ruins, including a living quarter complex, an ancient synagogue, and underground tunnels, and it can be accessed by foot.

Getting There

If you are venturing out to Herodium, you can go and return by bus, though you will also have to do a fair amount of walking. **Egged** bus (www.egged.co.il) number 266 toward Karmei Zur will get you close, followed by a 20-minute walk.

Herodium, the ancient ruins of King Herod's palace

LATRUN

Latrun is an easy side trip off Highway 1 if you have a car and are traveling between Jerusalem and Tel Aviv.

Sights

One way to cover a lot of ground in a short time is to see **Mini-Israel** (Latrun near Kahativa 7 Junction, tel. 700/559-559, www.minisrael.co.il, 10am-6pm Sun.-Thurs., 10am-2pm Fri. Sept.-June, 5pm-10pm Sun.-Thurs., 10am-2pm Fri. July-Aug., adult NIS79, child NIS59). The miniature theme park has 385 exact replica models on a 1:25 scale of Israel. The models are positioned among bonsai trees and miniature figurines of Israelis. There is also a 3D movie of Israeli landscapes, a restaurant and cafeteria, multimedia and play area for kids, and a new MiniMax aerial movie of Israeli sites.

Just off of Highway 1 between Jerusalem and Tel Aviv is the **Latrun Monastery** (tel. 08/922-0065, 9am-1pm and 2pm-5pm Mon.-Sat., free), founded in 1890 and home to an order of silent monks up until the 1960s. The site consists of a large church and living quarters on the monastery grounds, garden, vineyard, and orchards. In late 2012, the monastery was vandalized by Jewish settlers angry over being removed by the government from their settlement. As you enter the site, you will find a shop selling Domain de Latroun wines, liqueurs, spirits, and olive oil and honey made at the monastery.

Getting There

To get to Mini-Israel, take **Egged** bus (www.egged.co.il) number 433 to Mishamar Ayalon Junction (NIS24). To get to the Latrun Monastery, take Egged bus number 403, 433, or 434, a 25-minute ride from Jerusalem's Central Bus Station (NIS16).

ABU GHOSH

Abu Ghosh is a quiet Arab village just off the main highway between Jerusalem and Tel Aviv, famed for its hummus and other Arab delicacies. It's about 25 minutes northwest of Jerusalem.

Sights

Just outside of Jerusalem near the villages of Bet Nekofa and Abu Ghosh is **Ein Hemed**

(Aqua Bella) national park (off the main Hwy. 1 from the Hemed off-ramp, opposite Kibbutz Kiryat Anavim and the town of Abu Ghosh, tel. 02/534-2741, 9am-6pm daily, NIS20), which was once used as a way station for Crusaders. You can still find the remains of a ruined Crusader farmhouse and a park with an olive press.

Food

There are several good options in Abu Ghosh for Arab cuisine, including hummus, falafel, and shwarma. Try **The Original Abu Shukri** (15 Hashalom Way, tel. 02/652-6088, 8am-8pm daily, NIS45), which gets its name from a dispute with another restaurant. The dispute is that one (nobody is sure which anymore) is regarded as having the best hummus in all of Israel. The interior of the restaurant is very simple and homey, and the dining experience is, like most hummus dining, without much fanfare. But the food is delicious and comes to your table quickly, the service is good, and there is free parking.

The Lebanese Restaurant (65 Kvish Ha-Shalom, tel. 02/533-2019, 11am-11pm daily, NIS30) is another favorite for hummus. The decor is spartan but the food is divine, and you are guaranteed to leave with a full stomach and money still in your wallet.

If you're tired of Middle Eastern food, you can find the **Elvis American Diner** (near the Neve Ilan gas station, tel. 02/534-1275, 7am-midnight daily, NIS80) in Abu Ghosh, serving up what are widely reputed to be some of the best hamburgers in the area. A large statue of Elvis is outside the building, and Elvis pictures cover the walls inside.

Getting There and Around

To get to Abu Ghosh, take **Superbus** (www.superbus.co.il) number 185 or 186, about a 40-minute ride (NIS25). Once you are there everything is within fairly easy walking distance.

For the gorgeous parklands of Ein Hemed (Aqua Bella), the Superbus 185 leaves from Jerusalem every hour. It's about a 30-minute ride (NIS22). Just get off at Beit Nekufa and walk for 10 minutes over the bridge that goes over Road 1.

The major hub for Superbus in Jerusalem is in East Jerusalem near Damascus Gate.

Tel Aviv

Look for ★ to find recommended sights, activities, dining, and lodging.

Highlights

★ **Sarona:** Designed to be the cultural and culinary center of Tel Aviv, Sarona is one of the hottest spots in the city (page 112).

★ **White City:** One of the best examples of Bauhaus architecture in the world, Tel Aviv's White City is a UNESCO World Heritage Site. It's a draw for architecture, design, and urban enthusiasts (page 114).

★ **Neve Tzedek:** Nowhere in Tel Aviv does old-world European charm meet modern city life as it does in Neve Tzedek. The charming neighborhood is full of interesting shops, museums, and restaurants (page 115).

★ **Old Jaffa:** One of the oldest port cities in the world, Old Jaffa is also one of the best places in Tel Aviv to experience authentic Arab culture (page 117).

★ **Carmel Market:** Tel Aviv's answer to Jerusalem's famed *shuk,* the Carmel Market is a delight for the senses—filled with exotic spices, fruits, smells, and sounds (page 127).

★ **HaYarkon Park:** Along the northern border of Tel Aviv, the massive HaYarkon Park is a playground for all kinds of outdoor sports and recreation. When the sun goes down, it's a great place to take an evening stroll or drink outside (page 131).

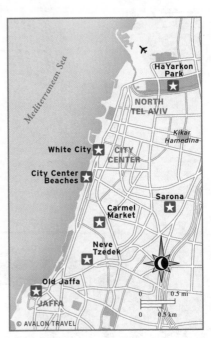

★ **City Center Beaches:** This coastline has a fantastic grouping of clean, easy-to-find beaches well-equipped with changing facilities, lockers, and restrooms (page 134).

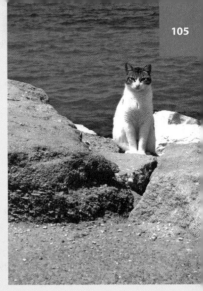

The first modern Jewish city, Tel Aviv plays an important role throughout Israel as a beacon of progress and modernity.

Tel Aviv is the ultimate combination of the old customs and traditions blended with the newness of the still relatively young country of Israel. Called "the center" by Israelis, Tel Aviv, like many major cities, is a melting pot of the best and worst from the entire country.

Tel Aviv is a bustling, incredibly humid (in the summer) mixture of commerce, beach-wear-clad people walking the streets, and great wealth with harsh pockets of poverty. The immigrant community from Ethiopia is much larger and more obvious here than in other parts of the country.

A magnet for talent and ambition from all over Israel, Tel Aviv boasts an impressive mixture of beaches, nightlife, business and commercial sectors, fashion and modeling industries, media and arts industries, high-tech and start-up companies, massive, gorgeous parks, and a largely secular lifestyle. Often described by Israelis as the place where everything happens and by visitors as just pure fun, Tel Aviv, on any given day of the week, has offerings for every taste and budget.

Its nightlife scene is legendary and infamous for not even really starting until after midnight—at the earliest.

Adjoining Tel Aviv and under the same municipality jurisdiction is Jaffa, one of the oldest cities in the world. Jaffa is predominately Arab and Christian and home to some of the best fine dining in town. Just after Israel became a state in 1948, the southern neighborhood of Jaffa was joined with Tel Aviv to form Tel Aviv-Yafo. Jaffa is home to some important Christian pilgrimage sites, ancient architecture, authentic Arab-style food, and interesting shopping opportunities. Adjacent to the beach, Jaffa makes for a great place to combine sightseeing, shopping, and dining in one afternoon.

Known as Israel's new city, Tel Aviv was founded before Israel was a state. Tel Aviv's name is, in a way, its defining characteristic. The word *tel* is the ancient word for "city," and the word *aviv* means "new." That very deliberate blend of old and new is what makes Tel Aviv so unique. It's a place where you can find

---

Previous: the modern buildings of Tel Aviv; an alley in Old Jaffa. **Above:** a cat sitting in the Tel Aviv sun.

the entire range of ancient Jewish traditions and customs alongside the new ways of doing things, the most advanced modern technology, and a hub of progressive thinking about the world. The metropolis is the center of arts, culture, and technology for the entire country.

ORIENTATION

Tel Aviv is about 30 minutes from Ben Gurion International Airport by car, and about one hour by train or bus. It is about one hour from Jerusalem by car, *sherut* (share taxi), bus, and about two hours by train to the City Center. The city is laid out in the shape of a rectangle with nothing but beach along the western border. Throughout all of Tel Aviv from north to south, there are miles of boardwalks, parks, and beaches.

North Tel Aviv

North Tel Aviv is generally made up of neighborhoods with pockets of shopping, entertainment, and food. The unofficial dividing line between the north and City Center is the Marina. The north section of the city is home to the massive HaYarkon Park, with all of its outdoor diversions as well as the Marina, with its shopping, sightseeing, dining, and nightlife options. The edge of North Tel Aviv is also home to some nice museums.

City Center

Tel Aviv's City Center is roughly south of the Marina and north of Charles Clore Park. A large majority of action happens in this part of the city, and it is where most of the designated beaches with lifeguards and hotels are located. Every type of shopping, dining, and entertainment option can be found in the center. If you are visiting the city for a few days, it is an excellent area for a base.

South Tel Aviv

South Tel Aviv is approximately from Charles Clore Park down to Jaffa and home to the lovely and entertaining Neve Tzedek neighborhood with its high-end shops, European-style cafés and restaurants, and varied nightlife options that include the converted HaTachana train station compound with shops, coffee, and live entertainment.

Jaffa

At the farthest south in Tel Aviv municipality is Jaffa, one of the oldest cities in the world. Today it is part of Tel Aviv and very much intertwined with the city's daily life. Jaffa's predominately Arab population gives it a completely unique flavor from the rest of the city, and it is famed for being home to some of Israel's best chefs, many of whom are internationally known.

PLANNING YOUR TIME

Particularly in the sweltering summer months, Tel Aviv really comes alive when the sun starts to go down. Plan to spend at least two days and nights in the city to get the right amount of sand, sun, food, and nightlife. In the summer, plan on air-conditioned downtime in the afternoon to keep your energy up for any late nights. The summer heat and humidity in Tel Aviv can be brutal, so pace yourself and keep drinking water. The city is active year-round, but as temperatures go down a bit during the winter months from November through March, people naturally move indoors.

Most of the sights and activities are concentrated in and near City Center, but it is a small city, so you don't have to go far to find a museum, a tour group, outdoor sports, or good food. If you stick somewhat close to the beach and promenade between Old Jaffa in the south and the port in the north, you won't run out of things to do. The best bet for getting around efficiently is to use the trains and buses.

Tel Aviv

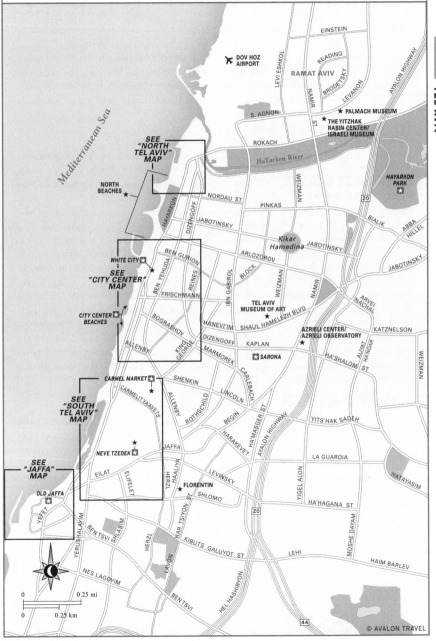

Sights

Tel Aviv proper is shaped like a rectangle with a curving eastern border and a pin-straight western border where the land meets the Mediterranean Sea, buffered by 13 beaches and boardwalks that stretch for almost nine miles. Each pocket of the city is generally known for its distinct offerings, such as world-class museums in the north, a huge variety of shopping and dining options in the center, and historical points of interest in the south.

NORTH TEL AVIV
Port of Tel Aviv

The object of a recent major transformation, the **Port of Tel Aviv** (where HaYarkon St.'s most northern point turns east and becomes HaTa'arucha St., tel. 03/544-1505, www.namal.co.il) was once desolate, but is now a hub of activity with its Marina and boardwalk. It is one of the most happening and family-friendly places in the city where you can get right up to the water's edge on the boardwalk. There is no swimming (legally) in the area, but Tel Avivians come out in droves in the evening to enjoy the seaside; the massive,

North Tel Aviv

sloping boardwalk; street performers; and the many restaurants and sweet shops.

During the hot summer months, the boardwalk is crowded late into the night with everyone—even children. Most of the restaurants serve typical Israeli food in the boardwalk area.

Ramat Aviv

The area of **Ramat Aviv,** at the northern tip of Tel Aviv, is home to some fantastic museums. Start with **The Yitzhak Rabin Center** (8 Chaim Levanon St., tel. 03/745-3322, www.rabincenter.org.il, 9am-5pm Sun.-Mon. and Wed., 9am-7pm Tues. and Thurs., 9am-2pm Fri., adult NIS50, senior and child NIS25), which includes the **Israeli Museum** (tel. 03/745-3345), which deals with the development of the State of Israel as a young democracy. Smart audio guides (NIS10) recognize where you are as you move in a downward spiral through the 1,500 striking photographs, extensive memorabilia, and documentary films on assassinated Prime Minister Yitzhak Rabin and the history of the State of Israel. The building is adjacent to the Eretz Israel Museum, and you should allow 2-3 hours for a visit.

The **Eretz Israel Museum** (2 Chaim Levanon St., tel. 03/641-5244, www.eretz-museum.org.il, 10am-4pm Sun.-Wed., 10am-8pm Thurs., 10am-2pm Fri.-Sat., adult NIS52, student NIS35, under 18 free) is an eclectic structure built partly on top of an archaeological site. It bills itself as a spiritual and cultural center of Tel Aviv and Israel. The museum includes several exhibition pavilions, each dedicated to a different cultural field and subject in Israel, including archaeology, Judaica, ethnography, as well as more modern art and cultural pieces. Some key permanent exhibitions are the ceramics exhibit and the ethnography and folklore pavilion. The museum's running theme is to highlight life in

Tel Aviv's Coastal Culture

Tel Aviv Marina

Israelis love to say that Tel Aviv is their "version of New York City" because of its bustling pace. In fact, it more closely resembles a beach town that just loves to party. Tel Aviv's surf-loving partying atmosphere is apparent everywhere, from the scantily clad to those crossing the street with a surfboard.

It is a city that has good reason to be so obsessed with the sea. Tel Aviv's entire western border is the Mediterranean, and it has a tremendous influence on the city's lifestyle, leisure activities, and atmosphere.

There are two types of Tel Aviv beaches: official and unofficial. Official beaches are designated as safe areas for swimming and have lifeguards. Unofficial beaches have no lifeguards and are often blocked off (such as at the Old Port of Tel Aviv). Some beaches, such as Hilton, are gay-friendly, while others are brimming with surfers, and others are jam-packed with tourists.

Four major points of reference on the Tel Aviv coast are the Jaffa Port, the Dolphinarium, the Tel Aviv Marina, and the Port of Tel Aviv.

The **Jaffa Port** is on the southern end of the city and near the Old City of Jaffa and the tip of Tel Aviv. Here you can find restaurants, ancient architecture, and general sightseeing in a scenic setting at what is believed to be one of the oldest ports in the entire world.

The **Dolphinarium Park** is just north of the oldest part of the *tayalet* (promenade) and the spacious Charles Clore Park, with gorgeous views of both Jaffa and Tel Aviv. The Dolphinarium was the site of a horrific terrorist bombing in 2001 during the Second Intifada. There is a park and playground there now that was established by the Tel Aviv Yafo Foundation. Nearby is the Israel Surf Club, where you can rent equipment and take lessons. Just southeast are the hip and happening adjacent districts of Shabazi Street, Neve Tzedek, and HaTachana.

Due north up the coast is the **Tel Aviv Marina,** another hub of activity and central launching point for activities. Here you will find the heated saltwater Gordon Swimming Pool, Atarim Square, and more excellent surfing spots and beaches.

Continue north to the **Port of Tel Aviv** to a tremendous center of activity, including a scenic boardwalk, restaurants, shops, a farmers market, and a couple of beaches. The area has been revitalized in recent years and is a beehive of activity, especially in the late summer evenings when locals looking to escape the stifling heat get out and about.

Israel from ancient up through modern times. It is easy to walk through the various exhibits. The outdoor archaeological exhibit is accessible even after closing hours. The gift shop's unique items and the building's open-air pavilions are popular draws that make an excellent spot for a leisurely visit.

The extremely popular **Palmach Museum** (10 Chaim Levanon St., tel. 03/643-6393, http://info.palmach.org.il, 9am-5pm Sun.-Mon. and Wed., 9am-8pm Tues., 9am-2pm Thurs., 9am-1pm Fri., adult NIS30, child NIS20) is an experiential museum documenting the history of the elite underground Jewish fighting forces in pre-state Israel. Instead of displays or documents, a 90-minute group tour includes fascinating personal accounts of historical characters alongside three-dimensional decor, films, and special effects that incorporate documentary materials. Visits must be arranged in advance, especially for English-speaking visitors.

A good way to combine a museum visit with a visit to the campus of Tel Aviv University is a stop at **Beit Hatfutsot, The Museum of the Jewish People** (Tel Aviv University

campus, Klausner St., in Ramat Aviv, entrance through Matatia Gate 2, tel. 03/745-7808, www.bh.org.il, 10am-4pm Sun.-Tues., 10am-7pm Wed.-Thurs., 9am-1pm Fri., adult NIS70, senior NIS30, child NIS55). The permanent and rotating exhibits that trace the story of the Jewish people over the last 2,500 years include models, short films, and texts on the history and ongoing stories of the Jewish Diaspora. A lack of upgrades in years past have now led the museum to initiate renovations, but it is still possible to spend hours exploring. Don't miss the miniature synagogue exhibit with models of famous synagogues from all over the world including Europe, Asia, and the Middle East. Also of interest is the genealogy section where you can research on computers and add information to the database.

CITY CENTER
Azrieli Observatory and Azrieli Center

The highest observation point in the Middle East is the **Azrieli Observatory** (132 Menachem Begin Rd., 3rd Fl. designated elevator, tel. 03/608-1990, http://mitzpe49.co.il/

A Brief History of Israel's "New City"

Tel Aviv draws at least some of its inspiration for being vibrant and exciting from its status as Israel's "new city." The name Tel Aviv literally translates as "spring mound" but the more intuitive meaning is "old new city," as its name was inspired by founding father Theodor Herzl's book bearing that title. The founding and creation of Tel Aviv was, and is, seen as the center of the revival of the new Jewish state in the ancient homeland.

Tel Aviv's official name, Tel Aviv-Yafo, stems from its connection to the ancient port city of Jaffa (or Yafo) that is at the southern end of the city. Jaffa, which is predominately Arab, is estimated to be about 4,000 years old.

The first modern Hebrew city, Tel Aviv was established in 1909 by a group of 60 families who simply took plots of land through a group self-assignment process. But as the population of Tel Aviv grew, so did tensions with Arab neighbors in Jaffa who had already been living there for years.

Suffering from a long history of instability and insecurity, on the eve of the establishment of an independent Jewish state in 1948 Jewish and Arab forces battled for control of Tel Aviv. Ultimately, Arab forces and residents were violently pushed into Jaffa. In 1949, Tel Aviv's second mayor, Israel Rokach, united Tel Aviv and Jaffa under the auspices of the Tel Aviv-Yafo municipality.

Today, Jaffa accounts for about 12 percent of Tel Aviv's total area and is home to about 45,000 Arab, Christian, and Jewish residents. It is famed for having some of the best fine dining in the country.

City Center

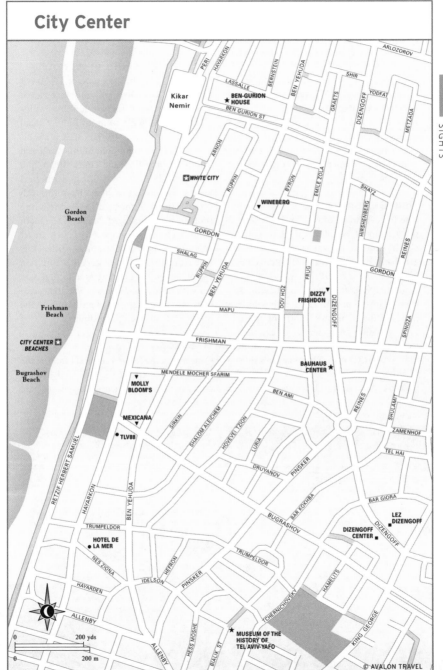

ARLOZOROV

Kikar
Nemir

BEN-GURION
★ HOUSE

BEN GURION ST

LASSALLE

★ WHITE CITY

▼ WINEBERG

Gordon
Beach

GORDON

SHALAG

▼ DIZZY
FRISHDON

Frishman
Beach

MAPU

FRISHMAN

CITY CENTER ✚
BEACHES

BAUHAUS ★
CENTER

Bugrashov
Beach

MENDELE MOCHER SFARIM

▼ MOLLY
BLOOM'S

BEN AMI

▼ MEXICANA

● TLV88

DRUYANOV

LEZ
DIZENGOFF ■

BUGRASHOV

DIZENGOFF
CENTER ■

TRUMPELDOR

HOTEL DE
● LA MER

TRUMPELDOR

NES ZIONA

HAYARDEN

ALLENBY

★ MUSEUM OF THE
HISTORY OF
TEL AVIV-YAFO

0   200 yds

0   200 m

© AVALON TRAVEL

home, adult NIS22, senior and child NIS17) on the 49th floor of **Azrieli Center,** a multi-level mall with a train stop and multiplex cinema. The observatory, located in the center's round tower, has a commanding view of the coastline from Gedera in the south to Hadera in the north and of Tel Aviv. Some vantage points are only accessible from the bar and restaurant, often closed for private events. It makes for a good sunset visit in combination with a trip to the mall in the same building or drinks and dinner at the 2C Restaurant on the same floor.

Ben-Gurion House

The former home of one of the fathers of the nation of Israel, David Ben-Gurion, is still intact for visitors. The very modest **Ben-Gurion House** (17 Ben-Gurion Blvd., tel. 03/522-1010, www.bg-house.org, 8am-3pm Sun. and Tues.-Thurs., 8am-5pm Mon., 8am-noon Fri., 11am-2pm Sat., free) includes Ben-Gurion's library of approximately 20,000 books and is an example of the Bauhaus/International design so well-preserved in Tel Aviv. The museum's signage is mostly in Hebrew, but it is still worth a visit to explore the residence and some of the

photos, letters, and gifts from world leaders. Call in advance to ask for a possible English-speaking guide.

Tel Aviv Museum of Art

Opened in 1932 in the home of Tel Aviv's first mayor, Meir Dizengoff, and since moved to a distinctive, futuristic-looking building, the **Tel Aviv Museum of Art** (27 Shaul HaMelech Blvd., tel. 03/607-7020, www.ta-museum.org.il, 10am-6pm Mon., Wed., and Sat., 10am-9pm Tues. and Thurs., 10am-2pm Fri., adult NIS50, senior NIS25, under 18 free) hosts a vast collection of art from the 16th century through modern times, including contemporary Israeli art. Made up of a main building, a new wing opened in 2011, an art education center, and a sculpture garden, this vast art museum hosts at least half a million visitors a year. The old masters collection is on par with European museums, and in general there is a surprising array of pieces in both the permanent and changing exhibits.

★ Sarona

Conceived as a renewed cultural center of the city, **Sarona** (http://saronatlv.co.il) is part popular village-like gathering place, part

the Tel Aviv Museum of Art

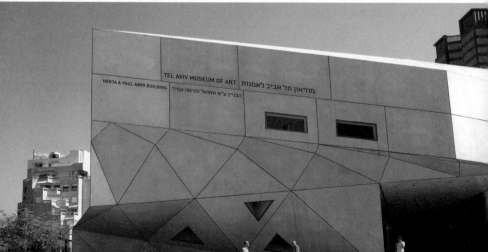

high-end food market. Designed to emulate similar ventures such as Eataly in New York City, Sarona is an open-air commercial center in the midst of a residential area. A former German Templar colony, Sarona was created from 37 renovated Templar-era buildings that were converted into upscale modern shopping and dining venues, and art galleries. The ample public space features live street music, and tours are offered at the visitors center. Nestled among lower-rise buildings, it is the perfect spot to get the old and new of Tel Aviv, with a clear view of the distinctive Azrieli Center high-rise building and tree-lined paths for a stroll on the way to have a drink or dinner outdoors.

A good place to start is the **Visitor Center** (14 Alber Mendler St.) which will help guide you through the restoration work done on the area and some of the history of Tel Aviv and the general area through its exhibitions. Maps of the area will also get you oriented, and you can check about available tours.

Helena Rubenstein Pavilion for Contemporary Art

Part of the Israel Museum, the **Helena Rubenstein Pavilion for Contemporary Art** (6 Tarsat Blvd., tel. 03/528-7196, www.tamuseum.org.il, 10am-6pm Mon.-Thurs., 10am-2pm Fri., NIS10) is home to contemporary art by Israeli and international artists. In addition to changing exhibits, the upper level houses permanent exhibits of porcelain and glassware artwork. The building is part of Tel Aviv's so-called "culture square" that includes the Habima Theater and the Bronfman Auditorium.

Israel Defense Forces History Museum

A good option for military history buffs and those who want to know a bit more about the Israeli military in particular is the **Israel Defense Forces History Museum** (Shimtat Shlush St. at the corner of Ashkelon St., tel. 03/517-2913, toldot_zahal_museum@mailto.mod.gov.il, 8:30am-3:30pm Sun.-Thurs., free) depicts the history of the Israeli army from 1948 through today. With a bunker-like exterior, the museum is spread out through five buildings and includes extensive outdoor pavilions with exhibits that include films, photographs, maps, historic documents, and authentic tanks, cars, and weapons.

TEL AVIV
SIGHTS

Sarona, an open-air shopping and dining center

The White City

In 1925, as Tel Aviv grew and developed, Scottish urban planner Sir Patrick Geddes was brought in to help design a modern urban city in response to the sprawling expansion with no overall cohesion. Geddes's vision for a Tel Aviv master plan was a garden city with clear separations between main streets, residential streets, and vegetation-filled pedestrian boulevards. One of the plan's key elements was creating shared public spaces in parks, squares, and in residential blocks. It was a significant part of the Bauhaus movement, a highly influential, modernist approach to art and design that manifested in architecture, as buildings (individually and as groups) centered on purpose, and integration with the needs of modern city life and its surroundings.

Using Geddes's urban plan, from the early 1930s until the 1950s, the White City came into being. Designed by architects who had trained and practiced in Europe, the White City reflects modern organic planning principles and ultimately became what UNESCO calls "an outstanding architectural ensemble of the Modern Movement in a new cultural context."

Bauhaus architecture comprises Tel Aviv's White City, a UNESCO World Heritage Site.

Declared a UNESCO World Heritage Site, the White City can be seen by guided tour, and its buildings are protected structures.

Old Town Hall

The beautiful, grand Bauhaus building that served as Tel Aviv's Old Town Hall (*Beit Ha'ir*) with grand colonnades and facing entrance staircases is home to the Beit Ha'ir (27 Bialik St., tel. 03/517-3052, http://beithair. org, 9am-5pm Mon.-Thurs., 10am-2pm Fri.-Sat. and holidays, free) and part of the Bialik Complex UNESCO World Heritage Site. The collection of photos and old video clips from Tel Aviv residents chronicles the history of the city in the last 100 years and includes an "old" and a "new" wing. The office of Tel Aviv's first mayor, Meir Dizengoff, has been restored with a view of Bialik Square and Bialik Street's Bauhaus architecture. Rotating exhibitions of local and international artists and designers are also on display. The museum is designed as an open house for area artists and thinkers, and is a pleasant, easy to reach stop on the way to see the White City.

★ White City

Tel Aviv's White City (between Allenby St. in the south, Begin Rd. and Ibn Gabirol St. in the east, the Yarkon River in the north, and the Mediterranean Sea in the west, www.white-city.co.il) is a UNESCO World Heritage Site and considered an outstanding example of new town planning and architecture in the early 20th century, adapted to the cultural and geographic context of Tel Aviv. It is a must-see for architecture aficionados. The Information Center (46 Herbert Samuel St. at the corner of 2 Geula St., tel. 03/516-6188) will assist in getting you oriented to tours and information about the area. Based on a design by Scottish Sir Patrick Geddes, the 4,000 buildings of the White City were built between the early 1930s through the 1950s. They are a definitive part of Tel Aviv's character and what UNESCO calls an "outstanding architectural ensemble of the Modern Movement in a new cultural context."

The buildings in the White City were designed by European-trained architects who practiced their profession abroad before immigrating to Israel. Most of the buildings are 3-4 stories high and have flat roofs, plaster rendering, some decorative features, and a monochromatic color scheme of cream to white. The buildings are located mainly along Rothschild Boulevard, around Dizengoff Circle and on Bialik Street.

On Fridays, the one-room **Bauhaus Foundation Museum** (21 Bialik St., tel. 03/620-4664, 11am-5pm Wed., 10am-2pm Fri., free) offers free two-hour tours, but call ahead for specific times. Otherwise, the one-room establishment dedicated to the Bauhaus movement through the display of Bauhaus objects and furniture is a worthwhile stop for architecture buffs. It is a housed on the ground floor of a renovated Bauhaus building and is also home to the Bauhaus Foundation.

The **Bauhaus Center** (99 Dizengoff St., tel. 03/522-0249, www.bauhaus-center.com, 10am-7:30pm Sat.-Thurs., 10am-2:30pm Fri., free) is dedicated to the public recognition of the White City as a unique architectural and cultural site. The center is small and tightly packed with an interesting array of Bauhaus memorabilia and a second-floor gallery with permanent and changing art exhibitions. The ground floor gift shop sells books in English on the subject of the White City and Bauhaus. Guided tours in English (10am Fri., NIS60) are available here either with a tour guide or by renting audio headphones (anytime, NIS60). Both types of tours take about two hours. The center also offers other tours in Tel Aviv and other areas of Israel.

The City of Tel Aviv also hosts a variety of free **Walk this Way Tours** (White City tour: meet at 46 Rothschild Blvd. on the corner of Shadal St., tel. 03/516-6188, www.visit-tlv. com, 11am Sat., free) that include a route of the White City. Other tours include Tel Aviv University, Tel Aviv by Night, Tel Aviv Art and Graffiti, and Old Jaffa. There is no need to book in advance; you just meet up at the starting point about 10 minutes before the scheduled departure time. Check the website for updated times before you go.

SOUTH TEL AVIV
★ Neve Tzedek

Decades before Tel Aviv was formally established as a city, **Neve Tzedek** (which means oasis of justice) had already sprung up in

Tel Aviv's Neve Tzedek neighborhood is full of charming European-style cafes.

South Tel Aviv

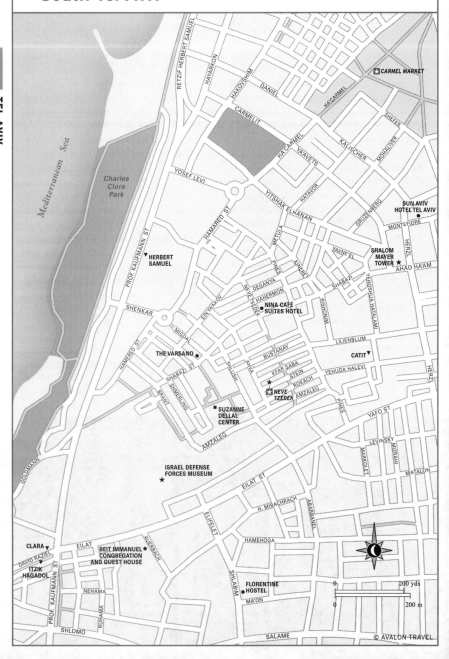

© AVALON TRAVEL

1887. It is Tel Aviv's oldest neighborhood, and the first one inhabited by Jewish residents. Prominent artists and writers like S. Y. Agnon and Nachum Gutman called Neve Tzedek home during the early 20th century, and it still has a distinctly bohemian, European vibe. It is by far one of the coolest places in the city to stroll around and take in the atmosphere; browse designer boutique stores, crafts shops, and bookstores; and enjoy one of the area's fine cafés or restaurants. The main (very narrow) throughway in Neve Tzedek is Shabazi Street, an excellent place to see historic Tel Aviv architecture.

Start at the **Nachum Gutman Museum of Art** (21 Shim'on Rokach St., tel. 03/516-1970, www.gutmanmuseum.co.il, 10am-4pm Sun.-Thurs., 10am-2pm Fri., 10am-3pm Sat., entrance fee, NIS24) with its distinctive bright yellow colonnade fence around an historic house dating to the founding of the neighborhood. The charming, small museum showcases works by Nachum Gutman, a beloved Israeli artist and children's author. You can see hundreds of his illustrations and drawings as well as oil, watercolor, and gouache paintings.

The **Rokach House Museum** (36 Shim'on Rokach St., tel. 03/516-8042, www.rokach-house.co.il, 10am-2pm daily, schedule English tours in advance, NIS10) was also built in 1887 and is famous for its domed roof. Now a museum named for Shim'on Rokach, a prominent Jewish public servant and cofounder of Neve Tzedek, the museum focuses on Rokach's notable artist and sculptor granddaughter, Lea Majaro-Mintz. There's also an English video and photographs depicting Neve Tzedek's history.

Shalom Mayer Tower

An interesting stop for art enthusiasts, the **Shalom Mayer Tower** (9 Ahad Ha'am St., tel. 03/510-0337, www.migdalshalom.co.il/eng, 8am-7pm Sun.-Thurs., 8am-2pm Fri. and holidays, free) has a spacious, modern layout that includes exhibits in the lobby and a first floor **art gallery** (10am-5pm Sun.-Thurs.,

10am-1pm Fri. and holidays, free). It is one of the largest nonprofit art galleries in Israel. Works include pieces from contemporary Israeli painters, sculptors, and photographers and a dozen permanent and alternating exhibits from Israel's best museums.

The tower also houses the **Discover Tel Aviv Center** (9 Ahad Ha'am St., for tours email tiki@discover-telaviv.co.il, 10am-5pm Sun.-Thurs., free) on the ground floor with an interactive multimedia display about Tel Aviv's development, history, and famous residents. It depicts the history of the city through paintings and photographs and offers professionally guided tours in Tel Aviv and throughout Israel.

The Rubin Museum

In the heart of old Tel Aviv, **The Rubin Museum** (14 Bialik St., tel. 03/525-5961, www.rubinmuseum.org.il, 10am-3pm Mon. and Wed.-Fri., 10am-8pm Tues., 11am-2pm Sat. and holidays, adult NIS20, senior NIS10, under 18 free) operates out of the house of famous and popular Israeli modern artist Reuven Rubin, and the four floors house works of Rubin, a reading room, a children's gallery, and changing exhibits of other Israeli artists.

JAFFA (YAFO)

The port city of Jaffa (Yafo) is believed to be one of the most ancient cities in the world. An area with a strong Arab flavor, Jaffa is an important part of a visit to Tel Aviv. It is directly adjacent to the rest of the city and easy to reach by bus or car. It is full of charming, interesting sights, restaurants, and shopping. For a scenic route to reach Jaffa, walk on the paved beachfront boardwalk at Charles Clore Park and cross the pedestrian bridge that is the unofficial boundary between Tel Aviv (the new city) and Jaffa (the old city).

★ Old Jaffa

Old Jaffa (access through the promenade or off of Yefet St.) is contained largely near the port on a hill overlooking the Mediterranean and has numerous corners to explore. You'll find archaeological sites here, but also upscale shops, some of the best fine dining in Tel Aviv, an artists' quarter, renovated Ottoman-era houses, and several important landmarks.

Start on the east side of Old Jaffa at **Clock Tower Square,** which is a popular meeting place and home to the **clock tower,** built in 1901 by Turkish Sultan Abed-el-Hamid II and one of Jaffa's most easily recognizable sites. Here you will also find the **former governor's house** and a jailhouse used by the Turks and British known as the **Kishle.** On Yefet Street in the immediate vicinity is the famous **Abulafia Bakery** (7 Yefet St., tel. 03/681-2340, NIS20), which also runs a 24-hour street bakery nearby. The plaza area is encircled by several galleries, restaurants, and souvenir shops, and you can hear free concerts here during the summer.

In the Clock Tower Square is the **Visitors Center** (Clock Tower Square, tel. 03/603-7686, www.oldjaffa.co.il, 10am-5pm Sun.-Thurs., 10am-3pm Fri., 10am-5pm Sat. Nov.-Mar.; 9am-7pm Sun.-Thurs., 9am-4pm Fri., 9am-7pm Sat. Apr.-Oct.), a good place to get started. It is also an archaeological site and a museum about the area's history. The Visitors Center is in an underground building that includes exhibits of archaeological ruins from the

Hellenistic and Roman eras and three-dimensional illustrations of Jaffa's legends and historical events of the past 2,000 years. There are also eight paintings done over the past 300 years of Jaffa from the perspective of the sea. The Visitors Center's light and sound show tells the story of the past and present of the Old City.

Along **Mifrats Shlomo Promenade** you will find a large structure that is historically and architecturally unique and

Old Jaffa

the landmark Jaffa clock tower

made up of several historical buildings, built over Crusader-era remnants. Dating to the 18th century, it has served as the seat of the Ottoman governor, a post office, and a guard house. A well-known Christian family by the name of Demiani bought part of the building in 1733 and converted it into a successful soap factory. Abandoned during Israel's War of Independence, it now houses the **Jaffa Museum of Antiquities** (10 Mifrats Shlomo St., tel. 03/682-5375, www.oldjaffa. co.il, 4pm-8pm Mon.-Wed., 4pm-9pm Thurs., 10am-4pm Fri.-Sat., NIS30) with permanent exhibits on archaeology and changing exhibits on modern art. It is small and comprehensive enough to be informative but not exhausting.

Built over medieval fortress remains and the ruins of a Byzantine church, **St. Peter's Monastery** (1 Mifrats Shlomo St. next to Clock Tower Square, tel. 03/682-2871, 8am-noon and 3pm-6pm daily Apr.-Oct., 8am-noon and 3pm-5pm daily Nov.-Mar., free) is a Franciscan church from the beginning of the 20th century. It features a unique brick facade and towering belfry that overlooks the sea from where it sits at the top of Jaffa mound. The iconic building's silhouette is visible from the southern end of Tel Aviv, and the picturesque view is frequently photographed. The location has been a center for Christianity for thousands of years, and it is believed that Napoleon once stayed here. The church has a spectacular interior with a vaulted ceiling, stained glass windows, and marble walls.

Old Port

From Jaffa's Clock Tower Square, you can find small winding streets leading down to the **Old Port** area, one of the most ancient ports in the world. The Bible's Book of Jonah mentions Jaffa's port; Napoleon's army destroyed it in 1799, and it was later rebuilt by the Ottomans. The port has served as the main point of entry for thousands of Jewish immigrants, and it has boating excursions and good seafood restaurants. The main hangars were restored to house art galleries, cafés, restaurants, and shops.

A highly popular draw is the startling and unusual **The Nalagaat Center** (Retsif Haaliya Hashniya at Jaffa Port, tel. 03/633-0808, www.nalagaat.org.il, call for reservations). It is an artistic complex operated by the deaf and blind community, complete with a unique restaurant and café.

Entertainment and Events

As soon as the sun goes down in Tel Aviv, residents come out in droves to party, eat, drink, and enjoy the beautiful evenings and wide array of entertainment. No matter what you are looking for, you will find it. Always carry some kind of ID and check the age range of the venue beforehand, as some places draw very young crowds or change the minimum age by the night. Have a backup plan, too, in case your destination is closed for that night or permanently.

BARS, CLUBS, PUBS, AND LIVE MUSIC

Tel Aviv nightlife is among the liveliest in the world, with parties of all kinds that go well into the wee hours of the night. Bars, clubs, pubs, and live music venues offer everything from beer and billiards to small venue rock concerts and are great hangouts for a few drinks. The entire spectrum of nightlife is available, from a low-key time sipping drinks in a cavernous jazz club to dancing all night at a beachfront megaclub.

North Tel Aviv

The seaside region just to the west of HaYarkon Park next to where the Yarkon River empties into the Mediterranean Sea has a nice variety of places for evening fun, many at or nearby the **Old Port of Tel Aviv.**

One of Tel Aviv's longest streets, Dizengoff Street runs from the north through the center of town, and is full of great spots all along the way. One of them, **Rosa Parks** (265 Dizengoff St., tel. 054/643-9958, 8pm-last customer daily, no cover), is a laid-back bar that caters to a 25-plus, sophisticated, and upwardly mobile crowd. It has two levels with a pool table and a small upstairs bar with a view of the street. It's known for its wide variety of DJ music, the kitchen is also open all night.

One of the oldest clubs in the city, the **TLV Club** (Old Port, tel. 03/544-4194, midnight-6am Mon. and Fri.-Sat., cover varies depending on who is performing) is a large discotheque and live music venue that features Israeli rock and pop stars. The age of the crowd varies widely, and the line to get in is usually fairly long. TLV Club's atmosphere is all about partying hard.

For a relatively low-key evening and change of pace in an intimate, high-end setting, the **Shablul Jazz Club** (Hangar 13 at the Port of Tel Aviv on Nemal St., tel. 03/546-1891, www.

shabluljazz.com, doors open 8pm, concerts start 9pm Sun.-Thurs., jam sessions 10:30pm, matinee shows 4pm Fri. and Sat., closed for Shabbat, cover NIS50-150, NIS60 for food menu) features live music nightly, including famous domestic acts and international acts like the group Harp Concert Jazz. On Friday afternoons they offer a bistro menu with their matinee show and always serve top-shelf alcohol.

City Center

City Center has a huge concentration of nightlife spots. The area around **Allenby Street** has some popular local spots and very posh and trendy clubs (think dress code and VIP rooms) while central **Dizengoff Street** is home to many popular hangouts of all speeds. Get extra dressed-up if you want to try your luck at getting into some of the more exclusive spots that have no qualms about turning customers away. One of the more artsy areas in Tel Aviv is near **King George Street** in close proximity to **Dizengoff Center.** On the upper side of King George you can find some alternative cafés and bars that make for a nice start to the evening before the clubs get going around 11pm or later.

Off of popular Allenby Street, **Beit Ha'amudim** (14 Rambam St., tel. 03/510-9228, 11am-2am Sun.-Thurs., 10am-sunset Fri., from 7pm Sat., NIS45), which means "house of columns," is a popular bar with jazz concerts, an intimate neighborhood crowd, and art exhibits. They are also known for their jazz brunches, and the food menu is all vegetarian.

The Prince (18 Nahalat Binyamin St., tel. 058/606-1818, 5pm-1am Sun.-Thurs., NIS30) is an artsy bar, bookstore, and coffee shop, with tons of books and wood paneling lining the walls. Not exactly a club or bar and not exactly a coffee shop or bookstore, it plays host to a hipster crowd that likes to hang out late. It is known for its central role in the young poetry revival movement and hosts writing salon groups and story slams (like poetry slams but with stories).

Along Dizengoff Street north of Dizengoff Center there is a nice variety of nightlife spots. On the northern end of the street is the bar-lounge **Dizzy Frishdon** (121 Dizengoff St., tel. 03/523-4111, 8pm-4am daily), a popular hangout with a fun-loving crowd. It's an easy place to get into if you're willing to wait in line and make new friends. The cozy interior is dimly lit with a bar and a food menu.

A bit on the pricey side but worth it for the famed ability of its bartenders to make practically any drink a customer orders, popular cocktail bar **French 57** (2 Brenner St., tel. 02/638-2621, 6pm-3am daily, NIS60) has a chilled-out atmosphere reminiscent of a New Orleans bar. Background jazz music and a menu that features surprises such as Philly cheesesteak and ceviche add to the overall experience of being transported into a world far from Tel Aviv.

A popular late-night hangout is **The Cat and the Dog** (23 Carlibach St., tel. 03/561-5595 and 052/449-9188 for reservations, www.thecatandthedog.com, about midnight-7am daily, free weekdays, sometimes NIS60-80 weekends). Known as one of the most popular spots in the city for international DJs, it doesn't really get going until superlate, around 3am. The club features underground and electronic music and enjoys a long-standing popularity for the party atmosphere and dancing with a state-of-the-art light and sound system. It's a bit of a mixed scene as far as customers, so come prepared to experience local flavor.

Right in the middle of City Center and down a dark, unmarked alley is **Radio E.P.G.B.** (7 Shadal St., tel. 03/560-3636, 9pm-6am daily, no cover, NIS20 for beer), a hipster dance club and music bar with a quirky atmosphere that includes a pinball machine and punk posters. Like many others, it attempts to lay claim to the best club/bar in the city, but in this case it might not be far off. The club features frequent live indie music performances, DJs spinning indie rock and electronic, and an overall extremely welcoming atmosphere for people of all types.

Starting at around 2am and ramping up

by 9am, the Tel Aviv after-party is largely a creature of Friday and Saturday nights. One of the best spots to experience this type of Tel Aviv nightlife culture is **Spice Melange** (113 Hashmonaim St., tel. 052/688-7706, marinaspice@gmail.com, 4am-2pm, NIS60) with its dress-to-impress atmosphere and food and drinks menu.

Just off of busy Dizengoff Street is the **Seret Club** (30 Ibn Gabirol St., inside the London Ministore mall, tel. 052/245-8600, eitan@seretbar.co.il, 9pm-4am daily, no cover). To get inside, go into the mall, go to floor minus 1 (one below ground floor) and find the entrance to the club off the parking lot. Once inside, you'll be in a movie-themed wonderland (*seret* means "movie" in Hebrew) that includes movie-theater chairs and marquee lights. It is crucial that you call or email in advance to book a table for your group, and they don't take traveler's checks.

A popular Irish pub is **Molly Bloom's** (2 Mendele St., at the corner of HaYarkon St., tel. 03/522-1558, www.molly-blooms.com, 4pm-last customer Sat.-Thurs., 2pm-last customer Fri., NIS55), whose claim to fame is that they were the first Irish pub in Tel Aviv when they opened in 2000. Still a neighborhood favorite, it has a standard pub and sports bar interior of wood, bar stools, and TVs. There's live Irish music every Monday starting around 9:30pm and open-microphone sessions on Fridays starting at 5pm.

If you're in the mood for a place with a smoking room, a pool table, and more of a neighborhood vibe, go to **Bar Giora** (4 Bar Giora St., at the corner of Dizengoff St., tel. 03/620-4880, http://bargiyora.co.il, 9am-2am daily, NIS45) with its café, bar, and live music, including a nightly "BBQ live music" from 9:30pm. There are multiple levels, and it is an old standard bar-coffee shop-restaurant that has survived the frequent changes of the Tel Aviv nightlife scene. There is a two-for-one happy hour (5pm-9pm daily), a food menu with Middle Eastern and Persian dishes, and comfortable booths to sit in. The pool tables are not always open, so call ahead if you want to play.

Just next to landmark Rabin Square, look for the swanky neighborhood **Otto Bar** (76 Ibn Gabirol St., tel. 077/414-5043, 9pm-5am daily, NIS45), known as a place where Israeli celebrities like to hang out. It is well lit with a pool table but definitely has the feel of a bar with a nicely decorated interior and tons of bar stools. It's not huge, but is one of three locations that Otto has in Tel Aviv (the other two are at 48 Ahad Ha'Am St. and 302 Dizengoff St.). The bar is restricted to ages 25 and older. Otto Bar is part of the growing trend in Tel Aviv to sell bracelets to customers who want an all you can drink option rather than spend a small fortune on one drink at a time.

South Tel Aviv

Just like the rest of the city, the southern part of Tel Aviv is hopping with a broad range of nightlife, including some spots popular with younger crowds that feature intense dance music and word-of-mouth only underground parties that change locations weekly.

The Penguin Club (43 Yehuda Halevi St., tel. 03/566-1450, penguinclubtlv@gmail.com, midnight-6am daily, technically member only, NIS50) is an underground haunt with electronic music and house DJs. It is a good spot to drop by on Wednesday and Thursday nights. The party doesn't really get going until about 2am or later and goes strong until closing time at 6am. Officially it is a member's only club and is only for the 25-plus crowd, but there seems to be some leeway for determined tourists. Just go with a backup plan.

The Block (157 Salame St., inside the Central Bus Station on the 4th Fl., tel. 03/537-8002, www.block-club.com, doors open around 11pm daily, NIS80 and up for DJs) has a high-quality analog sound system and a hefty lineup of international DJs. The urban atmosphere and on-trend customers help maintain its reputation as one of the coolest places in the city to party.

Just east of trendy Neve Tzedek near Allenby Street, there is a good selection of trendy spots with more sophisticated, polished crowds. The surrounding streets have dance bars that come and go and vary from slick and commercial to alternative. **Lilenblum Street** has a mixture of DJ clubs and bars. Tel Aviv's younger crowd (under 20) loves to hit the huge clubs and dance bars in the area near Ha'Masger to Ha'Rakevet Street. A popular spot is **Haoman 17** (88 Abarbanel St., tel. 03/681-3636, open only on select nights, usually weekends and holidays, call ahead for hours, NIS60-100), a megaclub that attracts top DJs from all over the world. It is one of the newest and biggest clubs in the city. There are multiple levels and three main dance areas.

The crowd at **Clara** (1 Kaufmann St. at Dolphinarium Beach, tel. 054/222-2260 or 03/510-2060, www.clara.co.il, 9pm-4am Mon. and Thurs. Apr.-Oct., no cover) is mostly younger with the age range mostly under 30. It is an open-air megabar right on the beach with a sophisticated atmosphere. Only open in the summer from April to October, Clara usually has a DJ and plenty of comfortable couches to hang out on, have a drink, and enjoy the ocean view.

GAY AND LESBIAN NIGHTLIFE

Tel Aviv is generally very gay- and lesbian-friendly. In addition, there is a nice selection of places that cater specifically to the gay and lesbian crowd.

Popular among those who know it's there, **Deli Bar** (47 Allenby St., tel. 03/642-5738 or 054/435-2834, 10am-8pm daily, no cover) is reached by passing through a sandwich shop to get to the back where the dancing is happening. Deli features hip-hop and electronica music by some of the city's best DJs and boasts a huge menu of cocktails and imported beers.

Tel Aviv's only men-only gay bar, **Apollo Sexy Bar** (46 Allenby St., tel. 03/774-1106, 10pm-5am daily, no cover minimum one drink purchase) is only for those looking for an especially intense experience. The basement area features a movie screen, there is a dark room, bar, and dance floor. Prior to midnight there is a reduced alcohol menu.

Formerly the Maxim Club, **Bootleg** (48 King George St., tel. 052/805-4448, 8pm-7am daily, NIS50 for special DJs) is a gay-friendly dance club with a relaxed atmosphere and house music. The crowd is generally comprised of people of all ages, and it has low light and loud music.

Evita (31 Yavne St., www.evita.co.il, 9pm-last customer daily, no cover) is the oldest gay bar in Tel Aviv just off of the major Rothschild Boulevard. The club has a huge wood bar, comfy couches, a dance floor, an outdoor area, and features an extensive alcohol menu as well as a food menu. On weekends the club has parties and is known for its high-end DJs.

PERFORMING ARTS, VISUAL ARTS, AND CULTURAL CENTERS
City Center

The **Z.O.A. House** (1 Daniel Frisch St., tel. 03/695-9341, 9am-11:30pm daily) is a charming mixture of cinema, theater, café, and history. With construction that was started in the presence of Israel's first prime minister, David Ben-Gurion, the Zionist Organization of America House now holds a movie theater, a theater for stage, and a ground-floor café that is reputed to serve some of the best cappuccino in all of Tel Aviv. There is a surprising array of performances that range from old Shakespeare classics to folk performances that are done in Yiddish.

There are several movie cinemas in the city; you can find current listings by searching online or buying an English newspaper. An easy cinema to reach is **Lev Dizengoff** (50 Dizengoff Center Mall, tel. 03/621-2222, NIS40). Most movie theaters in Israel will have some mainstream movies in English with Hebrew subtitles.

The **Tmuna Theatre** (8 Shonzino St., tel. 03/561-1211, www.tmu-na.org.il, tickets vary) is a community theater that hosts a variety of stage performances including plays, performing arts showcases, live music, literature, and fine art that are considered less mainstream and often fringe. Tmuna hosts over 550 theater shows, 80 dance performances, 270 music events, and 50 literature and poetry nights every year.

Part of one of Tel Aviv's largest cultural complexes is the renowned **Cameri Theatre** (19 Shaul HaMelech Blvd., tel. 03/606-0960, www.cameri.co.il). The theater puts on Israeli and classic plays, musicals, concerts, and modern theater.

The **Tel Aviv Performing Arts Center** (19 Shaul HaMelech Blvd., tel. 03/692-7777, www.israel-opera.co.il) is home to the Israeli Opera and the Israel Ballet and offers a wide variety of operatic performances for all ages, and hosts other varied performances almost nightly, year-round. It is particularly known for its dance performances by the Israel Ballet and the international performers and festivals it brings in throughout the year.

The country's second largest theater, **Beit Lessin Theater** (101 Dizengoff St., tel. 03/725-5333, www.lessin.co.il) was founded in the early 1980s as a club for Israel's Workers' Union. It is home to Israel's annual **New Israeli Drama Festival** called Open Stage. Numerous award-winning playwrights have shown their work at Beit Lessin or have been discovered on the venue's stage.

The **Habima Theater** (19 Leonardo da Vinci, tel. 03/526-6666, www.habima.co.il) is Israel's national theater and was rebuilt and reopened in 2009. All productions are in Hebrew, but you can call ahead for productions that are translated simultaneously into English.

South Tel Aviv

A centerpiece of the famed Neve Tzedek bohemian neighborhood is the **Suzanne Dellal Center** (5 Yehieli St., tel. 03/510-5656, www.suzannedellal.org.il), recipient of the prestigious Israel Prize and home to modern and experimental productions and top Israeli dance troupes. The carefully restored older buildings that make up the center play host

the Suzanne Dellal Center

to events, festivals, performances, a restaurant and coffee shop, and a large outer piazza.

ART AND PHOTOGRAPHY GALLERIES
City Center

The **Urban Gallery** (72 and 74 Ben Yehuda St., tel. 03/524-4110, www.urbangallery972. com, 9am-8pm Mon.-Thurs., 9am-3pm Fri., 9am-8pm Sun., free) has two locations in Tel Aviv and one in Jaffa and specializes in classic and contemporary Israeli and international art. It is also home to a large selection of works by famed Israeli artist Menashe Kadishman, known for his offbeat paintings of sheep.

Very near the center of town and easily accessible, the **Rothschild Fine Art Gallery** (48 Yehuda Halevi St., tel. 052/372-9431, www. rgfineart.com, 11am-6:30pm Mon.-Thurs., 11am-2pm Fri.-Sat., free) features a range of fine art by various Israeli and international artists, and displays mostly paintings.

The well-established and well-known **Gordon Gallery of Contemporary Art** (95 Ben Yehuda St., tel. 03/524-0323, www. gordongallery.co.il, 11am-2pm Mon.-Thurs., 10am-2pm Fri., 10am-1pm Sat., by appointment Sun., free) is a 45-year-old gallery with multiple locations; 95 Ben Yehuda Street is

their largest. A third location in South Tel Aviv is slated to open before the end of 2016. The gallery has published two of the most respected and authoritative art books in Israel, and is the father of Israel's first auction house. Today it emphasizes exhibitions of photography, works by top contemporary Israeli artists, and several permanent exhibitions.

The **Zalmania Pri-Or Photo House** (5 Tchernichovski St., tel. 03/517-7916, www. pri-or.com, 10am-6pm Sun.-Thurs., 10am-1pm Fri., free) is home to one of the largest and most important private photography archives in Israel with a collection of historical photographs and over one million negatives. It was established in 1940 by photographer Rudi Weissenstein, who documented the creation of the State of Israel.

At the heart of the Tel Aviv art scene is the **Shpilman Institute for Photography** (27 Shoken St., 3rd Fl., tel. 03/728-3737, http:// thesip.org, 10am-2pm Sun.-Thurs., free), a major modern photography institute with a vast exhibition space. The institute hosts lectures and exhibits by a range of international photographers.

Jaffa (Yafo)

An incubator project for Israeli artists,

ST-ART (3 Rabbi Pinkhas St., tel. 03/516-9599, www.st-art.co.il, 9:30am-6pm Sun.-Thurs., 10am-2pm Fri., free) supports mostly young graduates of Israel's leading art schools. It features largely contemporary Israeli art from 1986 onward.

The **Old Jaffa Artists' Colony** (Yefet St. in Jaffa Old Port area, free tour every Wed. at 10am, starts at visitors center office in Old Jaffa's clock square, tel. 03/603-7700) is a collection of several independent spaces centered around the port area of the old city.

FESTIVALS AND EVENTS
Spring
Tel Aviv comes alive with festivals and events in the spring. The new **White City Music Festival** (Hangar 11 at the Port of Tel Aviv, tel. 03/602-0888, May, ticket packages from NIS2,500) features major international and Israeli acts covering a range of musical genres including jazz, funk, rock and roll, and ethnic world music.

The **Taste of Tel Aviv Food Festival** (HaYarkon Park, tel. 03/642-2828, www.park.co.il, 8pm-midnight for three days in May, free entry) is the largest food festival in the country.

Also in May is the **Felija Blumenthal International Music Festival** (Tel Aviv Museum of Art, 27 Shaul HaMelech Blvd., tel. 03/620-1185, en.blumentalfestival.com, NIS45 and upward per show), a week-long classical array including chamber music, orchestras, solo ensembles, and folk music. Running since 1999, it's known for staging the debut of many Israeli artists who have gone on to become famous.

The only festival of its kind in the Middle East, the annual **Culture of Peace Festival** (Tzavta Theater, 30 Ibn Gabirol St., tel. 03/695-0156, www.havatzelet.org.il under project, three days in May, prices vary) includes Jewish, Muslim, and Christian traditional music.

Summer
The months of June through August are action-packed in Israel and Tel Aviv. The popular **Opera in the Park** (HaYarkon Park, tel. 03/692-7782, www.israel-opera.co.il under Outreach and Education, from 9pm in July, free) showcases performances by the renowned Israeli Opera. Typical crowds to the opera performances are about 80,000 or more from all across Israel, so go early and take a taxi or bus.

The famous **Tel Aviv Pride Parade** (www.gaytlvguide.com/the-guide/pride-parade, early June) hosts more than 50 events

The Tel Aviv Pride festival is a week-long party.

throughout the week-long festival (which is basically one big, nonstop party), finishing with the Gay Pride Parade. The parade starts at Meir Park and usually finishes near or at Gordon Beach.

The annual **Tel Aviv-Yafo's White Night** festival (www.tel-aviv.gov.il, June) is a celebration of UNESCO's 2003 recognition of Tel Aviv's Bauhaus White City as a World Heritage Site. The one-night festival features dozens of simultaneous indoor and outdoor events throughout the city, including music, art, dance, sports, workshops, and parades.

Fall

As the weather cools down, so do events. There are still some nice picks, including the **International Photography Festival** (locations vary, www.photographyfestival.co.il, Oct., buy tickets by dialing *8780 from Israel or go to www.leaan.co.il, NIS39 and up), a gathering of a couple hundred Israeli and international photographers for a week of workshops and events.

An annual event that marks the opening of Tel Aviv-Yafo's gallery season, the **Loving Art Making Art** festival (www.artyear.co.il, Sept. just before Sukkot, free) is a three-day event that is part of Tel Aviv Art Year. Sixty galleries, museums, and exhibition spaces open to the public for free, leading Israeli artists join in street exhibits, and there are artists' workshops and alternative art spaces.

The **Nike Night Run** (start at Rabin Square, spectators and supporters gather near the intersection of Ibn Gabirol St. and Rokach Blvd., www.nikerunning.co.il/nightrun-telaviv, run from 8pm-10:30pm, Oct., NIS120-180) is a 10K night run from Rabin Square in Tel Aviv's City Center to Tel Aviv North Sportek. About 15,000-20,000 runners have participated in recent years.

Winter

Israel's official **Tel Aviv Fashion Week** (HaTachana, http://fw.gindi.com, Nov.) includes receptions, parties, and fashion shows featuring some of the best Israeli designers from the country's lively fashion scene. An alternative fashion week also started running in recent years.

Piano Festival (tel. 03/762-6666, http://pianofestival.co.il, Nov.) has programming run completely in Hebrew, but features some big names among Israeli pianists.

International Exposure (Suzanne Dellal Center, 5 Yehieli St., tel. 03/510-5656, www.suzannedellal.org.il, Dec., tickets vary) showcases Israeli contemporary dance over the course of several days, with most performances at the Suzanne Dellal Center in Neve Tzedek.

Extremely popular, the **Feelin' Blues Festival** (info@feelinblues.com, www.feelinblues.com, Jan., NIS260-NIS830) is a daylong series of events, classes, live performances, parties, and competitions around the theme of blues music. An international contingency of performers takes part.

The annual **Jazz Festival** (Tel Aviv Cinematheque, tel. 03/606-0800, tlv.jazzfest@gmail.com, www.jazzfest.co.il, Feb., prices vary) has been running for about 25 years and hosts jazz musicians from throughout Israel and the world.

Shopping

Shopping in Tel Aviv is all about what kind of shopping you want to do, because every option under the sun is available. Beyond the common souvenir shops, you can find everything from outdoor markets to the showrooms of Israeli designers.

OUTDOOR, OPEN-AIR, AND FARMERS MARKETS
North Tel Aviv

For a down-to-earth experience outdoors at the port, the **Port Market** (Tel Aviv Hangar 12 at the Port of Tel Aviv, tel. 03/544-1505, www.namal.co.il, 8am-8pm Mon.-Sat.) features two levels of foodstuffs for sale. The emphasis is on the "slow food" movement, and options include organic cheese, handmade pasta, gelato, and more. Every Friday an open-air **Farmers Market** (Port of Tel Aviv, 7am-3pm Fri.) opens at the port, expanding the variety of delicious choices.

City Center
★ CARMEL MARKET

Tel Aviv's most well-known open-air market is **Carmel Market** (www.shuktlv.co.il, entrance

to the market is on Allenby St., 8am-dark Sun.-Thurs., 8am-2pm Fri.), named after its location on HaCarmel Street, between Magen David Square at the intersection of King George, Sheinkin, Nahalat Binyamin, and Allenby Streets, and also at HaKovshim Garden and the Carmelit bus terminal. It's an outstanding place to experience the local culture and buy fresh produce. Full of everything from spices to dry goods to clothing, the market is within walking distance to the beach. Vendors call out what they are selling by singing out unique songs, and you can buy everything from freshly squeezed juice to fresh-cut flowers.

There is a wide variety of things in the market to distract and amuse, including street musicians. But the best finds are farther inside the main entrances where there are tons of side alleys selling fresh fish, fruit, vegetables, and exotic spices and nuts.

South Tel Aviv

The spices, nuts, and dried fruits of the **Levinski Market** (Levinski St. in Florentin, tel. 054/226-8089, 8am-6pm Sun.-Thurs.,

TEL AVIV
SHOPPING

radishes for sale in the Carmel Market

The Heart of Israel's Fashion Industry

One of Israel's most surprising assets is its creative and daring fashion industry. Locally grown designers use creative tactics and approaches to create feminine, elegant, and extremely well-made clothing, shoes, bags, and accessories. Though only a lucky few Israeli designers have managed to go international, the range of items available inside of Israel is incredible.

The hallmark of Israeli fashion is simple and chic designs that feature minimal trimmings or flourishes. The designers let the materials speak for themselves, whether it's a leather handbag or an evening dress. Israeli jewelry is also extremely unique and can be found throughout the country.

Some of the more well-known designers include Lia, Gazelle, D and A, Liat Ginzburg, Sasson Kedem, Yosef, and Zaya by Avital Coorsh. Israel's technological advances have led to the creation of cutting-edge ultrasonic bonding equipment that cuts and seals fabric pieces without sewing a stitch. The method, called seamless construction, has put Israel on the map in the intimate apparel industry sector.

Boutique stores that sell almost exclusively Israeli designers can be found throughout the country, everywhere from trendy shopping districts to major shopping malls. Just ask shop owners selling upper-scale clothing and accessories if they have any items by Israeli designers, and the answer will likely be yes. Many stores are extremely supportive and proud of local designers and will choose to sell their products over imported items.

Tel Aviv is Israel's fashion center, and every year it hosts two international fashion week shows in the fall (a result of an industry-splintered professional relationship). Tel Aviv Fashion Week and Gindi TLV Fashion Week are within one month of each other.

Local designer shops are changing constantly, but former fashion industry professional **Galit Reismann** (tel. 054/814-1499, www.tlvstyle.com, tour rates vary based on size of group and length) takes customers on half-day tours (3-5 hours) with personal introductions to designers and personalized shopping experiences.

8am-4:30pm Fri.) make it a popular place for shopping for special treats. It's also the perfect place to do some last-minute souvenir shopping.

SHOPPING DISTRICTS
North Tel Aviv

The retail stores at the **Port of Tel Aviv** (northernmost end of HaYarkon St., tel. 03/544-1505, www.namal.co.il) are on the large side and are mostly chain stores, with a good selection of sporting goods items. The prices are on the high end, but they are also high-quality and include domestic name brands such as Fox, Shilav, and others. Aside from sports-related items, you can also find smaller items like shoes and jewelry.

Connecting Ibn Gabirol and Dizengoff Streets is **Basel Street,** a popular shopping and hangout area. The heart of the area is **Basel Square,** where you will find some of Tel Aviv's coolest boutique clothing stores. Start at about 34 Basel Street and work your way up or down the block. The farther north you go on Dizengoff Street in North Tel Aviv, the more expensive and fancier the designer boutiques, wedding gown stores, high-end clothing, jewelry, and shoe stores get.

City Center

Parallel to Dizengoff Street is **Bugrashov Street,** which is known for its offbeat and trendy fashion stores and selection of cafés.

Adjacent to Carmel Market, just one street parallel to the east is **Nahalat Binyamin Street,** which has a stretch of cafés, shops, and bars that runs from Allenby Street south into the **Florentin** neighborhood. Florentin has a mixture of hip designer shops, cafés, and housewares stores.

South Tel Aviv

Unquestionably one of the best places in Tel Aviv for window-shopping is the old, European-inspired neighborhood of **Neve Tzedek** (approx. Shabazi St. and north of Jaffa St. between Brant St. and Pines St.), with its high-end shops selling boutique jewelry, antiques, oriental rugs, clothing, and books.

Just a bit southeast of Neve Tzedek across the main drag of Jaffa Street is the neighborhood of **Florentin** (south of Jaffa St. and west of Hertsel St.), which was established in 1927 by Jews who emigrated from Greece. Today it is known as a hangout for hipsters and is full of upper-crust furniture and designer stores.

Due west from Florentin is the **Menashiya,** where you'll find the unique shopping experience of **HaTachana** (between Neve Tzedek and the sea, parking entrance at HaMered St. at the corner of Kaufmann St., www.hatachana.co.il, 10am-10pm Mon.-Sat., pubs, cafés, and restaurants open until midnight or last customer on Fri.), a hip shopping center with restaurants and cafés located at the Old Train Station Compound. The open space has incorporated elements from the original train station that opened in 1892. You can still see partial train tracks, cars, and freight terminals. You can find unique souvenirs at the **Made**

in TLV (tel. 03/510-4333) emporium and boutiques. On Thursdays (7pm-midnight), it hosts Israeli designers and artists for an open-air trade show that includes DJ music.

FLEA MARKETS
North Tel Aviv

The **Artists' and Collectors' Fair** (Port of Tel Aviv, on the pier, 10am-6pm Sat.) is a weekly flea market overlooking the Mediterranean. It's a good place to find locally made arts and crafts including jewelry and small trinkets. When you're done perusing the market, enjoy the good selection of restaurants nearby.

Jaffa (Yafo)

Probably the most fun you'd have shopping in Jaffa would be at the **Jaffa Flea Market** (east of the clock tower at the southern end of Old Jaffa, intersection of Olei Zion St. and Jerusalem Blvd., 10am-6pm Sun.-Thurs., 10am-2pm Fri.), with its combination of junk and unique finds including copper, antiques, Persian tiles and rugs, and Judaica. Considered one of the major attractions of Old Jaffa, the flea market also has a number of cafés and pubs. During the summer, there's live music on Thursday evenings.

TEL AVIV SHOPPING

the Jaffa Flea Market

WEEKLY FAIRS AND TRADE MARKETS
City Center

On Thursdays and Fridays, **Dizengoff Center** (intersection of King George St. and Dizengoff St.) hosts a popular international **food fair** (North building B, ground floor, tel. 03/621-2400, ext. 3003, idan@nihul-dc.co.il, noon-8pm Thurs., 10am-4pm Fri.) for a chance to try a variety of dishes.

Fashionably Late designer market (Dizengoff Square at intersection of Pinsker St. and Dizengoff St., 4pm-11pm Thurs., tel. 050/444-6861) is an open-air showcase of independent designers who put their work out in Dizengoff Square.

Dizengoff Square Vintage and Antiques Market (next to Dizengoff Square at Dizengoff and Reines Sts., noon-10pm Tues., 7am-4pm Fri.) features vendors selling clothes, accessories, books, and arts and crafts.

A section of Nahalat Binyamin Street that runs parallel to Carmel Market is open to foot traffic only and has an outdoor **craft fair** (10am-5pm Tues. and Fri.). Vendors sell wooden toys, jewelry, Judaica, photography, and trinkets of all kinds amid street performers.

SHOPPING MALLS
City Center

Azrieli Mall (132 Menachem Begin Rd., tel. 03/608-1179 www.azrielicenter.co.il, 10am-10pm Sun.-Thurs., 10am-4pm Fri., and 8pm-midnight Sat.) is a huge, multilevel mall that includes a train station stop, a multiplex cinema, and every type of store you can imagine from domestic chains such as Golf to international brands such as Gap. Convenient and well laid out, it includes coffee shop chains that are located throughout Israel (such as Aroma), cafés, and stands for manicures and pedicures. You can also easily travel from the mall by train or bus to and from other parts of the city.

With hundreds of stores, **Dizengoff Center** (50 Dizengoff St., near the intersection with King George St., tel. 03/621-2400, www.dizengof-center.co.il, 8am-2pm daily) straddles two sides of Dizengoff Street and is connected by underground passageways and an overhead bridge. It is the oldest mall in town, and hosts an odd mixture of high-end stores, cafés, and lower-end bargain shops that sell cheap goods; it also has two cinemas. Except for the cinemas, the entire center is closed on Shabbat. It is a good place to visit if you need clothing, makeup, and computer supplies.

On the more exclusive side is **Gan Ha'ir** (71 Ibn Gabirol St., tel. 03/527-9111, most shops 9am-9pm Sun.-Thurs. and 9am-2pm Fri.), a high-end mall centered around an open courtyard. Gan Ha'ir has a number of expensive stores that attract some of Tel Aviv's more sophisticated customers. You can find stores selling food, books, shoes, toys, and children's clothing. Inside the mall is a popular Hungarian café called Yehudith's and the rooftop Enav Cultural Center, where lectures, exhibits, concerts, and plays are often held.

Sports and Recreation

Tel Aviv's location on the sea and its sweltering summer days make it an incredibly active place after the sun goes down. Residents are known for showing a lot of skin, being somewhat image-conscious, and dedicated to staying in shape, which makes for a lot of sporting options. For more low-key options like outdoor hangout space, you'll find some of the largest and most well-designed parks in the country.

PARKS
Dizengoff Square

One of the most easily recognizable landmarks in Tel Aviv, **Dizengoff Square** (intersection of Pinsker St. and Dizengoff St., 24 hours daily, free) is a broad, split-level plaza at the center of the White City with a distinct raised platform above street level and a multicolored fountain in the center. Every Tuesday and Friday, the **Dizengoff Square Vintage and Antiques Market** (next to Dizengoff Square at Dizengoff and Reines Sts., noon-10pm Tues., 7am-4pm Fri.) sells clothes, accessories, books, arts, and crafts. The city plans to lower the square to street level.

Rabin Square

On November 4, 1995, Prime Minister Yitzhak Rabin was shot and killed by a Jewish assassin upon leaving a mass rally supporting the peace process. After his death, the location of the rally and assassination was renamed **Rabin Square** (69 Ibn Gabirol St., south of City Hall, 24 hours daily, free), and it still serves as a major staging ground for peace rallies, public music events, and annual book fairs. The **Yitzhak Rabin Memorial** (northeast corner on Ibn Gabirol St.) displays 16 basalt rocks from the Golan Heights sunk into the ground as a symbol of Rabin's roots and bond with Israel.

Meir Park

Featuring a fishpond with floating flora, a dog run, and huge, old trees **Meir Park** (35

King George St., 24 hours daily, free) is a green sanctuary. It is also home to Tel Aviv's gay community center, which often hosts lectures, sports events, and potlucks. It's a popular spot but is best to avoid at night.

★ HaYarkon Park

Among Tel Aviv's jewels, **HaYarkon Park** (Port of Tel Aviv and North Tel Aviv at Rokach Blvd., tel. 03/642-2828 or 03/642-0541, www. park.co.il, www.parkfun.co.il, 24 hours daily, free) stretches about 1,000 acres west to east from the Port of Tel Aviv to the neighboring city of Ramat Gan. The Yarkon River cuts through the park to the Mediterranean, and it is divided into several sections.

An elongated section on the eastern side of the park is perfect for long walks, especially in the late evenings because it is well-lit and active. There are two connecting bridges (the Ibn Gabirol Bridge on the west and the Derech Namir Bridge on the east). In this section, on the north side of the river is **Sportek** (Yarkon River north bank, tel. 03/699-0307, www.kir. co.il, 6:30am-10pm daily, prices vary based on activity), a sprawling collection of sports centers and playgrounds with tennis, volleyball, and basketball courts, baseball and soccer fields, inline skating courts (with equipment

HaYarkon Park

for rent), bungee and trampoline jumping, and an Olympic climbing wall. Both sides of the river have bicycle and walking paths.

The eastern side of the park extends into a huge circular pattern and includes a large artificial lake, a 5-acre **tropical garden** with a microclimate and orchids, and a 10-acre enclosed **rock garden** (10am-2:30pm Sun.-Thurs., 10am-1:30pm Fri., 10am-3:30pm Sat.), a showcase of Israel's geology and 3,500 species of plants, including 6 acres of cacti alone. On the banks of the Yarkon, **Ten Mills** (east Yarkon promenade), is a group of old flour mills that operated for centuries, some of them as recently as the 1920s. The mills are situated on landscaped paths near a wooden bridge and an old dam.

Near the lake is **Zapari** (tel. 03/642-2888, www.zapari.co.il, call ahead for hours, NIS50), a 7.5-acre oasis of tropical plantlife, including banana trees. Zapari is home to a variety of exotic reptiles and birds from around the world, a swan lake with tropical fish and waterfalls, parrots, and a recreation of a traditional African village.

The park hosts concerts and is home to two outdoor concert venues, **Wohl Amphitheater** (tel. 03/521-8210) and **Theater in the Park** (tel. 03/642-2828).

Just on the edges of the park's eastern side are **Luna Amusement Park** (Merkaz Hayeridim, enter from southern Rokach Blvd. across from HaYarkon Park, tel. 03/642-7080, 10am-8pm Sat. and holidays, NIS80), with a variety of rides for a wide range of ages, and **Meymadion Water Park** (near Ramat Gan stadium on eastern side of parking lot across from Luna Amusement Park, tel. 03/642-2777, www.meymadion.co.il, generally 9am-8pm daily but hours and open days vary, Apr.-early Oct., NIS99, after 1pm NIS85).

Hapisga (Summit) Park

Named for its location on the summit of Jaffa mound overlooking the sea, **Hapisga Park** (far southern end of promenade) is famed for its vista of Tel Aviv and the shoreline. In August the park's amphitheater hosts evening concerts, and the Zodiac Bridge is a place to make wishes according to your astrological sign.

Ha'atzmaut (Independence) Park

The massive coastal **Independence Park** (240 HaYarkon St.) is just under half a mile long and full of open spaces with breathtaking views of the sea, gay community-friendly, and

Scorpio sign on Hapisga Park's Zodiac Bridge

often used as a gathering spot. The southern end of the park abuts the Marina and is the access point for Nordau and Hilton Beaches.

Ramat Gan National Park

At almost 500 acres, the **Ramat Gan National Park** (access through Ahad Ha'Am St.) is full of lawns, walking and riding paths, a lake with an artificial waterfall, and a Parisian-style garden. At the center is the **Safari Park and Zoo** (1 Ha'Tsvi Ave. in Ramat Gan National Park, tel. 03/630-5328, 03/630-5327, or 03/630-5326, www.safari.co.il, call ahead for hours, adult NIS59, senior NIS52, add NIS7 Safari bus fee for visitors without cars) with about 1,600 animals from all over the world, including 68 species of mammals, 130 species of birds, and 25 species of reptiles. Check out Rotem the Sand Cat, a distinct regional species.

BEACHES

The beaches of Tel Aviv can be categorized by the types of crowds they attract and whether they are **official,** with lifeguards and changing facilities, or **unofficial,** without lifeguards or facilities and possibly with more dangerous currents or underwater conditions. Both types are free, but official beaches have some additional services such as lockers and equipment rental that cost money. Some of the prime beachfront is also taken up by outdoor seating for cafés, which will require you to buy something if you use one of their tables or chairs.

Hilton, Mezizim (Sheraton), Gordon, Frishman, Bugrashov, and Jerusalem Beaches all have sand courts available for **volleyball, beach handball,** and **soccer.** Aviv Beach has a designated area for surfing, kayaking, windsurfing, and kiteboarding.

North Tel Aviv

The northern locations inside the city limits include **Mezizim Beach** (unofficial, southern end of Nemal Tel Aviv St.) just near the old city port. Mezizim is known for its hip, trendy crowd of beautiful people and can be a bit boisterous.

Nordau Beach (official, off of Nordau St. and HaYarkon Rd.) is the city's only religious beach, with separate swimming areas for men and women. It's best to visit only if you are also religious or extremely conservative.

In the middle of the service road between Mezizim Beach and the Marina is popular **Hilton Beach** (unofficial, at Jabotinsky St. and HaYarkon St.), which is favored by surfers

Tel Aviv has a long stretch of beaches.

for its lights for night surfing, hippies, and dog owners and their pooches. It is also popular with Tel Aviv's gay community and has excellent access for people with physical disabilities. It is next to the Hilton Hotel.

★ City Center

A good place to start when visiting Tel Aviv beaches is the **City Center coastline** (tel. 03/724-0340), which runs roughly between Charles Clore Park and the Tel Aviv Marina. Along this stretch of coastline, there are about half a dozen beaches that are easy to access, free, quite clean, and safe.

One of the best spots for a little bit of everything is **Gordon Beach** (official, at J.L. Gordon St. and Herbert Samuel St.). Also known as Gordon-Frishman, it is extremely popular for its beach volleyball (even at night), hip beach bars, DJs, central location, and proximity to the Tel Aviv Marina. There are a large number of hotels nearby, shaded covers, public toilets and dressing rooms, sports facilities, cafés and restaurants, and a playground. You can rent lounge chairs and sunbathing beds, and there is a water sports area north of the sunbathing area for surfing, windsurfing, and kayaking.

Hip and full of bustling activity **Banana Beach** (8 Herbert Samuel St., tel. 03/510-7958, http://bananabeach.co.il) has options for playing in the sea and dining in style right on the shoreline. Options for refreshments and shade range from restaurants with deck seating to more casual setups chairs and low tables under some shade right on the sandy beach.

Easy to reach and within a four-minute walk of each other, **Frishman Beach** (unofficial, Frishman St. and Herbert Samuel St.) and **Bugrashov Beach** (unofficial, Bugrashov St. and Herbert Samuel St.) have nearby public restrooms and are close to public transportation.

Close to places to eat and paid parking is **Jerusalem Beach** (official, just across from the Opera Tower at 1 Allenby St.), where you can rent sunbathing chairs and lounge chairs. The nearby geometric-shaped shopping center that used to be home to the Israel Opera and is built on the site of the first Israeli parliament across the street is great place to get some air-conditioning if you need a break.

Toward the southern end of the beach scene, **Aviv Beach** (official, Herbert Samuel St. and Ezra HaSofer St.) is close to the major transportation hub at the Carmelit bus station

Tel Aviv Suburbs

The largely haphazard way that Tel Aviv was planned and grew (aside from the White City) created, by default, suburbs of the city. These suburbs, which include cities such as **Ramat Gan** in the east, **Holon** in the south, and **Ramat Aviv** in the north, were less outgrowths of Tel Aviv and more something the sprawling city ran into as it grew.

Upon visiting Tel Aviv, there might be a museum or restaurant you want to visit in one of these areas. While they are not part of Tel Aviv proper, they are still very much connected to the city's thriving day and night life.

Ramat Aviv is home to several worthwhile museums, and its position at the north border of HaYarkon Park makes it a natural stop to include if your sightseeing takes you in that direction.

There is enough to see between the Mediterranean Sea and the Ayalon Highway that you don't have to venture into Ramat Gan for fun. But if you happen to work your way to the far eastern side of HaYarkon Park, you'll find the 500-acre **Ramat Gan National Park** (Ramat Gan off of Hwy. 4 near Tel Aviv, tel. 03/631-3964). Inside the park is Safari Park, home to approximately 1,600 animals from all over the world, including 68 species of mammals, 130 species of birds, and 25 species of reptiles.

Also close by is **Meymadion Water Park** (150 Rokach Ave., at Ganei Yehoshua Park, tel. 03/642-2777, NIS99).

and paid parking. Aviv Beach is also known as Drummers' Beach for its popularity among drumming circles.

South Tel Aviv

Relatively isolated on the southern end of the city is peaceful **Charles Clore Beach** (unofficial, at HaMered St. and Kaufman St., tel. 03/724-0340), tucked into gorgeous, sprawling **Charles Clore Park** (12 Kaufmann St., from the south of the Dolphinarium Beach to Jaffa, http://clore-foundation.org.il) on the border of Jaffa. Popular with dog owners, the beach is near paid parking; a designated area for surfing, windsurfing, and kayaking; and a boardwalk with hotels, restaurants, and clubs. There is no lifeguard. The park has lush lawns and views of the Mediterranean, access to Charles Clore Beach, and connects Tel Aviv and Jaffa with the promenade.

WATER SPORTS
Swimming

The **Gordon Swimming Pool** (14 Eliezer Peri St. at the Tel Aviv Marina, tel. 03/762-3300, www.gordon-pool.co.il, 5am-7pm daily, weekdays NIS45, Sat. NIS50) is an unusual experience with its outdoor, Olympic-size swimming pool filled with saltwater. It is heated and open year-round. You can get access to the pool and workout equipment on the beach for an additional fee.

Surfing, Diving, Boating, and Beach Sports

For surfing lessons and equipment rentals of various types, go to the **Surf Point Beach Equipment** (off the promenade between Zrubavel and Nehemia Sts., tel. 03/517-0099, www.surf-point.co.il, 9:30am-6:30pm daily, NIS100/hour or NIS788 for 10 hours), which offers surfboard, boat, and windsurfing rentals. **Topsea** (165 HaYarkon St., tel. 050/432-9001, www.topsea.co.il, 8am-sunset daily, NIS50 and up for rentals, NIS150 and up for lessons) is the oldest surfing center in Tel Aviv. The **Israel Surf Club** (5 Herbert Samuel St., tel. 03/510-3439, http://israelsurfclub.co.il,

8am-8pm daily, NIS100/hour for lessons) near Charles Clore Beach also rents equipment and offers lessons.

For boating, the **Daniel Center** (2 Rokach Blvd., tel. 03/699-0484, www.drc.org.il, 8am-8pm Sun.-Thurs., 8:30am-1pm Fri.) in HaYarkon Park gives a free introductory **sea kayaking** lesson.

A popular water sport throughout Israel, diving has a number of good places and outfitters in Tel Aviv. The **Tel Aviv Diving Club** (145 HaYarkon St., tel. 054/662-7044, www.divetelaviv.com, 7am-8pm daily, NIS650 including gear rental) is the best place to start for dive lessons, custom dives, and advice.

For sailing information and recommendations, try the **Israel Sailing Association** (tel. 03/624-1112).

BICYCLING

Tel Aviv is a very bicycle-friendly city, and with its miles of boardwalk and relatively flat landscape, it is also an easy place to cycle even if you're not in great shape. Aside from renting bikes from a specialty shop, a very simple and cost-effective option is the city's bicycle rental system, **Tel-O-Fun** (www.tel-o-fun.co.il/en, NIS17 access fee, first 30 minutes free, and

Tel-O-Fun bikes at a rental station

NIS72 for up to 3.5 hours). You can pick up and drop off a rented bike at any of the docking points throughout the city. The distinctive green bikes with large frames are easy to spot and comfortable for most body types. There is no law in Tel Aviv that requires bicyclists to wear a helmet.

TENNIS

The Tel Aviv system for tennis dictates that you reserve a court in advance. There are several around town, including 18 courts at **The National Sports Center** (6 Sheetrit St., tel. 03/649-6464, http://nsc.org.il, tennis 6:30am-10pm Sun.-Thurs., 6:30am-8pm Fri.-Sat., call for prices as they vary by day and time). Contact the informal **Tennis Tel Aviv** (tel. 058/603-3370, http://tennis-telaviv.co.il, tennis@tennis-telaviv.co.il) for specific information and recommendations.

GYMS

Many hotels in Tel Aviv, particularly in City Center, are near gyms and some have an arrangement for discounted entry for hotel guests.

Otherwise, try **Sportek** (HaYarkon Park, Yarkon River north bank, tel. 03/699-0307, www.kir.co.il, 6:30am-10pm daily, prices vary based on activity), which includes a rock climbing center. Another option is **Cross Fit Tel Aviv** (167 HaYarkon St. at Atarim Sq., tel. 052/834-1247, http://crossfittelaviv.co.il, 6:30am-10pm daily, NIS200 and up), which is conveniently located just across from the Marina and caters to English-speaking customers.

SPECTATOR SPORTS

There are a couple of major sport arenas in Tel Aviv, including **Menora Mivtachim Arena** (51 Yigal Allon St., www.sportpalace.co.il., tel. 03/537-6376), home to Tel Aviv's Maccabi and Hapoel basketball teams. **Bloomfield Stadium** (8 She'erit Israel St. in Jaffa, tel. 03/637-6000) is the professional soccer arena and also hosts major international performers who draw huge crowds, such as Barbra Streisand. The major sports stadium is **Hadar Yosef Stadium** (10 Sheetrit St., tel. 03/649-7474), which hosts all kinds of sports including soccer.

Food

You could try a different restaurant for every meal, every day in Tel Aviv and you won't run out of incredible options. The best picks range from high-end fine dining to casual fare fit for a picnic in the park. One of the hallmarks of Tel Aviv restaurants is that many (particularly the higher-end places) are open only for lunch and dinner. Lunch menus often have a special business menu, which indicates a lower price for an inclusive food and drink option. Most restaurants are open until very late, and some are 24 hours, 7 days a week, but fewer open very early in the morning. Kosher Tel Aviv restaurants are not the majority, and it is fairly easy to find many options open during Shabbat. One thing to keep in mind about the hours that restaurants advertise is that they fluctuate slightly according to the level

of business, particularly during the winter. If you plan to be early or late to an establishment, call in advance.

NORTH TEL AVIV
Mediterranean and European Fusion

Right on the water at the port, **White Pergola** (Yordei Hasira 1, Port of Tel Aviv Hangar 4, tel. 03/546-4747, www.hasuka-halevana. co.il, 10am-last customer daily, NIS100), or *Hasukkah Halevana* in Hebrew, is an elegant and popular restaurant that specializes in, and is known for, its wide array of seafood dishes, but they also serve beef and lamb. Some offerings include lobster, mussels, crab, and shrimp. There is seaside outdoor seating, and part of the restaurant's spacious interior has floor-to-ceiling blond wood paneling that gives the feel of being inside the belly of a ship. The service can be quite slow, and the wine and alcohol menu is small, but selective.

The unparalleled open seaside atmosphere of **Shalvata Restaurant** (Port of Tel Aviv Hangar 28, tel. 03/544-1279, www.shalvata. co.il, 5pm-11pm Sun.-Thurs., 9am-11pm Fri.-Sat., NIS70) is a popular place for events. The 360-degree bar and restaurant spread out over a wooden deck face the sea with shade from straw parasols. There are different sections with varied heights and types of seats, some directly on sand where you can kick your shoes off and dig your toes in. The menu is mainly pizza, pasta, chicken, and hamburgers, and there is menu with varied options for alcohol, cocktails, and beer.

Italian

A kosher establishment that specializes in thin-crust pizza and calzones, **Pizza Fino** (169 Ben Yehuda St., tel. 03/522-8165, noon-midnight Sun.-Thurs., noon-3pm Fri., about 6pm-midnight Sat., NIS60) is a favorite among Tel Avivians who love pizza. Its redbrick storefront is situated very obviously at the intersection of Ben Yehuda and Jabotinsky Streets. The very casual atmosphere includes a window for walkup takeout, some indoor seating, and several outdoor sidewalk tables.

Meat and Seafood

At ★ **Gilly's** (Port of Tel Aviv Hangar 15, tel. 03/605-7777, www.gillys.co.il, 10am-10pm daily, NIS100), you must make reservations to experience this Jerusalem transplant known for its savory meat dishes, including a French-style steak. The owner, Gilly Pepperman, is famous for introducing his Jerusalem customers to high-quality, well-prepared meat. The restaurant and bar boast large windows that look out onto the sea and a balcony, and the warm atmosphere and spacious outdoor seating on the sea somehow manage to evoke a decidedly Jerusalem vibe. Hugely popular for their "Breakfast Royal" (10am-5pm daily), which includes a champagne cocktail, freshly baked

bread, eggs, bacon, and more, Gilly's presents extensive menu selections from appetizers to alcohol and dessert.

CITY CENTER
Middle Eastern

The highly inventive **Shakshukia** (94 Ben Yehuda St., tel. 03/522-3433, 10am-10pm Sun.-Thurs., 10am-4pm Fri., NIS60) offers many creative takes on *shakshuka* (a staple Middle Eastern egg and vegetable dish), including one option with turkey.

Mediterranean and European Fusion

A very subdued, classy atmosphere that gives the feel of dining in someone's home is a hallmark of ★ **Messa** (19 Ha'arbaa St., tel. 03/685-6859, http://messa.rest.co.il, noon-2:30pm and 7pm-11:30pm daily, bar 7pm-last customer daily, NIS160), a European-style restaurant known for its outstanding service and presentation. The entrance is hidden behind a large door on the corner of a building with a modern exterior. The interior's layout includes a huge, long dining table for numerous customers and a bar. Known to attract customers from the upper echelons of society, Messa's food is based in French Provencal techniques and local ingredients. The restaurant emphasizes using high-quality raw ingredients in their dishes.

Housed in a 129-year-old restored building that once belonged to a Turkish sheik, **Kimmel** (6 HaShachar St., tel. 03/510-5204, http://kimmelrest.co.il.en, noon-midnight daily, NIS125) uses its setting for its take on the "rustic" French country approach to food, drink, and atmosphere, largely succeeding. The arrangement of tables feels a bit like a cafeteria, but the overall warmth of the setting, down to the types of glasses used, overpowers the slightly utilitarian seating arrangements. Vegetables, wine bottles, and antique knick-knacks adorn the walls and alcoves, and the dishes place emphasis on cheeses, meat, and fish in rich sauces, herbs, creams, and olive oil. Don't be shy about asking one of Kimmel's friendly waitstaff to explain certain menu items that border on exotic.

American

Known and loved for its hamburgers (which some say are the best in Tel Aviv), **Moses** (35 Rothschild Blvd., tel. 03/566-4949, www.mosesrest.co.il, noon-4am daily, NIS65) is a popular and trendy American-style eatery near the Tel Aviv Stock Exchange, Independence Hall, and a couple of smaller museums and galleries. The slightly pricey combination beef, lamb, and veal hamburger is recommended, but the service tends to be a bit slow in the afternoons. The interior is simple and fashioned after an American diner.

The spacious layout, exposed brick, and huge bar give **Dixie** (120 Igal Alon St., corner of 3 Totzeret Ha'aretz, tel. 03/696-6123, www.dixie.co.il, 24 hours daily, NIS65) a very American (particularly New York City) vibe. Add the large portions of steak, chicken sandwiches, and hamburgers to the mix and you could almost forget you're in Israel. The menu changes three times a year, and a range of wines from leading Israeli and international wineries, beer, and cocktails is available. Known as the grandfather of the 24/7 restaurant concept in Israel, its clientele is very trendy Tel Aviv and it is a favorite of late-night clubbers. The restaurant also delivers takeout orders. Its main downside for visitors to Tel Aviv (unless you're hanging out with locals) is the location, as it is a bit off the beaten path of sightseeing, though it is close to HaShalom train station.

Italian

Considered one of the best Italian restaurants in Tel Aviv, **Rustico** (15 Rothschild Ave., tel. 03/510-0039, www.rustico.co.il, noon-midnight daily, NIS60) has another location (42 Basel St.) and has a selection of fresh pizzas and focaccia dishes that are baked in a large stone oven in view of patrons. They also serve homemade pasta, seafood, and risotto. The rustic Italian countryside interior includes a large bar in the center of the restaurant and

windows with views of the avenue. Outdoor seating includes a beautiful wooden porch, but overall it is not the best place for an intimate meal, as it can get very loud and lively, with tables positioned relatively close together.

Meat and Seafood

One of Tel Aviv's most famous restaurants, **Manta Ray** (Alma Beach on the Tel Aviv Promenade, west of Charles Clore Park, near the Intercontinental David Hotel at 12 Kaufmann St., tel. 03/517-4773, www.manta-ray.co.il, 9am-midnight daily, NIS110) lives up to the hype. A place where Madonna and other stars are said to have eaten, this gourmet seafood restaurant serves items like mullet ceviche and baked blue bream. On weekends, they also serve fresh oysters from Paris. The breakfast menu is available until noon and surprisingly affordable and very popular (make reservations). The exterior of the building literally looks like a gray, cement hut on the beach, but the interior is spacious and welcoming, even though the clientele and staff tend to be on the yuppie side. It's a great place to have a bite and then hang out on the beach, though there is no swimming.

Mexican and South American

Full of savory dishes, **Mescal** (2 Vital St., tel. 03/518-7925, http://mezcal.rest.co.il, noon-2:30am daily, NIS50) specializes in Mexican street food and has a hip interior that is very reminiscent of Mexican restaurants in North America. The specialties include a variety of tacos, burritos, tostadas, and all the classic sides and starters ranging from guacamole to two varieties of nachos. Try the bistec-con-papas, a hefty amount of filet mignon steak served on a sizzling platter with potatoes and toasted corn. Mescal also has a fairly large alcohol menu with drinks ranging from beer in the bottle and on tap to mojito and tequila-inspired beverages.

If you're in the mood for deliciously satisfying and spicy, spicy, spicy, **Mexicana** (7 Bugrashov St., 03/527-9911, www.mexicana.co.il, noon-midnight daily, NIS60) has a Mexican menu that could quell most Americans' cravings for something familiar. The atmosphere is always bustling, especially on Shabbat, when it is one of the few places on its particular stretch of street that is open. The prices are not on the easily affordable end of Mexican restaurants, but one of the best items on the menu, and best priced, is the tortilla soup. The fajitas and chips are also excellent. There is a bit of outdoor sidewalk seating, and the indoor seating is brightly and cheerfully decorated. Overall, space is rather limited so you could end up at a cozy distance from other diners. The service is unfailingly friendly, upbeat, and accommodating, though you might have to make special requests a few times because they are so busy.

Thai

Thai House (8 Bugrashov St., tel. 03/517-8568, www.thai-house.co.il, noon-11pm daily, NIS75) serves up northwest Thai food and classics from the Bangkok and southern islands regions, including curry coconut dishes, street-stall dishes, organic green papaya salad, and farm-grown eggplant. Managed by a husband-wife team with roots in a long line of Thai restaurateurs, the restaurant also offers special fish dishes on request that are not listed on the menu. The somewhat shabby exterior belies the unique bamboo-walled interior that gives the feeling of being in a bamboo hut. Though small, just by reputation for its outstanding authentic Thai food, the restaurant attracts a large number of repeat customers. Reservations are recommended.

Wine and Tapas

Incredibly popular and in a great location near the Tel Aviv Marina, **Wineberg** (106 Ben Yehuda St., tel. 03/522-3939, lunch 11:30am-last customer, dinner 5:30pm-last customer, NIS70) has a rustic, friendly atmosphere replete with a wooden antler head on the wall. Wineberg's food is focused on tapas, cold dishes, meat sandwiches, soup, pasta, and some seafood. Try the lamb siniya, with steamed burghul and eggplant cream, and the gnocchi la romana hot tapas. There is also a large menu of spirits, wine, and beer. Wineberg is loved by customers for its winning combination of good food, good atmosphere, and good value for the money.

Mentioned again and again by locals and tourists as a favorite, ★ **Vicky & Cristina** (HaTachana Bldg. 17 at 1 Kaufmann St., tel. 03/736-7272 and 057/944-4144, http://vickycristina.rest.co.il, 5pm-last customer Sun.-Thurs., noon-last customer Fri.-Sat., NIS90) is a Spanish tapas (Vicky) and wine bar (Cristina), located in a spacious patio under an ancient rubber tree. The atmosphere is intimate and understated, with Latin background music. A wine bar with more than 120 selections (from 7pm daily) is on the back side of the patio with high bar stools and a garden of mosaic-covered sculptures inspired by Barcelona's famous Park Güell.

Cafés and Bistros

Situated behind a customized tropical garden patio near Dizengoff Center, **Bar Giora** (4 Bar Giora St., corner of 64 Dizengoff St., tel. 03/620-4880, http://bargiyora.co.il, 10am-last customer Sun.-Thurs., 11am-last customer Fri.-Sat., NIS55) somehow combines a beach atmosphere with the comforts of a bistro. It's a favorite among locals, which adds to its reputation as a neighborhood institution. The multilevel establishment attracts a younger crowd and has live music in the evenings in the basement. The menu provides a wide range of salads, sandwiches, hamburgers, and Persian, Moroccan, and pasta dishes. There are also a variety of homemade pastries and desserts and a menu of specials.

Known for its chicken schnitzel, great service, and excellent views of the sea, **Café Metzada** (83 HaYarkon St., with entrance on the promenade, tel. 03/510-3353, 24 hours daily, NIS60) is just on the promenade and has a relaxed, calm atmosphere with indoor and outdoor seating. The menu and food preparation are simple, but the portions are large and there are a variety of items such as chicken wings, hamburgers, steak, salad, and dessert.

SOUTH TEL AVIV

Mediterranean and European Fusion

A French gourmet meets Mediterranean fine dining experience and long considered one of Tel Aviv's best restaurants, Catit (57 Nahlat Binyamin St., tel. 03/510-7001, www.catit. co.il, 6:30pm-11pm daily, NIS180) is a transplant from a small village where it earned a reputation as a must-visit restaurant. It is now one of the most highly-regarded restaurants in Tel Aviv after almost a decade. Chef Meir Adoni is still known for his unique touch with food, including risotto in wine, veal fillet with Mediterranean olives and za'atar tapenade, and lamb with bulgur and spice seeds. Housed in a historical building with an upscale interior, the venue has an atmosphere that evokes elegant country. Due to its wide reputation, Catit attracts discerning locals and curious tourists alike.

A local favorite, Suzanna (9 Shabazi St., tel. 057/944-3060, http://suzana.rest-e.co.il, 10am-1am daily, NIS70) serves Greek and Mediterranean dishes that feature a wide variety of stuffed items. Housed in a distinctive yellow building in Neve Tzedek that includes a very inviting shaded terrace, Suzanna's menu includes traditional Moroccan soup, stuffed vegetables and fruits, stews, and grilled dishes. The outdoor bar is open nightly (7pm-1am).

Italian

Boasting the reputation as one of the best Italian restaurants in Tel Aviv, Pronto (4 Hertsel St., tel. 03/566-0915, www.pronto. co.il, 12:30pm-3pm and 6:30pm-11:30pm daily, NIS90) has had more than 20 years to establish its stature in the local restaurant scene. A favorite place for doing business and entertaining clients, Pronto has a generous wine menu, and serves mostly pasta for main dishes with a few specialties, including braised duck and lamb chops. The spacious and modern interior includes a small bar and huge floor-to-ceiling windows that are right on street level.

Japanese

A rare find in the neighborhood where it lives, Okinawa (46 Shabazi St., tel. 03/510-1099, www.okinawatlv.co.il, noon-midnight Sun.-Fri., 5:30pm-midnight Sat., NIS60) seems to be the lone sushi bar and Japanese restaurant in the Neve Tzedek area. Serving a sashimi and sushi menu, the restaurant has a relaxed and friendly atmosphere with an accommodating staff, and they have a large cocktail menu to boot. It attracts mostly locals who enjoy sushi restaurants but haven't found a favorite yet.

Meat and Seafood

One of a group of three leading restaurants in Israel, Herbert Samuel (6 Kaufmann St. at the Gaon House, tel. 03/516-6516, http:// herbertsamuel.co.il, 12:30pm-4pm and 6pm-midnight Sun.-Wed., 12:30pm-midnight Thurs.-Sat., NIS150) is just across the street from the beach and promenade and specializes in meat and seafood dishes. Chef Yonatan Roshfeld is known for his reality TV show, which contributes to the huge buzz the restaurant enjoys as one of the best in Tel Aviv. Renowned for its outstanding service, the upscale and contemporary setting includes tables with window views of the sea and a bar. Specialty items on the menu include duck, shrimp lasagna, and an artichoke, chestnut, and truffle soup.

Famed for its massive porterhouse steak that weighs in somewhere between 70-170 ounces and piglet in maple sauce and apples, NG (6 Ahad Ha'Am St., corner of Yehuda Ha'hasid St., up the staircase, tel. 052/839-3119 and 03/516-7888, www.ngrestaurant. co.il, 6pm-1am Sun.-Thurs., 4pm-1am Fri., noon-1am Sat., NIS110) was voted Best Meat Restaurant for three years in a row by *Time Out* magazine. Set in picturesque Neve Tzedek, the restaurant's atmosphere is quaint and romantic, with friendly, down-to-earth service (one of the owners might wait on you). There is a generous wine list and a selection of several beers from local breweries to round out the hefty food at this self-labeled "meat bar."

Wine and Tapas

A warm, muted atmosphere featuring Mediterranean tiles and ropes of hanging garlic is what you'll find at **Tapas 1** (27 Ahad Ha'Am St., tel. 03/566-6966, www. tapas1haam.co.il, 6:30pm-12:30am daily, NIS60) with its Spanish tapas and other Spanish cuisine. Also known as Ahad Ha'Am Tapas Bar, the restaurant serves dozens of types of tapas and is an extremely popular hangout for young people and culinary enthusiasts. On Mondays specialty seafood dishes are available.

JAFFA (YAFO)
Middle Eastern

It doesn't have a fancy appearance inside or out, but ★ **Itzik HaGadol** (3 Razi'el St., tel. 057/943-8970, www.itzikhagadol.co.il, noon-midnight daily, NIS70) is legendary among generations of local Tel Avivians. Also known as Big Itzik, because of its extension on the other side of the narrow street, it has been in business for decades. Neither the interior nor the general atmosphere boasts warmth and relaxation, but it is impossible to dine here and leave hungry. With an emphasis on meat and *mezze* (Middle Eastern appetizers and hummus), you can order lamb chops, goose liver, kebab, grilled eggplant, and more to your heart's content. But watch out for racking up a huge bill and too much food because it accumulates quickly. You will start getting falafel, hummus, and *mezze* almost immediately after sitting down, so pace yourself and try one thing at a time.

With a name like **Dr. Shakshuka** (3 Beit Eshel St., tel. 057/944-4193, http://shakshuka. rest.co.il, 8am-midnight Sun.-Thurs., NIS45), there is bound to be a lot of hype. But as one of the few kosher Libyan restaurants in town that specializes in very large portions of the staple Middle Eastern egg and vegetable dish called *shakshuka,* Dr. Shakshuka has somewhat of a corner on the market in their location. Skipping fancy presentation in both their food and decor, the restaurant's interior features old copper items like lamps hanging from the ceiling, exposed stone walls, and large palm plants. Popular with locals and tourists, the atmosphere is 100 percent Middle Eastern.

Seafood

Very popular for its sparkling service and delicious food, **Yona** (Jaffa Port on the Pier, tel. 03/774-2222, www.yona.be, noon-midnight daily, NIS110) has taken the vast interior of an old container warehouse and somehow made it inviting and fun. Huge wooden shipping barrels filled with fresh loaves of bread baked on the premises and lampshades reminiscent of seashells add to the seafaring atmosphere. Not unlike its sister restaurant Manta Ray, Yona is known for its seafood dishes. The restaurant's presentation is based on the "open source" trend that allows customers visual access to the chefs at work. Yona also makes their own yogurt and ricotta, and smokes their salmon and meat on the premises. Vegetarian dishes are also available. There is a large bar and outdoor seating in the summer months with a view of the sunset and fishing boats.

Cafés

The Nalaga'at Center's **BlackOut Restaurant** (Retsif Haaliya Hashniya at Jaffa Port, tel. 03/633-0808, www.nalagaat.org.il, first sitting 6:30pm, second sitting 9pm Sun., Tues., Wed., and Thurs., NIS120) serves meals in complete darkness employing waiters who are blind. Also at the Nalaga'at Center, **Café Kapish** (Retsif Haaliya Hashniya at Jaffa Port, tel. 03/633-0808, www.nalagaat.org.il, 6pm-11pm Sun.-Thurs., NIS18) deaf and hearing-impaired staff interact with customers using sign language. You can get coffee, beer, wine, and other drinks and snacks.

Accommodations

In Tel Aviv four- and five-star hotels abound, particularly along the coastline. But there is a broad range of other options throughout the city for every budget, even near the sea. Some pitfalls of Tel Aviv hotels to watch out for include rooms that are extremely small but advertised as suitable for two people, accommodations that are not hostels but have shared bathrooms and showers, and places that might make you try to pay VAT, which is a tax only Israeli citizens or residents are required to pay. There are also often lower rates for tourists, and the best rates are usually found through online travel websites, which often offer discounts, and not through the accommodations themselves. Avoid phone reservations, as you might arrive and find your room has been given away. If you stay in Jaffa, keep in mind you might be awakened by the sound of 4am calls to prayer. If you are close to a mosque, the singing from the loudspeakers can wake you up very easily. Parking is extremely hard to come by in Tel Aviv, so if you have a rental car, ask in advance about the parking options, as not every hotel offers space.

NORTH TEL AVIV
US$100-150
The small but accommodating **Port Hotel** (4 Yirmeyahu St., tel. 03/544-5544, www.porthoteltelaviv.com, US$149 d) is a newer, 21-room boutique hotel with free wireless Internet, refrigerators, and modern decor and interiors. The hotel has a rooftop lounge area with an outstanding view of the sea. The rooms are simple and very spare on trimmings, but with clean, modern lines. There are numerous nightlife options nearby, and it is just a five-minute walk to the Port of Tel Aviv.

US$150-200
The **Armon HaYarkon** (268 HaYarkon St., tel. 03/605-5271, www.armon-hotel.com, US$165 d) is a small hotel with an unremarkable exterior, but it has all the amenities you need, including breakfast, wireless Internet, TV, and refrigerator. It's also just a few minutes from the sea and the exciting Port of Tel Aviv with its bars, clubs, shopping, nightlife, and restaurants. It's also a short drive to Israel's domestic airport, Sde Dov, where you can catch flights to the popular southern tourist city of Eilat.

Over US$200
Right on the edge of the massive Ha'atzmaut (Independence) Park, ★ **Melody Hotel** (220 HaYarkon St., tel. 03/542-5555, www.atlas.co.il, US$250 d) is within easy walking distance of some of Tel Aviv's most popular beaches. A 2012 Travelers' Choice selection for Trendiest Hotel, this 55-room property has views of the sea and the park. The lobby lounge is open throughout the day, and Sunday to Thursday, it serves free snacks and drinks in the evening. During warmer months, the eighth-floor rooftop lounge is open. Amenities include LCD TV, wireless Internet, a safe, fridge, beach towels, bike and beach chair rental, and some discounts for sightseeing tickets and dessert and wine vouchers from the reception desk.

Conveniently located directly across from the Tel Aviv Marina and the Gordon Swimming Pool, the **Marina Tel Aviv** (167 HaYarkon St., tel. 03/521-1777, www.marina-telaviv.com, US$260 d) is a 160-room hotel with sea views and family-friendly rooms that caters to business travelers. Every room has air-conditioning, a bathtub, fridge, safe, and LCD TV. Hangout spaces include a lobby bar, a rooftop sundeck and swimming pool (in season), and a business lounge bar deck. Underground parking is available.

CITY CENTER
Under US$100
Of the many options in City Center, the **Mugraby Hostel** (19 Allenby St., tel.

03/510-2443, www.mugraby-hostel.com, US$70 d) is one of the least expensive hotels if being near the beach is a higher priority for you than privacy and creature comforts. Owned and operated by two brothers, Nimrod and Avi Katorza, the hostel has been in business since 1996 and relocated in 2011. The dorm-style accommodations and some private rooms include shared showers and toilets, linens, kitchen, and lounge with cable TV. The English-speaking staff can offer travel and tour advice, and there is an Internet café on the premises. A nearby laundry service and two 24-hour supermarkets make it convenient for the low-budget traveler.

US$150-200

If you want to roll out of bed and into the sea, **Abratel Suites Hotel** (3 Geula St., tel. 03/516-9966, www.abratelsuiteshotel.com, US$200 d) is a small but good option. With only 24 suites and six standard rooms, the hotel faces the sea and promenade; a room with a sea view costs extra. There are free parking and beach towels, and the entire hotel has central air-conditioning. Rates include breakfast and free coffee, tea, and cookies in the lobby.

An extremely hip option that exudes Tel Aviv's modern style is the **City Hotel** (9 Mapu St., tel. 03/542-5555, www.atlas.co.il, US$195 d). The hotel is known for its cozy but swank atmosphere and excellent restaurant. The 96-room hotel has a bright, modern interior, free wireless Internet throughout, an outdoor coffee shop on the terrace, room service, free parking, and event space. Guests can use a nearby gym for a fee, and several of the rooms feature a small balcony that can seat up to four. The hotel is a very short walk to the beach, and you can rent a bike or get beach towels from reception. Bed-and-breakfast options are also available for the spacious rooms that have a fridge, safe, and LCD TV.

Part of a regional group of hotels, the **Deborah Hotel** (87 Ben Yehuda St., tel. 03/527-8282, www.arcadiahotels.co.il, US$160 d) is a 69-room establishment just between lively Dizengoff Street and the sea. About two blocks from the sea promenade and the Tel Aviv Marina, Deborah Hotel is kosher and has a hotel synagogue and a Shabbat elevator. wireless Internet, business traveler services, and a nearby gym at a discount are also available. The interior of the rooms is not spectacular but includes all the basic amenities. The height of the building also allows for some great views of Tel Aviv.

Situated along a row of hotels just one block from the sea and promenade, **TLV88** (88 HaYarkon St., tel. 03/620-4676, www.tlv88.co.il, US$160 d) is a Bauhaus building from 1936 that gives the feeling of being right on the beach. Renovated in 2012, TLV88 is one of the trendier options in the area, and is self-described as "an intimate boutique hotel with a Monte Carlo style and a French Riviera flavor." The nautical decor of the rooms creates a sporty, seafaring atmosphere, and amenities include a 24-hour concierge service and free parking. Every room has a sea or city view and there is a seaside restaurant on the ground floor and a wide variety of other restaurants and entertainment venues nearby.

★ **Hotel De La Mer** (2 Ness Tsiyona St., corner of 62 HaYarkon St., tel. 03/510-0011, www.delamer.co.il, US$179 d) is an exclusive European-style boutique hotel. The exterior is restored historic Bauhaus and the interior has been arranged using feng shui techniques. Extremely close to the sea and beach, the units are nonsmoking rooms and suites with a range of options, including sea views and in-room whirlpool tubs. The range of services at De La Mer is huge, and includes wireless Internet, a coffee lounge where you can have breakfast, a sunbathing rooftop terrace, currency conversion, basic postal services, babysitting, clerical services, and 24/7 free coffee and tea service in the lobby. Some rooms have a balcony for an additional charge, and rooms have satellite TV, a writing desk, and a wardrobe closet. You can get adaptors, hair dryers, and irons at the front desk.

Over US$200

Even though it only has 21 rooms, **Dizengoff Suites** (39 Gordon St., tel. 03/523-4363, www.dizengoffsuites.co.il, US$215 d) makes the most of their amazing location close to some of the highlights of Tel Aviv shopping and entertainment. The three available varieties of suites are recently renovated and include a fully equipped kitchenette, mini-fridge, air-conditioning, cable TV, and free wireless Internet. The elevator can only fit about two people at a time, and there is an unusual card-key system for electricity in the rooms, some of which have a balcony or rooftop terrace. The overall feel is very homey, and the staff is friendly and accommodating. An excellent breakfast in the downstairs restaurant with a distinctly Parisian atmosphere, Café Marco, is included.

A newer 62-room hotel dedicated to Israeli art, ★ **Artplus Hotel** (35 Ben Yehuda St., tel. 03/542-5555, www.atlas.co.il, US$210 d) is like one big work of art from floor to ceiling and throughout the hotel. Murals on every floor were commissioned by five famous local artists, and the hotel's foyer and lobby feature works by two internationally renowned Israeli artists Zadok Ben-David and Sigalit Landau. The overall design is retro modern. It is within easy walking distance to the beach. Amenities include tons of freebies, including parking, bicycle rental, breakfast, refreshments and snacks in the hotel's library every evening, a sun roof terrace, and coupons to local restaurants. Rooms include air-conditioning, a fridge and safe, an LCD TV, and hair dryer.

The atmosphere, location, and price of the **Bell Hotel** (50 HaYarkon St., tel. 03/517-4291, www.bellhotel-telaviv.com, US$209 d) are all right on the mark. This seaside boutique hotel is near some of Tel Aviv's best nightlife and beach life. A double room includes free parking, wireless Internet, air-conditioning, fridge, coffee and tea service, and breakfast. The rooms are comfortably and artfully designed to reflect Tel Aviv's vibe of sand and sea, with a sandstone-based color scheme and some rooms with balcony seaside views and whirlpool tubs.

With 227 rooms, the **Hotel Metropolitan and Metropolitan Suites** (11-15 Trumpeldor St., tel. 03/519-2727, www.hotel-metropolitan.co.il, US$219 d) is big enough to give the experience of hotel luxury but still maintains a warm atmosphere. Some of the decor in the rooms is a bit dated, but the lobby bar and restaurant both have a modern feel and are open until the wee hours. It is right on the sea. Adjacent to the hotel are sister suites for longer-term stays. With services catered toward business travelers, the hotel has rooms with phones that allow for international calls, a business center (for an extra cost), laundry service, minibars, and car rental. There is also room service, and rooms are available for guests with disabilities. Guests have free access to a health club and to private parking for a fee. An outdoor pool is open April-October.

SOUTH TEL AVIV
Under US$100

A home-style hostel in the trendy Florentin neighborhood, **Florentine Backpackers Hostel** (10 Elifelet St., tel. 03/518-7551, florentinehostel.com, US$60 d private room for two, US$25 one dorm bed) has an unusual age restriction that only allows guests between the ages of 18 and 40. Private rooms have a double bed, air-conditioning, linens, and a shared bathroom and shower. There is also free wireless Internet, coffee and tea, a barbecue area, free parking, cell phone and bicycle rental, luggage storage, an indoor lounge, a fully equipped communal kitchen, and a rooftop terrace. It is within walking distance to Old Jaffa and the flea market, the beach and boardwalk, and the historic but hip Neve Tzedek neighborhood. Near the hostel there are numerous cafés, nightclubs, and pubs.

Part of a small domestic chain, the **Sun Aviv Hotel Tel Aviv** (9A Montefiori St., tel. 03/517-4847, www.sun-aviv.co.il, US$95 d) has 20 tidy rooms and is located in between Carmel Market, Nahalat Binyamin outdoor mall, and trendy Shabazi Street in Neve

Tzedek. A room includes continental breakfast, air-conditioning, minibar, satellite TV, laundry service, and car rental. The hotel is decorated in a very spare manner, with few trimmings or luxurious touches. There is a cafeteria on the ground floor, a 24-hour reception desk, and, during the day, cold and hot drinks can be ordered by room service.

Over US$200

Luxurious in a way that is unique to Tel Aviv, the ★ **Neve Tzedek Hotel** (4 Deganya St., off of Shabazi St., tel. 054/207-0706, www. nevetzedekhotel.com, US$760 d) has spacious, airy rooms with endless small touches that make it both visually appealing and comfortable. Some highlights include garden suites with private outdoor garden terraces, plush beds, huge windows, and luxurious furnishings that are both beautiful and comfortable. Opened in 2009 in a historic building, the hotel is near Nana Bar restaurant and Pri Hagefen wine bar, owned by Golan Dor and Tommy Ben-David, neighborhood residents, and the renowned Suzanne Dellal Center, Jaffa, and Zappa Club. In addition to all the usual amenities, a stay here will get you handmade chocolates, cakes, and baked goods; superb cheeses and wines; exotic fruits; spa treatments and kits; beach bags; flowers; house and bath robes; and literature, art, and access to tickets for shows and attractions.

Styled in a decidedly European fashion, the **Nina Café Suites Hotel** (29 Shabazi St., tel. 03/510-5239, http://ninacafehotel.com, US$250 d) is a luxury boutique hotel in the heart of Neve Tzedek. Both suites and studios are available. All rooms include a minibar, cable TV, DVD, wireless Internet, laundry services, air-conditioning, and breakfast at the nearby Nina Café, or breakfast can be ordered to the room.

Within easy walking distance to the beach and Jaffa and nearby to the trendy and happening HaTachana complex, **The Varsano** (15 Hevrat Shass St., tel. 077/554-5500, www. hotel-tel-aviv.net, US$475 d) is a stylish and modern luxury boutique hotel that is perfect for longer stays with all the comforts of home. The rooms are designed as suites, with living space and a loft atmosphere, and have fully-equipped kitchens, dining areas, and bedrooms. There is also free wireless Internet, LCD TVs, high-end kitchen appliances, a washer and dryer on premises, and parking (for a fee).

JAFFA (YAFO)
Under US$100

Among some of the more homey picks in Jaffa, the ★ **Beit Immanuel Congregation and Guest House** (8 Auerbach St., tel. 03/682-1459, www.beitimmanuel.org, US$92 d) is a good fit for all types of travelers on a budget and welcoming to couples and families with kids, as well as groups. The small 13-room guesthouse has simple and plain private rooms with bathrooms and dormitory rooms, all with coffee and tea service, air-conditioning, and heat, and some rooms have balconies. Just next to the ancient Jaffa Port and some outstanding (and a bit less crowded) beaches, Beit Immanuel caters to special prayer tour groups or people traveling on short-term religious missions. There is free wireless Internet in the lobby and a quiet garden area on the ground floor. The included breakfast can be eaten in the garden between May and October. Luggage storage, free secure parking, conference facilities, and a prayer room are available, as well as a Hebrew-language worship service on Friday evenings with English translation.

The **Old Jaffa Hostel and Guesthouse** (13 Amiad St., tel. 03/682-2370, www.telaviv-hostel.com, US$80d) is in an older building with touches that evoke a distinctly Middle Eastern flavor. Located across the street from the Jaffa flea market, a 10-minute walk from the Old City of Jaffa, and 15 minutes from the Jaffa Port, the hostel has a sizable rooftop garden and is close to several new cafés, wine bars, pubs, and restaurants. Housed in an old renovated building with high ceilings, colorful floor tiles, and balconies overlooking the flea market, the hostel is closed on national holidays. Amenities include free wireless

Internet, a fee-based Internet station, a fully equipped kitchen, free coffee, tea, and cookies in the morning, and coin laundry service. There is also a storage safe and a code-locked entrance gate.

Over US$200

If you're planning on staying four nights or more in one place, **Andromeda Hill** (3 Andromeda Hill Louis Pasteur St., tel. 03/683-8448, www.andromeda.co.il, US$220 d) is a pick that includes a notably long list of amenities, such as a saltwater swimming pool and tremendous views of the sea. Just at the southern tip of Old Jaffa and close to numerous historical sites, beaches, and restaurants, the Andromeda Hill apartment-style stone complex is built on top of a buttress named for Greek mythology's Andromeda. The rooms are modern, simple, and functional, and some of the comforts include a lounge deck, free towel service, a fitness spa, a poolside café, an open promenade and gardens, en-suite kitchenettes, a conference room, parking, and 24-hour security. Some rooms include a balcony. Massage services, a steam room and dry sauna, luggage storage, and wireless Internet are also available.

Information and Services

Tel Aviv caters to tourists and visitors from all over the world and presents information and services regularly in English, including at ATMs, post offices, and websites. It is also one of the most Wi-Fi-friendly cities in the world, so if you have a device like a tablet from a foreign country that works on a wireless network, it should also work in Tel Aviv.

INFORMATION
Tourist and Travel Information

There are three major tourist information centers in Tel Aviv, and one of the most centrally located and easily accessible is **HaTachana Train Station Complex Tourist Center** (HaTachana Bldg. 5, tel. 03/776-4005 or 03/516-6188, ext. 3, www.hatachana.co.il, 10am-8pm Sun.-Thurs., 9am-2pm Fri., closed on Jewish holidays). You can also have some fun shopping and eating at HaTachana.

The **Herbert Samuel Promenade Tourist Center** (46 Herbert Samuel St., tel. 03/516-6317, ext. 1, www.visit-tlv.co.il, 9:30am-6:30pm Sun.-Thurs., 9am-1pm Fri. Apr.-Oct., 9:30am-5:30pm Sun.-Thurs., 9am-1pm Fri. Nov.-Mar., closed on Jewish holidays) is a reasonable stop to combine with going to the beach, as it is directly on the promenade and near swimming.

Down in Old Jaffa is the **Jaffa Clock Tower Tourist Center** (2 Marzuk at Azar St., tel. 03/516-6188, jaffainfo11@bezeqint.net, 9:30am-6:30pm Sun.-Thurs., 9am-2pm Fri., 10am-4pm Sat. Apr.-Oct., 9:30am-5:30pm Sun.-Thurs., 9am-2pm Fri. Nov.-Mar., closed on Jewish holidays).

Maps and Guides

There are some useful online maps of Tel Aviv, including several very detailed options on the website for the **Israel Ministry of Tourism** (www.goisrael.com). They are especially helpful if you have access to a color printer.

Tel Aviv City Guide (www.cityguide.co.il) has an interactive map that allows you to pinpoint accommodations, food, entertainment, and more in the surrounding vicinity of your search with clickable thumbtacks.

Hospitals and Emergency Services

Very close to the center of Tel Aviv near Hamedim Square is **Ichilov Hospital** (6 Weitzman St., tel. 03/697-4444), which has some of the best facilities in Israel.

For emergencies 24 hours a day and transportation to the nearest emergency room, contact **Magen David Adom** (dial 101 or tel.

03/546-0111, www.mdais.com). Ambulance service is available by dialing 101.

For non-medical emergencies, contact the **Tourist Police** (tel. 03/516-5382, corner of Geula and Herbert Samuel Sts.) or dial 100 for the police in general. For a fire, dial 102 for the **fire department.**.

Media
The home offices for most of Israel's domestic media companies are located in Tel Aviv, including the general news and interest **Ha'aretz** and **Yediot Ahronoth,** which have editions in English, as well as the English business publication **Globes.** Some publications only found here include **Time Out Tel Aviv.**

English-language radio can be found on 88FM.

SERVICES
Currency Services and Money Exchange
Banks and post offices will change money, but **post offices** (www.israelpost.co.il) charge no commission and have services that include buying foreign currency with a credit card (up to US$1,000), changing traveler's checks for the U.S. dollar and the euro, and changing cash. Some post office branches also have **Western Union** services.

There are also several money-changing locations in the center of the city. **Moneygram** (www.moneygram.com) is a popular company that has about three dozen locations throughout Tel Aviv. You can find exact addresses and contact information for Moneygram locations by visiting their website.

Banks and ATMs
All banks have branches or headquarters in Tel Aviv, the financial capital of the country. Most bank branches or buildings are on Allenby Street, Rothschild Boulevard, Herbert Samuel Street, and Yehuda Halevy Street. ATMs are also very easy to find in small shops and near commercial centers. Look for the green and white machines of **Israel Discount Bank** (27-31 Yehuda Halevi St., tel. 03/514-5555), which generally charge the lowest fee for withdrawing money from a foreign account. ATMs bearing the red, white, and black colors of **Bank Hapoalim** (50 Rothschild Blvd., tel. 03/567-3333) are also fairly easy to find.

For a specific listing of commercial bank addresses, go to the "Aliyahpedia" page on www.nbn.org.il and look under banking.

Postal Service
Post office locations can be found **online** (www.israelpost.co.il). The **main post office** branch is at 132 Allenby Street, and there are some conveniently located but smaller branches around town (286 Dizengoff St., 61 HaYarkon St., 3 Zamenhoff St., 3 Mendele St. and 138 Yeffet St. in Jaffa).

Internet
More than five years ago, Tel Aviv began a free Wi-Fi hotspot program throughout the city, starting with Ben Gurion Boulevard. The hotspots don't allow visits to file-sharing websites and will block you if you try to download files that are too big. If you can't find a city hotspot, most cafés and coffee shops in Tel Aviv have free wireless access. The network now includes parks, city shores, main streets, and commercial centers.

Embassies
The **American Embassy** (71 HaYarkon St., tel. 03/519-7475, http://israel.usembassy. gov), **Canadian Embassy** (3/5 Nirim St., tel. 03/636-3300, www.canadainternational. gc.ca), and **Embassy of Australia** (Discount Bank Tower, Level 28, 23 Yehuda Halevi St., tel. 03/693-5000, www.israel.embassy.gov.au) are located in Tel Aviv.

Transportation

It's very easy to get to Tel Aviv, to travel within the city, and to take short trips in the vicinity. Tel Aviv itself is only about 20 square miles, and is one hour from both Jerusalem and Haifa, the two other major urban centers of Israel. Public transportation does not run on Shabbat, and will stop about mid-afternoon on Friday and resume after dark on Saturday evening.

GETTING THERE

Air

Tel Aviv's **Ben Gurion International Airport** (www.iaa.gov.il, tel. 03/975-2386) is about a 15-minute drive from the City Center. From the airport, you can get into the city by hotel shuttle, train, taxi, and bus.

The public transportation depot is on the second floor near Gates 21 and 23. Buses go from there to the **Egged** (www.egged.co.il) station at nearby Airport City, and then you can transfer to regular Egged bus lines. To get from Airport City to the airport there are free passes.

Train

Once on the **Israel Railways** train (www. rail.co.il, NIS20), you can be in Tel Aviv's City Center in 10 minutes from the airport, and in about 90 minutes from Jerusalem. There are several bus lines that leave about every 20-30 minutes from the airport and stop at four stations.

Tel Aviv's most southerly stop, HaHagana, will get you closest to Jaffa, Florentin, and Neve Tzedek in the south. The next stop, HaShalom, will drop you off at Azrieli Center, and get you near Dizengoff and some of the best beaches in the city. Savidor Station gets you in proximity of Jabotinsky Street and the Marina and Old Port. University Station is quite far north and actually gets you just outside of the city.

You can buy a daily or multi-journey ticket; kids under five travel for free.

Car

If you are driving into Tel Aviv, you are going to take Highway 1 from Jerusalem and Highway 2 from Haifa. You will run through the center of the city on Ayalon (North or South), also known as Highway 20. Ayalon

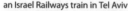
an Israel Railways train in Tel Aviv

has about half a dozen exits that lead to different parts of the city.

Share Taxi

Sherut, or share taxis, also travel to and from Tel Aviv and are your best (and almost only) option during the weekend. A *sherut* from Jerusalem is about NIS35 or less, and leaves from City Center on Yafo Street, seven days a week. The end point for most *sherut* is the Tel Aviv Central Bus Station (106 Levinski St.), just east of Neve Tzedek and Florentin. If you are paying close attention and know where you are, you can call out to the *sherut* driver at certain points along the route to hop out after they have exited the freeway and are in Tel Aviv. If you are on the freeway and have some type of emergency and need to get off the bus, it's also acceptable to ask the driver to pull over and they will if there is a place to stop.

Bus

The green-and-white Egged (www.egged. co.il) buses travel into south Tel Aviv to the Central Bus Station. From Jerusalem's Central Bus Station, it is about an hour ride without traffic. Try to avoid making the trip on a Friday afternoon, as the traffic is usually the worst at that time. Once in Tel Aviv, there are tons of taxis outside the front doors of the bus station.

GETTING AROUND
Driving

Tel Aviv is relatively easy to navigate by car, except that there is usually quite a bit of traffic. Since the western border of the city is the Mediterranean, and Ayalon Highway essentially forms the eastern border, you always have landmarks for orientation.

The parking system in Israel is universal: gray curbs are free parking, blue and white stripes are paid (look for the pay station and keep change on hand), and red and white stripes mean no parking. If you have a phone that operates inside Israel you can use the Payngo app to pay for parking.

Aside from renting a car at the airport,

there is a group of car rental company offices on HaYarkon Street just north of Frishman Street. They include Eldan (114 HaYarkon St., tel. 03/527-1166, www.eldan.co.il), Avis (113 HaYarkon St., tel. 03/527-1752, http://avis. co.il), and Shlomo Sixt (122 HaYarkon St., tel. 03/524-4935, www.shlomo.co.il).

Public Transportation

The city bus line, Dan (tel. 03/639-4444, www.dan.co.il/english) operates a series of very convenient lines throughout the city, and they have detailed information on their English language website. They shut down for the weekend. A multi-trip Rav Kav Card offers a small discount per ride if you know you will be taking more than one ride. It can be purchased from the bus driver and works in both Tel Aviv and Jerusalem.

The Central Bus Station (106 Levinski St.) is a multilevel hub that looks a little bit like a low-end shopping mall. From here you can buy tickets and take buses that travel all over the country.

Taxis

Recommended by the Tel Aviv Tourism Bureau are Gordon Taxi (tel. 03/527-2999), Habima Taxi (tel. 03/528-3131), and Kastel (tel. 03/633-2253).

Rental Bikes

One of Tel Aviv's coolest features is Tel-O-Fun (www.tel-o-fun.co.il/en), a bicycle rental system. You can pick up and drop off a rented bike at any point throughout the city. There is no law in Tel Aviv that requires bicyclists to wear a helmet.

Shabbat and Holidays

For the most part, most venues in Tel Aviv are open on Shabbat and holidays, but public transportation shuts down. You can find *sherut* (share taxis) at the Central Bus Station (106 Levinski St.) that will take you to a variety of places for a price, including to Jerusalem. They leave when the taxi is full, not on a set schedule.

Haifa and the North Coast

The north coast of Israel has a subtle, seductive charm that makes it a place where you could easily lose track of time for days.

Whether you are in Haifa, Akko, Caesarea, Zichron Ya'akov, Nahariya, or Rosh Hanikra, there are options for indoor and outdoor activities and excursions, a surprising number of high-end boutique hotels, and some world-class wineries.

One of the best jumping-off places for exploring the region is Haifa, Israel's third largest city, situated on the coast a short drive north of Tel Aviv. The city is built up on the side of Mount Carmel and revolves around the massive, dominating Baha'i Gardens and Golden Dome from a social, economic, and spiritual perspective. Haifa is full of scenic vistas around every corner, excellent restaurants of all kinds, and a range of interesting activities such as long walks on the promenade by the beach and world-class museums. It is also home to the "MIT of Israel," the Technion, and is known as a tolerant and inclusive place, where Arabs, Jews, and Christians live together peacefully.

Not far from Haifa are some of Israel's most memorable coastal spots, including Akko (a UNESCO World Heritage Site), Caesarea and the ruins of the Roman aqueduct, and the quaint, picturesque artist village of Zichron Ya'akov. A notable stopping point that is a bit off the beaten path is the little seaside town of Nahariya, where you'll find some of Israel's best surfing year-round and townspeople who will warm your heart with their hospitality.

Throughout the coastal region north of Tel Aviv, there is such a wide variety of things to see and do that it's hard to leave once you're here, so try to keep things open-ended. You might plan to spend just one night in Nahariya, but if you find yourself riding a free bike rental from your hotel down the miles-long promenade by the beach, plans could change.

ORIENTATION

Haifa is Israel's third largest city and is directly north of Tel Aviv by about one hour and northwest of Jerusalem by about two hours. The city is built on and around Mount Carmel, and is full of winding, steep streets

---

Look for ★ to find recommended
sights, activities, dining, and lodging.

Highlights

★ **Baha'i Gardens and Golden Dome:**
Everyone talks about the Baha'i dome and gardens, but it's not until you see them that you understand why. A marvel of terraced landscaping and a reminder of the power of faith, they stand out among Haifa's sights (page 155).

★ **Louis Promenade:** There's no better place to get your first glimpse of Haifa than from the Louis Promenade. It's difficult to tear yourself away from the gorgeous vistas of the Port of Haifa and the lower city (page 162).

★ **Acre Old City:** If you make only one side trip on the north coast, go to the Old City in Akko (Acre). The centuries-old structures and odd, winding streets illuminate layers of history critical to understanding the region (page 172).

★ **Caesarea National Antiquities Park:**
Not far from Tel Aviv, you'll find surviving examples of Roman civilization, including an amphitheater, the hippodrome, and Hellenistic and Crusader ruins (page 181).

★ **Roman and Byzantine Aqueduct:**
The aqueduct outside of Caesarea is an excellent place to combine sightseeing with outdoor play. The ancient aqueduct creates a sort of barrier for the popular beach, which is an easy place to slow down to enjoy wading or swimming in the sea (page 183).

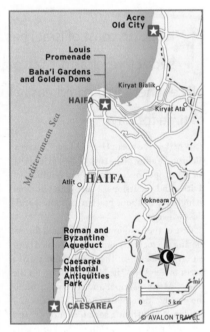

Haifa and the North Coast

Mediterranean Sea

Shlomi

899

GROTTO CAVES ★

SEE "NAHARIYA" MAP

89

Nahariya

Ma'alot-Tarshiha

89

NORTHERN

854

864

70

SEE "AKKO" MAP

Akko

85

Karmiel

85

ACRE OLD CITY ★

4

784

805

Sakhanin

805

BAHA'I GARDENS AND GOLDEN DOME ★

Kiryat Bialik

79

SEE "HAIFA" MAP ★ HAIFA

22

Kiryat Ata

LOUIS PROMENADE ★

780

784

70

672

75

77

79

754

Atlit

721

672

70

HAIFA

Nazareth Illit

Nazareth

Migdal HaEmek

73

60

2 4

66

Yokneam

SEE "ZICHRON YA'AKOV" MAP

70

Afula

Zichron Ya'akov

6

653

65

675

60

SEE "CAESAREA" MAP

Caesarea

ROMAN AND BYZANTINE AQUEDUCT ★

CAESAREA NATIONAL ANTIQUITIES PARK ★

652

596

66

Jenin

Hadera

65

585

581

CENTRAL

6

WEST BANK

60

0   5 mi

0   5 km

2   4

57

Tulkarm

© AVALON TRAVEL

Haifa's Topography and Neighborhoods

The first time you enter Haifa it is easy to understand why it is known as "the San Francisco of Israel." The city's winding streets are extremely steep in the places where the city climbs up Mount Carmel. There are three major tiers of the city. The lowest is the old city center, **Wadi Salib,** which extends to **Wadi Nisnas** and is commonly called downtown. The area is the hub of Arab life and culture. In the same vicinity toward the **Port of Haifa** is the **German Colony** with its Templar-period buildings, visitors center, and restaurants.

The next tier up is the **Hadar** neighborhood, which dates back to the 1900s and is about halfway up Mount Carmel. Hadar is home to a large Jewish synagogue and block after block of closely situated, lower-end shops of all kinds. During Shabbat, part of a major street near the synagogue is closed to traffic and the entire area shuts down from late Friday afternoon until well after dark on Saturday night.

One of the most prestigious areas in town that is also highest up on the mountainside is **Carmel,** which includes the French Carmel, Merkaz HaCarmel, Romema, Carmeliya, and more. Carmel is home to some of Haifa's finest restaurants with the most remarkable views.

and main roads that sweep around the base of the mountain, following the shore of the sea.

Haifa is the gateway to the Galilee and Israel's north coast, and makes an excellent base for excursions within an hour radius, including north to Akko, Rosh Hanikra, Nahariya; south to Zichron Ya'akov, Caesarea, and Tel Aviv; and east to Nazareth.

PLANNING YOUR TIME

Haifa is the perfect place to base yourself while exploring this region and make day trips to the north coast. There are also some nice options for hotels in nearby areas, but this will require a bit more of a sense of adventure to navigate. The best way to get around this region is by car, but regional bus lines are also quite accessible (though perhaps not very frequent).

At least two nights are advisable for Haifa and nearby environs. Depending on how many trips you want to make to the surrounding areas, three nights and four days in the area may be best. Anywhere in between 2-5 days will give you a good but quick sampling of Haifa and its region.

The trick to seeing and experiencing a satisfying amount of Haifa is to plan your time according to which neighborhoods you are traversing. The neighborhoods and related sights are situated like steps up and down Mount Carmel.

A good approach is to plan a walking route that eventually leads to a resting place, such as following the Louis Promenade to the Baha'i Gardens as far down as you can go and ending up at the base of the gardens in the German Colony. You can also plan a route around the city's subway stops for easy getting in and out.

Haifa

One of Haifa's main distinguishing features is its reputation as a model of peaceful coexistence among different faiths and ethnicities within Israel; you'll often hear Israelis remark on it. When you're in Haifa, you can feel it. At the foot of the Baha'i Gardens and Golden Dome, significant for followers of the Baha'i faith, you can hear the bells of a nearby Christian church and see Arabs and Jews eating in the same restaurants in the German Colony.

The life of the city revolves around several major points, including the Baha'i Gardens and Golden Dome, the beaches, and the distinct neighborhoods on multiple ascending tiers from the seaside to the top of Mount Carmel. Many areas of Haifa remain open on the weekend (except for the Hadar district), so there are many options of things to do, see, and experience on Friday and Saturday.

HISTORY

The earliest evidence of human settlements in the region of Haifa goes back to the 14th century BC. Haifa is mentioned in 3rd century BC Jewish Talmudic literature as a small fishing village and the home of several Jewish scholars. The Haifa of that time is believed to have existed from the Jaffa Street Jewish cemetery to Ramban Hospital.

Its seaside position and port encouraged the capture and governance of Haifa by a variety of rulers throughout the ages, including Byzantine, Arab, Crusader, Mamluk, Ottoman, and Egyptian.

In 1909, around the same time that Haifa was emerging as a major industrial port and center of population, the city became a central place for followers of the Baha'i faith, when the remains of their religious leader, the Bab, were moved to nearby Akko (Acre) and a shrine was built on Mount Carmel by 'Abdu'l-Baha. Today Haifa is a central site of worship, pilgrimage, and administration for the Baha'i religion.

After the Israeli War of Independence in 1948, Haifa became a gateway for waves of Jewish immigrants from all over the world coming to the newly established Jewish state. Several neighborhoods sprang up very quickly as a result to accommodate the new residents, and by 1970, Haifa's population was about 200,000. With the fall of the former Soviet Union, a huge influx of 35,000 more immigrants came to the city.

SIGHTS
★ Baha'i Gardens and Golden Dome

Haifa's Baha'i World Center includes the golden Shrine of the Bab, terraced gardens, and administrative buildings, covering the northern slope on Mount Carmel all the way to the foot of the mountain where it abuts

the Baha'i Gardens and Golden Dome

Haifa

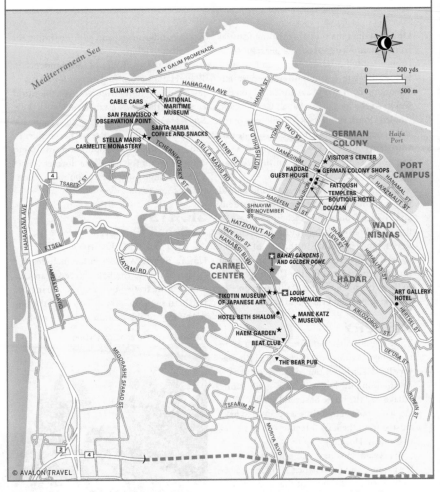

the German Colony. The **Baha'i Gardens and Golden Dome** (Baha'i World Center, 80 Hatzionut Ave., tel. 04/831-3131, www.ganbahai.org.il/en, inner gardens 9am-noon Tues.-Thurs., outer gardens 9am-7pm daily, closed Wed., free entrance and free tours) is so massive and dominating that it acts as the unofficial center of Haifa.

An extended staircase that goes up the side of Mount Carmel is divided into 19 terraces

and the golden Baha'i Shrine of the Bab is situated in a dominating position in the middle. The golden-domed shrine marks the burial place of one of the two prophets of the Baha'i faith and can be seen from multiple points throughout the city.

The garden is an intricate work of art that exudes a calm and peaceful atmosphere. The outer gardens can be accessed from the top and bottom entrances, and free guided tours in English begin at noon from the top entrance.

The smaller but also very pretty and peaceful Baha'i gardens in Akko are the resting place and former residence of the second prophet of the Baha'i faith.

Mane Katz Museum

In a small and distinguished house with views of the Bay of Haifa, the Mane Katz Museum (89 Yafe Nof St., tel. 04/911-9372, www.mkm. org.il, 10am-4pm Sun.-Wed., 4pm-7pm Thurs., 10am-1pm Fri., 10am-3pm Sat., adult NIS35, senior NIS17.5, child NIS23, combined Haifa museum ticket NIS60) is tucked away at the southern end of Louis Promenade. The museum was the home of the artist Mane Katz at the end of his life and features some of his work. Also on display are Jewish religious and ceremonial pieces and works by Marc Chagall.

Haifa Educational Zoo

Situated high up enough in Haifa to afford gorgeous views of nearby mountains and on one of the Carmelit subway stops, the Haifa Educational Zoo (124 HaTishbi St., tel. 04/837-2390, www.haifazoo.co.il, 9am-4pm Sun.-Thurs., 9am-4pm Sat. and holidays fall and spring, 9am-1:30pm Fri. and holiday evenings summer, 9am-6pm Sun.-Thurs., 9am-6pm Sat. and holidays, 9am-3pm Fri. and holiday evenings winter, adult and child NIS35, senior NIS25) is home to more than 100 types of animals including bears, wolves, hyenas, and monkeys and spread out over some very hilly terrain. It is a great place for a family visit, especially with the carousel, sweet treats, and playground just outside the zoo entrance, which is part of a popular park.

Haifa Museum of Art

Among the three largest museums in Israel, the Haifa Museum of Art (26 Shabbetai Levi St., tel. 04/911-5997, www.hma.org.il, 10am-4pm Sun.-Wed., 10am-7pm Thurs., 10am-1pm Fri., 10am-3pm Sat., adult NIS45, senior NIS22.5, child NIS30, combined Haifa museum ticket NIS60) covers three floors and more than 3,500 square meters. The artwork ranges from Israeli to international contemporary permanent and changing exhibitions.

Haifa City Museum

The Haifa City Museum (11 Ben Gurion Ave., tel. 04/911-5888, www.hcm.org.il, 10am-4pm Sun.-Wed., 4pm-7pm Thurs., 10am-1pm Fri., 10am-3pm Sat., adult NIS35, senior NIS17.5, child NIS23, combined Haifa museum ticket NIS60) is a good place to get some background on the history of Haifa. Located in a former Templar school building in the historic German Colony, the museum recently underwent renovations and additions. The museum's changing exhibitions focus on topics of regional interest including architecture, history, and residents.

Stella Maris Carmelite Monastery

Whether you go to see the vistas or the Stella Maris Carmelite Monastery (top of Stella Maris Rd., off of Tchernikovsky St. and adjacent to the upper station of the Haifa cable car, tel. 04/833-7758, 6am-noon and 3pm-6pm daily, free), heading to the top of Mount Carmel on Stella Maris Road is well worth it. The Carmelites are a religious order of the Catholic Church that took their name from Mount Carmel, where they originated. From about 1631 onward, the monastery was built and destroyed several times. The current structure was opened in 1836, and the interior is full of beautiful, detailed paintings that grace the small but exquisite interior's vaulted ceiling.

San Francisco Observation Point

The blue dome cage of the San Francisco Observation Point (across from Stella Maris Carmelite Monastery on Tchernikovsky St., free audio guide at site) provides a gorgeous view. A recording, in multiple languages, provides detailed background information on the area.

the interior of the Stella Maris Carmelite Monastery

The National Maritime Museum

It can be a bit confusing to find, but **The National Maritime Museum** (198 Allenby St., tel. 04/853-6622, www.nmm.org.il, 10am-4pm Sun.-Thurs., 10am-1pm Fri., 10am-3pm Sat., adult NIS35, senior NIS17.5, child NIS23, combined Haifa museum ticket NIS60) features a collection that covers 5,000 years of maritime history of the Mediterranean basin, the Red Sea, and the Nile. The museum has three levels with permanent and changing exhibitions, and is an interesting window into the region's maritime history. It is just down the road from the more obscure **Clandestine Immigration and Naval Museum** (204 Allenby St.), which can be confusing. Look for the large ships on display outside to lead you to the general area of the museums.

Elijah's Cave

Situated about midway up a mountainside is the humble religious and spiritual destination of **Elijah's Cave** (230 Allenby St., tel. 04/852-7430, 8am-5pm Sun.-Thurs., 8:30am-12:45pm Fri., free). Expect to see people here praying, as it is an important site to followers of Christianity, Judaism, and Islam. It is widely accepted to be a cave where the prophet

Elijah lived, and ceremonies are sometimes held here on religious days. The site is accessible from the top of the mountain at Stella Maris Monastery, but much easier to reach from Allenby Street, and there are separate male and female entrances.

Cable Car

If you have no fear of heights, the **cable car** (top entrance at Stella Maris Carmelite Monastery area at Tchernikovsky St. and bottom entrance at Bat Galim Promenade, tel. 04/833-5970, www.visit-haifa.org, 10am-6pm daily, NIS32 round-trip, NIS21 one-way) is one of the best ways to get great views of Haifa, Mount Carmel, and Haifa Port. The slightly rickety and globe-shaped cars dangle from cables that go up and down the mountainside on a regular basis during the day. The bottom car can be found nearby the Clandestine Immigration and Naval Museum and its huge outdoor ships. The lower cars drop you off at the slightly-worse-for-wear Bat Galim beach and promenade. The upper cars are a quick walk from the Stella Maris Carmelite Monastery. The top terminal also has three restaurants with amazing views that are somewhat pricey but popular among locals.

German Colony

Good for simply strolling about and taking in a variety of scenery and restaurants, the **German Colony** is the area roughly between the base of the Baha'i Gardens and the port. Numerous buildings here were built during the 1800s by the German Templars, and the area provides a calm and charming respite from a day of more intense sightseeing. There are guided tours in multiple languages through the German Colony; check with the **information center** (48 Ben Gurion St., tel. 04/853-5606, www.visit-haifa.org, 9am-5pm Sun.-Thurs., 9am-1pm Fri., 10am-3pm Sat.).

Madatech: National Museum of Science, Technology, and Space

A good option if traveling with kids, **Madatech: National Museum of Science, Technology, and Space** (25 Shmariyahu Levine St., tel. 04/861-4444, www.madatech.org.il, 10am-3pm Sun.-Wed., 10am-5pm Thurs., 10am-1pm Fri., 11am-6pm Sat., adult NIS89, under 5 free) is a massive, hands-on, experiential science museum geared toward enhancing science- and technology-based education. Housed in a restored historic 1912 building, the museum includes over a dozen interactive exhibits, a science park, and an interactive "edutainment" movie theater called Cinematrix.

Reuben Hecht Museum Haifa

A small, but beautifully appointed, museum on the University of Haifa campus, the **Reuben Hecht Museum Haifa** (University of Haifa, Mt. Carmel, tel. 04/825-7773, http://mushecht.haifa.ac.il, 10am-4pm Sun.-Mon. and Wed.-Thurs., 10am-7pm Tues., 10am-1pm Fri., 10am-2pm Sat., guided tours for groups, free) will satisfy the archaeologist in any traveler. Some of the exhibits create the experience of being in a town under siege by the Romans. The Canaanite mummies and remnants of an ancient ship that was discovered underwater in the 1980s are interesting touches, as is the exhibit of l'Ecole de Paris artwork. The museum affords a wonderful vista of Haifa and a chance to wander about the university campus.

TOURS

Route of 1,000 Steps

If you are in very good shape, adventurous, and good with maps, you can try the **Route of 1,000 Steps,** a self-guided tour that goes from the top of Mount Carmel down through

Haifa's cable cars carry people up and down the mountainside.

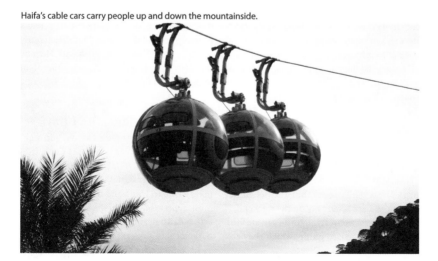

The Influence of the German Templars

Throughout Haifa and the north coast, the influence of the German Templars can still be seen in the form of entire neighborhoods that exhibit graceful architectural design and exude an atmosphere of antique elegance.

German Templars of the late 19th century who settled in what was then Palestine are not the same thing as the Templar knights, a monastic military order of the 12th century that guarded European pilgrims in the Holy Land. Today there are Templars neighborhoods in Jerusalem, Tel Aviv, and Haifa.

The German Templars' neighborhood in Haifa (called the German Colony, just like in Jerusalem) is not large, but its unique character has been carefully preserved and walking tours regularly explore it. It runs from the foot of the Baha'i Gardens roughly to the port between Rothschild and Ben Gurion Streets.

Haifa's German Colony has been recently restored in a major undertaking by the city and is one of the best places in the city to have a relaxing meal (the businesses are open seven days a week), especially in combination with a visit to the Baha'i Gardens. It is also home to some of the city's best boutique hotels.

One odd aspect of the German Templars' history is that around the time of World War II, they were sympathetic to the Nazis and were ultimately expelled from Palestine.

several major neighborhoods of the city, ending at the German Colony. The route starts from Savyonim Lookout Point near Yefe Nof Street. You want to be in the vicinity of the Crowne Plaza Hotel Haifa (124 Yefe Nof St.) to get started. There are four routes along the way that are marked by steps and color-coded.

Free Tours

Many hotels in Haifa offer free tours as a courtesy to their guests. Tour times and availability vary; so when you check in, ask the front desk of your hotel if they have anything available and what the tour schedule is. It is worthwhile to try and book a hotel that offers free tours, as buying a private tour is expensive. You can also stop into any hotel (there are several close to each other in the German Colony) and ask for information.

Private Tours

The **Haifa Tourist Board** (www.visit-haifa. org) offers some tours, but the schedules change and are often only on the weekend. If you are interested in arranging a private tour, stick with a licensed guide, which they can recommend.

ENTERTAINMENT AND EVENTS

Haifa is home to a wide variety of things to do when the sun goes down, from wine-tastings (wine lovers will enjoy the surprisingly wide variety of regional vintages), to live music, festivals, and the largest movie theater in Israel.

Cinema

Billed as one of the largest movie theaters in Israel, **Yes Planet** (55 HaHistadrut St., tel. 04/841-6898, http://yesplanet.co.il) screens contemporary American and European movies. Films are shown in English with Hebrew subtitles, or in a foreign language other than Hebrew with English and/or Hebrew subtitles. Check in advance.

Live Music, Clubs, and Bars

Part of the variety of options for day and night on Hanassi Boulevard, the **Beat Club** (124 Hanassi Blvd., tel. 04/866-2244 and 04/810-7107, daily, cover varies) is a top live performance club in Haifa and the north, with live musical performances of the leading domestic artists daily. Beat Club sometimes hosts international acts.

Recommended by locals who like to party

(in typical laid-back Haifa style), **Syncopa** (5 Khayat St., tel. 054/614-2643, 8pm-last customer daily, NIS40) is a bar with a crowd that is generally over 25. Mostly playing funk music, the bar has a softly lit interior and is a popular spot for simply hanging out.

Easy to spot on busy Hanassi Boulevard, just near a Carmelit station, **The Bear Inn Pub** (135 Hanassi Blvd., tel. 04/838-1703, 5pm-3am Sat.-Wed., 11pm-4am Thurs.-Fri., NIS60) is a popular local spot for a drink and a hamburger. They have a rich, woody interior that looks and feels like an English pub. Most of the customers are locals and expatriates, and the large alcohol menu and wide variety of beers attracts a more mature crowd. They serve standard pub food, but the range of choices includes everything from a burger to salmon carpaccio.

Festivals

FIRST FRUITS WINE AND CHEESE TASTING FESTIVAL

Held annually around May or June, the **First Fruits Wine and Cheese Tasting Festival** (Haifa Auditorium Park near the Haifa Cinematheque in the Hacarmel neighborhood, tel. 04/853-5606, www.visit-haifa.org, 6pm-11pm daily) showcases regional wineries, wines, and foodstuffs with an emphasis on Haifa and the north. In addition to wines from vineyards of all sizes, there are booths of boutique cheese makers, chocolatiers, olive oil, and wine accessories; workshops and lectures are also given.

BEER CITY FESTIVAL

During the last week of August thousands of people gather in Haifa for the annual **Beer City Festival** (Students Beach) that includes beers from all over Israel and the world and live music.

PUPPET FESTIVAL

The end of August brings the completely free **Puppet Festival** (Haifa Auditorium in Central Carmel, tel. 052/389-7487, yaeln@012.net.il, free) that includes children's performances, puppet shows, outdoor events, and an exhibition of masterpiece artistic puppets.

HAIFA INTERNATIONAL FILM FESTIVAL

Held in late September or early October, the **Haifa International Film Festival** (multiple venues, tel. 04/801-3471, www.haifaff.co.il) has been operating for more than 30 years. It includes events, lectures, and awards.

FESTIVAL OF FESTIVALS

This popular December event is a multicultural food and folklore festival that bills itself as the only one of its kind in the Middle East. Also known as the Holiday of Holidays, the **Festival of Festivals** (tel. 04/853-5606, www.visit-haifa.org, 9am-8pm Thurs.-Sat.) for several weekends throughout December makes use of the numerous religious holidays that occur among different faiths and cultures in the region in that month. The

Haifa decorates for the multicultural Festival of Festivals in December.

festival is held in the Wadi Nisnas neighborhood of Haifa, between the neighborhoods of Hadar and the downtown area around the German Colony. The main staging areas are on Khoury Street, Hatzionut Street, Shabbtai Levi Street, and HaWadi Street.

SHOPPING

Haifa has some great shopping and specific districts that are dedicated to shopping.

German Colony

Along Ben Gurion Boulevard near the waterfront in the **German Colony** are a variety of high-end shops, art galleries, souvenir shops, coffeehouses, and restaurants housed in historic 19th-century Templar buildings. Most of the shops are open by 10am and close around 8pm on weekdays, with some closed or operating on more limited hours on Friday and Saturday.

Merkaz Panorama

Conveniently located on Hanassi Boulevard within an easy walk to all the hotels in the area, **Merkaz Panorama** (109 Hanassi Blvd., tel. 04/837-5011, 9am-8pm Sun.-Thurs., 9am-2pm Fri.) is a small, upscale shopping mall that offers a surprising variety of clothes, shoes, and coffee shops with sandwiches and salads.

SPORTS AND RECREATION

As a coastal city, Haifa is home to numerous parks, promenades, and outdoor activities. Its proximity to Mount Carmel also affords good hiking opportunities.

Parks, Gardens, and Beaches

DADO BEACH

You might want to take a car or taxi to get here, but **Dado Beach** (southwest Haifa coast) is the best place in town for enjoying the beach, whether or not you go in the water. The promenade is long, there are beach chairs with shade, and it has numerous options for eating. It's even pleasant in good winter weather.

SCULPTURE GARDEN

At the **Sculpture Garden** (Mitzpor Shalom or Peace Park, upper section of Hatzionut Ave., corner of Shnayim Be'November St., 8am-6pm daily, free), 29 bronze sculptures by Israeli artist Ursula Malbin line the walkways and are scattered about the lawns. The garden has a sweeping view of Haifa, the Mediterranean Sea, and the hills of the Galilee and Lebanon on a clear day. It is a 10-minute walk to the midsection level of the Baha'i Gardens.

★ LOUIS PROMENADE

One of the best places in the city for a long walk full of incredible vistas of Haifa, the port, and the lower city, **Louis Promenade** (off of Yefe Nof St. in the Carmel district) runs through the center of the Carmel district parallel to Yefe Nof Street. There are plenty of places to sit and enjoy the view, take photographs, and enjoy the scenery. It is close to the main cluster of hotels on Hanassi Boulevard, which makes it an easy walk if you're staying in the area.

Along Yefe Nof Street just off of the promenade, there are a couple of small, but nice museums, including the **Tikotin Museum of Japanese Art** (89 Hanassi St., tel. 04/838-3554, www.tmja.org.il, 10am-7pm Sun.-Thurs., 10am-1pm Fri., 10am-3pm Sat., adult NIS35, senior and child NIS23) and the **Mane Katz Museum** (89 Yafe Nof St., tel. 04/911-9372, www.mkm.org.il, 10am-4pm Sun.-Wed., 4pm-7pm Thurs., 10am-1pm Fri., 10am-3pm Sat., adult NIS35, senior NIS17.5, child NIS23, combined Haifa museum ticket NIS60). If you follow Yefe Nof Street by foot for about 15 minutes or less past the end of the promenade, you'll find the upper entrance to the Baha'i Gardens.

HANGING BRIDGES AT NESHER PARK

If you have the means to get here, the **Hanging Bridges at Nesher Park** (Carmel National Forest, arrive from Haruv St. in Nesher off Rte. 4, tel. 04/823-1452, www.

Israel's National Trail in Haifa

If you look closely, you will see signs in Haifa for the **Israel National Trail** (*Shevil Israel* in Hebrew, www.israelnationaltrail.com and www.israeltrail.net), a hiking footpath that runs 580-620 miles (depending on the routes) from the Red Sea in the south to the border with Lebanon in the north.

The trail, which takes about 45 days to complete, can be seen at various points in Haifa, where it can be identified by subtle trail markings of three stripes of white, blue, and orange. It is listed among National Geographic's World's Best Hikes.

The trail also passes through Jerusalem, Tel Aviv, Nazareth, the Negev, and the Sea of Galilee.

parks.org.il, NIS38) can give you the experience of being up in the trees. Not for the faint of heart or those who are afraid of heights, the bridges are suspended between canyons in the midst of the forest. There is a picnic and play area for kids, and it's about 25 minutes by car almost directly southeast out of Haifa.

HECHT PARK

The largest area of greenery inside Haifa city limits, **Hecht Park** (Ha'hagana St., www.visithaifa.org) is at the north end of Dado Beach and promenade and hugs the coast with continuous views of the sea. The park has a path for walking and running that spans an almost two-mile perimeter.

X-PARK

Attracting every skill level, from families to professionals, the **X-Park** (southern entrance to Haifa in the Congress Center, tel. 054/788-3812, www.xpark.co.il, call for pricing as it depends on activity) includes a skating park complex, an Olympic climbing wall, a rope park, paintball, and more. If you have extra time in the Haifa area or want to do something active on your way in or out of the city, this is a good option.

FOOD

Haifa's food scene offers two unique experiences: Druze cuisine and winery restaurants. Aside from that it also offers a wide variety

Louis Promenade affords spectacular vistas of Haifa.

of seafood restaurants, pubs, and standard Israeli fare of salads, toasted cheese sandwiches, and meat dishes. There is a decidedly Russian influence to some of the restaurants, including in the style the food is prepared and the amount of meat dishes offered.

Mediterranean

The key word when describing **Tsfarim 1** (1 Tsfarim St., tel. 04/811-2235, www.zafririm1.co.il, noon-last customer daily, NIS55) is "cool." Everything from the atmosphere to the menu presentation and the unique preparation of dishes makes it a lively option for breakfast or lunch. Situated in the Carmel district, Tsfarim 1 serves up dishes with a Mediterranean flair, such as Taboon chicken and Baladi eggplant. The restaurant's exposed brick interior walls and black-lacquer tables with overhead lighting give it an overall feel of a New York spot you might find in SoHo.

Middle Eastern

Just next to the slightly gritty Hadar district of Haifa is the mostly Arab section of town, Wadi Nisnas, which is home to several delicious options for falafel, hummus, shwarma, and the like. Around the area of Hanevi'im and Hehaluts Streets there is a nice selection of small falafel shops and stands, most of which are open from late morning (10am) to evening (about 9pm). They are excellent options for takeout or a quick, cheap bite to eat, but offer almost nothing in terms of atmosphere.

One of the most popular spots in the German Colony for both its food and atmosphere, ★ **Fattoush** (38 Ben Gurion St., tel. 04/852-4930, 8am-1am daily, NIS70) serves up a tasty variety of Middle Eastern food and the best cappuccino in town. The massive outdoor patio seating is situated in a grove of trees and decorated with tons of tiny touches, including colorful hanging beads, glass lamps, and brass finishes just like the cave-like interior of the restaurant. It all adds up to give the feel of an exotic locale that enhances the experience of the delicious food. A handwritten sign at the entrance states that all types of people of all backgrounds and beliefs are welcome. It is the type of place that you will want to go back to again and again.

At the family-run, French-Arab fusion restaurant **Douzan** (35 Ben Gurion St., tel. 04/852-5444, http://douzan.rest.co.il, 9am-midnight daily, NIS60) the whole aim is to make customers feel at home and relaxed. Decorated with whimsical touches that

Douzan restaurant in Haifa's German Colony

include old clocks, musical instruments, and velvety cushions, it is known for its surprising specialties that include small meat pies with pine nuts (called *sfeeha*).

An excellent choice for Arab food in the midst of the German Colony, **Allenby Restaurant** (43 Allenby St., tel. 04/852-9928, 7am-7pm Sat.-Thurs., 7am-5pm Fri., NIS45) is simple with few frills and fast, efficient service. The exterior and interior are also simple and unassuming, with a plain storefront and a more cafeteria-like interior. Catering to a more mature, working-class crowd, the restaurant is famous for the various presentations and side dishes that accompany its hummus, vegetable dishes, and Turkish coffee.

Bistro

The open, split-level, loft-like floor plan of **Sinta Bar** (127 Moriya Blvd., tel. 04/834-1170, www.sinta-bar.co.il, noon-11pm daily, NIS 90) gives this meat-lover's paradise in Haifa's Ahuza district a cool and relaxed atmosphere. At more than a decade old, the restaurant is considered one of Haifa's longer-running institutions and is a very short drive from the Carmel district. Serving up seafood and meat dishes with a nice selection of desserts made in-house, it is a low-key and classy option for dinner, especially if you're staying on the mountain.

Italian

Inspired by Tuscany, the upscale and renowned **Hanamal 24** (24 Hanamal St., tel. 057/944-2262, http://hanamal24.rest.co.il/en, noon-midnight Mon.-Sat., NIS110) has several different rooms throughout the restaurant's space, including a lounge, piazza, and wine cellar. Touches of brick in the flooring and rich, warm wood tones throughout give it a welcoming atmosphere. Some highlights of the gourmet dinner menu include salmon and drum fish ceviche, pork with white wine risotto, and a very inventive and broad menu of meat and seafood dishes. The extensive wine list includes choices from Israel and beyond.

Latin

You wouldn't expect to find Cuban-themed food in the German Colony in Haifa, but **Havana Plus** (25 Ben Gurion St., tel. 053/809-4797, www.2eat.co.il/havana-plus, 10am-3am daily, NIS80) ably takes the role on. With a richly decorated atmosphere that includes comfy pillows and hookahs, soft lighting and wood finishes, Havana has a very relaxing and warm atmosphere. Most of the menu items include meat and fish dishes, with an occasional pasta dish. They cater to Haifa's hipper and younger crowd. As long as you don't go expecting to find fried plantains and refried beans, you won't be disappointed.

Winery Restaurants and Wine Bars

A classy choice for a nice dinner and glass of fine wine is **107 Brasserie Wine Bar** (107 Yefe Nof St., tel. 073/759-8501, 5pm-last customer Sun.-Thurs., noon-last customer Fri., NIS55). The huge wine selection is complemented by the wide range of prices and options from the food menu and the subdued interior with wine bottles lining the walls and a long, rich mahogany bar. The lovely selection of meat and fish dishes includes traditional dishes with an original twist, including the shrimp risotto.

Coffee Shops and Cafés

If you find yourself at the **Stella Maris Carmelite Monastery,** you won't miss the obviously positioned **Santa Maria Coffee and Snacks** (entrance to Stella Maris Carmelite Monastery on Tchernikovsky St., tel. 04/859-7518, 8am-8pm daily, NIS55) at the entrance. Relaxed and casual in both its atmosphere and location with a bright and airy feel, it makes a terrific place to have a leisurely cup of coffee and enjoy a piece of their famous apple strudel. They also have a nice selection of sandwiches, desserts, and breakfast items. The staff is incredibly friendly and upbeat, and there is a beautiful view of the open sky and sea.

With its fresh, bright atmosphere and

emphasis on the healthiest of dishes including some gluten-free food options, **Café Louise** (58 Moriya Blvd., tel. 04/834-9950, www. cafelouise.co.il, 10am-10pm Sun.-Thurs., 9am-3pm Fri., NIS60) has another location in Haifa at the Grand Canyon Mall and one in Tel Aviv. The seafood and meat dishes are punctuated with some vegan menu choices and detailed touches like whole wheat pasta. Catering to the health-conscious of Haifa, it offers a nice alternative to somewhat standard options at cafés that include things like salads and bread.

With their claim to fame that they were the first coffee shop/café in Haifa, ★ **Café HaBank** (119 Hanassi Blvd., Carmel Center, tel. 04/836-3363, http://habank.rest.co.il, 8:30am-midnight Sun.-Thurs., 8:30am-after midnight Sat., NIS65) is a kosher restaurant that serves up fairly standard, but really delicious fare that includes salad and meat dishes. Seating is creatively arranged with an outdoor patio, an inside greenhouse-like area, and an inner area with a bar, flat-screen TVs, and fish tanks. They make their desserts (try the banana crumble or the huge slice of unbaked cheesecake) and are known for their lamb pastry dish (NIS80). The crowd is very local and pretty subdued, and the staff is friendly and laid-back.

One of many seaside cafés along the promenade at Dado Beach, **Camel Restaurant** (Dado Beach, tel. 04/852-2990, 9am-2am daily, NIS55) is easy to spot with its huge yellow sign that is reminiscent of a certain famous cigarette brand. Like many of the restaurants along the strip, it has a spacious, simple interior suitable for sandy feet and wet towels. There is also tons of outdoor seating on the beach with comfy, cushioned chairs and umbrellas where you can order food even on nice days in the winter months. It's a great place to get a large pizza to feed several people, and the staff is friendly and accommodating.

ACCOMMODATIONS

There are many hotel options in Haifa and the north coast, ranging from five-star luxury resort hotels to bed-and-breakfast options to very simple and affordable hostels. The only note of caution is to beware of booking a room in the Hadar district over the weekend. Though there are some affordable options there, the entire area shuts down from late Friday afternoon through late Saturday evening, and you'll be hard-pressed to even find a place to eat.

Under US$100

With 50 rooms and its slightly removed position from the hustle of central Haifa, the **Haifa Marom Hotel** (51 Palmach St., tel. 04/825-4355, marom.hotelasp.com, US$85 d) is situated in a peaceful location amid pine trees on top of Mount Carmel, with a sundeck and surrounded by gardens. The plain but comfortably furnished rooms are air-conditioned and all include a bathroom, free wireless Internet, phone, and satellite TV. Deluxe rooms have a whirlpool bath. Other amenities include free covered parking and 24-hour room service. The hotel has dining rooms, large halls for conferences and events, a gym, and a spa. It is in close proximity to the Technion and Haifa University, the Horev Center, the Grand Canyon Shopping Center, and the City's Sports Hall.

Situated in a renovated Arabic-style building in downtown Haifa, the **Port Inn Hostel** (34 Jaffa Rd., tel. 04/852-4401, http://portinn.net, US$99 d) is a cross between a hostel and a motel, with 18 vacation apartment rentals, room rentals, and dormitory rentals to choose from. The inn's central location is close to the Haifa Port passenger terminal, the Haifa Merkaz-Hasmona train station, and the Carmelit subway. It is also near the Baha'i Gardens, the German Colony, and numerous restaurants. The inn is decorated in a simple, homey manner and with a common lounge area with a multilingual satellite TV, a kitchen with free coffee and tea all day, and a lush tropical garden area for sitting and relaxing. There are coin-operated washing machines.

Near the National Museum of Science, the Hadar Shopping District, and the Carmelit subway, the **Loui M. Apartments** (35

HeHaluts St., tel. 054/837-1342, http://loui-hotelhaifa.com, US$72 d) is a 14-room motel with a simple, boxy exterior and a plain interior with rooms and studios laid out with the feel of apartments. Rooms include an LCD TV, a small dining area, and a private bathroom. The building has a roof terrace and is about 10 minutes from Haifa Port.

US$100-150

The family-run **Hotel Beth-Shalom** (110 Hanassi Blvd., tel. 04/837-3480, www.beth-shalom.co.il, US$110 d) is a small 10-room hotel tucked away on busy Hanassi Boulevard that caters to pilgrims. It is conveniently located near a number of sights, shopping, food, and an area of town that stays open during the weekend. The rooms are very small, but spotlessly clean, and every inch is so well-utilized that you have room for everything. The staff is extremely warm and accommodating, and there is some space at the front of the hotel for parking. Some rooms include a small balcony with a bit of canopy from the trees. Wireless Internet access costs US$5 from the front desk.

The ★ **Art Gallery Hotel** (61 Hertsel St., tel. 04/861-6161, http://haifa.hotelgallery.co.il, US$115 d) is a 40-room boutique hotel designed around the theme of art and scenery, and art galleries are integrated into the interior. The Bauhaus building has a clean, modern interior, 24-hour concierge service, and parking is available. Two computers with Internet are available in the lobby, and there are free guided tours of the hotel art galleries. Though small by American standards, all of the rooms include free wireless Internet, air-conditioning, LCD cable TV, and wooden floors, while suites feature a separate sleeping area, a balcony overlooking the city, and a spa bath. The 24-hour fitness center overlooks Haifa Bay, and the hotel offers free tour services. Slightly off the beaten path, the hotel is an excellent choice for a bit of luxury at an extremely affordable price, especially if you are traveling with a car. Beware about booking here over the weekend, though, as you'll be in an area that shuts down on Friday and Saturday.

Situated in the bustling downtown Turkish market area, the **1926 Designed Apartments** (36 Moshe Aron, tel. 054/539-9040, http://1926.co.il, US$118 d) is a very

the 1926 Designed Apartments

small eight-room apartment suite that comes highly recommended by travelers for its location, modern atmosphere, and central location. The building is within easy walking distance from the Carmelit, direct buses throughout Haifa, Haifa Port, the Dagon Grain Museum, and the History of the City of Haifa Museum. The modern, bright, and pretty apartments in the renovated building include a sitting area with a sofa; a kitchen with a refrigerator, microwave, hot plate, electric kettle, cutlery, and dishes; air-conditioning; a 32-inch cable satellite TV; and free wireless Internet. Each studio apartment can accommodate two or three people.

The **Theodor Hotel** (63 Hertsel St., tel. 04/867-7325, www.theodorhotel.co.il, US$115 d) is a 98-room hotel in Haifa's Hadar neighborhood the one that shuts down on the weekend). The hotel has free wireless Internet, small collections of books on all 11 floors, and a very comfortable, spacious lobby that feels more like a coffee shop. The modern, bright, and comfortably furnished rooms are geared toward couples and include cable TV, a kettle for tea and coffee, a safe, air-conditioning, and telephones for direct inbound calls. The hotel is slightly off the beaten path, but has views of the Carmel Mountains and Haifa Bay, and includes a lobby bar, restaurant, lobby TV, and laundry services. You can also buy postage and change money at the front desk. Hotel staff can assist with arranging for a doctor or babysitter, and there are on-site spa treatments.

The small and rustic **Haddad Guest House** (26 Ben Gurion St., tel. 077/201-0618, www.haddadguesthouse.com, US$110 d) makes up in services what it lacks in flash. Some of the 13 rooms have a view of Mount Carmel, the Baha'i Gardens, or Haifa Bay. Rooms have a double or twin beds, a closet, private shower and toilet, a small, fully-equipped kitchen, a small TV, hair dryer, and air-conditioning. An extra bed can be added to a room on request. Guest services include wireless Internet, laundry, and office services. Haddad's interior is extremely simple and a bit utilitarian, but it is located in the heart of the main street of the German Colony, the center of Haifa's nightlife, art gallery scene, shopping, museums, and cafés, and is 15 minutes by foot to the Baha'i Gardens. Ask the front desk for discount coupons for nearby restaurants.

US$150-200

Conveniently located just a 15-minute walk from the Baha'i Gardens in the center of Carmel neighborhood and a few minutes from the Carmelit subway, the recently renovated and renamed **Haifa Bay View Hotel** (101 Hanassi Blvd., tel. 04/835-4311, www.nofhotel.co.il, US$157 d) has a sleek, modern decor, fantastic views of the water, and a late checkout. Most of the 91 rooms have outstanding views of Haifa Bay, the Baha'i Gardens, and the western Galilee. Parking is free and there are coffee shops, restaurants, and stores nearby. Inside the hotel there is a cafeteria, a piano bar with live music, and a kosher Chinese restaurant. Room amenities include cable TV, a hair dryer, a direct-dial phone, air-conditioning, and a minibar. Lobby services include a coffee and tea corner, computers with Internet for free use, and personal safes at reception. The hotel can also assist with car rental, laundry services, and taxis.

The **Colony Hotel Haifa** (28 Ben Gurion St., tel. 04/851-3344, www.colonyhaifa.com, US$195 d), a 103-year-old restored boutique hotel in Haifa's historic German Colony, is known for its friendly staff. The building's lovely exterior is limestone with green shuttered windows, and inside there are 40 rooms and mini-suites with tiling accents and comfortable, modern furnishings that give an overall feel of historic luxury. The hotel's terrace overlooks the Baha'i Gardens, which are a straight 10-minute walk up Ben Gurion Street. The hotel has a 24-hour lobby bar, a spa room, gardens, and free wireless Internet in all the rooms. Concierge services help with reserving tours, laundry services, and takeout orders from nearby restaurants. The hotel is also near cafés, shopping, and Haifa Port.

There is something unforgettable about the ★ **Templers Boutique Hotel** (36 Ben Gurion Blvd., tel. 077/500-3110, www.templershaifa.com, US$179 d) set back a bit from the main street in the German Colony. The privately-owned boutique hotel has one of the best locations, as well as a huge private parking lot in the back and an indoor-outdoor café with a gorgeous patio and covered tables in the front. Some of the beautiful, classy, modern rooms feature massive freestanding bathtubs, whirlpool tubs, or huge showers, alongside luxurious and comfortable decor with sitting chairs and large, soft beds. Just at the foot of the Baha'i Gardens, the building dates back to 1870 and won first place in the German Colony's building renovation competition. Each room is designed in a different style, and the hotel offers last-minute deals and free Baha'i Gardens walking tours. It is near public transportation and all rooms have a kitchenette, a coffee and tea maker, a flat-screen satellite TV, free wireless Internet, and air-conditioning.

Over US$200

Villa Carmel Boutique Hotel (1 Heinrich Heine St. off 30 Moriah Blvd., tel. 04/837-5777, www.villacarmel.co.il, US$220 d) is a 15-room boutique hotel with a modern, sleek interior that includes comfortable couches in the rooms and a pretty dining room. Situated in the middle of Haifa's prestigious Carmel district, the Villa was built as Haifa's most luxurious hotel in the 1940s and has been renovated with modern conveniences. Surrounded by a small glen of trees, the hotel was a regular choice of Israel's first prime minister, David Ben-Gurion, and his wife. The hotel is quite far off the beaten path and tucked away in a residential neighborhood. It's a good fit if you're looking for an immersed escape. Room amenities include Egyptian cotton linens, cozy beds, free wireless Internet, a desk and phone with conference call capability, and wide-screen HD TVs. Most rooms have a whirlpool bath or computerized jet shower. The hotel has a restaurant, lush garden, rooftop sundeck with a large whirlpool tub and sauna, and massages

by appointment. There is also a fully-equipped business center and private meeting space with screen and projector.

INFORMATION AND SERVICES

Haifa is a tourist destination among those who live in the region as well as those who come from abroad, and is well-equipped for visitors.

Tourist Information

You will see signs for it all over town, but there is only one **Haifa Tourist Information Office** (48 Ben Gurion St., www.visit-haifa.org, 9am-5pm Sun.-Thurs., 9am-1pm Fri., 10am-3pm Sat.), conveniently located in the German Colony. The office is full of flyers, maps, and information about the area. The real wealth of information, though, can be found in the staff working here: they will give you as many details as you can handle.

Online Resources

The most robust website for online resources about Haifa and the surrounding areas is the **Haifa Tourist Board** (www.visit-haifa.org). Don't worry about downloading their tourist guide, though. You will get offered the compact printed version at every turn once you are in Haifa.

Also useful is the **Haifa Aliya Website** (www1.haifa.muni.il/aliya) with tons of information on services, transportation, and the makeup of different neighborhoods for new residents of the area.

Hospitals and Emergency Services

Fairly centrally located and with an emergency room, the **Bnai Zion Medical Center** (47 Golomb St., tel. 04/837-1973, www.b-zion.org.il) is between the Hadar and Carmel districts.

You can also call **Magen David Adom** (tel. 04/851-2233) 24 hours a day for emergency services, including for an ambulance to the nearest emergency room.

Public Transportation Surprises

A pleasantly surprising aspect of Haifa, Israel's third largest city, is that it features some unique public transportation options that cannot be found anywhere else in Israel.

The first surprise is that during **Shabbat,** there is some public transportation running, something that not even Tel Aviv can claim. Public bus service on the green Egged buses still runs, though on a less frequent schedule.

The second surprise is that Haifa is home to Israel's only subway, the **Carmelit.** Even though the Carmelit's range and distance is extremely limited (it goes in a straight line from the lower city to the upper city in just six stops), it offers a convenient transportation option. The route the Carmelit travels goes directly through a major section of Haifa's tourist areas and is a less-intimidating option for a first-time visitor than taking a bus or taxi.

Haifa's final public transportation surprise is the **cable car** that traverses the side of Mount Carmel at a daring angle. It leaves every 15 minutes or less and has one stop at the top of the mountain and one stop at the bottom. It is yet another option for tourists looking for the quickest and least expensive route between some of the city's attractions, including Stella Maris Carmelite Monastery, San Francisco Observation Point, Elijah's Cave, and the National Maritime Museum.

Police

The **tourist police** in nearby Tel Aviv can be reached by phone (tel. 03/516-5382) if the need arises, and they should be able to direct you to the appropriate location or service.

ATMs, Banks, and Currency Exchange

The most robust areas in town for ATMs, banks, and money-changing services are on Hanassi Boulevard near Yefe Nof Street and Ha'em Park, as well as on Ben Gurion Street in the center of the German Colony.

Inside the **Panorama Mall** (109 Hanassi Blvd., tel. 04/837-5011, 9am-8pm Sun.-Thurs., 9am-2pm Fri.) is a currency exchange desk.

GETTING THERE AND AROUND

Most visitors to Haifa arrive by car or the national Israeli intercity train. Egged buses that travel all over the country also go here. Once here, you can get around by city bus, taxi, or Israel's only underground subway—the Carmelit.

Car

Driving into Haifa is fairly simple, but once you get into the city you really need to have a GPS to navigate around Mount Carmel and through the winding, hilly streets. Take Highway 2 straight north from Tel Aviv, or Highway 1 to 2 or 6 from Jerusalem. Highway 2 is a very pretty drive along the coast in good weather, and you can even see some ancient ruins if you keep an eye out.

There are three car rental companies lined up next to each other at the northern entrance to the city. **Avis** (34 HaHistadrut St., tel. 04/861-0444, http://avis.co.il) is a familiar option, and if they cannot accommodate you, the competition is literally next door, including **Eldan** (164 HaHistadrut St., tel. 04/841-0910, www.eldan.co.il) and **Shlomo Sixt Car Rental** (48 HaHistadrut St., tel. 04/872-5525, en.shlomo.co.il).

Bus

There are buses leaving multiple times a day from Jerusalem, Tel Aviv, and elsewhere to get you into Haifa. Watch out: there are five stations within Haifa, and you could end up on the wrong side of town if you don't know where you're going. It's about a two-hour ride from Jerusalem and can be crowded on Thursdays and Fridays, especially in the late afternoon.

From Jerusalem or Tel Aviv, take an **Egged** bus (www.egged.co.il, NIS42 and up) from the Central Bus Station. Once in Haifa, there are more public Egged buses that run all over the city and even operate on the weekend, though not as frequently.

Boat

Some visitors to Haifa arrive and stay for a day or two due to a scheduled stop on their cruise ship or boat trip. The **Port of Haifa** (www.haifaport.co.il) is in the downtown area and about a 10-minute drive or 30-minute walk to the German Colony.

Train

The **Israel Railways** (www.rail.co.il) train station is a 70-minute ride from Tel Aviv and at least a three-hour ride from Jerusalem.

Cable Car

If you find yourself at Haifa's Bat Galim Promenade on the waterfront and want to get up the side of the mountain to see Stella Maris Carmelite Monastery, the **cable car** (top station on Tchernikovsky St. opposite the Stella Maris Carmelite Monastery, bottom station at the northern end of Bat Galim Promenade, www.visit-haifa.org, 10am-6pm daily, NIS29 round-trip, NIS19 one-way) is the quickest and cheapest way to go. The ride only takes about seven minutes one way, but the dangling cars are slightly rickety and it is very high up.

Subway (Carmelit)

Haifa proudly boasts the only subway in Israel, but in practice the area the **Carmelit** (http://carmelithaifa.com, 6am-midnight Sun.-Thurs., 6am-3pm Fri., after sunset-midnight Sat., single ticket about NIS7, daily ticket NIS15) covers is very limited. It can be an easy way to experience various parts of the city, and there are restaurants along the way. It is most convenient if you're traveling in a straight line between the different stations at the lower city, Wadi Nisnas, and straight up the mountain until Hanassi Boulevard. In all there are only six stations. You can buy a single, daily, or 10-ride ticket.

the Carmelit subway in Haifa

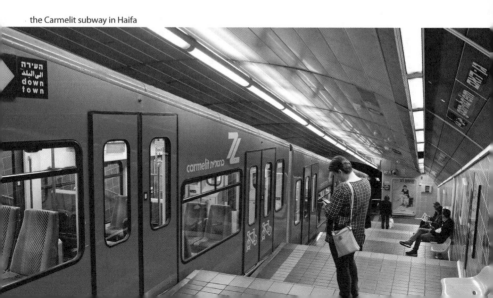

Akko (Acre)

Akko is beautiful and full of interesting nooks and crannies as well as a long and rich history. Repeatedly conquered and occupied by different civilizations throughout the ages, the Old City of Akko (also called Acre) is a UNESCO World Heritage Site. To visit Akko's Old City and wander through the ancient halls of stone with their massive, arching ceilings is to step straight into the past.

Also a favorite locale to get world-class seafood (one of the region's most famous seafood chefs operates here) and within easy driving distance of Haifa, Akko is the perfect place to spend the afternoon sightseeing and then have a delicious meal.

SIGHTS
Baha'i Gardens
Smaller than its Haifa counterpart but

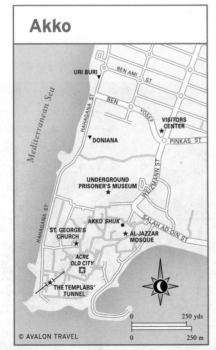

similarly designed and landscaped, the **Baha'i Gardens** (just off Hwy. 4 when entering Akko, tel. 04/831-3131, www.ganbahai.org.il/en/akko, inner gardens 9am-noon Fri.-Mon., outer gardens 9am-4pm daily, free) is the resting place of the founder of the Baha'i religion, and the location of the house where he lived during the last years of his life. The immaculate, circular gardens create a peaceful cocoon of tranquility.

★ Acre Old City
Akko's magnificent **Acre Old City** (1 Weizmann St. at southern end of HaHagana St., www.akko.org.il/en, NIS15 and up for sites, combination ticket options available, ticket office at the Enchanted Garden) is a UNESCO World Heritage Site and comprised of a complex network of buildings, sites, and museums that would take about two days to tour completely. The Crusader city is a network of walls and fortresses, knights' halls, and beautiful, golden stone that seem to whisper stories from its past as you walk through the main complex of halls, buildings, and courtyards. There are some areas that are in the process of ongoing renovations, but the collective impact is akin to stepping straight into the past.

The main buildings of the Old City, the **Hospitaller's Fortress** (8:30am-6pm Sun.-Thurs., Sat., and holidays, 8:30am-5pm Fri. and holiday eves, NIS66 for part of combined ticket) and its courtyard, were the main fortress of a monastic military order that was established to treat the sick in the Holy Land. The order had its headquarters in Akko from 1191 to 1291.

Fascinating and a bit haunting is the **Underground Prisoner's Museum** (The Citadel, tour reservations in advance at tel. 04/991-1375, 8:30am-4:30pm Sun.-Thurs., 8:30am-1:30pm Fri.), which features tons of life-size bronze statues of prisoners and other

The World of Old Acre

In 2010, UNESCO declared the Old City of Acre (Akko) a World Heritage Site of outstanding universal value, and with good reason. The designation is international recognition of its history as home to a number of different cultures throughout the centuries, and guarantees a certain degree of protection and preservation for the sake of global humanity.

Acre Old City is a historic, walled, port city that has been populated—without interruption—since the time of the Phoenicians (about 1500-300 BC) until the modern day.

Acre Old City's position on a peninsula with a natural bay made it internationally important during the time of the Crusaders. Its strategic port became a center for international trade. In the 18th century, it became the regional capital of the Ottoman Empire after a long period of decline.

One of Acre Old City's most impressive monuments to its storied history is the remains of the Crusader City (AD 1104-1291) that have stayed almost completely intact above and below the modern street level. Since the 18th century, Acre Old City in its current state has fit the characteristics of a fortified Ottoman city with typical urban elements of a citadel, mosques, *khans* (roadside inns), and baths.

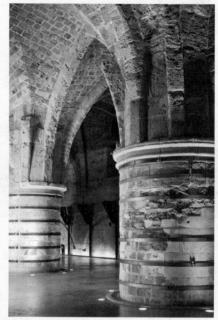

knights' halls at Acre Old City

characters who played roles in the prison's history, positioned throughout different rooms.

The **Al Basha Turkish Bath** (8:30am-6pm Sun.-Thurs., Sat., and holidays, 9am-5pm Fri. and holiday eves, NIS25) also features bronze, life-size statues of people going about their business in the bathhouse, including props and scenes of what life was like in the intact six rooms.

It takes about a 20-minute walk through backstreets to reach **The Templars' Tunnel** (9:30am-5:30pm Sun.-Thurs., Sat., and holidays, 9:30am-4:30pm Fri. and holiday eves, NIS15), used by the monastic military order called Templars that guarded European pilgrims while they were visiting the Holy Land. The main fortress of the Templars was built at the western end of the tunnel, and the tunnel extends for 350 meters underground.

The route to reach the tunnel is not well-marked, and it is necessary to ask for directions along the way. Set out by about 2pm to give yourself enough time to find the tunnel, explore it, and find your way back. You must have a ticket to enter, which you can purchase at the main ticket booth of the Old City.

Churches and Mosques

There are several ancient churches and mosques in Akko, most of which can be found on the very well-organized **website for the Old City** (www.akko.org.il/en). One of the

Akko's Al-Jazzar Mosque

churches considered among the most beautiful in the Levant is **Saint George's Church** (tel. 04/991-0563, call in advance for a visit), a Greek Orthodox establishment that was likely Akko's first Christian house of worship built during the Turkish period.

Dominating and beautiful, the **Al-Jazzar Mosque** (tel. 04/991-3039, NIS15) is brilliant green and white and looks stunning from a distance. The entrance to the mosque, one of the second largest in Israel, is up some steep steps just at the beginning of the pathway that leads to the Templars' Tunnel. According to an Arabic inscription above the front door, the mosque was inaugurated around 1781. The interior has beautiful pillars and arching below a second-floor open walkway, with inlaid inscriptions on the circumference of the inner building. There are no specific hours, but try to visit between 9am-4pm Saturday-Thursday, and avoid Fridays.

ENTERTAINMENT AND EVENTS

Renowned domestically and internationally, the **Acre Fringe Theater Festival** (Acre Old City, during the intermediate days of the Sukkot holiday in the fall, www.accofestival.

co.il, NIS40-75) has been held every year since 1979 in the Old City. The festival's events include plays, street performances, booths, and fire demonstrations. The main events are held in the Hospitaller's Fortress.

SHOPPING

Akko's two main shopping areas can be found easily by looking for the green and white Al-Jazzar Mosque. Get to the far eastern side of the Old City, and as you face the mosque, go to the left to find some shops and stores that sell a variety of items like food and basic amenities. Go to the right (with the mosque on your left) and you'll pass through a small plaza that leads into the *shuk* (outdoor market).

FOOD
Middle Eastern

A good place to stop off for lunch, **Hummus Said** (middle of the Old City market area, off of Salah ad Din St., tel. 04/991-3945, 6am-2:30pm Sun.-Fri., NIS30) serves up piles of pita, pickled *mezze* dishes, and other appetizers, as well as hummus. It has a small, humble interior with just a few tables and is extremely popular among locals and tourists. Expect a crowd if you go during the height of mealtime.

Seafood

Set up in an old Turkish house converted into a restaurant and facing the Mediterranean, ★ **Uri Buri** (11 HaHagana St., waterfront, tel. 04/955-2212, www.2eat.co.il/eng/uriburi, noon-11pm daily, NIS115) specializes in unique and masterful seafood preparation and presentation thanks to their iconic chef-owner Uri Yurmias. The interior is set up with individual rooms with Arab decor for an intimate atmosphere with limited seating, so reservations are recommended for this widely acclaimed seafood restaurant destination. Outdoor terrace seating facing the sea is also available in good weather. The dishes are inventive—Creole shrimp with spicy sauce and mangoes and fried calamari rings with three dips—and the half-orders allow you to sample more.

Also on the waterfront and situated on the third floor of the building, **Doniana** (6 HaHagana St., waterfront, tel. 04/991-0001, noon-2am daily, NIS70) is an Arab-style fish and meat restaurant with an atmosphere defined by its views of the sea and the city. The *mezze* selection has an extensive number of dishes and can be filling enough for a meal, especially around midday.

ACCOMMODATIONS

Places to stay in Akko are very few and largely limited to luxury accommodations that might not be open in the low season. It is a very short drive from Akko to other nearby cities and towns that offer more options for places to stay at a range of prices.

Over US$200

If you plan to spring for a night in Akko, try **The Efendi Hotel** (Louis XI St., P.O.B 2503, Acre Old City, tel. 074/729-9799, www.efendi-hotel.com, US$400 d), a five-star luxury boutique hotel with just 12 rooms in the historic Old City. The palatial hotel has views of the historic city walls and the Mediterranean Sea. Built from two ancient houses that were combined and restored over a period of eight years, the hotel has rooms spread out over three levels with different designs and some feature illustrations, preserved wood, sea views, and views of the ancient city of Akko and the scenic mountains of the western Galilee. Hotel services include a spa room, a 400-year-old Turkish bath, a wine bar, and a cellar from the Crusader era. Rooms feature Egyptian cotton linens, goose down pillows and blankets,

The Efendi Hotel's reception area

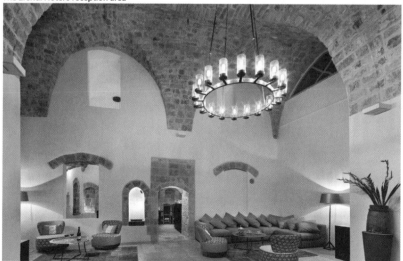

robes and slippers, marble-lined bathrooms with large showers, freestanding bathtubs, and towel warmers. There is also free wireless Internet, a minibar, and an espresso machine.

INFORMATION AND SERVICES

Akko is a tourist destination, and once you get anywhere near the Old City and Al-Jazzar Mosque, it is well-equipped to meet your needs.

Old Acre Visitors' Center

Just to the right as you enter the Enchanted Garden, the **Old Acre Visitors' Center** (1 Weizmann St., tel. 04/995-6706, 8:30am-4pm Sun.-Thurs. and Sat., 8:30am-3:30pm Fri. and holiday eves) has some useful maps and a seven-minute free introductory movie about Akko in English.

Online Resources

By far the best website about Akko, put up by the Old Acre Development Company, is www.akko.org.il/en. The website includes maps, site introductions, operating times, and background information.

ATMs and Money Exchange

The plaza in front of Al-Jazzar Mosque has a convenient combination of an ATM, bank, and money exchange services.

Police and Emergency Services

Just around the corner from the Al-Jazzar Mosque you'll find the extremely friendly and accommodating volunteer **tourist police** (9am-5pm daily).

GETTING THERE AND AROUND

Akko is very easy to reach by car by way of Highway 4 from either the north or the south. There is plenty of parking around town and plenty of signage in English to direct you to the Old City.

If you are taking a bus, from Haifa board **Egged** bus (www.egged.co.il) numbers 251 and 271. Coming from the north, take bus numbers 501 and 360. Once in the city, you can get from city center to the Old City on bus numbers 61 and 62.

The **Israel Railways** (www.rail.co.il) Akko train station is an 80-minute ride from Tel Aviv and up to 3.5 hours from Jerusalem; from the station, it is a 15-minute walk to the Old City.

Nahariya

Nahariya is a surprisingly charming little town where everyone seems to know each other. It is brimming with sweet details such as decorative lamps that line the streets. It's the perfect place to spend a low-key afternoon and evening while getting in some surfing, swimming, bike riding, or a long walk. Nahariya's city center is compact and quaint, with a nice selection of restaurants, shops, and scenery. The most enchanting aspect by day or night is the Ga'aton River that runs through the center of town and is bordered by graceful trees and a white railing. Burdened by its history as a nuclear waste dumping ground that has been in the process of getting cleaned up for years, Nahariya is small and quiet.

SIGHTS
Promenade

Pleasant even in the winter, Nahariya's long **promenade** (off of HaMa'apalim St.) is very close to the town's center and has space for running, biking, and strolling. The buildings along the promenade are well maintained, and at some points there are restaurants and coffee shops. The promenade extends south for about five miles, almost to Akko.

Grotto Caves at Rosh Hanikra

A 10-minute drive from Nahariya are the gorgeous, sparkling blue **Grotto Caves** (Rte. 4 to the northernmost part of Israel, tel. 073/271-0100, www.rosh-hanikra.com, 9am-6pm Sun.-Thurs., 9am-4pm Fri. and holiday eves, 9am-6pm Sat. and holidays Apr.-Oct.; 9am-4pm Sun.-Fri. and holiday eves, 9am-6pm Sat. and holidays mid-Oct.-Mar.; adult NIS50, senior and child NIS37) at Rosh Hanikra. About 220 yards of walking track lead down to the natural grottoes, which are lit. Located at Israel's northernmost point at the border with Lebanon, the grottoes also have a few other attractions, including a promenade, a cable car, and sea-view restaurants. The entire site of the grottoes is set up so you can experience both the grottoes and the sea at an extremely close proximity through a network of paved walkways and cable cars. Note that it's not particularly accessible to people with disabilities.

The Lieberman House Museum

Showcasing the history of the city of Nahariya and housed in the former home of one of the

Rosh Hanikra's cliffside

Nahariya

© AVALON TRAVEL

HAIFA AND THE NORTH COAST
NAHARIYA

town's first settlers, **The Lieberman House Museum** (21 Hagedud St., tel. 04/982-1516, nahariyamuseums@gmail.com, 9am-1pm Sun., Tues., and Thurs., 9am-1pm and 4pm-7pm Mon. and Wed., 9am-noon Fri., 10am-2pm Sat., free) includes an archive of photos, posters, announcements, and correspondence from Nahariya's past and the Lieberman house's past, dating from pre-1948 through today.

SHOPPING
Nahariya Mall

The very small **Nahariya Mall** (2 Irish St., Ein Sara, tel. 04/992-9977, www.nahariya-mall.co.il, 10am-9:30pm Sun.-Thurs., 9am-2:30pm Fri.) sells a variety of shoes, bags, and clothes and has a surf shop that sells equipment and might be willing to rent pieces out.

SPORTS AND RECREATION

There are several outdoor and recreational sports in and around Nahariya, including swimming, bicycling, surfing, and hiking.

Surfing

A popular pastime in Nahariya is surfing, particularly at **Sokolow (Sokolov) Beach**

(Nahum Sokolow St. at the beach end of HaGa'aton Blvd.). The beaches are clean and easily accessible. On a day with good waves (even in the middle of a workday during the week), you can expect to see at least a dozen surfers in the water. Sokolow is considered a very consistent break, with waves that can get up to about seven feet or higher.

Swimming

Look for HaGa'aton Boulevard and follow it to the sea to find plenty of spots to swim. If you need a landmark on the shore, look for the large structure that looks like boat sails. Some of the beaches cost a small fee (about NIS10) and others are free.

You'll likely see locals swimming in areas with warnings posted to not swim there, but don't be tempted to follow suit. The undertow of the Mediterranean can be very strong, even in shallow water and on a calm day. Stick to areas that are designated beaches with lifeguards. Try your luck at **Galei Galil Beach.**

Bicycling

A favorite pastime in Nahariya, biking is a good way to take in a lot of the seaside and hop into a café for lunch without tiring yourself out. Try the front desk at the centrally located Shtarkman Erna Boutique Hotel for **bicycle rentals** (29 Jabotinsky St., tel. 04/992-0170, www.sernahotel.co.il).

FOOD

Dining options in Nahariya are surprisingly plentiful, easy to access, and provide a variety of options, even late at night.

American

The **Sogo Sushi and Grill Bar** (1 Jabotinsky St., corner of HaGa'aton Blvd., tel. 04/900-0001, www.sogo-bar.co.il, 9am-3am daily, NIS55) is a restaurant by day and a dance bar by night. The interior is huge and spacious, with a massive bar and modern finishes on all of the decor. The food is a fairly standard fare of burgers, sandwiches, and salads. If you're looking for some nightlife, this is a good place to start.

Cafés

One of the oldest restaurants in town and always hopping, **Penguin** (21 HaGa'aton Blvd., tel. 04/992-8855, 9am-midnight daily, NIS55) is easy to find with the life-size penguins at the front door. The interior is simple, spacious, clean, and classy, with tons of outdoor seating and a nice wine and liquor selection. Their signature dish is schnitzel, and they also serve a wide variety of sandwiches and do a typical hearty Israeli breakfast.

ACCOMMODATIONS

Though small, Nahariya has a relatively large number of accommodations that vary from cheap motels to upscale boutique hotels. There is no reason to settle for something you're unhappy with if you wind up staying here for a night or two. Most hotels are within very easy walking distance of the beach and promenade.

US$100-150

Near the popular Galilee Beach and the train station, the ★ **Shtarkman Erna Boutique Hotel** (29 Jabotinsky St., tel. 04/992-0170, www.sernahotel.co.il, US$130 d) is a classy, understated 26-room boutique hotel. Originally opened in 1959 and since renovated and remodeled, this multi-generation, family-run hotel has air-conditioned rooms with free wireless Internet, cable TV, a telephone, and a small fridge. Some rooms have a spa bath, drinks are served in the hotel's private garden, bicycles are available for free, and there is free parking. The owners that run Shtarkman are quintessential locals and know every possible detail about their town and the surrounding area. Excursions can be arranged through the hotel staff, and guests get discounts on local restaurants and tickets to nearby historic Akko. In the month of August, guests get free entrance to a private beach and country club with swimming pools and tennis courts. Some of the rooms are on the small side by American standards, but every inch of the place makes you feel perfectly at home, including the lavish breakfast that's included in your stay.

Travel Hotel at Kibbutz Gesher Haziv (Kibbutz Gesher Haziv on HaOranim St., just north of Nahariya, tel. 04/995-8568, www.zimmeril.com, US$140 d) is a bed-and-breakfast situated north of Nahariya near the cliffs of Rosh Hanikra and a short drive from Achziv Beach. Located on a kibbutz overlooking the Mediterranean, the atmosphere of Gesher Haziv is pure Israel countryside. All 32 rooms are plainly decorated but have a warm atmosphere and include private bathrooms, air-conditioning, a television, refrigerator, microwave, and free coffee and cookies. There are several nature reserves nearby that can be explored by foot, donkey, horseback, or by jeep with a guide and driver. Located in the western Galilee, a main center of Crusader activities, the kibbutz makes it convenient to explore Crusader castles at Montfort and Yechiam and the underground Crusader city in Akko. The kibbutz offers discount coupons for all attractions and restaurants in the area, free wireless Internet in common areas, and free entrance to their pool, sports facilities, and children's playgrounds.

Camping

Just a bit north of Nahariya is the popular **Achziv National Park** (about three miles north of Nahariya on the way to Rosh Hanikra, tel. 04/982-3263, www.parks.org.il, sign in and out for camping is by noon, adult NIS37, child NIS20), which has space for camping as well as beautiful, secluded beaches. There is also a Crusader fortress in the area and the ruins of ancient Achziv.

INFORMATION AND SERVICES

As a small, coastal town, Nahariya has all the basic services you might need. The residents are extremely friendly and most speak English. If you have questions, you should feel comfortable to ask anyone you encounter on the street.

Online Resources

The best source of online information about Nahariya is the **Israel Ministry of Tourism** website (www.goisrael.com). Also full of useful information is the family-run **Shtarkman Erna Boutique Hotel**'s website (www.sernahotel.co.il), which has tons of tips and information about tourism in the area.

ATMs and Currency Exchange

Your best bet for an ATM and for changing money is the **Nahariya Mall** (2 Irish St., Ein Sara, tel. 04/992-9977, www.nahariya-mall.co.il, 10am-9:30pm Sun.-Thurs., 9am-2:30pm Fri.).

Police, Emergency, and Tourist Services

Dial 100 for the **police** and 101 for **emergency medical services** from any phone. Dial *3888 from any phone for tourism, the Israel Police, the Ministry of Interior services, the Airport Authority, and more.

GETTING THERE AND AROUND
Car

You can reach Nahariya very easily by taking Highway 4 north. It's about 40 minutes from Haifa and just over two hours from Jerusalem. Once here, it's a remarkably easy place to navigate, with tons of free parking. It's basically impossible to get lost with the Ga'aton River as a guidepost in the center of town.

Bus

The **Egged** bus (www.egged.co.il) number 960 takes about 3 hours from Jerusalem (NIS65 one-way) and bus number 910 takes about 3.5 hours from Tel Aviv (NIS73 one-way). Both have transfers in Haifa.

Once you are in Nahariya, several Egged bus lines operate throughout town.

Train

The **Israel Railways** (www.rail.co.il) train takes about three hours from Jerusalem (NIS65 one-way), and about 90 minutes from Tel Aviv (NIS48 one-way).

Netanya

A seaside resort spot that is known for its oddly 1970s-themed atmosphere and popularity among French visitors, Netanya is not a major destination for Israelis or overseas visitors. However, it is just about equidistant between Haifa and Tel Aviv and offers an alternative for exploring some low-key spots or just relaxing on the beach without the crowds you find in Tel Aviv.

SIGHTS
Parks and Nature Reserves

Netanya has several natural attractions in its vicinity that the Tourist Information Office should be able to tell you about. The **Utopia Tropical Orchard Park** (Kibbutz Bahan, tel. 09/878-2191, www.utopiapark.co.il/english, 8:30am-6pm Sun.-Thurs., 8:30am-3pm Fri., 8:30am-7pm Sat. and holidays summer, 8:30am-5pm Sun.-Thurs., 8:30am-3pm Fri., 8:30am-6pm Sat. and holidays winter, adult NIS59, senior NIS54, child NIS44) is a good option because it can be reached by bus from the Netanya Central Bus station (#33 Native Express). Kibbutz Bahan, home of the park, is the last stop on the line. The park is an incredible, lush oasis near Netanya that boasts waterfalls, a massive indoor greenhouse with tropical plants, gardens of roses, carnivorous plants, herbs, a musical water fountain, and a deck area for eating and drinking. A late morning or afternoon visit to Utopia could be a welcome respite, especially during Israel's hot, muggy summer months.

SPORTS AND RECREATION
Beaches

One of Netanya's cool features is that it has eight beaches. At the most central, **Sironit Beach** (base of Rishonim Promenade), there is a **transparent elevator** down to the beach. Buffered by piers, the water is safe for swimming almost the entire year. In the summer months, nearby restaurants provide entertainment, and there are sports tournaments and games on the beach.

Hiking

The **Israel National Trail** (www.israelnationaltrail.com, www.netanya.muni.il) passes

Netanya has safe swimming areas almost the entire year.

through Netanya, winding through some scenic areas that include the urban **purple Iris reserve,** several of the area's beaches, and the cliffs next to the city. The entire trail is about 620 miles from the Red Sea to the border with Lebanon.

INFORMATION AND SERVICES

The **Tourist Information Office** (12 Ha'azmaut Sq., tel. 09/882-7286, 8am-4pm Sun.-Thurs., 9am-2pm Fri.) is right at the town center and offers information about Netanya and the surrounding area.

The **Netanya Board of Tourism** (www. gonetanya.com) has a great website that provides a lot of basic information for visitors.

GETTING THERE AND AROUND

Israel Railways (www.rail.co.il) has a train station in Netanya. The train ride is about 30 minutes from Tel Aviv (NIS16 one-way) and two hours from Jerusalem (NIS38 one-way).

Netanya is a 30-minute drive from Tel Aviv just off of Highway 2, or 45 minutes off of Highway 4.

From Jerusalem, take **Egged** bus (www. egged.co.il) number 947 from the Central Bus Station (NIS32 one-way), which takes about 90 minutes. From Tel Aviv, take bus number 641 (NIS20 one-way), which takes close to 2 hours.

Caesarea (Qesarya)

Caesarea is two towns: the ancient city and the modern, rural town that is a favorite vacation home site for wealthy Israelis. The ruins of ancient Caesarea can be seen alongside the modern town. The main highlight is the massive Antiquities Park with a few other smaller, but notable attractions.

SIGHTS
★ Caesarea National Antiquities Park

The **Caesarea National Antiquities Park** (off Hwy. 2 near Kibbutz Sdot Yam, tel. 04/626-7080, www.parks.org.il, 8am-6pm Sun.-Thurs., 8am-5pm Fri. Apr.-Sept., 8am-4pm Sun.-Thurs., 8am-3pm Fri. Oct.-Mar., NIS40) is unique in that it has buildings from different historical periods. Spanning a time period of about 2,300 years, the park covers an area of about 125 acres and includes archaeological remnants from the Hellenistic period (the 3rd century BC) to the Crusader period (the 12th century AD), during a time when Caesarea was a port city and Israel's capital.

Named for Augustus Caesar, who gave the city to King Herod, Caesarea was built up by

the Roman baths in the Caesarea National Antiquities Park

Caesarea (Qesarya)

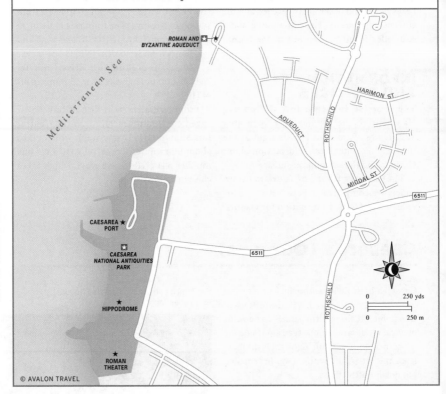

© AVALON TRAVEL

Herod to include venues for entertainment, bathhouses, and places of worship. Touring through the Antiquities Park allows you to wander in between ancient buildings and ruins, including the **Hippodrome** and the still used **Roman Amphitheater.**

Situated inside the national park, the **Caesarea Port** (tel. 04/626-8882, www. caesarea.com) is an intoxicating mixture of ancient and modern, including the ancient **Crusader City.** Aside from the ancient port itself, there is a beach, restaurants, galleries, and more. Here you can also find the multimedia **Travel Through Time** (long building next to the jetty, English presentation every 15 min.) that tells Caesarea's history in three stations: a short movie of the city's history from ancient times through today, a 3D interactive presentation on the impact of different historical figures, and a computer-generated show that depicts the city's construction masterpieces throughout history from the time of Herod onward.

Caesarea Antiquities Museum

Just at the southern entrance of Caesarea is the **Caesarea Antiquities Museum** (Kibbutz Sdot Yam, tel. 04/636-4367, www. parks.org.il, 10am-4pm Sun.-Thurs., 10am-1pm Fri., NIS15), home to a wealth of treasures from the Mediterranean Sea and the surrounding area, including ancient coins, late Roman sculptures, Roman and Byzantine gems and jewelry, and pottery.

Many of the finds here were dug up from the ground in the surrounding area by residents on the kibbutz over the past several decades.

★ Roman and Byzantine Aqueduct

More part of the scenery than a destination, the **Roman and Byzantine Aqueduct** (shore of the Mediterranean Sea, end point in Caesarea at Aqueduct Beach, 24 hours, free) is just a few miles east of modern Caesarea proper. It runs along the seashore in a stunning display of ancient engineering.

There are several portions of the aqueduct, some of which are underground. You can see another section along Highway 2 between Caesarea and Haifa. The portion nearest Caesarea was built by the Romans in the 2nd century AD and was repaired many times, so portions of the still-remaining aqueduct are different ages.

The raised stone aqueduct was used to bring water to the old city of Caesarea, and a large portion of it is still intact. The incredible architecture and engineering of the aqueduct is apparent despite its somewhat crumbling facade. But overall, it has held up remarkably well and is still incredibly beautiful, especially against the backdrop of the Mediterranean Sea. It stops short of reaching Caesarea because part of the aqueduct has not survived.

If you're adventurous and in good enough shape, you can climb up on top of the aqueduct at Aqueduct Beach in Caesarea, and walk along the top.

Birds Mosaic Floor

Believed to be part of a large villa dating back to the 6th or 7th century BC, the **Birds Mosaic Floor** (about 0.25 miles from the Antiquities Park, free) was likely part of a large, open courtyard. Several other parts of the villa had mosaic floors and have also been discovered at the site. The area is open, you can walk on the mosaic, and it is easy to spot.

Tours

For a guided day trip to Caesarea plus a couple of other areas, **Egged Tours** (www.egged-tours.com, Sun., Tues., and Fri., US$115 from Jerusalem, US$102 from Tel Aviv) has a one-day tour that also includes Akko and Rosh Hanikra. The tours depart from Jerusalem at 5:50am and from Tel Aviv at 7:15am.

the ancient Roman and Byzantine Aqueduct at Caesarea

ENTERTAINMENT AND EVENTS

Particularly in the summer, Caesarea is fun to experience in the evenings with its natural ambience of the ancient port and outdoor seating at cafés. It's not Tel Aviv, but it has a nice rhythm to it.

Concerts at the Roman Amphitheater

During the summer months, the ancient **Roman Amphitheater** (Caesarea National Antiquities Park, tel. 04/626-7080, www.parks.org.il) holds outdoor concerts in a magical, unforgettable setting. There is no official website for upcoming concerts, but you can try searching **Eventim** (www.eventim.co.il) close to the date you are interested in.

Festivals

Every year during the months of July and August on Tuesday nights, different events are held at the port near the art gallery market and food stands for **Caesarea Nights.** Events, which include movie screenings, are scattered throughout the port area.

SHOPPING

A great place to shop for gifts and souvenirs is the **Caesarea Port** where you can find jewelry, ceramics, and Judaica items.

SPORTS AND RECREATION

Caesarea's main distinction for sports enthusiasts is its 18-hole international golf course, the only one of its kind in Israel. There are also some great places to go swimming and diving.

Parks and Beaches

One of the best beaches to visit in the Caesarea area is **Aqueduct Beach** (free), which you will see signs for as you drive through town. There is free parking, but there are no restrooms or places to change.

Golf

The **Caesarea Golf Club and Professional Golf Course** (Golf neighborhood, tel. 04/610-9600, golf@caesarea.com, 6am-6:30pm Tues.-Sun. summer, 6am-5pm Tues.-Sun. winter, NIS480 for 18 holes) was established in the 1960s by the Baron Edmond de Rothschild family and is the only international golf club in Israel. The grounds of the club include training ranges, a perfectly groomed course, a pro shop, and a gourmet restaurant. In 2009, the course was redesigned by internationally renowned golf course designer Pete Dye.

Diving

The **Old Caesarea Diving Center** (Caesarea National Antiquities Park main entrance, tel. 04/626-5898, www.caesarea-diving.com) is in a unique location on the ancient ruins of Herod's now-submerged port. The center operates the **Underwater Archaeological Park** with preserved underwater treasures and marine flora and fauna. Both certified and inexperienced divers are welcome, and you can get guided and independent diving and snorkeling, lessons, and gear for rent.

FOOD
Seafood

In the heart of Caesarea's old town is the delightful **Helena** (Old Town Caesarea Port, tel. 053/809-4915, www.2eat.co.il/eng/helena, noon-11pm daily, NIS110), a gourmet restaurant run by two leading chefs in Israel. The star of the restaurant's decor is the view of the sea and port from the massive outdoor deck that is mostly covered from the hot sun. The interior is extremely simple with hardwood floors and ceiling fans. The menu's Mediterranean style features mainly seafood dishes, including a rich bouillabaisse. They also do a nice fish fillet that is served on a bed of gnocchi with cream sauce, mushrooms, and spinach and offer an extensive wine and alcohol menu as well as a discounted business lunch.

Cafés

Port Café (The Port, tel. 04/610-0221, www.portcafe.co.il, 8:30am-last customer daily, NIS70) has a great view and delectable dishes for any time of the day or night. It's a good bet for breakfast omelets and other egg dishes, salads, tapas, pizza, and seafood entrées. The exterior has an ancient stone look, and the interior furniture gives the feeling of being on a ship, with heavy, worn wooden tables, deck, and railings. The café has an extensive wine and alcohol menu, including cocktails.

ACCOMMODATIONS

It is a tempting place to stay overnight, but Caesarea is strangely lacking choices for accommodations, particularly in the summer months. The only real hotel in the area is the extremely expensive Dan Caesarea.

Over US$200

Luxury and location combine to make the Dan Caesarea (1 Rothschild St., tel. 04/626-9111, www.danhotels.com/caesareahotels, US$300 d) an oasis-like experience. Surrounded by acres of private landscaped gardens, the hotel is just next door to Israel's only 18-hole golf course. The four-star hotel is less than a mile from the Mediterranean Sea and offers a large outdoor swimming pool, supervised activities for children, a spa, and sports courts. Many of the sleek, clean rooms in this 114-room hotel include views of the golf course and surrounding grounds and spacious private patios. The rooms are simply furnished and flooded with light, and every guest gets free wireless Internet, buffet breakfast, and parking. There are also four restaurants, 24-hour front desk, and town car service.

Two other great options if you want to stay in the area for a few nights are to go to nearby Zichron Ya'akov or to get a vacation rental through Aloha Caesarea Vacation Rentals (tel. 054/425-8045, www.aloha.co.il, US$170 d and up), which can accommodate a variety of needs and groups. They also have accommodations in nearby areas.

INFORMATION AND SERVICES

The Caesarea Development Corporation (www.caesarea.com) has a useful website with plenty of photos and basic information about visiting the area.

GETTING THERE AND AROUND

It is very easy to get to Caesarea by car, but there is no direct train and the bus involves a transfer at a junction.

Car

Take Highway 2 about 30 minutes past Tel Aviv and follow the exit signs for Caesarea. Follow the road until you see the anchor sculpture, turn right, and go to the end of the road to the visitors' parking lot.

Bus

From Jerusalem, take the Egged bus (www.egged.co.il) number 972 from Jerusalem to Hadera (about an hour and 45 minutes, NIS32), and then transfer to the Nateev Express (www.nateevexpress.com) bus number 76 or 77.

Train

From Jerusalem it is a 2.5-hour train ride on Israel Railways (www.rail.co.il) to the Binyamina station (NIS46 one-way). From Tel Aviv it is only 30 minutes (NIS27) to Binyamina. From the train station, take one of the waiting taxis to your destination (approx. NIS45). It's about a 15-20-minute taxi ride.

Zichron Ya'akov

Situated on a mountainside overlooking the sea, Zichron Ya'akov is a sweet oasis in the hills just off the highway. It makes for a perfect place to stop for a meal or stay for a night. It has the feel of a village, and the town center's pedestrian mall has been carefully cultivated in a European style with a pedestrian restaurant and shopping area complete with live street performances during the warm summer months.

SIGHTS
Town Center
The main point of interest in town is the quaint, idyllic **Town Center** (Hameyasdim St.), also known as the Midrahov. Once you're in Zichron Ya'akov, just follow the many signs to find the *Midrahov*, or ask anybody. The place is so small you can't get lost.

Once in Zichron Ya'akov, you can easily spend a leisurely afternoon or evening enjoying a meal and coffee, browsing through the many interesting shops for souvenirs, and listening to street musicians perform.

First Aliyah Museum
It is very small, but the **First Aliyah Museum** (2 Hanadiv St., tel. 04/629-4777, 9am-2pm Mon. and Wed.-Fri., 9am-3pm Tues., NIS15) is interesting for a look at how early settlers dealt with life in Israel. Directly across the street from the gorgeous Gan Tiyyul (Strolling Garden), the museum tells stories of immigrants who came to then-Palestine, particularly Zichron Ya'akov, in the first wave of Jewish immigration that began in 1882. There are multimedia presentations, sculptures, photographs, and English descriptions of the exhibits on two floors in the tightly packed quarters.

Carmel Wine and Culture
Housed in a wine cellar that was built in 1892 by Baron Edmond de Rothschild, the **Carmel Wine and Culture** (20 Derech Ha'Yayin/ Winery St., tel. 04/629-0977, www.carmel-wines.co.il, 9:30am-5pm Sun.-Thurs., 9am-2pm Fri. and holiday eves, NIS25 and up for tastings) is a must-see for any wine enthusiast.

Carmel Wine and Culture, built by Baron Edmond de Rothschild

Zichron Ya'akov

© AVALON TRAVEL

The complex includes a wine shop, a wine and culture center, a restaurant, two specialist tasting rooms, a small cinema, and a barrel room in one of Rothschild's historic underground cellars. A variety of wine workshops, winery tours, and tutored tastings are available, some of which require reservations.

SPORTS AND RECREATION
Parks and Beaches

At the southeastern entrance to Zichron Ya'akov is **Ramat Hanadiv Nature Reserve** (Rte. 652 between Zichron Ya'akov and Binyamina, tel. 04/629-8111, www.ramat-hanadiv.org.il, 8am-4pm Sun.-Thurs., 8am-2pm Fri., 8am-4pm Sat., crypt closed on Sat., free), which includes a memorial garden and a nature reserve. It is also the final resting place of Baron Edmond de Rothschild and his wife. The reserve has four circular routes with gorgeous vistas. There are also archaeological relics scattered throughout and the Ein Tzur spring. The park is home to a kosher dairy restaurant (04/844-9979) and a snack kiosk.

There are a few beaches nearby, but the closest authorized one is **Dor Beach** (just off Hwy. 4, NIS12), which is very clean, pretty, and has plenty of nice sand.

FOOD

Throw a rock in the town center and you'll hit a restaurant, coffee shop, pub, or café of almost every size and type. The hard part is making a choice.

The extremely popular **Nili Wine** (43 HaMeyasdim St., tel. 04/629-2899, www.nili-restaurant.com, 8am-11pm Sun.-Thurs., 8am-1:30pm Fri., NIS70) serves kosher food with Italian, Japanese, and European touches, and an array of regional wines. The egg dishes have a decidedly French influence, while the various pasta dishes are reminiscent of Tuscany. Nili's Japanese dishes include seafood dishes and seaweed salad. A specialty is the cheese plate with five types of regional cheeses on a platter with raw vegetables, dips, and bread.

ACCOMMODATIONS
US$150-200

Distinguished largely because of its charm but in part because of its lack of competition, the ★ **Hotel Beit Maimon** (4 Zahal St., tel. 04/629-0390, www.maimon.com, US$190 d) is located in the hills of lovely and picturesque Zichron Ya'akov, just half an hour south of Haifa. The small, 25-room hotel has an on-premises restaurant, room service for drinks, and some rooms with breathtaking views of the Mediterranean Sea. Every room has air-conditioning, a 32-inch LCD TV, direct-dial telephone, wireless Internet, a refrigerator, and bathroom with a shower, and some rooms have a connecting door and a large whirlpool bathtub overlooking the sea. There is also an outdoor whirlpool tub on the second floor.

Over US$200

An option about 20 minutes from Zichron Ya'akov is **The Castle** (Old Tel Aviv Haifa Rd. 4-10, Kerem Maharal, tel. 054/720-0661, www.thecastle.co.il, US$350 d), which makes up for in uniqueness what it lacks in available rooms—there are only four. The 900-year-old Crusader fort from the 11th century is just 30 minutes south of Haifa near the coast, and caters to travelers seeking a unique vacation. The only structure in Israel from this period that is privately owned, The Castle was built as a home for the ruler of the area and has been painstakingly restored. Two suites have a balcony and two have a garden. The interior features massive stone bathtubs, and paintings and artwork created by one of the owners. There is free wireless Internet throughout (when it's working), free parking, 24-hour concierge service, a dining area, a fully equipped shared kitchen, and a panoramic balcony with an incredible view of the countryside. Nearby activities include horseback riding, cookout facilities, bicycle rental, and picnic lunches.

Part hotel and part arts hub is the **Elma Arts Complex Luxury Hotel** (1 Yair St., tel. 04/630-0111, www.elma-hotel.com, US$370 d), a 95-room property that has many rooms divided into distinct buildings and cottages, each with its own style. The advance purchase rates directly through the hotel website offer significantly lower prices on rooms, and the modern, spacious interiors include many options with views of the sea. A stay here includes free wireless Internet, a pool with a poolside restaurant and bar, a spa, an espresso bar, and room service. Some of the rooms are used by artists for extended periods of creative work, and the hotel is home to the Elstein Gallery with 750 square meters of exhibition space.

INFORMATION AND SERVICES

Just next to the Founder's Monument on Hameyasdim Street is the **Gidonim Tourism Information Centre** (tel. 04/639-8811, gidonim@bezeqint.net, 8:30am-1pm Mon.-Thurs.), where you can inquire—in advance—about arranging a tour in English.

The **Tourism Development Agency of Zichron Ya'akov** (www.zy1882.co.il) has some useful information.

Hanadiv Street pedestrian mall is the best place to find most services, including ATMs.

GETTING THERE AND AROUND

Zichron Ya'akov is relatively easy to reach, especially if you remember that the spelling of the town's name changes from sign to sign as you drive. It is well known, though, so there is no problem asking for directions.

Car

If traveling by car, take Highway 2 to Route 70 and the exit for Zichron Ya'akov. It is about an hour from Tel Aviv. From Jerusalem, take Highway 6 to Route 70, which takes about 90 minutes.

Train

Binyamina Train Station is about a 12-minute drive from Zichron Ya'akov. The **Israel Railways** (www.rail.co.il) train takes 2.5 hours from Jerusalem (NIS85 round-trip) and 50 minutes from Tel Aviv (NIS40 round-trip).

Bus

From Jerusalem the **Egged** bus (www.egged.co.il) to Zichron Ya'akov transfers at Tel Aviv, stops at the Binyamina Train Station, and takes 2.5 hours (NIS46 one-way). From Tel Aviv it is a 90-minute ride (NIS28 one-way) that also lands you at the train station. From there you will need to take a taxi.

The Galilee and the Golan Heights

Highlights

★ **Mount of Beatitudes:** The site where Jesus gave the Sermon on the Mount near Tiberias is one of the most peaceful spots in all of Israel (page 197).

★ **Capernaum:** The ruins and church at Capernaum, a city where Jesus once lived and taught, weave a magical web of mystery on the shores of the Sea of Galilee (page 198).

★ **Basilica of the Annunciation:** This cavernous, modern church in Nazareth yields a wealth of lovely details, including a huge collection of wall mosaics from all over the world depicting the Virgin Mary and Jesus (page 206).

★ **Beit She'an:** Tucked into a crevice between the borders with Jordan and the West Bank, magnificent Beit She'an has massive and remarkably well-preserved Roman columns (page 211).

★ **Gan Garoo Australia-Israel Park:** Animal lovers will enjoy the pure fun that awaits them at Gan Garoo, where kangaroos and other Australian animals live (page 212).

Northern Israel has vast spaces of nothing but rolling green hills, punctuated by significant cultural and religious sites such as Nazareth, Tiberias, and Capernaum, to name a few.

This is one of the most beautiful parts of the region and a perfect place to escape for an excursion into the countryside. Aside from religious attractions, northern Israel has beautiful scenery, world-class wine, archaeological and historical sites, outstanding sports and recreation, and interesting people.

East of Haifa is Nazareth, the town where Jesus lived for much of his life. Also built up the side of a mountain, upper Nazareth has some incredibly steep and narrow roads. The Old City of Nazareth is full of interesting sights including an outdoor market, but the main attraction is the Church of the Annunciation, a modern Catholic church built over the ruins of Byzantine and Crusader churches.

Though the Golan Heights (both upper and lower) and the Galilee are full of hiking, biking, camping, and swimming spots, the anchor of the region is the Sea of Galilee. The sea is the main water source for Israel and home to a number of significant sights, including the ancient town of Tiberias and the ruins at Capernaum, where Jesus once taught and lived. It was near Capernaum that Jesus gave the Sermon on the Mount and turned a few fish and loaves of bread into enough food to feed thousands. There are so many legends and so much history in the Golan and Galilee that after spending a few nights here, it's easy to slip into an introspective, philosophical state of mind.

ORIENTATION

The Sea of Galilee (*Kinneret* in Hebrew) is home to one of the lowest-lying lakes in the world and is only about 31 miles around, with its eastern shore in the Golan Heights and its western shore in the Galilee. The area is full of religious history and legends, and numerous very well-preserved archaeological sites. The two main cities in the region are Nazareth, situated essentially in the middle of the region, and Tiberias, on the western shore of the sea.

Previous: a boat on the Sea of Galilee; the hills of Golan. **Above:** pilgrims at the chapel at the Mount of Beatitudes.

The Galilee and the Golan Heights

Mediterranean Sea

LEBANON

GOLAN HEIGHTS

KIRYAT SHMONA

Shlomi

Ma'alot-Tarshiha

Sasa

JISH
Jish
Dalton

Nahariya

Tsafat
Elifelet

SEE "TIBERIAS AND THE SEA OF GALILEE" MAP

Akko

Karmiel

Korazim
MOUNT OF BEATITUDES

CAPERNAUM

Sakhanin

Arraba

Migdal

Sea of Galilee

Kiryat Ata

NORTHERN DISTRICT

HAIFA DISTRICT

Tur'an

Tiberias

SEE "NAZARETH" MAP

Nazareth Illit

Nazareth

Kinneret

Migdal HaEmek

BASILICA OF THE ANNUNCIATION

MT PRECIPICE

Kfar Tavor

Afikim

JORDAN

Yokneam

Ahuzat Barak

ISRAEL

AFULA

MEGIDDO NATIONAL PARK

GILBOA GUEST HOUSE-BENHARIM

SHE'AN NIGHTS

WEST BANK

GAN GAROO AUSTRALIA-ISRAEL PARK

BEIT SHE'AN

© AVALON TRAVEL

0   5 mi
0   5 km

The Undefined Territory of the Golan Heights

Depending on who you ask about the status of the Golan Heights, you'll get a different answer; the geography alone can be confusing.

The area known as the Golan Heights runs from Mount Hermon in the north, at the intersection of the borders of Lebanon, Syria, and Israel, to the south at Hamat Gader and the intersection of the borders of Jordan, Israel, and the West Bank. The western side of the Golan Heights hugs the shoreline of the Sea of Galilee and the 1949 Israel-Syria armistice line. On the eastern border of the Golan Heights is the complex, layered border of the 1974 ceasefire maintained by the United Nations Disengagement Observer Force, then as a DMZ buffer zone, and then the official border of Syria.

Israel considers the Golan Heights of significant strategic importance for three reasons: the presence of a defensible land border, a buffer for northern Israel from artillery fire, and access to the country's most significant water source in the Sea of Galilee. In 1981, Israel officially put the Golan Heights under Israeli law, jurisdiction, and administration, but its status as part of Israel is not universally accepted in the international community. There are some security considerations here, particularly in respect to bordering Syria.

Much of the region has year-round hiking trails, hot springs, and different types of ecotourism. A major baptismal site for pilgrims in the Jordan River is here, at Yardenit. The entire region seems vast on a map, but is actually relatively easy to navigate from one point to another by car or bus and even by foot in some areas.

PLANNING YOUR TIME

Set aside about three days and nights to explore the Golan and the Galilee. A rental car is highly recommended in the interest of time and for the flexibility of seeing different sights, but you can also get around to most areas by bus.

Good options for a base include Tiberias, which allows for a high degree of accessibility to nearby sites and towns. Ginosar is also a good, lower-cost option. If you're feeling adventurous, it is feasible to hop across the Galilee and Golan by staying in Nazareth, Tiberias, Ginosar, and other small towns.

Tiberias and the Sea of Galilee

Tiberias is a medium-size town of about 40,000 on the western shore of the Sea of Galilee and the largest town on the Galilee. It caters to domestic and international tourists, though some of its ancient sites are abandoned or not well preserved. It has been continuously occupied for thousands of years and encompasses historical and religious sites of Christian, Jewish, and Muslim origin in the town and nearby. The majority of the population is Jewish, and at more than 656 feet below sea level, it is the lowest city in Israel and gets extremely hot and humid in the summer.

The Sea of Galilee has a very narrow strip of land along most of the eastern shore that is on the Israeli side of the 1949 Israeli-Syrian armistice line. Most activities on the eastern shore include water sports and outdoor adventures. Past the 1949 line toward Syria is the territory known as the Golan.

Tiberias and the Sea of Galilee

CANAAN GALLERY CAFE
Tsafat
ROSH PINNA
890
90
Elifelet
89
GOLAN HEIGHTS
888
87
827
92
85
Korazim
90
87
NORTHERN
MOUNT OF BEATITUDES
MONASTERY OF THE TWELVE APOSTLES
65
CAPERNAUM
CHURCH OF THE MULTIPLICATION
Tabgha
RAMOT RESORT HOTEL
Ramot
807
Ginosar
90
Migdal
Sea of Galilee
789
ISRAEL'S KITCHEN AT ARBEL GUEST HOUSE
SEE "TIBERIAS" MAP
7717
92
77
Tiberias
TOMB OF RABBI MEIR
768
EIN GEV HOLIDAY RESORT
98
90
Kinneret
0   2.5 mi
767
RIVER BISTRO BAR
Ma-agan
92
0   2.5 km
YARDENIT
90

© AVALON TRAVEL

HISTORY

Believed to be one of the earliest settlements dating back to the Early Bronze Age in the land known today as Israel, Tiberias was named in honor of the Roman emperor in AD 18. Following the destruction of the Second Temple in Jerusalem, many Jews fled to Tiberias, and the city eventually became an important center of religious Jewish learning. Tiberias is where the Mishnah, a commentary on the Torah, is believed to have been put together by powerful rabbis of the day. The Jewish Great Rabbinical Court was also located in Tiberias.

Key to the city's development is the nearby natural hot springs, renowned for its curative and therapeutic properties. Throughout the ages, Tiberias became known as one of Judaism's four holy cities.

The area around the Sea of Galilee is also deeply important to Christians. At a certain point in his life, Jesus is believed to have moved his base of activities to the northern shore of the Galilee, where several widely recognized miracles took place, including the multiplication of the bread and fish for the masses and walking on water. The significance of Jesus's activities here led to the establishment of many churches in the area after Christianity began to spread.

SIGHTS

Many of the more remarkable and interesting sights in Tiberias are just to the north, while the main attractions of the town are centered around the beautiful, long waterfront promenade with its many restaurants and cafés. Near the black basalt walls of the old city you'll see some ruins that are abandoned and lacking in any explanation of their history. Most of the sites in the area are Christian holy sites and burial sites of Jewish sages.

Tomb of Rabbi Akiva

Just up the mountainside behind the Kiryat Moshe neighborhood of Tiberias is the small, domed **Tomb of Rabbi Akiva** (off Yohanan Ben Zakai St., on Trumpeldor St. north of town center, 24 hours daily, reception hours vary, free), a Jewish sage born in AD 50 who was killed for supporting the Bar Kochba revolt. The tomb has long been a pilgrimage site where devout believers pray for rain during drought years.

Tomb of Maimonides

Near the Tomb of Rabbi Akiva is the final resting place of a popular sage and philosopher. The **Tomb of Maimonides** (off Yohanan Ben Zakai St., north of Tiberias town center, 24 hours daily, free) is known as a place to pray for good fortune, especially for a family. Also known as Ramban, Maimonides was employed in the court of the revered Muslim leader Saladin as his physician. The site features a symbolic walkway to the tomb with seven columns on each side with religious inscriptions and a stream of water next to them.

The Black Stones of Tiberias

While visiting Tiberias and the surrounding region, you'll likely notice that many of the buildings are constructed with a distinctive black stone. The stone is volcanic black basalt, typical of the region and commonly found in Tiberias and nearby, particularly in older buildings.

The old tradition of using black basalt to construct buildings is fading away in modern times due to the need for structures to be more durable and less susceptible to damage during earthquakes. Though black basalt is beautiful and unique, it is not as safe or hard-wearing as modern building materials.

The old city of Tiberias is easy to distinguish from the newer areas by the clear demarcation of medieval black basalt walls and the contrasting white plaster in between the stones.

Tiberias

There is a large metal structure covering the tomb complex that symbolizes a crown, a mark of respect in Jewish tradition.

Tomb of Rabbi Meir

The resting place of a well-known sage and one of Judaism's holiest sites is the **Tomb of Rabbi Meir** (south end of Tiberias near Ha'Marchatzaot Rd., just below the Tiberias hot springs, 8am-5pm Sun.-Thurs., 8am-2pm Fri., free), a Sephardic tomb with a blue-domed roof that overlooks the Galilee. Meir's nickname Ba'al Haneis means "miracle worker," based on a legend that he saved his sister-in-law from the Romans with a single prayer. Jews around the world give charity in Rabbi Meir's name, and his tomb is a popular place for religious Jews to celebrate the first haircut of their three-year-old boys and pray for divine intervention. Every year, one month after Passover and four days before the holiday of Lag b'Omer, thousands of believers flock to the tomb and light huge bonfires.

Marina and Old City

Along the shore of the Sea of Galilee in Tiberias is the lively and bustling **marina** and its wide selection of restaurants, shops, and beautiful views. The boats docked in the marina used to sell regular rides across the Sea of Galilee, but in recent years the tradition has declined and now it can be hard to hire a ride on the water, particularly in the low season or unless you are with a group.

The **old city** sits at the southern end of town and consists of a partial wall and a few buildings mixed in with the modern architecture. The end of the old city marks the beginning of the promenade.

Dona Gracia Hotel and Museum

A former castle holds the **Dona Gracia Hotel and Museum** (3 Haprachim St., tel. 04/671-7176, www.donagracia.com), dedicated to a Jewish woman named Dona Gracia, who used her wealth to save many Jews from the Spanish Inquisition and establish a Jewish city in Tiberias. The different halls of the museum tell Gracia's story using scenery, visuals, and audio, and the main exhibit uses miniatures to depict different scenes. It is possible to request to dress in one of the hotel-museum's 16th-century-style costumes for a souvenir picture.

Tabgha

Tabgha is a Greek word that means seven springs. In a cove on the northwestern shore of the Sea of Galilee is **Tabgha** (Rte. 87, Ginosar), known for being where many miracles recorded in the Bible occurred, including the miracle of Jesus multiplying three loaves of bread and two fish into enough to feed 5,000.

The event is marked by the **Church of the Multiplication** (tel. 04/670-0180, 10am-5pm Sun., 8:30am-5pm Mon.-Sat., free), a Christian church with a very simple interior that is a replica of a 4th-century basilica, with an outer courtyard and fish pond. The highlights of the church include a famed mosaic floor of a basket of bread flanked by two fish, and a rock underneath the church's main altar, which is believed to be the actual rock that Jesus blessed and broke the bread on.

From the church you can walk along a promenade about 200 yards to the very simple and boxy black basalt **Church of the Primacy of St. Peter** (tel. 04/672-4767, 8am-noon and 2pm-5pm daily, free), the site where Jesus is said to have appeared to his disciples after his resurrection and forgiven Peter for denying him on the night of his trial. The church is built over a flat rock called the Table of Christ where it's believed a fire was lit for Jesus to have breakfast with his disciples. The church is also at the site where the miraculous catch of fish is said to have occurred.

★ Mount of Beatitudes

Situated atop the **Mount of Beatitudes**, where Jesus is believed to have given the

the Church of the Multiplication

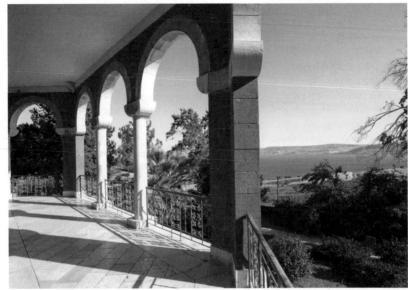
view of the Sea of Galilee from the church at the Mount of Beatitudes

Sermon on the Mount, is a gray-domed **Roman-Catholic church** (Rte. 8177, off Rte. 90, tel. 04/679-0978, 8am-noon and 2:30pm-5pm daily Apr.-Sept., 8am-noon and 2:30pm-4pm daily Oct.-Mar., NIS5 parking per car), surrounded by colonnaded walkways at the end of a garden.

The gardens are dotted with fountains and decorative tablets inscribed with excerpts from the sermon, and the hillside slopes down toward the Galilee, forming a natural amphitheater. This is where people believe Jesus gave the sermon, and there are plenty of benches and places to sit in the gardens and look out over the sea and quietly contemplate the surroundings.

The interior of the church is small and simple and features a beautiful gold-ceilinged dome and a colonnaded portico that looks out over the Galilee. The site is run by warm and friendly nuns who are available to answer questions.

★ Capernaum

A large parking lot by the Galilee and a long path along the shoreline leads to **Capernaum** (off Rte. 87 north of Tiberias, tel. 04/672-1059, 8:30am-11:30am and 3:30pm-4:45pm daily, NIS5), one of the most astonishing sites in the area. Something about the ruins, which include remarkable foundations, colonnades, and even seats of an ancient synagogue, evokes a living feeling of the ancient past.

Not far from the foundation of the synagogue are the remains of a large limestone relief that used to be on the exterior of the synagogue. The detailed carved pictures on the stone include typical religious Jewish symbols and images of a synagogue.

Capernaum is the town where Jesus is said to have lived for three years and performed numerous miracles, including healing Peter's mother-in-law and raising the synagogue leader's daughter from the dead.

A modern church sits above the ruins of a church that was built on the site of Peter's house. You can see the ruins of the old church and its mosaic floor through a glass viewing floor. Throughout the site you can see small pieces of white paper with prayers written on them that have been folded up and placed in areas that are considered holy.

the ruins of the synagogue at Capernaum

Capernaum is relatively small and easy to walk about; it includes an information desk and a snack shop. Modest dress is required: Keep your shoulders and legs covered.

Monastery of the Twelve Apostles

The Greek Orthodox **Monastery of the Twelve Apostles** (Rte. 87 at Kfar Nahum Junction, tel. 04/672-2282, capernaum1@ gmail.com, 10am-5pm daily but call in advance because hours vary, free) is easy to spot by its unusual pink-domed roof. The church isn't large, but its interior is remarkably detailed and ornate, and every inch of the walls seems to be adorned with paintings of the 12 apostles and scenes from their lives.

Yardenit

At the point where the Jordan River starts to flow out of the Sea of Galilee is the **Yardenit** baptismal site (Kibbutz Kinneret off Rte. 90, tel. 04/675-9111, www.yardenit.com, 8am-6pm Sun.-Thurs., 8am-4pm Fri. Mar.-Nov., 8am-5pm Sun.-Thurs., 8am-4pm Fri. Dec.-Feb., last baptism one hour before closing,

closed on Yom Kippur, free entrance, $10 robe rental). A large limestone building marks the entrance, and baptisms can be performed in the river or in one of the 12 baptismal pools, though you should bring something to wear underneath if you plan on wearing a baptism robe. There are changing facilities, a gift shop, and snacks on-site. The general atmosphere of Yardenit is a bit commercial and touristy, though scores of pilgrims do visit every year to enter the waters. This is one location on the Jordan River that claims to be the site where Jesus was baptized by John, though there are other baptismal sites that are easy to reach.

Magdala

Recently uncovered archaeological remains revealed the site of **Magdala** (Migdal Junction on the western coast of Sea of Galilee at Mt. Arbel, tel. 04/620-9900, www.magdala. org, 8am-6pm daily, NIS15, children under 12 free), a 1st-century synagogue and city. The oldest archaeological site excavated in the Galilee, and one of only seven 1st-century synagogues ever found in Israel, Magdala is believed to be a former location where Jesus

the Monastery of the Twelve Apostles

taught. The site includes an archaeological park, modern chapels, and a visitors center, seaside chapel, and more facilities that are under construction.

ENTERTAINMENT AND EVENTS

There is not a lot to speak of when it comes to entertainment and events in and around Tiberias. It is a fairly low-key area, but one exception is the annual **Jacob's Ladder Festival** (Ginosar, tel. 04/685-0403, www.jlfestival.com, May, NIS225 and up), a three-day festival of food, wine, and live music in Ginosar, just a 15-minute drive up the Galilee shore from Tiberias.

SHOPPING

Tiberias is a good place to do a bit of shopping if you need clothes, shoes, or other basic items.

Once you get to the **Town Center** (you'll know it by the long outdoor chairs and counters under the covered sidewalk promenade), you can find a surprising variety of shops and stores at reasonable prices. Near the marina and promenade, the shopping is concentrated around the town's main streets, Hagalil and HaBannim. You can find everything from shoe stores to small grocery stores to national chain stores such as Fox and souvenir shops.

SPORTS AND RECREATION
Parks and Nature Reserves

Boasting 17 natural hot springs that have long been renowned for their health benefits, **Hamat Tiberias National Park** (Rte. 7677, 20 minutes south of Tiberias, tel. 04/672-5287, 8am-5pm daily Apr.-Sept., 8am-4pm daily Oct.-Mar., last entry one hour before closing, adult NIS17, child NIS9) is worth venturing out of Tiberias to see. Inside the park you will find a synagogue with a mosaic floor built between 286 and 337 BC, and the **Hammam Suleiman Museum** inside an ancient Turkish bathhouse at the entrance.

Beaches

There are two important things to note about the beaches on the Galilee. One is that even if you are a strong swimmer, stick to designated beaches that have lifeguards. Even though it just looks like a big lake, there is a notoriously strong undertow, and swimmers at unsupervised beaches have drowned. The other thing is that in recent years there has been a proliferation of privatized beaches, so many areas are completely restricted. Others charge for entrance. Wherever you are in the area, ask locals in the shops and restaurants for directions to the best beaches.

Noting the dangers and restrictions of beach access in the area, most swimming beaches are located on the eastern shore of the Galilee. Among them are the well-maintained Ein Gev Beach (Kibbutz Ein Gev on the eastern shore of the Sea of Galilee, tel. 04/665-8008, adult NIS33, child NIS27), adjacent to a restroom, lockers, and changing rooms. Another option just south of Tiberias is the very popular Tzemach Beach (southern tip of the Sea of Galilee off Hwy. 90, tel. 04/675-2440 and 052/303-3777, 9am-5pm Sun.-Thurs. or call in advance for groups on weekends, NIS55, NIS70 for night and day lodging). There are tons of events here in the summer, beach umbrellas, and water sports galore, and it's an easy drive if you're staying in a hotel in Tiberias.

On the Water

In the past couple of years, it has become increasingly difficult to spontaneously hop on a boat in the Tiberias marina for a ride around the Sea of Galilee, especially in the low season. Your best bet is to inquire at one of the upscale hotels, such as the Scots Hotel, on the waterfront, about possible boat trips. Otherwise, you can try Jesus Boats (Tiberias Marina, tel. 057/775-8562, www.jesusboats.com, inquire for price).

Expeditions

For a two-hour carriage ride adventure into the Galilean countryside, contact Jordan Carriages (near the entrance to Kibbutz Kinneret off Rte. 90 south, tel. 052/370-1662, merkavot@nana.co.il, year-round, adult NIS60, child NIS50, book in advance). The carriages are not plush by any means, but the experience includes stops along the way in the Jordan Valley for things like baking pita bread, walks across rope bridges, and other activities.

It gets superhot and humid during the summer months, but riding a bicycle around town is highly recommended as a fun way to see the area. Some hotels rent out bicycles by the day, try the Aviv Hotel and Hostel (66 HaGalil St. in town center, tel. 04/672-3510, NIS45 and up). Just remember to start early and drink a lot of water.

There is a wide variety of other sporting and countryside adventures that you can take while in the area of Tiberias and the Sea of Galilee. A long list of possibilities can be found at www.zimmeril.com.

FOOD
Israeli Kitchen Cooking

A wide variety of customers from locals to tourists frequent ★ Little Tiberias (2 HaKishon St., Tiberias, tel. 04/679-2806, http://littletiberias.rest-e.co.il, noon-midnight daily, NIS85). Tucked into a building that forms part of the wall of the old city, it is just off the town's main street and next door to a score of other options. The interior is modern and has a homey feeling with tons of seating, and the staff is warm and friendly. Among the specialties is a beef Stroganoff. The types of dishes that are served here include standard favorites that can be found in Israeli kitchens: schnitzel, cucumber and tomato salad, pita, and more.

Kibbutz Dining

Located on one of the oldest kibbutzim in the area, Kibbutz Ein Gev's restaurant Marinado at the Port (Kibbutz Ein Gev, tel. 057/944-4106, http://marinadoattheport.rest-e.co.il, noon-last customer Sun.-Thurs., noon-one hour before sunset Fri., NIS95) has an incomparable view for outdoor dining. Not only are you sitting on the waterfront, you are in a semiprivate, idyllic setting. The restaurant itself is nothing fancy in its interior and general presentation, and serves the typical seafood fare of the area, including whole St. Peter's fish, but perfect for a last-minute decision or a larger group. The only real problem with Marinado is that it's difficult to tear yourself away, especially if you go around sunset.

Mediterranean

A family restaurant and one of the best known in town with an extremely loyal customer base, **Avi's Restaurant** (1 HaKishon St., Tiberias, tel. 04/679-1797, www.avi.rest.co.il, noon-midnight Sun.-Thurs., one hour after sunset-midnight Sat., NIS58) serves Israeli-style meat and vegetarian dishes, and free *mezze* (appetizers). Their specialty is meat dishes, and the owner will probably send more food to your table than you can eat. The homey environment of Avi's (which is the name of the owner) includes arched windows, stone walls, stained glass windows, and a large aquarium.

A nice option just outside of Tiberias, **Israel's Kitchen at Arbel Guest House** (Arbel Village just west of Tiberias on Rte. 7717, tel. 04/679-4919, 7:30pm-last customer daily, NIS120, call in advance for reservation) is fine dining in a country farmhouse atmosphere, set in a small village. Known for their delicious meat dishes and fresh ingredients in an idyllic garden setting, Arbel mainly exists to feed their guests, but can accommodate outside customers who make advance reservations.

Middle Eastern

A Lebanese restaurant with friendly staff that caters to families, **Ktze Hanahal** (Kibbutz Ginosar, off Rte. 90 north, tel. 04/671-7776, 9:30am-9:30pm Sun.-Thurs., 9:30am-midnight Fri.-Sat., NIS70) is situated in the middle of a kibbutz about 15 minutes north of Tiberias. The restaurant's dishes blend local Galilee-style food with Lebanese home cooking. The food is served in large portions, which are best enjoyed family-style. The specialty of Ktze Hanahal is their kebab preparation, put together while you watch. A fun feature of the restaurant is the playroom where weary parents can deposit their kids;

the atmosphere is generally family-friendly and simple.

If you're heading out of Tiberias, just 15 minutes to the north is the Lebanese **Tanureen** (off Rte. 90 north at Migdal Crossroads, tel. 04/671-2896, noon-midnight daily, NIS88), which serves seafood and meat prepared in a distinctively Middle Eastern style. Some of their specialties include grilled eggplant and Lebanese-style kebab. The restaurant's interior is spacious, modern, and upscale. It's not exactly what you'd expect to find off the beaten path and makes for a refreshing dining experience when you want to get off the road and relax.

Fine Dining

If you're looking for gourmet dining and romantic atmosphere at its very best while in Tiberias, **Decks Restaurant** (Gdud Barak St. at the Lido Beach, Tiberias, tel. 04/672-1538, www.lido.co.il, noon-last customer Sun.-Thurs., noon-1pm Fri., one hour after sunset-after midnight Sat., NIS100, reservations needed) should be your first stop. Their meticulous attention to detail includes grilling meat cooked over citrus, olive, and other kinds of wood. The restaurant's interior features a long deck that extends out over the Galilee; the deck is covered in the winter. It's an especially good place for a romantic meal, though it's easy to rack up a large bill.

Seafood

Both family-run and family-friendly, **Galei Gil Restaurant** (Old Promenade, Tiberias, tel. 04/672-0699, 11am-3pm Sun.-Thurs., 7pm-last customer Fri.-Sat., NIS60) is one of the oldest seafood restaurants in Tiberias and known for its tilapia cooked over coals. Conveniently located in the town center on the shores of the Galilee with a view of the water, it has a welcoming and warm atmosphere. The menu is reasonably priced, and you should easily get your fill of food. They are only open for lunch during the week and only open for dinner on the weekend.

Steaks and Burgers

Specializing in South American-style meats, the kosher ★ **El Rancho's** (3 HaKishon St., tel. 053/809-4609, www.2eat.co.il/elrancho, noon-last evening customer Sun.-Thurs., noon-3pm Fri., NIS85) claim to fame is that it serves the best steak in Israel, and everyone knows it. While the steak is very well done, it is typical by American standards. The friendly staff is accommodating and upbeat, and the interior is huge with exposed brick walls and wood touches, giving it a ranch house feeling. A nice touch to the interior is bottles of Israeli wine on display.

If you happen to have taken an afternoon to visit the baptismal site at Yardenit, stop off at the **River Bistro Bar** (Yardenit, Kibbutz Kinneret, tel. 057/944-3619, onhadas@walla. co.il, 7pm-3am daily, NIS80) afterward for dinner. The combination of going to a riverside bar and grill after visiting the possible baptismal site of Jesus might seem odd, but it is one of the few decent options in the area. The interior has high, cabana-like ceilings, and tables are lined up against huge windows. The centerpiece is the bar, with its wide variety of alcoholic drinks and several types of beer on tap. The kitchen at the River Bistro Bar is obsessed with hamburgers, so your best bet here is probably a burger and a beer.

ACCOMMODATIONS

The town of Tiberias alone has a range of about 30 different accommodations, from youth hostels to luxury hotels, with most options on or within easy walking distance to the beach or the promenade, restaurants, and shopping. Near Tiberias, around the shore of the Sea of Galilee, other options range from *zimmers* (private semi-luxury cabins to rent) to camping.

Under US$100

Located in Old Town Tiberias, **Maman Mansion** (Atzmon St. in Schunat Achva Atzmon, tel. 04/679-2986, www.mamanmansion.co.il, US$85 d) subscribes to the less-is-more philosophy by featuring a small sampling of choice amenities, including an outdoor pool, a great view of the Sea of Galilee, bike rentals, and free parking and wireless Internet. The small hotel houses 23 rooms in a 19th-century building. The rooms are bright and air-conditioned with a TV. There is also a garden and chapel.

It is very bare-bones on creature comforts, but **Aviv Hostel** (66 Hagalil St., tel. 04/671-2272, avivhotel@walla.com, US$65 d) fits the bill nicely for a clean, quiet, centrally located place to stay in Tiberias. The hotel/hostel shares restaurant facilities with its more upscale sister hotel next door, where your included breakfast is served from a massive, gourmet spread. The rooms offer a kitchen with a small fridge, private bathrooms, free parking, and balconies and views of the Sea of Galilee. It's a pretty good bang for your buck, especially if you're on a tight budget.

US$100-150

For the price, the family-run **Restal Hotel** (Yehuda Halevi St., tel. 04/679-0555, www. restal.co.il, US$135 d) is a comfortable fit for a couple nights' stay in the center of Tiberias. The recently refurbished hotel has an outdoor swimming pool and modern decor with wood floors and a flat-screen TV in the rooms. The hotel is on the larger side, with 174 rooms, a bar, a 24-hour front desk, and a fitness center. There is free wireless Internet in all public areas.

On the hillside in central Tiberias and close to shops, restaurants, and 20 minutes by foot to the Sea of Galilee, the **Berger Hotel** (27 Neiberg St., tel. 04/671-5151, www.bergerhotel.co.il, US$115 d) is a medium-size hotel that features balconies with a view of the city in most rooms. Kitchenette rooms are available on request at booking, and rooms include cable TV with international channels, a private bathroom, and a telephone for incoming calls. There is also a restaurant, 24-hour front desk, and free wireless Internet in public areas.

Overlooking Tiberias, the **Astoria Galilee Hotel** (13 Ohel Yaakov St., tel. 04/672-2351/2, www.astoria.co.il, US$103 d) is one of the oldest hotels in the city, and about 20 minutes by foot to the seashore. The hotel has 88 rooms, free wireless Internet, and modern updated rooms. There is also an outdoor pool, table tennis, and a sauna. The location makes it convenient to hop out of town and explore nearby sights and towns, including Safed and the Jordan River.

Bookings fill up months in advance, but **Karei Deshe Youth Hostel & Guest House** (D.N. Hevel Korazim, tel. 02/594-5633, www.iyha.org.il, US$105 d) is a great option if you want location and a low price. This youth hostel is situated on the western shore of the Galilee with a private beach, just about 20 minutes north of Tiberias. It has an inner courtyard, buffet breakfast, basketball court, and wireless Internet. Rooms here book quickly year-round. It is also near the popular Yardenit baptismal site at the Jordan River and hot springs. The rooms come either as dormitories or private rooms with private bathrooms. There is a walking path nearby that leads through four major sites in the area: the Church of the Multiplication, the Mount of Beatitudes, Capernaum, and the Monastery of the Twelve Apostles.

US$150-200

With an outdoor pool overlooking the Sea of Galilee and a hot tub, the **Golan Hotel** (14 Ahad Ha'Am St., tel. 04/671-1555, www.go-lanhotel.co.il, US$180 d) is just at the northern end of Tiberias. There's also a fitness center with a gym and sauna where guests can book massages and other treatments. With almost 100 rooms, the Golan Hotel also has a 24-hour front desk, garden, and terrace.

The **Nof Ginosar Hotel** (off of Rte. 90 north just before Ginosar, tel. 04/670-0320, www.ginosar.co.il, US$200 d) is a resort-style hotel on the western shore of the Galilee with a private beach and extensive grounds that are part of Kibbutz Ginosar. The arrangement is somewhat unusual with a 161-room hotel plus a holiday village nearby with 75 ground-floor rooms spread out throughout the area and an outdoor pool. The complex also has basketball and tennis courts and a jogging track that runs along a river. The friendly, English-speaking hotel staff can also help arrange excursions into the surrounding area.

Over US$200

Ramot Resort Hotel (eastern Sea of Galilee, tel. 04/673-2636, www.ramotresort.com, US$220 d) is more like a resort compound of cabins than a hotel. Just at the foot of the Golan, the hotel has 123 rooms spread out through cabins and chalets on grounds that overlook the Galilee through a canopy of palm trees. The rooms in the cabins are like small houses, with most of the amenities of home, including a kitchen, coffee service, a flat-screen TV, and huge, comfy beds. The area has hiking trails, and you can drive about 30 minutes south around the shore of the Galilee to reach Tiberias. The hotel sells out for the coming summer at least six months or more in advance.

On the eastern shore of the Galilee, the **Ein Gev Holiday Resort** (Kibbutz Ein Gev, tel. 04/665-8035, tourist department tel. 04/665-8030, www.eingev.com, US$224 d) not only has extremely reasonable rates and is in an idyllic location, it can accommodate families and groups. Ein Gev, with a total of 166 rooms, is set up as a series of cabins spread over the grounds plus 40 rooms situated around the hotel's reception area in the main building. Ein Gev's specialty is organized tours for international visitors. Situated in the oldest kibbutz on the Galilee, their restaurant is famous for their St. Peter's fish. They offer free wireless Internet, comfortably furnished (though not fancy) rooms, and special offers throughout the year on their website. There is a game room, a playground, a spa treatment room, and beachfront access.

One of the most prestigious and popular hotels in Tiberias, ★ **The Scots Hotel** (1 Gdud Barak Rd., tel. 04/671-0710, www.scot-shotels.co.il, US$475 d) is situated just steps away from the promenade that runs along the Sea of Galilee. It is in a historic building that used to be a hospital and has been remade into a medium-size hotel with some rooms that have views of the water. The hotel's restaurant serves gourmet food, and there is a wine cellar and art gallery on-site. You can also take advantage of the outdoor pool, in-room breakfast, currency exchange desk, and an ATM. Wireless Internet costs an extra US$18.

It only has 11 rooms, but the **Shirat Hayam Boutique Hotel**'s (Yigal Alon Promenade, tel. 04/672-1122, US$320 d) pretty exterior and charming location on the Tiberias promenade make it a hot commodity. The rooms and suites all have an LCD cable TV, a fridge, and a tea kettle. The 19th-century building has been equipped to also allow for hot tubs and balconies in some suites, and there is room service and a 24-hour front desk. It is in a central location, so ask for a quieter room when booking if you need it.

Beach Camping

The shores of the Sea of Galilee make a great place for camping, especially during the summer months when the weather is extremely warm. Most of them have some kind of entrance fee, which varies, but is generally about NIS20 per night. It is best to call the campground in advance and verify their entrance fee and hours of operation.

Along the eastern shore of the Sea of Galilee, some campsites that include amenities like running water, toilets, and showers are **Gofra Beach** (tel. 04/673-1942), **Halukim Beach** (tel. 04/673-2185), **Duga Beach** (tel. 04/673-1214), and **Sussita Beach** (tel. 04/665-8199). Visit www.camingil.org.il for more information.

At the northern end of the Sea of Galilee is **Amnon Beach** (northern tip of the Sea of Galilee near the Amnun 2000 Recreation Village, tel. 050/710-3420), and on the western shore is **Tamar Beach** (western shore of the Sea of Galilee, near Ginosar and 15 minutes north of Tiberias, tel. 04/679-0630 or 050/585-2101).

INFORMATION

The most useful online information about Tiberias, the Golan, and the Sea of Galilee can be found on the website of the **Israel Ministry of Tourism** (www.goisrael.com). The independent, tourist-minded **Go Visit Israel** (www.govisitisrael.com) has tons of useful information in a simple format, but the website is a bit hard to navigate. The very useful **Zimmer Israel** (www.zimmeril.com) has extremely helpful information from locals.

GETTING THERE AND AROUND
Car

Tiberias is located about two hours north of Jerusalem by car. Most of the drive is along Highway 6, which skirts the West Bank. It is about 90 minutes from Tel Aviv, also mostly along Highway 6.

Once you are in the area, Tiberias makes an excellent base to travel to other sites and towns along the shore of the Sea of Galilee, which has a circumference of only about 31 miles. With a car, you can easily leave your hotel in the late morning, see several sites at a leisurely pace, and be back in time for an early dinner. Tiberias itself is not that large and is very easy to navigate. If you are going to rent a car while visiting the region, this is a good time to do so.

Bus

You can travel to Tiberias from Jerusalem by **Egged** bus (www.egged.co.il, bus 963 or 962, NIS45 one-way) in about 2.5 hours. From Tel Aviv (bus 835 or 841, NIS45 one-way), it is approximately a three-hour trip.

Once you are in Tiberias, there are city buses and some bus companies that operate exclusively in the north of Israel. In Tiberias call *6686 from a local phone, or check out a useful alternative (in English) for buses anywhere in the country, **Bus.Co.Il** (www.bus.co.il), which provides detailed transportation information and timetables for Tiberias and the surrounding areas.

Nazareth and Vicinity

Nazareth is an important city to both religious Christians and Arabs, and the main draw for visitors is religious sites. Built up the side of a mountain, some of Nazareth's streets become increasingly steep and narrow the higher up you go, which can make it a bit difficult to navigate if you are driving. With a predominately Arab population, Nazareth is also home to good Middle Eastern restaurants, an Arab *shuk* (outdoor market), and an old city region.

SIGHTS
The Old City Market

In the course of visiting sites in Nazareth, you'll likely find yourself in the **Old City,** which includes a **market** (tel. 04/601-1072, board@nazarethboard.org, 9am-5pm Mon.-Fri., 9am-2pm Sat.) and a grouping of about 100 very impressive **Ottoman period homes.** You also might come upon the 18th-century **Saraya or Government House** (top of Aliyah Bet St.), built by a famous governor of the Galilee in 1740 as his summer home and currently undergoing renovations to become the Museum of Nazareth.

Nazareth Village

A careful recreation of life in Nazareth during biblical times, **Nazareth Village** (5079 St. in the Old City, opposite the French Hospital, tel. 04/645-6042, www.nazarethvillage.com, 9am-5pm Mon.-Sat., last tour at 3pm, adult NIS55, senior NIS37, child NIS25) is something similar to a living and breathing museum with guides in period dress who lead you through what life was like here 2,000 years ago.

★ Basilica of the Annunciation

The **Basilica of the Annunciation** (southwestern corner of the Old City, tel. 04/657-2501, www.basilicanazareth.org, 8am-5pm Mon.-Sat. Oct.-Mar., 8am-6pm daily Apr.-Sept., modest dress, free) is one of the largest churches in the Middle East. It is a bit difficult to find it on your own, as it's located about halfway up the mountainside of very steep and narrow roads. It's best to reach it with a tour group or via a taxi.

The Catholic church was established in

the ancient city of Nazareth

Nazareth

1969, and built on the site of what is believed to be the Virgin Mary's original home. The cavernous, two-story church engulfs a cave and the remains of previous churches, including a stone wall behind the cave from a 12th-century Crusader church. There are two stories to the church, with the upper level overlooking the main worship area.

Among the most engaging and dynamic features in the church, on the walls and throughout the massive courtyard surrounding the building, is an extensive collection of mosaic pictures from all over the world, each depicting scenes of the Virgin Mary with baby Jesus. There is also a small archaeological museum on-site that includes items from the Middle Bronze Age and Byzantine and Crusader times.

St. Gabriel's Church

One of the loveliest among the many churches in town, the Greek Orthodox **St. Gabriel's Church** (Paulus VI St., tel. 04/656-8488, www.nazarethinfo.org, 8am-noon and 2pm-5pm Mon.-Sat., free) is just at the entrance to the city as you are coming from the north. This is the spot where, according to the Greek Orthodox tradition, Gabriel announced the future birth of Christ to the Virgin Mary. The church has a high, arched ceiling, and between the colonnades the ceiling is painted with religious images against a blue backdrop.

the Basilica of the Annunciation

Church of Saint Joseph

The **Church of Saint Joseph** (northwestern corner of the Old City near the Basilica of the Annunciation, tel. 04/657-2501, www.nazarethinfo.org, 8am-5pm Mon.-Sat. Oct.-Mar., 8am-6pm Mon.-Sat. Apr.-Sept., free) is said to be built over the carpentry workshop of Joseph, Jesus's father. The Franciscan church that is now on the site was established in 1914 over the ruins of older churches and the lower level has an ancient water pit, mosaics, caves, and barns from ancient Nazareth of the 1st and 2nd centuries BC.

Roman Bathhouse

The beginnings of the Cactus souvenir shop in 1993 brought with it the discovery of the **Roman Bathhouse** (Mary's Well Square under the Cactus souvenir shop, tel. 04/657-8539, www.nazarethbathhouse.org, 9am-7pm Mon.-Sat., NIS120 for private tours of up to four people, NIS28 pp up to four people), a 2,000-year-old bathhouse under the shop.

Excavations have revealed underground heating tunnels, a hot room, and furnace. The tour fee includes refreshments.

Megiddo National Park

One of Israel's several UNESCO World Heritage Sites, **Megiddo National Park** (Megiddo and Yokne'am Junctions on Rte. 66, tel. 04/659-0316, www.parks.org.il, 8am-5pm daily Apr.-Sept., 8am-4pm daily Oct.-Mar., last entry one hour before closing, NIS27) surrounds the ancient ruins of the biblical town Megiddo. A historically strategically important city that went from ruler to ruler throughout the ages, it is today a national park that makes for a relatively easy hike. Abandoned after the Persian period, Megiddo is identified with Armageddon, the scene of the battle of the End of Days according to Revelation 16:14-21. The park includes a souvenir shop, a museum with an audiovisual presentation, and guided tours by reservation. The site is good for visits year-round, and it takes about one to two hours to tour it.

the Church of Saint Joseph

Byzantine church, and an excavated 4,500-seat Roman amphitheater. It is also home to several mosaic floorings, including the Mona Lisa of the Galilee, a remarkable depiction of a woman made from mosaic tiling. There is a visitors center at the entrance. As you leave the park you can explore the water channel and cistern.

FOOD
Middle Eastern

Just uphill from the Basilica of the Annunciation, **El-Reda** (21 Al-Bishara St., Old City Nazareth, tel. 04/608-4408, 7pm-2am Sun., 1pm-2am Mon.-Sat., NIS60) is an Arab-style café with a great view and an authentic atmosphere. Dishes prepared by the owner, Dehar Zaidani, reflect his enthusiasm for regional cuisine, and it comes through in the range of flavors and varied types of dishes such as mushrooms with almonds and sweet potatoes, various chicken dishes, a range of wines, and hot apple cider. The bohemian atmosphere of the El-Reda, considered one of the best restaurants in Nazareth's lively restaurant scene, is amplified from time to time with live music and poetry.

An upscale Middle Eastern restaurant in Nazareth's Old City, **Tishreen** (56 Al-Bishara St., tel. 04/608-4666, http://tishreen.rest-e. co.il, noon-midnight daily, NIS115) serves seafood, vegetarian dishes, and some tasty Arab-style pizza. Popular among locals for leisurely lunches and dinners, Tishreen's interior is muted and low-key with stone walls throughout, and a massive stone hearth oven.

A gorgeous, massive, stone-walled interior is the first thing you notice upon entering **Sudfeh** (Al-Bishara St., tel. 04/656-6611, www.sudfeh.com, noon-midnight Mon.-Sat., 6pm-midnight Sun., NIS80), which is inside a former stone Arab house. The lively restaurant-bar recently underwent major renovations, so it is best to call in advance to make sure it is open. It has a creative selection of salads and local flavors in a European-style package. At just a 10-minute walk from the

Mount Precipice

Just about 1.5 miles outside of Nazareth is **Mount Precipice** (second exit off Rte. 60 south out of Nazareth), also known as the Mount of the Leap of the Lord, one of the city's highest points. Mount Precipice is where the people of Nazareth took Jesus to be thrown off the cliff. There is a viewing platform to see the landscape below, and at the same spot is the **Cave of the Leap,** a 50,000-year-old cave that has the remains of 13 human skeletons and over 15,000 artifacts from the Stone Age.

Zippori National Park

About three miles west of Nazareth is the well-laid out **Zippori National Park** (2.5 miles east of Hamovil junction on Rte. 79 between Hamovil junction and Nazareth, tel. 04/656-8272, www.parks.org.il, 8am-5pm daily Apr.-Sept., 8am-4pm daily Oct.-Mar., last entry one hour before closing, adult NIS30, child NIS17), which is home to the ruins of a Crusader castle, foundations of a

Basilica of the Annunciation, Sudfeh is an affordable, yet upscale, dining option that sometimes hosts live performances by local musicians.

When you're in the mood for a huge spread of Middle Eastern food, head to **Diana** (51 Paulos VI St., tel. 04/657-2919, www.2eat. co.il/eng/diana, noon-midnight daily, NIS70), where you'll find unusual twists to common dishes, such as kebab on cinnamon sticks. Some of the ingredients used in the dishes are local to the Nazareth region. The lamb is particularly succulent and tender. Diana is a bit hard to find, so don't be shy about asking for directions; it is well known.

ACCOMMODATIONS
US$100-150

Fauzi Azar Inn (6091 Al-Bishara in Old City Nazareth, near Tishreen Restaurant, tel. 04/602-0469, www.fauziazarinn.com, US$115 d) is a small, 10-room guesthouse in Old City Nazareth that exudes Arab charm because of its location and the architecture of arched outer colonnades and cave-like rooms. Housed in a 200-year-old Arab mansion, the inn has free wireless Internet, a common area terrace, and air-conditioning. Located near the *shuk,* vegetable market, restaurants and coffee shops, and the Basilica of the Annunciation, it works well as a base to explore Nazareth.

Tabar Hotel (5053 El Mutran St., tel. 04/608-5400, www.tabarhotel.com, US$130 d) is a 90-room, five-floor hotel on a hillside of a largely residential area overlooking the city of Nazareth. The hotel has a modern, clean, simple interior, and every room has free wireless Internet, air-conditioning, and private balconies with views of the city and the Jezreel Valley. The hotel has a restaurant and coffee bar and is within walking distance to the Old City markets.

A bit off the beaten path, **Rosary Guest House** (6141/2 El-Dabas St., tel. 04/655-4435, www.rsisters.com, US$130 d) is a restored monastery with 24 air-conditioned rooms that all have a balcony with garden

views and a private bathroom. The Church of the Annunciation is a 10-minute walk away. The rooms are simply furnished, and there is free wireless Internet and a TV in the shared lounge. You can book tours directly at the guesthouse, and there is a chapel on-site.

US$150-200

The **Golden Crown Old City Hotel** (16 Galilee St., tel. 04/650-8000, www.golden-crown.co.il, US$150 d) is close to most major attractions in the Old City and has all the comforts of a midsize hotel, including gorgeous city-view rooms with satellite TV, a restaurant, a pool, and free private parking. The rooms are sleek, modern, and upscale with free wireless Internet, room service, and the option of having the included breakfast brought to your room.

Over US$200

Nazareth Ilit Plaza Hotel (2 Hermon St., tel. 04/602-8200, www.plaza-nazarethilit.co.il, US$240 d) is a midsize luxury hotel with 184 rooms just on the outskirts of Nazareth. The hotel has a pastoral atmosphere amidst pine trees and gardens with views of the Jezreel Valley, Mount Tabor, and Gilboa Heights and is a 10-minute drive from Nazareth. The hotel's rooms are comfortably equipped with large, soft beds and updated, modern interiors, a safe, minibar, wireless Internet, and hair dryer. The hotel has a VIP lounge, gym, and assistance for tourism activities.

GETTING THERE AND AROUND
Car

Nazareth is just under two hours north of Jerusalem by car. Most of the drive is along Highway 6, which skirts the West Bank. It is about an hour and 20 minutes from Tel Aviv, also mostly along Highway 6.

Driving within Nazareth is an incomparable nightmare, unless you are accustomed to extremely steep, narrow streets that are sometimes not clearly marked as one-way. Using a GPS in Nazareth to navigate can make matters worse because certain parts of the city are so tightly packed. Nazareth Illit, or Upper Nazareth, and the Old City area have many of the more troublesome streets but also many of the major sights. If you must drive to Nazareth, park near the entrance to the city and take cabs to your destinations.

Bus

Getting to the center of Nazareth, near the Basilica of the Annunciation, from Jerusalem by **Egged** bus (www.egged.co.il, bus 955, NIS42 one-way) is just under 2.5 hours. From Tel Aviv, it takes three hours (bus 702, NIS37.5 one-way).

Once you are in Nazareth, you can take city buses to get around. Visit **Bus.Co.Il** (www.bus.co.il) for information. But it is always best to ask for specific information at the front desk of any hotel in town.

The Galilee

There are numerous sites and things to do scattered throughout the Galilee, but the main attractions are outdoor activities, such as hiking.

SIGHTS
Tsfat (Safed) and Vicinity

Tsfat (off Rte. 89 west, tel. 04/692-4427, www.safed.co.il) is an ancient town in the Upper Galilee 3,200 feet above sea level with commanding views of the Golan, the Hermon, Lebanon, and Syria. About 40 minutes north of Tiberias, Tsfat is a great place for short hikes to archaeological sites, such as **Montfort Castle** (24 hours daily), the Crusader fortress at the top of the town. Tsfat is also considered the center of Jewish mysticism and one of Judaism's holy cities.

Jish

A small town about 40 minutes northwest of Tiberias, **Jish** (from Tiberias, take Rte. 90 and then Rte. 89) sits near Dalton Lake and has a few archaeological sites, two historical synagogues, and a unique mausoleum and burial caves.

Rosh Pina

A 120-year-old moshav situated on the northeastern slope of Mount Canaan overlooking the Hula Valley and the Golan, **Rosh Pina** (Rte. 90 about 30 minutes northeast of Tiberias) has a well-developed tourism industry that caters to high-end customers. It has a variety of restaurants and hotels. Farmers started the moshav in the late 1800s with the support of Baron Edmond de Rothschild. The town makes a good base for touring the upper Galilee and the Golan. Its historic **town center** has some spots worth exploring, including an audiovisual presentation about the town's history at the **House of Officials** (center of Rosh Pina, HaChalutzim St., also known as the Old Rosh Pina Office, tel. 04/693-6603, 8:30am-5pm Sun.-Thurs. and 8:30am-1pm Fri.-Sat., NIS20).

Kiryat Shmona

In the heart of the Hula Valley, **Kiryat Shmona**'s (take Rte. 90 north, one hour from Tiberias) main attraction is the **scenic cable car** (Kibbutz Manara, Rte. 90, Kiryat Shmona, tel. 04/690-5830, 9:30am-5pm daily Mar.-July and Sept.-Oct., 9:30am-7pm daily Aug., 11am-4pm daily Nov.-Feb., NIS59 weekdays and NIS69 weekends, last car is half an hour before closing). It is the longest cable car in Israel, going from Kiryat Shmona up to the cliffs of Kibbutz Manara. At the observation point at the top of the cable car is a restaurant, hiking path, and sports center.

★ Beit She'an

Just at the southern edge of the Galilee where it meets the West Bank is 6,000-year-old **Beit She'an**, home to **ancient ruins** that

the ruins at Beit She'an National Park

are scattered throughout the modern city and **Beit She'an National Park** (off Shaul HaMelech St., Afula, tel. 04/658-7189, www. parks.org.il, www.goisrael.org, 8am-5pm Sat.-Thurs. Apr.-Sept., 8am-4pm Sun.-Fri., 8am-5pm Sat. Oct.-Mar., NIS27).

Another of Israel's UNESCO World Heritage Sites, Beit She'an is one of the oldest cities of the Ancient Near East and sits at the crossroads to the Fertile Crescent. Incredibly, about 20 layers of settlement have been found at Beit She'an that go as far back as the 5th millennium BC. Beit She'an rose to its height under the Romans and the Byzantines before being destroyed by an earthquake in AD 749. The colonnaded streets, a bathhouse, theater, and shrines were reconstructed in Beit She'an National Park.

You can pick up a free map at the entrance and tour around this remarkable archaeological site that was known as Scythopolis during the late Roman and Byzantine periods (2nd-6th centuries AD). Excavations that started here in the 1960s revealed a **Roman Amphitheater.** More recent work to uncover the city has exposed a beautiful **downtown,** with colonnaded main streets, a central plaza, fountain, a Byzantine bathhouse, and more.

In the evenings, a few hours after the park closes, the park hosts a multimedia **night show** for an extra fee. The night show comes with the added benefit of enjoying the park when the sun and the temperature, which can get up to over 100°F in the summer, have gone down.

Beit Alpha Synagogue and Mosaic

The 6th-century **Beit Alpha Synagogue and Mosaic** (Kibbutz Heftziba, Rte. 669, tel. 04/653-2004, 8am-4pm daily and until 5pm in the summer, adult NIS18, child NIS9) features a magnificent mosaic floor. It is considered simplistic compared to other mosaics in the region, but it is one of Israel's great archaeological treasures. One of the first archaeological discoveries in modern Israel, the mosaic has images from the zodiac arranged in reverse order, which does not correspond to the region's seasons.

★ Gan Garoo Australia-Israel Park

One of the more unusual places you'll find in Israel is the four-acre **Gan Garoo Australia-Israel Park** (Kibbutz Nir David, off Rte. 669 at Gan Ha-Shlosha, tel. 04/648-8080, www. nirtours.co.il, 9am-4pm Mon.-Fri., 9am-5pm Sat., NIS45) in Beit She'an Valley. The park a koala at Gan Garoo Australia-Israel Park

is full of a variety of Australian animals including kangaroos, flying foxes, cassowaries, koalas, and more.

In typical Israeli fashion, the operation isn't too tightly controlled, which makes it possible to mingle a bit with the animals and get a close look at wildlife that you might never see otherwise. You can hand feed the kangaroos and pet the goats. The park is a nice change of pace from the ancient ruins, parks, and religious sites that dominate the area. It is also great fun for kids, though you might want to closely supervise any children with you.

ENTERTAINMENT AND EVENTS

The annual **She'an Nights Festival** (Beit She'an Foundation for Culture and Tourism, tel. 04/658-8892, www.goisrael.org, prices vary) is not to be confused with the She'an Nights multimedia show that runs in the evenings on a regular basis in Beit She'an National Park. The festival is held annually, usually around the time of Sukkot (Oct.) and includes food, wine, street performers, and music.

SPORTS AND RECREATION
Parks, Nature Reserves, and Mountains

Full of different outdoor pursuits from hiking to paragliding, **Mount Gilboa** is at the southernmost part of the Lower Galilee. Some of its features include the **Gilboa Iris Nature Reserve** (Mar.-Apr.), **hiking trails,** and a **scenic road** (Rte. 667) that includes places to stop and look at the vista.

Hula Nature Reserve (Upper Galilee, tel. 04/681-7137 and 04/693-7069, www.agamonhula.co.il, 9am-4pm Sun.-Thurs., 6:30am-4pm Fri.-Sat., depending on activity NIS23 and up) is a world-class site for observing nesting and migrating birds in a natural habitat. The reserve is right in the heart of the Hula Valley and offers a wide range of activities for nature lovers, including guided night tours.

Noted for its exceptionally breathtaking view, **Mount Tabor** is about 30 minutes east of Nazareth and said to be the place of Jesus's transfiguration. On the mountaintop is the **Basilica of the Transfiguration** (tel. 04/673-2283, www.goisrael.com), a complex that includes a Greek Orthodox church and a gorgeous Franciscan church with a colonnaded interior of white stone and high ceilings. There are also Crusader and Byzantine ruins on the mountaintop.

More than just a nice, long cable car ride over the hills, **Manara Cliff** (Rte. 90, Kiryat Shmona, tel. 04/690-5830, www.cliff.co.il, 10am-4pm Mon.-Thurs., call in advance because prices and hours of operation vary) is like a huge indoor-outdoor playground that also offers mountain slides, scenic trains, rock climbing, archery, hiking, bungee trampolines, zipline rides, and extreme mountain biking. Situated in the Upper Galilee with a view of the Hula Valley, a restaurant, and a sports center, Manara Cliff also offers a guided hiking tour of the area.

Offering a variety of ranch-themed activities, **Bat Ya'ar Ranch** (tel. 04/692-1788, www.batyaar.co.il) has short horseback rides, family activities, and a ranch house-style restaurant.

The Jesus Trail

on the Jesus Trail along the Sea of Galilee

Throughout the Galilee, there are scores of sights that were significant in the course of the life and teachings of Jesus. Even sights that have more obscure connections to Jesus are advertised as places where relatives of Jesus lived, worked, or were born. Some of the most significant points along the trail are Nazareth, Cana, Migdal, Tabgha, Magdala, and Capernaum.

It is possible to have a guided experience along what has become known as the **Jesus Trail** (http://jesustrail.com) and literally walk in the footsteps of where Jesus is historically recorded to have lived, traveled, and spread his teachings. The 40-mile trail connects Nazareth to Capernaum. There are a variety of accommodations along the trail, and portions can be explored by bicycle.

The Jesus Trail website provides a significant amount of information about hiking routes between biblical sites significant to Jesus and his activities in the Galilee region. A combination of ecotourism and religious tourism, the Jesus Trail covers several significant points between Nazareth and Capernaum. You can also take a self-guided tour that includes hiking guidance and prearranged accommodations along the way for six days and five nights.

It is conveniently located just about 10 minutes from Safed.

FOOD
Mediterranean

If you're in the mood for an expedition that ends with a unique dining experience, try **Goats with the Wind** (near Moshav Yodfat, Har Hashabi, tel. 050/532-7387, www.goatswiththewind.com, 10:30am-3pm daily, call one day in advance for reservations, NIS90), an organic cheese and goat farm and restaurant in the heartland of the Upper Galilee. The restaurant is at the end of a dirt track. It is privately owned and operated, so you get a truly unique, Israeli experience. The goat cheese comes from goat milk on the farm and is presented elegantly. All seating is on private verandas where you can feast on dishes like tomato and eggplant salad, *labaneh*, fried eggplant, cabbage salad, and other Mediterranean delights.

Steak and Seafood

In the middle of the pastoral Galilean countryside is **Dag al HaDan** (Tel Dan in Kiryat Shmona, tel. 04/695-0225, www.dagaldan. co.il, noon-last customer daily Sept.-June, 9am-last customer daily July-Aug., NIS95), a kosher dairy restaurant next to the Dan River known throughout Israel. The restaurant's emphasis is on fish, especially trout, which is fitting because its name means fish on the Dan River. You can also get *mezze,* sandwiches, and other standard Mediterranean café fare, and the layout is housed in a rustic, barnlike structure with plenty of seating.

With a reputation as an outstanding place to get a steak, **Hatahana** (1 HaRishonim St., Metula town center, tel. 04/694-4810, 1pm-10:30pm Mon.-Thurs., 1pm-midnight Sat.-Sun., NIS90), which means "the mill," raises its own cattle and serves up a variety of scrumptious meat dishes including T-bone steaks, lamb chops, and hamburgers. It tends to get packed with meat lovers, so reservations are recommended.

Cafés

The steady stream of tourists to Safed ensures that there are several options for places to eat, but none are quite as charming as the ★ **Geffen Courtyard** (55 Alkabetz St., Safed, tel. 050/881-8104, 10am-6:30pm Sun.-Thurs., 10am-3pm Fri., NIS50). Replete with a winery, a vineyard, an art museum, and a scenic view, Geffen is overflowing with entrancing details. Considered a must-stop location in the region, they serve a lovely selection of wines, regionally made cheeses, and fresh breads. The stone interior is accented by a nice setup of wooden tables and a breathtaking view.

A relatively new kid on the block that has quickly become popular, **Haari 8** (8 Haari St., Safed, tel. 04/692-0033, http://haari8.rest.co.il, noon-10pm Sun.-Thurs., NIS45) is a standout for its unusually accommodating service and generous portions that include options even for vegans. This kosher restaurant is just at the edge of Safed's Old City, making it a

convenient stop for an American-style hamburger for lunch after a morning of touring. The menu has a variety of other meat options, including Moroccan cigars, a lamb-filled dish in the shape of a cigar.

ACCOMMODATIONS
US$100-150

The **Tabor Land Guest House** (Kfar Kisch, tel. 050/544-1972, www.taborland.com, US$100 d) boasts views of the Jordanian Gilead Mountains to the east and Mount Tabor to the west. The accommodations are clean and extremely simple with four rooms (some dormitory-style), and there is free wireless Internet throughout the premises. The location is a good jumping-off point for hikes in the Lower Galilee. Guests can use the kitchen, garden, terrace, and living room with a TV and DVD player.

US$150-200

Situated in a quaint village, **Gilboa Guest House Benharim** (Harod Spring Nature Reserve, Gid'ona, tel. 050/336-0061, www. benharim.com, US$173 d) is a very simple, eight-room establishment with free wireless Internet, an outdoor area equipped for barbecues, and an on-site spa and wellness center. The simply decorated rooms have views of the Gilboa Mountains and include a TV. Some rooms are dormitory-style with a shared bathroom, and there is a fully-equipped common kitchen and reading area. The guesthouse is near numerous outdoor attractions, including the Harod Spring Nature Reserve and Beit She'an National Park.

Over US$200

Country luxury is the specialty of **Noach Batavor Cabins** (Kfar Kisch, tel. 052/283-7397, www.zimmeril.com, US$245 d), at the Kfar Kisch Moshav where they cater to couples. Three luxury wooden cabins include hot tubs, panoramic views of Mount Tabor, free wireless Internet, and an LCD TV and DVD player. Every cabin has a kitchenette and luxury amenities like robes and slippers.

The moshav has an olive oil plant with guided tours and tastings. Nearby attractions include the church on top of Mount Tabor and the Nahal Tabor Nature Reserve. It is a great area for outdoor sports including canoeing, hiking, biking, and horseback riding.

With only four rooms, booking well in advance at the extremely popular **Artists' Colony Inn Zefat** (9 Simtat Yud Zayin, Safed, tel. 04/604-1101, www.artcol.co.il, US$230 d) is a must. The bed-and-breakfast is in a fully renovated stone villa with rooms that have been converted into comfortable, modern suites that include free wireless Internet, a large breakfast, and espresso. Located in the artist colony district of the ancient city of Safed, the villa has a garden and terrace with views. All custom-designed suites have a flat-screen TV, and there is free coffee and snacks in the lobby. The International Centre for Tzfat Kabbalah is a five-minute walk away, and it is 25 minutes by car to the Sea of Galilee.

GETTING THERE AND AROUND
Car
The Upper and Lower Galilee make up a broad swath of land that is relatively easy to cross by car, and many of the roads and highways between towns and cities have been recently or are in the process of being widened and improved. It takes about 90 minutes to get to the Lower Galilee from Jerusalem and a little over an hour from Tel Aviv.

Once you are in the Galilee, because of the empty expanses between towns and cities, you might encounter people hitchhiking by pointing their index finger toward the ground or just standing near a bus stop and trying to catch your eye as you pass. It is legal to hitchhike in Israel and frequently used for transportation in more deserted areas, but the typical cautionary notes about hitchhiking or picking up hitchhikers still apply.

Bus
As in the rest of the country, the easiest and most convenient bus service around the Galilee is **Egged** (www.egged.co.il), which lists schedules, bus numbers, and times in English. You can also check **Bus.Co.Il** (www.bus.co.il).

There are bus stops near some major sights, but you will need to plan ahead and communicate with your driver about where you need to go.

Taxis and Share Taxis
You can order a taxi in this region by going through any hotel or hostel, and often local businesses will know drivers in the area. Share taxis are also a popular mode of transportation. It is imperative to tell your driver at the outset where you want to go.

The Golan Heights

The Golan is situated in the northernmost region of Israel and shares borders with Lebanon and Syria. It is a popular domestic weekend getaway spot and also a favored spot for hiking and other outdoor pursuits. The Golan Heights is home to fine wineries and apple and cherry orchards and the source of much of the beef and dairy in the region.

SIGHTS
Druze Villages
Throughout the internationally disputed territory of the Golan there are several **Druze villages** inhabited by a total of about 20,000 Druze, an Arab people of Syrian descent who have Israeli citizenship. The Druze are known by reputation as warm and willing hosts to visitors. They make up about half of the sparsely populated Golan.

The Mysterious Druze

The people of the Golan Heights, in particular the Druze, are just as complex as the division of borders and land. Previously Syrian residents, the Druze in the Golan follow a mystical religion that is largely secret and has its own courts, laws in personal matters, and leadership.

The approximately 20,000 Druze in the Golan (the majority population in the region) have a unique status as a minority group and have been serving in the Israeli military and border police since 1948, even though their passports read "undefined" as their nationality. The Druze culture is Arab, but they don't follow mainstream Arab culture, and have held high-level positions in the political, public, and military life of Israel.

The Druze religion allows for women to attain high positions, and its major aspects are considered secret, though they will allow that they believe in reincarnation.

Druze villages are renowned for their warm hospitality, and are located mainly in the Galilee and the Golan. The largest Druze village in Israel is in Daliyat el-Carmel, on Mount Carmel in the heart of the Carmel National Park, just southeast of Haifa. In the Golan, the center of Druze life is the village of Majdal al-Shams, with a population of 8,000 at the foot of Mount Hermon. Misada, Bukata, and Ein Kinya are also important Druze villages in the Golan.

Druze villages include **Ein Kinya** (near Mt. Hermon next to the Sahar River), which is the smallest but the most popular among tourists. The other villages are **Majdal al-Shams** (near intersection of Rte. 98 north and Hwy. 989 north), **Bukata,** and **Misada.** You can freely enter any of the villages, which are safe and welcoming to visitors.

Katsrin

The capital of the Golan Heights, **Katsrin** (take Rte. 87 north to Hwy. 9088 west), or

Qatsrin, was founded in 1977 and is considered the tourism center of the region.

The town's features include the **Golan Archaeological Museum** (Rte. 87, Merom Golan, tel. 04/696-2412, www.ilmuseums. com, 8am-5pm Sun.-Thurs., 8am-3pm Fri., 10am-4pm Sat., NIS27 with the Ancient Katsrin Park). The modern, well-maintained museum is small but laid out well. It has a short film and exhibit about the Golan. You can also learn about the destruction of Gamla, a stronghold during the First Revolt against Rome that the Romans destroyed in AD 67.

In the immediate vicinity is the **Ancient Katsrin Park** (Rte. 87, Merom Golan, tel. 04/696-2412, 9am-4pm Sun.-Thurs., 9am-2pm Fri. Sept.-May; 9am-6pm Sun.-Thurs., 9am-4pm Fri., 10am-4pm Sat. June-Aug., NIS27 with the Golan Archaeological Museum). The park features the remains of a 3rd-century Jewish village, including an ancient synagogue. Two reconstructed houses are set up with props of common objects that might have been used when the village, which was likely struck by an earthquake, was inhabited.

Golan Heights Winery

The producer of several popular domestic brands, the world-famous **Golan Heights Winery** (Rte. 87, south of Katsrin, tel. 04/683-8435, www.golanwines.co.il, 8:30am-5:30pm Sun., 8:30am-6:30pm Mon.-Thurs., 8:30am-1:30pm Fri. and holiday eves, NIS20) is less than two miles from Katsrin. It features a visitors center that offers tours (book in advance) and a gift shop with the full range of wines and wine accessories.

Dolmens (Prehistoric Megalith Tombs)

As you are traveling about the Golan, you will likely see **dolmens,** or prehistoric megalith tombs, that date to about 30 BC and are believed to have been used for burial by nomadic tribes, and then possibly reused for secondary burial long later. The dolmens look like flat rocks stacked on top of each other in partially

Israel's Wine Country

the Golan Heights Winery

The history of wine in Israel is a long one. For thousands of years, Jews have been using wine for mostly sacramental purposes. The development of wine and the wine industry today has reached the point that some wines made in Israel are recognized internationally and even win international awards. There is the added element in Israel of a wide variety of kosher wines.

Israeli wine country is concentrated in a few areas: in the foothills of Jerusalem and the surrounding areas, the Negev Desert, the Golan, and the Galilee. Unfortunately the industry is still young enough that wine-related tourism hasn't developed to the point where you can take a wine tour of any regions. But you can make arrangements through a tour guide, by request, to visit different wineries. Many wineries have visiting centers and offer the chance to take a tour and have tastings for about NIS40.

In the Golan Heights, the center of tourism, Katsrin, is also the center of the regional wine industry, led by the **Golan Heights Winery** (www.golanwines.co.il), which is considered by many to be the grandfather of Israel's modern-day wine industry. The visitors center offers a variety of tours and tastings in multiple languages, and has a gift shop.

In the Upper Galilee, particularly in the area of Carmel Mountain, there are a variety of wineries of all sizes. An excellent website that gives an overview of Israel's wine country is **Israeli Wines** (www.winesisrael.com/en), where you can get current news and information about the industry as well as product information.

freestanding formations; they appear in the middle of desolate areas.

SPORTS AND RECREATION
Parks and Nature Reserves

At the foot of Mount Hermon is the Banias Spring that leads through a canyon to the magnificent Banias Waterfall. It's all part of

Banias Nature Reserve (east of Kibbutz Snir on Rte. 99, tel. 04/690-2577 for spring, tel. 04/695-0272 for waterfall, 8am-5pm Sat.-Thurs., 8am-4pm Fri. and holidays Apr.-Sept., 8am-4pm Sat.-Thurs., 8am-3pm Fri. and holidays Oct.-Mar., adult NIS30, child NIS15, combination tickets available for Nimrod Fortress and Banias for adult NIS40, child NIS20). The reserve has some very scenic the Banias Waterfall at Banias Nature Reserve

trails that are highlighted with archaeological ruins.

Within the reserve there are several sites to visit, depending on which route you take. Once called Caesarea Philippi, you can take a 45-minute trail to go through **Roman and Crusader ruins,** including a Roman bridge. Farther along is the **waterfall,** and a backtrack route will take you toward **Agrippas' Palace.**

The relatively easy two-hour hike in **Nimrod Fortress National Park** (Rte. 989 between Kiryat Shmona and Mt. Hermon, tel. 04/694-9277, 8am-5pm Sat.-Thurs., 8am-4pm Fri. and holidays Apr.-Sept., 8am-4pm Sat.-Thurs., 8am-3pm Fri. and holidays Oct.-Mar., adult NIS22, child NIS10, combination tickets available for Nimrod Fortress and Banias for adult NIS40, child NIS20) leads to the unique offerings of a vulture nesting site and a secret passageway at Nimrod Fortress. Situated above Banias Spring on the slopes of Mount Hermon, the 13th-century fortress was gradually built up over time and the hiking path passes by a huge gate, an ancient toilet, guard towers, and cisterns.

Not what you'd expect to find in the Middle East, but when in season, **Mount Hermon** (off of Rte. 98, www.skihermon.co.il, 8am-4pm daily, adult NIS55, child NIS45) has a functioning ski resort complete with a ski lift. If you don't ski, you can play on snow sleds, ride the cable car, or hang out in the restaurant. In the summer, the area has gorgeous vistas of Syria, Lebanon, the Galilee, and the Hula Valley, and you can take guided tours, ride mountain sleds, and tool around the mountain bike park.

Gamla Nature Reserve (Rte. 869 from Gamla Junction to Daliyot Junction on the eastern side of the Sea of Galilee, tel. 04/682-2282/3, 8am-5pm Sat.-Thurs., 8am-4pm Fri. and holidays Apr.-Sept., 8am-4pm Sat.-Thurs., 8am-3pm Fri. and holidays Oct.-Mar., adult NIS30, child NIS16) has relatively easy hikes that run 1-4 hours. The site includes observation plazas, a snack bar, and binoculars for rent. The reserve is famed for its griffon vulture observation point and views of an ancient city and the remains of a Byzantine church. It is also home to one of the most ancient synagogues in Israel.

Gamla Nature Reserve

FOOD
Farm Restaurants
The **Dubrovin Farm Restaurant** (Rte. 90, Merom Golan, grounds of Dubrovin Farm, tel. 04/693-7371, dubrovinfarm@bezeqint.net, call in advance for reservations as hours vary, NIS125) on the grounds of a reconstructed farm founded in 1909 near the Hula Nature Reserve. There is a complete farmhouse and a small museum with interactive exhibits and activities for kids (tel. 04/693-7371, NIS12). The restaurant serves a prix fixe menu featuring meat dishes and nondairy ice cream for dessert. It is best enjoyed by groups.

Middle Eastern Fusion
If you get as far north as Majdal al-Shams near the Syrian border, check out the local sophisticated **Undefined** (Majdal al-Shams main road, tel. 050/764-1699, 11am-10pm Wed.-Mon., NIS55), named for the description that most Syrian Druze have on their IDs under the identifying factor for nationality. Serving an interesting mix of Asian and Middle Eastern dishes, steaks, and fresh fruit desserts,

the café setting has a friendly atmosphere that sometimes hosts live acoustic performances.

Moshav Dining
Conveniently located and with a simple, warm, atmosphere and very extensive regional wine menu, **Moshbutz** (third turn inside Moshav Ramot, eastern shore of the Galilee, tel. 04/679-5095, http://mushbutz. rest-e.co.il, 6pm-last customer daily, NIS80) takes its name from the combination of the words *moshav* and *kibbutz,* reflecting its roots in connection with the moshav. Try to get a seat near the windows and enjoy the view of the eastern shore of the Sea of Galilee. They do serve dishes such as hamburgers, but the beef is in the aged style and may not appeal to an American palate. A better bet is the beef stew in wine stock or the pork spareribs (a rare find in this part of the world).

ACCOMMODATIONS
US$100-150
One of the more unique experiences available for accommodations, **Ghengis Khan in the**

Golan (Givat Yoav, Neot Golan, tel. 052/371-5687, www.gkhan.co.il, US$122 d) is a popular specialty lodging spot with just five rooms (or tents, rather) along the Golan Trail. Family-run with handmade tents and free wireless Internet, it is a contradiction between technology and nature. It provides an area to cook out, a garden with seating, and a shared kitchen with an option to buy food supplies. The tents are equipped with mattresses, pillows, and private or shared bathrooms nearby. Nearby excursions include horseback riding, hiking, and jeep trips for hire. The Galilee is just 15 minutes by car, and buses to and from Tel Aviv and Jerusalem stop nearby.

The Society for the Protection of Nature in Israel (SPNI) has field schools throughout Israel and the Golan, and they make a great option if you are looking for something affordable, conveniently located, and only need the most basic in amenities and comfort. Even in the high season of summer, the Golan SPNI Field School (Katsrin, tel. 04/696-1234, field school reservations hotline tel. 03/638-8688, www.teva.org.il, US$141 d) is reasonable. The simple, ground-floor accommodations are surrounded by trees, and it caters to groups of travelers, including touring and Birthright groups, so you might have a lively crowd of young people there with you. Every room is air-conditioned and can hold about six people. Breakfast is included in the price.

US$150-200

The mystical grounds of Between Water and Sky (Neot Golan, tel. 054/488-2299, www.a-hotel.com/israel/neot-golan, US$200 d) cater to couples looking for a romantic getaway and offer three cabin suites that come with a hot tub, a flat-screen TV with satellite, a furnished balcony with views of the Sea of Galilee, free wireless Internet, a minibar with free nonalcoholic drinks, and a DVD library. Basically every element of pampering is covered, including flowers, chocolate, wine, and

cookies when you arrive. There is an olive press on the property that can be toured to see how olive oil is made, and it is just five minutes from the Sea of Galilee.

Situated on the side of Mount Hermon is the Chalet Nimrod Castle Hostel (Nachal Nimrod, tel. 04/698-4218, www.bikta.net, US$159 d) with varied types of cabins that were built by owners Guy and Lilach. The independent cabins are void of technology and surround a central lodge where you can get breakfast (for an extra fee) and maps and travel guides to the surrounding area. The whole vibe of the chalet is peace and calm, and its location on the Golan Trail makes for easy access to hiking. The cabins are air-conditioned and include a kitchenette, and there is a restaurant on-site. Additional amenities can be found nearby.

Over US$200

Best for families and couples, the Sanabl Druze Hospitality Center (Ein Kinya, Golan Heights, Nimrod, tel. 050/577-8850, www.zimmeril.com, US$275 d) is a small religious property in the Druze village of Ein Kinya in the Golan Heights with a selection of suites and villas. A stay here includes access to a Druze restaurant (ask for the stew) and options for suites and villas that all have a TV and DVD player, a hot tub, balcony, and modern, luxurious furnishings. There are also cooking facilities, and a traditional Druze buffet breakfast is included. There is free parking and wireless Internet, and you can arrange for horseback riding, hiking, and jeep excursions through the center. If there's snow, it's a five-minute drive to skiing on Mount Hermon. It's also near Banias Nature Reserve and Nimrod Fortress National Park.

To the north of the Galilee with just four suites, Tenebagolan Suites Zimmers (293 Gan Hashiqmim, Had Nes, tel. 04/697-0027, www.tenebagolan.co.il, US$275 d) is a luxury experience that caters to people who want a rustic experience with individualized pampering. Every suite has a hot tub, a terrace view of the Golan Heights, and a flat-screen TV. You can borrow a bicycle for free, and there is also free wireless Internet. A common kitchen is open for use, and a prepared Israeli breakfast is included. It is five minutes to the Galilee and about 30 minutes from Tiberias.

One of several luxury accommodations on the Ramot Moshav, **Naomi's Place** (Kochal, Moshav Ramot, tel. 04/673-2157, www.zimmeril.com, US$250) is a bed-and-breakfast in the midst of a date plantation. The four wood cabins are set on spacious grounds that include a swimming pool, playground, and an area to cook out. About five minutes from the Galilee and 20 minutes from the holy city of Safed, it is very close to hiking trails. Every cabin has a cozy, warm interior with soft lighting and large, luxurious beds, a private garden, hammock, a kitchenette, and fireplace. Though breakfast is provided, there are also restaurants nearby.

Conveniently located near a bus stop and just five minutes from the Golan Heights Winery, **Vila Golan** (Inbar St. on the outskirts of Katsrin, tel. 050/957-5758, www.zimmeril.com, US$230 d) is a very small luxury bed-and-breakfast in the sweet little town of Katsrin. The four suites all have a fully loaded kitchenette, a huge bed, a TV-DVD player, and free wireless Internet. You get a free bottle of wine on arrival and breakfast is included. There is an option for a room with a hot tub. The town's country club gives guests of Vila Golan a discount, and it's a short drive to the Galilee.

GETTING THERE AND AROUND
Car
If you can manage it, the best way to get around the Golan Heights is by car. Any other independent mode of transportation might prove a bit tricky. One option is to rent a car in Tiberias from **Eldan Car Rental** (1 HaBannim St., tel. 04/672-2831, www.eldan.co.il), the largest domestic car rental company in Israel.

Bus
Egged buses (www.egged.co.il) do travel into the Golan, and a trip to Katsrin (Qatsrin), a city about 40 minutes north of Tiberias is possible. To Katsrin from Tel Aviv is about 3.5 hours (bus 843, NIS46 one-way), and from Jerusalem it is closer to 4 hours (bus 966, NIS46 one-way). Once you are in the Golan, there are Egged routes that traverse between the towns on a regular basis.

The West Bank

Highlights

★ **Church of the Nativity:** This ancient church in Bethlehem, believed to be the birthplace of Jesus, has an atmosphere of mystery and wonder (page 229).

★ **Jacob's Well:** Way off the beaten path, Jacob's Well is where Jesus is said to have once stopped for a drink of water. It is housed deep under a massive church that's set amidst vast, lushly landscaped grounds (page 238).

★ **Mount of Temptation Monastery:** High above Jericho is the place where Jesus is said to have been tempted by Satan. This spot is now home to a monastery, which you can reach by a cable car that travels over the biblical-era ruins of Jericho (page 241).

★ **Hisham Palace:** A mosque, massive mosaic floors, decorative touches, and fountains are the highlights of these ruins near Jericho, still in the process of being restored and preserved (page 243).

★ **Wadi Qelt and St. George Monastery:** Hike a canyon next to flowing streams that lead to an ancient Greek Orthodox monastery (page 244).

I n spite of the complicated legal, political, and human rights situation in the West Bank, it remains home to some important archaeological and spiritual sites—holy to Muslims, Jews, and Christians.

The West Bank also encompasses significant, ancient biblical cities such as Jericho, Bethlehem, Hebron, and Nablus, alongside more modern cities like Ramallah and Ariel.

Situated between Israel and the border with Jordan, the West Bank is an area of about 2,200 square miles. The separation barrier constructed by Israel running along much of the highway is a physical border that continues to be extended, while the legal border is a based on the 1949 Armistice Agreement Line.

The actual landscape of the West Bank is a patchwork of olive and lemon tree groves, Arab villages and cities, and Jewish settlements, with the occasional checkpoint or fence with concertina wire. While the West Bank is not part of Israel proper, different interpretations of borders, the increasing presence of Jewish settlements, and the decreasing holdings of Arab villages have seriously complicated its status both regionally and internationally. Israel maintains a strong military presence in many areas of the West Bank, particularly in areas where there are Jewish settlements.

SPECIAL TRAVEL CONSIDERATIONS

Some parts of the West Bank are completely under Palestinian control, some are under shared control with Israel, and some are completely under Israeli control; these are known as Areas A, B, and C, respectively. Many people also refer to the area collectively as Palestine or as Judea and Samaria. It's important to understand whether you are in Area A, B, or C, as it will impact how you move about and what the generally accepted customs are. Some areas of the West Bank are extremely religiously conservative and have significant security concerns (such as Hebron), and other areas are tricky to navigate unless you connect with a group of some kind (such as Nablus).

When traveling in the region, keep in mind

Previous: prayer at the Tomb of the Patriarchs in Hebron; the old city of Hebron. **Above:** the Mount of Temptation Monastery in Jericho.

The West Bank

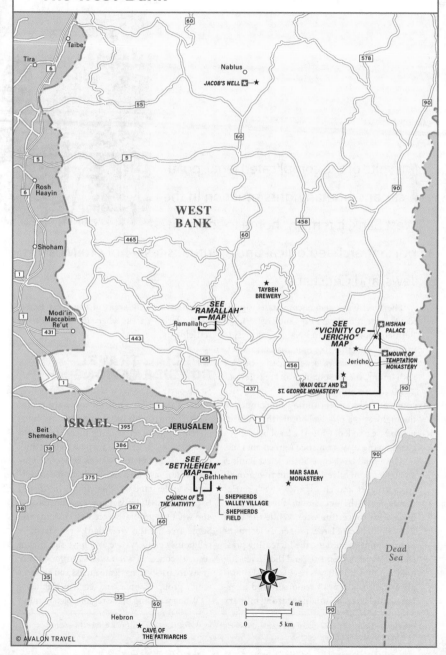

Taibe

Tira

6

60

Nablus

JACOB'S WELL

578

55

60

90

5

5

Rosh Haayin

6

WEST BANK

465

60

458

Shoham

90

1

Modi'in Maccabim Re'ut

431

TAYBEH BREWERY

443

45

SEE "RAMALLAH" MAP

Ramallah

SEE "VICINITY OF JERICHO" MAP

HISHAM PALACE

458

MOUNT OF TEMPTATION MONASTERY

Jericho

437

WADI QELT AND ST. GEORGE MONASTERY

90

1

1

Beit Shemesh

395

ISRAEL

JERUSALEM

38

386

90

375

SEE "BETHLEHEM" MAP

Bethlehem

MAR SABA MONASTERY

38

367

CHURCH OF THE NATIVITY

SHEPHERDS VALLEY VILLAGE

SHEPHERDS FIELD

35

Dead Sea

35

90

60

Hebron

CAVE OF THE PATRIARCHS

0   4 mi

0   5 km

© AVALON TRAVEL

Areas A, B, and C

The West Bank is divided into three sections: Palestinian Authority-controlled (Area A); Palestinian Authority and Israeli military joint control (Area B); and Israeli military-controlled (Area C). If you looked at a map of the West Bank that was coded according to these three areas, you would see a complex division of shaded zones indicating territory and control. The divisions are part of the reason that while traveling through the West Bank, you will find checkpoints, fences, and gates in certain areas.

An easy way to remember who is in control where goes something like this: the Palestinian Authority (PA) has an A in its acronym, and controls Area A. Both the PA and Israel control area B and the word "both" starts with B. By process of elimination, Area C is fully Israeli controlled.

It is important to take into account safety precautions before you go to any area in the West Bank and know whether you are going to Area A, B, or C. For example, Nablus is in the very center of a large Area A section and the city of Ariel (which started as a small settlement) is in an Area C section. Hebron is a special case; it is an occupied city under Israeli military control.

Some Arab villages and Jewish settlements are partially in more than one area, or in an area that is not controlled by their respective government. Most of the West Bank is Area C, and every major Arab town in the region, even if it is in Area A or B, is surrounded on almost every side by Area C territory.

that it is important to wear conservative clothing (especially for women), which generally means nothing too tight or revealing, and it's best to keep arms and legs covered. Using Israeli currency is recommended, though U.S. currency is also taken (but you will likely get hugely overcharged). When traveling in the West Bank, the general rule of thumb is to always err on the side of caution in all things. Keep any electronics or camera equipment out of sight and close by.

Complications and special considerations aside, the West Bank is one of the most fascinating areas of the region. It is a bit on the wild side and evokes a feeling of being in untamed territory. But it's also an easy place to

graffiti on a wall in Ramallah

connect with a rich historical past. Looking out over the rugged, sparsely populated landscape with its patchwork of gray-green olive trees and minarets, it is easy to see why so many people of different faiths want to maintain a connection to this part of the land.

HISTORY

The recent history of the West Bank is the most relevant for the purpose of travel. The current border of the West Bank was created in a 1949 armistice agreement that divided the newly created Jewish state from the other parts of the Mandatory Palestine.

In the 1948 War of Independence, Israel took control of the western part of Jerusalem, and Jordan took control of the eastern part, including the Old City, home to dozens of sites that are deeply important to the Christian, Jewish, and Muslim faiths. Until 1967, the West Bank was ruled by Jordan. In 1967, the Six Day War between Israel, Egypt, Jordan, and Syria led to Israel's capture of the eastern side of Jerusalem. The result of that war is essentially the reason for today's existence of East and West Jerusalem. According to international law, East Jerusalem is part of the West Bank, and situated inside of the 1949 armistice lines. According to Israeli practice, East Jerusalem is under the control and governance of the Jerusalem Municipality and the Israeli government. The complexity of this background is why border police patrol the area around and inside of Jerusalem's Old City; it is technically situated on a border zone.

The West Bank (except for Jerusalem) of today is divided into three zones: Palestinian Authority-controlled (Area A); joint Palestinian Authority and Israeli-controlled (Area B); and Israeli-controlled (Area C). The status of both Jerusalem and the West Bank is one of the most contentious issues impeding progress toward a peace agreement between the Palestinian Authority and Israel.

ORIENTATION

The West Bank is the area to the west of the Jordan River and east of Israel. To enter or exit the West Bank, you will have to pass through checkpoints. Under normal circumstances, the checkpoints are cursory and you are not stopped. The West Bank extends just to the north of Jenin, covers much of the Dead Sea, and its southernmost point is just 25 minutes from Beer Sheva, the largest city in the Negev. The border between Israel and the West Bank north of Jerusalem is roughly along Highway 6 which runs north to south, and circles around Nablus just south of Afula. South of Jerusalem, the West Bank border extends south between Highway 35 and Highway 60 until it circles east before reaching the city of Beer Sheva.

PLANNING YOUR TIME

In spite of the tangled legal situation, the West Bank remains home to some important historical and religious sites and it is worth spending a couple of days exploring the more notable sights. There are also some fantastic day hikes in the region.

There are countless places to enter and exit the West Bank, and most checkpoints consist of guard huts manned by soldiers who may or may not stop vehicles. Taxis are often stopped. It is always wise to have your passport handy for inspection.

If you plan to stay in the West Bank for a couple of nights, a good place to base yourself is Bethlehem or Ramallah. Both places have a range of options.

The best way to get around the region is by car or share taxi. Many parts of the West Bank are much better experienced as part of an organized tour group or with a hired private tour guide who speaks Arabic and can drive. Hire a guide in Jerusalem; the odds of getting ripped off are high if you hire someone in Bethlehem.

Bethlehem

Bethlehem is a city of about 75,000 people that depends largely on tourists and pilgrims who are attracted by its religious and historical sites, chief among them the place where Jesus was born. It is 15 minutes from Jerusalem and completely controlled by the Palestinian Authority. It is illegal for Israelis to enter Bethlehem.

SAFETY

Bethlehem is 15 minutes from Jerusalem's city center, and the entrance is through a fairly strict checkpoint. You must bring your passport with you and be prepared for a wait when leaving the city. Though it is basically safe, tensions can run high there from time to time, so check your embassy website before going.

Once in Bethlehem, you will notice a number of heavily armed Palestinian Authority troops standing on the street. Though they may look intimidating, they are actually extremely friendly to tourists and are a great resource for information.

Despite the paranoia some people have about visiting Bethlehem, it is a generally safe and friendly city, though if you are driving you might get lost, even with a GPS.

SIGHTS
Manger Square

The heart of Bethlehem's Old City and the jumping-off point for the town's most popular attractions and events is **Manger Square** (center of Bethlehem off of Manger St.). A large number of hotels and places to eat are also located here.

★ Church of the Nativity

Not overly impressive from the outside, the **Church of the Nativity** (Manger Sq. in the Old City, tel. 02/274-2440; church hours 6:30am-7:30pm Mon.-Sat. Apr.-Sept., 5:30am-5pm Mon.-Sat. Oct.-Mar.; grotto hours 6am-noon and 2pm-7:30pm Mon.-Sat. Apr.-Sept., 5am-noon and 2pm-5pm Mon.-Sat. Oct.-Mar.; on Sun. church is open for holy mass and grotto is open only in afternoon; free) is imposing and affecting once you duck through the low main entrance door. Basically

the interior of the Church of the Nativity

Bethlehem

0
0
250 yds
250 m

PALESTINE ST.

DERECH BEIT JALA

ANGEL
HOTEL

MARTYR

JAMAL ABDUL NASER ST.

CHILDREN

AL-SAFF ST.

DERECH HEVRON

SCHOOLS

JACIR PALACE
INTERCONTINENTAL

DERECH BEIT JALA

CHILDREN

CHILDREN ST.

DERECH HEVRON

RACHEL'S
TOMB ★

AL-SAFF ST.

BOULOS ST.

SIXTH ST.

UNIVERSITY ST.

MANGER

WAD MAALI ST.

SCHOOLS

WAD AL-TAHIR

CHURCH
OF THE NATIVITY

MILK GROTTO ST.

DERECH S.O.S.

MANGER

DERECH S.O.S.

ANFRA

ST. CATHERINE'S
CHURCH

ST. JOSEPH

WAD AL-SAWAHRA

BEIT BASSA ST.

JINNA ST.

JERUSALEM ST.

SHEPHERD'S FIELD ST.

SHEPHERDS VALLEY
VILLAGE

EFRAT ST.

SHEPHERDS
FIELD

SHEPHERD
HOUSE
HOTEL

© AVALON TRAVEL

The Settlement Issue

Israeli soldiers guard a settlement in Hebron.

One of the most confusing and complicated issues of the West Bank is the settlements: groups of Jews who have settled in homes throughout the region. The population of Jewish settlers in the West Bank is well over 350,000 and growing all the time. That number does not include about 300,000 Jews who live in East Jerusalem and developments around the Jerusalem area.

The presence of settlements in some parts of the West Bank is illegal according to international law. The continued support (and in some cases encouragement) of settlements by the Israeli government is interpreted by many as an act of bad faith in the peace process with the Palestinian Authority and has been a major stumbling block in that process. The Israeli government has forcibly removed settlements when they are on land controlled fully by the Palestinian Authority and also forcibly removed Palestinians from their homes in other areas. Some settlers live peacefully next to their Arab neighbors, whose villages often surround them, but there have been many cases of violence from both sides.

The range of types of settlements is enormous. They can be anything from a small group of 10 families living on a hilltop in fairly makeshift accommodations to well-established cities with a full infrastructure and municipal government services. In areas that are not fully under Israeli military control, the government provides armed soldiers for protection, basic services such as electricity, and builds roads.

The issue of settlements is extremely contentious both domestically and internationally. The unsatisfactory resolution of the situation and continued building of new settlements are regarded as a major impediment to peace between Arabs and Jews in the region. The very existence of Jewish settlements throughout the West Bank creates a serious problem in the question of the formal establishment of a Palestinian state. If the armistice line that demarcates the West Bank were to become the legal border of a Palestinian state, a quarter of a million Jews would find themselves living in a foreign country.

Several excellent books have been written on the topic; one of the most recent is called *Lords of the Land* by Idith Zirtal and Akiva Eldar.

at the center of Bethlehem in the Old City, it is one of the oldest working churches in the world, having been constructed by the Roman emperor Constantine in the 4th century AD. The modern church is under the control and guardianship of the Greek Orthodox Church, the Roman Catholics, and the Armenians.

The church building is over the grotto where Mary is believed to have given birth to Jesus. The pillared interior is dark with shafts of light streaming through the high windows and low-hanging ceremonial lamps. The entire atmosphere is quite solemn and mysterious.

Due to its popularity among tourists and pilgrims, you might run into people selling their tour guide services just outside the entrance of the church. They charge NIS80 or more. If you hire a guide, it's best to make arrangements in advance and go with them to the site.

To get to the grotto, you need to go down some stairs where you'll see a 14-pointed silver star with the inscription *Hic de Virgin Maria Jesus Christus Natus Est* (Here Jesus Christ was born to the Virgin Mary). Nearby is the **cloister of St. Jerome,** who is known for translating the Bible into Latin.

St. Catherine's Church

The location of the annual Catholic midnight Christmas mass that is broadcast on television globally is the Roman Catholic **St. Catherine's Church** (Manger Sq. in the Old City center, 6am-noon and 2pm-7pm daily Apr.-Sept., 5:30am-5:30pm daily Oct.-Mar., free), attached to the Church of the Nativity. The late 19th-century church was built by Franciscans and has a series of grottoes that were once used as places to live.

Rachel's Tomb

The third holiest site to the Jewish religion, **Rachel's Tomb** (Jerusalem-Hebron Rd. near the entrance to Bethlehem, 7:30am-4pm Sun.-Thurs., 7:30am-3:30pm Fri., free) is the burial site of Rachel, wife of Jacob, who died giving birth to his second son. Over the years, the

Mar Saba Monastery

The West Bank vs. Palestine

The language used to describe the land to the east of Jerusalem commonly referred to as either the West Bank or Palestine tends to be vague.

The west in the name refers to its western proximity to the Jordan River, as it used to be part of the Hashemite Kingdom of Jordan. A reference to the area as Palestine is more of a political statement than a formal name. The hope for many is that this will change, however.

In November 2012, the United Nations granted Palestine non-member observer status, while still urging efforts for a formal, two-state solution between Israel and the Palestinians. At the time of publication, no such solution had been reached.

The most neutral way to refer to the region is to call it the West Bank.

domed structure of the tomb has been gradually enclosed in a walled compound due to the deteriorating security situation in the area. Access to the tomb is very limited, and it might not be possible to enter unless you are with a tour group that has been preapproved.

Mar Saba Monastery

Only men are allowed to enter, but the 5th-century Greek Orthodox **Mar Saba Monastery** (about 9 miles from Bethlehem, tel. 02/277-3135, 8am-5pm daily, free) is a beautiful building that has existed in its current state for 1,500 years and overlooks the Kidron Valley. There is no electricity or running water in the monastery, and it is full of passages, alcoves, cells, and stairs that add to its ambience.

ENTERTAINMENT AND EVENTS
Christmas Eve

One of the main events in Bethlehem is **Christmas Eve,** which includes a midnight mass in St. Catherine's Church, visiting the birthplace of Jesus in the Church of the Nativity, and celebrations and live music in Manger Square, around the stage and enormous Christmas tree that are set up for the event.

SHOPPING

There is a surprising amount of shopping to be had in Bethlehem, but the main draw is directly surrounding **Manger Square.** There are several shops that cater to pilgrims and sell postcards and handmade trinkets, boxes, and nativity scene pieces made from olive wood, many with inlaid mother-of-pearl. Shop owners try to sell the pieces for very high prices, but feel free to bargain with them if you're interested in something.

Well worth a stop is the **Palestinian Heritage Center** (Maha Saca, Manger St., tel. 02/274-2381, www.phc.ps, 10am-8pm Mon.-Sat., call ahead to confirm if open), which sells embroidery and other handcrafted products. The center employs women from refugee camps in the West Bank and aims to preserve Palestinian heritage through the display and sale of authentic dresses, jewelry, furniture and more. They also sell a range of embroidered items and house a permanent exhibition of Palestinian cultural heritage.

Just off of Manger Square is a pedestrian street full of shops selling all kinds of goods, from handwoven rugs to soda. The shopkeepers try to sell products for a price that is based on the product's status as an antique. If you plan on shopping here, do not pay the first

items for sale in Bethlehem

price you're offered; instead, be willing to walk away to get the lowest possible bid from the vendor.

A great place to shop for locally made products including ceramics and blown glass and olive-based products including soap and wood is the **Bethlehem Fair Trade Artisans** (Milk Grotto St., tel. 02/275-0365, www.bethlehemfairtrade.org, 10am-5pm Mon.-Sat.). Contact them for more information about their tour guide services and educational programs about their products and the area.

FOOD

If you visit Bethlehem just for the day, the easiest place to get something to eat is in one of the restaurants that surround the plaza area of Manger Square. Another option, though pricier, is any of the nicer hotels, as most have some kind of dining option, especially in the evenings. If you are traveling with a tour group, the tour will probably make arrangements with a particular place in advance, eliminating the guesswork for you.

Middle Eastern

Known for their very consistent and delicious falafel, **Afteem Al-Yafawi** (Manger Sq. in the Old City, tel. 02/274-7940, afteemrestaurant@ yahoo.com, 8am-9pm Mon.-Sat., NIS60) is a family-owned restaurant that has been in business since 1948. The restaurant is in an old Arab-style building of stone, and they serve generous helpings of hummus, falafel, and other traditional Middle Eastern foods.

You can experience Bedouin hospitality at **Shepherds Valley Village** (Shepherds Field St., Beit Sahour, tel. 02/277-3875, 11am-5pm Mon.-Sat., NIS55). You can lunch inside a huge Bedouin tent on *mezze* (appetizers) and grilled meat and vegetables, with a view of the area that, according to tradition, is where the shepherds saw the star above Bethlehem that led them to baby Jesus.

For an experience that will get you some interaction with locals, **Ka'abar** (Beit Jala St., near Municipality Bldg., Beit Jala, tel. 02/274-1419, 11am-9pm Mon.-Sat., NIS40) is in the village just west of Bethlehem called Beit Jala. Ka'abar grills chicken outdoors, but has no menu. When you order, you get a prix fixe menu with meat and five side dishes and mint tea to finish. It's just a taxi ride from Manger Square.

Italian

For some really delicious pizza made with high-quality ingredients, **Mundo**

street near Manger Square in Bethlehem

Restaurant (Manger St., tel. 02/274-2299, 11am-11pm daily, NIS55) is family-friendly and a popular spot for both tourists and locals. They serve all kinds of other Italian food, mostly pasta dishes, and the interior of the restaurant is lined with floor to ceiling wood. An entire wall is comprised of huge windows that afford a fantastic view of the area.

Cafés and Coffee Shops

The sweet little Dar Jdoudna Coffee Shop (Manger Sq. in the Old City, tel. 02/274-3212, 9am-8pm Mon.-Sat., NIS40) is housed in an old textile factory building with an olive oil press. It's a good place to have a coffee with something sweet. Dar Jdoudna means "our grandfather's house," which is symbolic of the Palestinian expression of returning to their ancestral homes.

ACCOMMODATIONS

Bethlehem is highly accustomed to international visitors, including pilgrims and tourists of all kinds, and set up with a range of accommodation options from five-star hotels to hostels and guesthouses.

Under US$100

If you are on a budget but still want to be close to the action, Al-Salam Hotel (Manger St., opposite the Church of the Nativity, tel. 02/276-4083/4, samhotel@p-ol.com, US$60 d) has the location and price that outweigh the very sparse setup. Every room has a bathroom, shower, TV, and phone. The hotel is on the small side with only about two dozen rooms and very plain, spare furnishings. It is a good option if you are making a last-minute booking and want a budget price.

With a great atmosphere and an affordable price, the Angel Hotel (184 Al-Sahel St., Beit Jala, tel. 02/276-6880, www.angelhotel.ps, US$90 d) is one of Bethlehem's more well-known and popular places to stay. It is a bit off the beaten path in nearby Beit Jala, but the hotel has a rooftop restaurant with incredible views, free wireless Internet, a breakfast buffet, and a bar with an outdoor terrace.

The rooms are decorated very simply with tile flooring and have basic amenities.

The Bethlehem Star Hotel (Freres St., tel. 02/274-3249, www.bethlehemstarhotel.com, US$80 d) is on the plain side and known as a favorite spot for foreign journalists to stay. Close to Bethlehem's city center, the midsize hotel has a fantastic view of the city from its breakfast room, and there is also a rooftop restaurant and free wireless Internet. Every double room comes with a minibar, hair dryer, direct dial phone, and an LCD TV. The hotel has a lobby coffee shop and the rooftop restaurant has views of Shepherd's Field and other sites around the city. There is live music once a week.

US$100-150

The midsize Shepherd House Hotel (Shepherds Field St., tel. 02/274-0656, 02/274-0657, or 02/274-0658, www.shepherdbethlehem.com, US$125 d) is in a pastoral setting and a short drive to the Church of the Nativity and other Christian sites. Billed as "the only four-star hotel in Bethlehem," the hotel has a 24-hour front desk, dry cleaning and laundry service, free wireless Internet, and some of the more than 100 rooms have a balcony with a view of the lovely mountain landscape that surrounds Bethlehem. The exterior of the building is simple, but the rooms are comfortably furnished and spacious, and the elegant lobby is full of comfortable chairs and nice corners to sit.

US$150-200

The Jacir Palace Intercontinental (Jerusalem-Hebron Rd., tel. 02/276-6777, www.jacirpalace.ps, US$150 d) gets its name from its former status as a palace. The perfectly beautiful, classy hotel has a soothing atmosphere and is full of elegant touches. Even if you're not a guest here, it's worthwhile to have a cappuccino in the lobby coffee shop amid the massive stone pillars and skylight atrium. All of the 250 rooms at the Jacir are decorated in a warm, yet elegant fashion with comfortable touches like loveseats and coffee

Alternative Tours

In recent years, there has been a proliferation of alternative tour companies, offering options other than the standard tour guide or group. Many of the alternative tours emphasize a participatory experience, such as helping to pick olives during the harvest, or have a political agenda or slant. Either way, they can give you a fresh perspective on the West Bank.

One of the most popular and well-known social enterprise alternative tour companies is **Green Olive Tours** (tel. 03/721-9540 in Israel, U.S. tel. 612/276-2077, www.toursinenglish.com). The company gives tours that deal with the culture, history, and political geography of the West Bank for groups and individuals. The work the company does also aims to support the local population in the areas it tours by working with local tour guides, overnight host family stays, and encouraging the purchase of local crafts.

Another option is the well-established and reputable **Alternative Tourism Group (ATG)** (74 Star St. in Beit Sahour, tel. 02/277-2151, www.atg.ps), a Palestinian NGO that specializes in taking a critical look at the historical, cultural, and political situation in the West Bank. The company is based in Beit Sahour, near Bethlehem. They also launched a smartphone app called Palestine and Palestinians, available in the Google Play store, which provides comprehensive information on the region and its people.

Though Green Olive Tours and ATG are separate companies, they sometimes work in cooperation with one another.

tables, bathtubs, balconies overlooking the hotel grounds, and a sitting area with satellite TV. The hotel has a restaurant, coffee shop, gym, bar, a massive lobby that doubles as a coffee shop, and a pool. Make reservations as far in advance as possible; it is far and away the nicest place in town and books early, especially during December. It is a short drive to the Church of the Nativity.

About as close as you can get to the main action in town is **Manger Square Hotel** (Manger St., tel. 02/277-8888, http://mangersquarehotel.com, US$150 d), an upscale hotel with 220 rooms that caters to international visitors. The hotel has a spacious lobby and dining room that serves buffet-style meals, free wireless Internet throughout, and modern rooms with wooden furniture, satellite TV, and rooms with a minibar. Though it is just steps from the main tourist attractions of Bethlehem, the hotel may entice you to stay inside and relax at the bar or get room service.

INFORMATION AND SERVICES
Tour Guides

Visiting Bethlehem with a tour guide is a good way to experience the city and avoid many of the hassles you might encounter on your own. **(John) Hanna Awwad** (PO Box 51340, Jerusalem, 91513, tel. 02/289-9305 or 054/445-2824, awwadhanna@yahoo.com) is based in Jerusalem, which is best because you would not want to go to Bethlehem and then try to hire a guide. John is so well-known and connected in Jerusalem that if he happens to not be available, he will be able to recommend an alternative.

GETTING THERE AND AROUND

There are several ways to get into Bethlehem, and all of them involve going through a checkpoint.

Checkpoint

The main checkpoint entrance to Bethlehem is 15 minutes from Jerusalem city center at the end of Hebron Road. Going into the city is easier than getting out because the guards check the cars going into Jerusalem a bit more closely.

Taxis and Share Taxis

Taking a taxi into Bethlehem might prove difficult. The easiest thing to do is take a taxi to the checkpoint, walk through, and find another taxi on the other side. It is a bit confusing where the checkpoint is exactly because of the lack of signs into or out of the city. Just follow the general flow of traffic, or keep asking until you get the right directions.

Damascus Gate Buses and Taxis

If you go to Damascus Gate in Jerusalem near the Old City, you should be able to find a bus or *sherut* (share taxi) that will take you to Bethlehem. Just be confident about what you're doing, and don't get tricked into being driven for a fixed price by a taxi: Insist that they use the meter; it's the law.

Buses

You can also take a Jerusalem city bus straight down Hebron Road (buses 71, 72, 73, 74) to the end, walk through the checkpoint, and pick up a taxi on the other side. Bus routes change, so check in advance what goes in that direction.

Nablus and Vicinity

Mentioned many times in the Bible by the name Shechem and once a flashpoint of violence during the Second Intifada, over the past decade-plus Nablus has been steadily growing and stabilizing, though it still sometimes has violence. There is also a sizable *shuk* (outdoor market), An-Najah National University, and Nablus is famed as the home to the best version of the Arab treat, *knafe,* that you will ever eat (not an overstatement).

Situated at the center of the Palestinian-controlled area of the West Bank, Nablus is avoided by most Israelis, and in times of regional unrest, scheduled tours to the area are usually canceled. If you can manage the trip, Nablus has a unique charm and very warm residents. But check your embassy's website for any travel warnings before going.

aerial view of Nablus

SIGHTS

There are very few sights in Nablus unless you are interested in an intensive tour with highlights of the complicated political situation and some modern history about what happened during the Second Intifada and afterward. Once you are here, however, it's a fun place to stroll, buy some souvenirs for a great price, and try *knafe*.

Old City Market

The center of Nablus is home to the **Old City,** which serves as a destination for shopping, eating, and sightseeing. There are six quarters to the very densely populated Old City: Yasmina, Gharb, Qaryun, Aqaba, Qaysariyya, and Habala. You can find six Turkish baths here and a few historic monuments. Note the fading posters plastered about the area and remembrance plaques of people who died during fighting with Israeli forces, including occasional bullet holes on walls and unrepaired windows.

A Samaritan man prepares the Passover lamb.

Mount Gerizim

Overlooking Nablus is **Mount Gerizim,** home to the last remaining community of Samaritans, who are guardians of some of the region's strictest and most ancient religious traditions. They believe that the earth of the mountain they live on was used by God to create Adam, and thus it is extremely holy to them. The area has numerous archaeological ruins. It is possible to visit the area, including the Samaritan community that lives here, but you should arrange for a guide familiar with the area to take you. On Passover, you can see a traditional lamb sacrifice at the community center.

★ Jacob's Well

Well worth the side trip of about 10 minutes by car from Nablus city center, **Jacob's Well** (off of Rte. 5487 at the entrance to Nablus, tel. 09/237-5123, 9am-noon and 2pm-4pm daily, until 5pm in the summer, free) is said to be the same well that a Samaritan woman gave Jesus a drink of water from during a long journey 2,000 years ago. The well (also known as the Well of Sychar) is an object of pilgrimage and housed deep inside the caverns of a massive Eastern Orthodox Church on the grounds of Bir Ya'qub monastery built over and around a 4th-century church.

Beneath the high altar at the center of the church is the crypt that houses the well. You can descend into the cavernous crypt and draw a drink of cool, clear water from the same well Jesus drank from. The well has been measured as about 130 feet deep, adding to its reputation as one of the more authentic sites in the Holy Land because it would have been almost impossible to move.

Even though it is immediately off of a main road, the gate and high stone wall keep the area protected and give the very pretty grounds of the church the atmosphere of a calm oasis.

The church, grounds, and well are closely guarded. You should call in advance of a visit to make sure it is open. Only call if you are certain you will visit, as they might open it especially for you and await your arrival.

Refugee Camps That Became Permanent

markets in Balata Refugee Camp

Since the establishment of the State of Israel, various regional wars and conflicts and disputes over land have forced displaced Arab residents into refugee camps. In many cases, the refugee camps have perpetuated a situation of instability, poverty, and dependence for the people living there.

According to the United Nations, the West Bank is home to 771,000 registered refugees, and about a quarter of them live in refugee camps.

One of the largest, Balata Refugee Camp, is just outside of Nablus. It was established in 1950 and has continued to exist through today, with a current population of about 23,000 and an unemployment rate of 25 percent. Balata's population is larger than most towns in the region. Balata's civil society is extremely active and parts of its landscape are small, rough alleys between tightly packed stone buildings with piles of rubble instead of a simple playground or park.

Much of the support for residents of refugee camps comes from international bodies such as the United Nations, nonprofits, and nongovernmental organizations.

Balata Refugee Camp

You won't notice it unless you ask around, but almost directly across the street from Jacob's Well is the **Balata Refugee Camp Community Center,** the largest refugee camp in the West Bank and home to about 23,000 people. If you're interested in seeing their community center, you can ask someone from the church for an introduction. The people running the community center are very friendly and willing to chat about their living situation and the general conditions in the area. They also sell a number of nice, handmade items that are small, lightweight, and easy to pack for a return trip. The profit from the sale of the goods goes to support the community center and women artisans in the community.

FOOD

For a wide variety of things to eat in Nablus, just head anywhere near the Old City. Here you will find everything from restaurants to snacks and sweets.

A very nice spot to sit for some light food and tea or coffee is **Zeit Ou Zaatar** (City Center downtown, inside the Al Yasmeen Hotel, tel. 09/233-3555, 9am-9pm daily, NIS55). The furniture and appointments in the sitting area are mixed antiques and modern pieces, and the atmosphere is very Middle Eastern with old lamps and mirrors. It is the perfect spot for an intimate discussion, and the impeccable service is on par with a four-star hotel.

Partly charming for its atmosphere and partly for its food, **Al Saraya** (Hiteen St. just east of the Nablus Mall, tel. 09/233-5444, http://visitpalestine.ps, 11am-9pm daily, NIS55) serves up delightful Arabic dishes, such as *mansaf* (lamb in fermented dried yogurt) and *musakhan* (roasted chicken cooked with onions, sumac, allspice, and saffron), in the setting of a 140-year-old house. Old copper lights and oriental window frames add to the ambience of this favorite neighborhood spot. It is just on the outskirts of the Old City, making it an easy stop after an afternoon of sightseeing.

ACCOMMODATIONS

There isn't much reason to stay overnight in Nablus, but if you do need a hotel, it would be advisable to gravitate toward an area where foreigners gather.

The **International Friends' Guest House** (Annajah Al Qadeem St., tel. 09/238-1064, www.guesthouse.ps, US$55 d) can provide both an affordable place to stay and historical and current information about the political situation in the region. The guesthouse offers a variety of resources for researchers and those who want to make a trip to the Old City of Nablus and nearby refugee camps. There are also activities and seminars on a weekly basis. The building is a lovely, older stone house with some nice gardens and not far from the center of the city.

Knafe

Whatever else you eat, go in search of *knafe* (pronounced ka-nah-feh), a flat Arab cheese and biscuit-type creation cooked up on large, shallow pans and served fresh out of the oven. There are several shops in the Old City that sell it; ask anybody to point you in the direction of the nearest *knafe* shop. A happy warning: the variation of *knafe* served in Nablus is considered the best of the best, so once you have it here, you will likely be ruined for eating it anywhere else.

INFORMATION AND SERVICES

Two very useful websites about Nablus are www.nablusguide.com and http://visitpalestine.ps.

Most Israelis will not go to Nablus, nor do they want to, but it is safe place for a foreign visitor. Keep in mind that it is a conservative, mostly Muslim town and you should always check your embassy website in advance.

GETTING THERE AND AROUND

The two best ways to get to Nablus are by hired taxi or share taxi. Don't be surprised when your hired taxi stops along the way to pass you off to another taxi at a large taxi parking lot just outside of the city limits. It is related to the security situation in the region.

The easiest, cheapest, and safest way to get around Nablus is by hired taxi.

Checkpoints

The checkpoint situation surrounding Nablus changes according to the severity of the security situation. You will go through at least one checkpoint, maybe more, before arriving. Be prepared with a very clear, simple answer about the purpose of your visit and keep your passport handy.

Jericho

The ancient and low-lying city of Jericho is situated at about 853 feet below sea level. There are some amazing archaeological and biblical sites here, reflecting its thousands of years of history as a continuously inhabited city.

Jericho has been conquered repeatedly over the millennia, first by the Israelites after 40 years of desert wandering when, according to the Bible, Joshua made the walls come tumbling down. It was also conquered by the Babylonians, Romans, Byzantines, Crusaders, and Christians.

SIGHTS

★ Mount of Temptation Monastery

Perched about 1,140 feet above Jericho and seemingly etched into the side of a cliff is the Greek Orthodox **Mount of Temptation Monastery** (8am-1pm and 3pm-4pm Mon.-Fri., one hour later in the summer, 8am-2pm Sat., free), also called Jabel Quruntul, which dates back to the 12th century. The Crusaders originally built one church in a cave partway up the cliff and another church on the summit.

The current monastery dates back to the 19th century. The mountain is believed to be the place where Jesus was tempted by Satan. If you take the cable car ride, you will pass over excavations of biblical-era Jericho.

You can take the 30-minute hike up the mountainside or ride the **cable car** (tel. 02/232-1590, 8:30am-6:30pm Mon.-Sat., adult NIS40, child NIS22) to reach the monastery in about five minutes, but the view from below can also satisfy.

Museum of the Good Samaritan

Situated on the main highway between Jerusalem and Jericho, the **Museum of the Good Samaritan** (off Hwy. 1 at Kfar Adumim Junction, www.parks.org.il, 9am-5pm Sun.-Thurs., NIS20) offers a chance to see some detailed mosaics from around Israel and

Mount of Temptation Monastery

Vicinity of Jericho

HISHAM
PALACE

90

AYN
AL-SULTAN

GREEN
VALLEY

HISHAN PALACE

MOUNT OF
TEMPTATION
MONASTERY

LIMONAH

AIN ES-SULTAN

JERICHO

AHINAD ASHUGAERI

WADI AL-QEIT

AQABAT
JABR

WADI QELT AND
ST. GEORGE MONASTERY

VERED
YERICHO

0   500 yds

0   500 m

© AVALON TRAVEL

the West Bank. Also on display indoors and alongside the mosaics that range from quite small to massive are stones with ancient engravings. The museum offers a chance to learn a bit of the history of the Samaritans and their contributions to the region.

★ Hisham Palace

The gorgeous ruins of **Hisham Palace** (about 2 miles off Qasr Hisham St., follow guidepost signs, tel. 09/232-2522, 8am-5pm daily Oct.-Mar., 8am-6pm daily Apr.-Sept., NIS15) are a major archaeological site in Jericho. The palace was built in the 8th century, possibly as a seasonal retreat of some kind.

It's just a mile north of Jericho proper, and the excavated site shows the remains that were destroyed in an earthquake in AD 747. Among the site's treasures are a mosque, water fountains, enormous mosaic floors, and decorative accents like the often-photographed carved six-pointed star window.

Restoration and preservation work have been carried out with the cooperation and support of the Italian government, UNESCO, the Palestinian Department of Antiquities, and the Franciscan Archaeological Institute. There is a small museum just to the right of the entrance that has a collection of pottery found at the site. You can see a short video about the site with a ticket at the visitors center.

Bethany on the Jordan Baptismal Site

Situated on the main highway between Jerusalem and Jericho, the **Bethany on the Jordan Baptismal Site** (off Hwy. 1 at Kfar Adumim Junction, www.parks.org.il, Sun.-Fri. 9am-dusk, free) is an easy to reach baptismal site that doesn't offer the trappings of other more touristy baptism sites, but the spiritual dimensions remain intact. The site has stairs with rails to go into the Jordan River and is patrolled by Israeli soldiers. Just a stone's throw away across the water is Jordan, and their baptismal site with a Jordanian soldier. It is an easy stop on the road between the Dead Sea and Jerusalem.

Hisham Palace

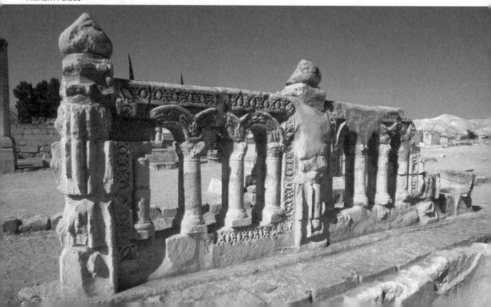

★ Wadi Qelt and St. George Monastery

If you are up for a 90-minute hike through a canyon that has year-round flowing water fed by three streams, pass through **Wadi Qelt** (at Kosiba), where there are plenty of shady spots to stop and even play or swim in the water to cool off.

Along the way you will come upon the Greek Orthodox **St. George Monastery** (Wadi Qelt Rd. in Kosiba, tel. 05/025-9949, 8am-11am and 3pm-5pm Mon.-Fri., 9am-noon Sat., 9am-5pm Sun., but hours can change so call in advance, free), which you can also get to by car. While the original dates back to AD 420, the current structure is a restoration that was done by the Greek Orthodox Church in the 19th century. The upper floor of the monastery, which looks like it is clinging to the side of a cliff, is an ancient cave and there are three churches and a bell tower built around it. The building is about three miles from Jericho.

FOOD

On a main road, **Limonah Restaurant** (Muntazhat St., tel. 02/231-2977, call for hours as they vary, NIS55) serves up a wide variety of food that ranges from hummus to pizza and is known for ridiculously large portions. The staff is helpful and friendly, and it's a spotlessly clean establishment.

Time-tested and popular, **Al Rawda** (Ketf Al-Wad St., tel. 02/232-2555, 8am-8pm daily, NIS50) is the oldest restaurant in Jericho and serves barbecue and boasts beautiful views of the city.

An easy stop is **Green Valley Park** (Ein Al-Sultan St., tel. 02/232-2349, noon-9pm daily, NIS60), an indoor-outdoor restaurant owned by a respected local family and partially supported by international charity. They serve up Middle Eastern dishes, *mezze*, and meat grilled outdoors.

ACCOMMODATIONS

If you are passing through and want to stay a night in Jericho, there are a variety of options but the lower-end accommodations come and

the baptismal site at Bethany on the Jordan, with Jordan on the opposite shore

the Greek Orthodox monastery of St. George, located in Wadi Qelt go. The safest bet is something on the higher end with international connections.

US$150-200
The **Bab Al Shams Resort** (Al-Maghtas Rd., tel. 02/231-3733, US$170 d) is not quite a resort, but this smaller hotel does have an outdoor pool on pretty grounds encircled by palm trees and a bar. The rooms are very basic with simple beds and very little furnishings or creature comforts, but with private bathrooms. The well-kept rooms also have air-conditioning, a mini-fridge, and a flat-screen TV. The hotel offers a breakfast buffet and a space to barbecue on hotel grounds.

Over US$200
The **Oasis Hotel Jericho** (Jericho-Jerusalem Rd., tel. 02/231-1200, US$220 d) offers every amenity typical of a luxury hotel, including a variety of options for dining, beautifully landscaped grounds, a Dead Sea water pool, a full-service spa, and outdoor tennis courts. Set on the outskirts of Jericho, it is 30 minutes from

the Dead Sea and an hour from Jerusalem. It also has a full suite of business services. The 181 rooms are modern with nice furnishings, desks, TVs, and comfortable, large beds. Room service and free continental breakfast are also available.

INFORMATION AND SERVICES
The **Alternative Tourism Group** (www.atg. ps) has a very useful app for smartphones and a helpful website, both with plenty of relevant information.

GETTING THERE AND AROUND
As with everywhere else in the West Bank, keep your passport handy in case you need it at checkpoints. The easiest way to get to Jericho if you don't have a rental car is to go from Ramallah via buses that travel several times during the day. The schedules are fairly informal, so you might need to ask around once you are in Ramallah.

Hebron

Known as the City of the Patriarchs, Hebron is thousands of years old and full of historical and religious significance and tension. Situated on four hills at an elevation of about 3,000 feet, it is holy to Muslims, Christians, and Jews alike because it is home to the tomb of Abraham and other patriarchs and matriarchs.

More than a dozen Jewish settlements surround the city, and several hundred Jewish settlers live in the city, which is within the jurisdiction of the Palestinian Authority but under Israeli military control. The settlers who live in the city are accompanied by armed Israeli military guards.

VISITING HEBRON
It is recommended that you visit Hebron with a tour guide or with a tour group, as it will

take all of the guesswork out of where to go and what to do, and will give you smoother access to the sites because of the complicated security situation. A centrally located local tour company called **Explore West Bank** (base of street at the Tomb of the Patriarchs, tel. 059/824-4150, zzzaa_2009@hotmail. com, $150 per day or $75 half day) can ferry you around the city and the region very easily. Other good tour companies are **Green Olive Tours** (tel. 03/721-9540 in Israel, U.S. tel. 612/276-2077, www.toursinenglish.com) and **Abraham Tours** (67 Hanevi'im St. in Jerusalem, tel. 02/566-0045, http://abraham-tours.com).

SIGHTS
Old City
One of the oldest of its kind in the West Bank,

Hebron's **Old City** includes a large *shuk* with gorgeous arched ceilings. Hebron is one of the only Islamic cities that has maintained its original urban layout, and is dominated by the Mamluk architectural style.

Tomb of the Patriarchs (Cave of Machpelah) and Ibrahimi Mosque

The traditional burial site of Abraham and other patriarchs and matriarchs, the **Tomb of the Patriarchs** (end of the street in the Old City, tel. 052/429-5554 or 052/431-7055, 4am-8pm Sun.-Thurs., dress modestly, including head covering for women, free) is one of the most sacred sites in Judaism, Islam, and Christianity. The **Ibrahimi Mosque,** second only to Jerusalem's Al Aqsa Mosque in terms of regional significance to Muslims, is located here.

The existence of the mosque came about after the tombs were enclosed by Herod the Great, who built a huge wall around the burial sites and the cave. The structure was later turned into a church and then a mosque with four Mamluk minarets on the corners of the building (only two remain). The current structure includes prayer halls, inner and outer areas, and extremely steep stairs, which lead to the rooftop area where domes mark the burial sites.

In 1994, there was a shooting of Muslims at prayer in the mosque. Since then, there has been ongoing tension and violence in Hebron, and the site, as well as the city, is tightly guarded and controlled. The visiting hours of the cave and the mosque vary, especially during religious holidays, so it is best to call in advance. If you visit during a time when regional tensions are flaring, it might also be difficult to gain entrance; be sure to take your passport.

SHOPPING

Hebron is known for its grapes, leatherwork, glassblowing, colorful and attractive ceramics, and carpets. The *shuk* is unfortunately a bit of a touchy area because it is adjacent to a part of town that is tightly controlled, but you can find a great deal of local handiwork here.

Shuk

Boasting arched rooftops and vast alleys, Hebron's *shuk* (in the town center) is a site to explore for treats, souvenirs, or just for the fun of it. Things on sale include fresh and dried fruit, olive wood items, pottery, glass craftwork, and leather products.

the exterior of the Tomb of the Patriarchs in Hebron

jewelry for sale in Hebron

Glassblowing

Hebron is famed throughout Israel and the West Bank for ceramics and glassblowing. The major glassblowing workshops of Hebron are near the northern entrance to the city in the direction of Bethlehem. One of these, the **Hebron Glass and Ceramics Factory** (Ras al Jora St., in the northern part of Hebron, tel. 02/222-8502, hebronglass@yahoo.com, 10am-5pm Mon.-Fri.) sells beautiful, original pieces that range from multicolored goblets to dishes and decorative boxes. You can take photographs, watch glassblowers using ancient techniques (probably imported to the area by Venetians), and buy products.

FOOD

The *shuk* is always a good place to pick up snacks, and you can usually find things like falafel there. If that isn't enough to satisfy your appetite, Hebron has a few other options for something quick and inexpensive, particularly on and around Nimra Street.

Middle Eastern

The very popular **Abu Mazen** (Nimra St., tel. 02/222-6168, 11am-9pm daily, NIS30) has a great reputation and is a good option for a delicious, affordable meal. It gets very crowded at lunchtime as it serves up salads, fresh bread, Middle Eastern lamb dishes, and vegetarian choices, including soup. The atmosphere is that of a fairly typical home-style restaurant with simple furnishings and a lot of regulars.

INFORMATION AND SERVICES

Online Resources

There are a couple of websites with information about Hebron, the **Hebron Municipality** site (www.hebron-city.ps) and the site of the **Jewish Community of Hebron** (www.hebron.com/english).

Safety and Security

Hebron's central Shuhada Street was closed years ago because of violence in the area. The street, which used to be a main thoroughfare and full of shops, now has restricted access, despite the fact that it leads to the Tomb of the Patriarchs and Ibrahimi Mosque. International visitors can walk and drive down it, though be aware that there are sometimes clashes in this area.

GETTING THERE AND AROUND

From Jerusalem, take the bus from next to Damascus Gate at the Old City to Abu Dis, and make sure to tell the bus driver you are going to Khalil (Arabic for Hebron). From Beer Sheva's central bus station, there are several options for buses, but make sure you don't get a ride on the bus that's going to the nearby settlement of Kiryat Arba. From Ramallah and Bethlehem, take a *sherut* (share taxi) from the town centers.

Once you're in Hebron, you will need to choose different transportation routes for either the Palestinian Authority-controlled side or Israel-controlled side. For the Palestinian Authority-controlled side (which is most of the city), go from the bus station by Damascus Gate in Jerusalem on bus number 21 (NIS15). You will transfer at the Bethlehem bus station and switch to a *sherut* (NIS15). The Israeli-controlled side, including the Tomb of the Patriarchs, requires bus number 160 from the Jerusalem Central Bus station (NIS12).

The simplest thing to do is take a *sherut* from Jerusalem to Bethlehem, and then ask your driver where to find another *sherut* to Hebron.

Ramallah and Al Bireh

Ramallah (and its twin city Al Bireh) is just a 15-minute drive from Jerusalem and known as an Arab cultural and arts hub, rather than a hot spot for archaeological or religious sightseeing. There are also a number of excellent restaurants in this area and some good hotels. Although Ramallah might seem like a good alternative place to stay if you are planning on sightseeing in Jerusalem, be aware that you will have to go back and forth through a checkpoint.

SIGHTS
Taybeh Brewery

A truly original stop on a trip to the Middle East is **Taybeh Brewery** (1 Taybeh Rd., Taybeh, just outside of Ramallah, tel. 02/289-8868, www.taybehbeer.com, 8am-4pm

Ramallah

Ramallah

AL BIRA

THE POPULAR ART
CENTRE (PAC)

STARS &
BUCKS CAFÉ

ZAMN ▼   AL MANARA
ROUNDABOUT

■ AL-KASABA THEATRE
AND CINEMATHÈQUE

● ROYAL COURT
HOTEL

PSAGOT

0   200 yds
0   200 m

© AVALON TRAVEL

Mon.-Sat., 30-minute tours 9am-2:30pm Mon.-Sat., free), the only Palestinian brewery in existence. Taybeh, a town of about 1,500 people, is the only majority-Christian Palestinian community in the Holy Land. The driving force behind the family-run brewery is a father-daughter team, and they are the main sponsors and advocates of Taybeh's annual Oktoberfest.

ARTS AND CULTURE CENTERS

Ramallah is home to several arts and culture centers that are NGOs and operate with international assistance. The centers put on all kinds of arts-related events throughout the year.

Most notable among these centers is **The Popular Art Centre (PAC)** (Al Bireh, tel. 02/240-3891, www.popularartcentre.org), which is also home of the renowned Palestine International Festival. PAC runs a number of arts programs for children, has a cinemathéque, and promotes traditional music and dance.

Established originally in 1970 in Jerusalem, the **Al-Kasaba Theatre and Cinemathéque** (Hospital St. in Ramallah, tel. 02/296-5292/3, www.alkasaba.org) works on a local and international level in arts promotion, including a past international film festival, theater productions, and hosting international artists.

Established in 2005, the **Ramallah Cultural Palace** (Industrial Zone, tel. 02/298-4704, http://culture.ramallah.ps) executes a mission similar to the other centers in the area in its promotion and support of arts, poetry, and music programs in the community.

ENTERTAINMENT AND EVENTS
Taybeh Oktoberfest

Yes, there is a beer festival in the West Bank even though it only has one brewery. The annual **Oktoberfest** (Taybeh, just outside of Ramallah, www.visitpalestine.ps, first Sat.-Sun. in Oct.) features an interesting mix of local folk musicians, hip-hop, and brass bands as well as local dishes for the food portion of the two-day event.

Palestine International Festival

Founded in 1993 to host and showcase international arts in the West Bank, the **Palestine International Festival** (various locations, www.popularartcentre.org, tickets vary) includes a wide array of music, poetry, and performance events in surrounding Arab villages and refugee camps.

PalFest

The Palestine Festival of Literature, known as **PalFest** (http://palfest.org, free), was founded in 2008 and showcases the Middle Eastern love for the written word with domestic and international writers, poets, and songwriters. They facilitate workshops and put on musical performances. Some events are in English, and the festival is held in various locations throughout the West Bank and East Jerusalem.

FOOD
Fine Dining

Locally grown food and handmade pasta are the highlights of **Orjuwan Lounge** (Hope St. in central Ramallah, tel. 02/297-6870, www. orjuwanlounge.com, 10:30am-midnight daily, NIS75), which has a classy, upscale atmosphere on par with something you'd find in Tel Aviv or Jerusalem. They were among the restaurants chosen to participate in the annual French Culinary Week in Palestine sponsored by the French government. Serving a range of dishes that includes everything from

Oktoberfest at Taybeh Brewery

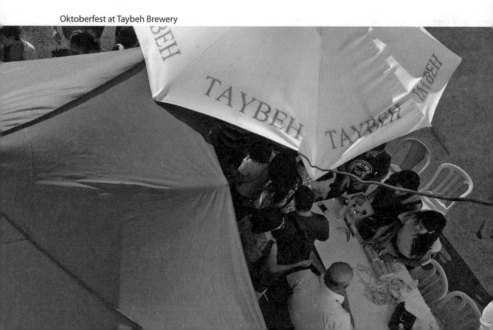

arugula salad to lamb and chicken dishes, Orjuwan is decidedly Western food with an Asian flair. Their main offerings are soups and appetizers, salads, risottos, seafood, and favorite Italian dishes such as ravioli, prepared inventively with local flavors and ingredients, but they also have a surprising range of inventive main dishes. They are known for their weekend brunch and an experimental tasting menu of 12 dishes that requires a reservation 24 hours in advance.

Cafés and Coffee Shops

ZAMN Premium Coffee House (Al Teereh St. roundabout, tel. 02/295-0600, 24 hours daily, NIS45) is one branch of a very successful local chain of upper-end coffee shops. It is a popular gathering place and serves up excellent coffee and sweets.

Just for the novelty and bizarre experience of it, try **Stars & Bucks Café** (City Center, tel. 02/297-5674, 9am-midnight Sat.-Thurs., 3pm-midnight Fri., NIS75) right in the center of Ramallah. You'll find yourself marveling at how they have managed to get away with such blatant spoofing of an international brand. Many tourists visit just to buy souvenir evidence to show people back home. It's a fairly large place (and a regional chain) that has decent coffee on the second floor of a building at the center of the first major roundabout in town. They serve a wide variety of main dishes in addition to their coffee offerings, including noodle dishes, sandwiches, and Chinese food. It operates as both a coffee shop and a hookah lounge, so you can also smoke a water pipe while you're here.

ACCOMMODATIONS
Under US$100

The **Area D Hostel** (Maliki Bldg. top floor, Jamal Abdel Nasser St., tel. 056/934-9042, http://ramallahhostel.com, US$65 d) is a youth hostel that caters to independent backpackers who want a good base in the region to do some exploring. The hostel features private and dorm rooms with shared bathrooms and private apartments with private bathrooms, free wireless Internet, a 24-hour front desk, and a snack desk. The rooms are simply furnished with tile floors. It is situated in a central location near the bus to Jerusalem, and tours can be arranged through the front desk.

US$100-150

A very nice option that includes semi-luxury accommodations and rooms with balconies big enough to dine on, the **Royal Court Suite Hotel** (24 Jaffa St., tel. 02/296-4040, www.rc-shotel.com, US$150 d) is a small hotel with only suites in Ramallah's business district, across from the city park and near the new city center. There is a roof restaurant, whirlpool tubs and kitchenettes in the comfortably furnished suites, balconies with views of the city, and a complimentary buffet breakfast. There are many restaurants nearby, but you can also dine at the hotel's bar with outdoor seating, which is frequented by both locals and tourists.

INFORMATION AND SERVICES
Online Resources

The **Municipality of Ramallah** (www.ramallah.ps) has a multilingual website, but the functions are a bit limited and it will basically provide you with some background information and a few pictures.

Safety and Security

Violence sometimes erupts in Ramallah, particularly near the Qalandia Checkpoint. It is always best to check with your embassy in advance of a visit.

GETTING THERE AND AROUND
Checkpoints

Ramallah's main drawback for visitors coming from Jerusalem is going through the infamous **Qalandia Checkpoint,** which involves a complex series of checks, especially in times of unrest. By far the easiest thing to do is get to

252

THE WEST BANK
INFORMATION AND SERVICES

the checkpoint, walk through, and take a taxi on the other side.

There are alternative routes that are longer and more circuitous, but unless you are riding in a *sherut* (share taxi) or a bus, just go through Qalandia.

Taxis and Share Taxis
Many taxis from Jerusalem won't go through the Qalandia Checkpoint because of the trouble in getting back through. No matter what you do, if you take a taxi insist that they set their meter. The driver might insist on a large sum of money on delivering you to Ramallah with the reasoning that they have to go to the trouble of driving back through the checkpoint. Your best bet is to take a taxi to the checkpoint, walk through, and catch another taxi on the other side.

Damascus Gate Buses
Ramallah is just 15 minutes from Jerusalem, so you can always find a bus at Damascus Gate that is going here, though the ride might be longer as they go around Qalandia to avoid the lines.

Information and Services

While tourism is being promoted more heavily in the West Bank in recent years, it is nowhere near the level of tourism in Israel. There are some good online resources and a governmental agency to visit for more information.

ONLINE RESOURCES
An excellent online guide for all things in the West Bank is **Visit Palestine** (www.visit-palestine.ps/en). The **Official Tourism Site** (http://travelpalestine.ps) for the region is less robust, but also has some good tips and information.

More of a West Bank version of Time Out than a tourism site, **This Week in Palestine** (www.thisweekinpalestine.com) is a great guide for events and happenings in the region.

TOUR GUIDE SERVICES
Offering a wide variety of tourism services, **BeinHarim Tourism Services Ltd.** (tel. 03/542-2000, www.beinharimtours.com) has an online chat service and arranges tours to most areas in the West Bank. **Explore West Bank** (tel. 059/824-4150, zzzaa_2009@hotmail.com) can also provide tour services in Ramallah and elsewhere.

NEWSPAPERS AND PRINT PUBLICATIONS
There are three major Arabic dailies in the region: *Al Quds, Al Ayyam,* and *Al Hayyat* newspapers. Many shops and markets also sell foreign English newspapers and magazines. A popular English periodical, *This Week in Palestine,* has listings of major events, happenings, and tourism services and can be found throughout the region for free.

BUSINESS HOURS
Keep in mind that the Muslim holy day of the week is Friday, so most businesses and services are shut down for at least part or all of that day.

LANGUAGE
The major languages spoken in the West Bank are Arabic and Hebrew; English is less common. It is advisable to learn a few key phrases in Arabic before traveling to the region, including common greetings and pleasantries. It will help break the ice and make it easier to communicate about more complicated topics.

Eilat and the Negev

Look for ★ to find recommended
sights, activities, dining, and lodging.

Highlights

★ **Masada National Park:** Arguably the most dramatic vista in the region is from atop this hilltop fortress of Herod the Great that served as the last stand for a band of rebel Jews facing off against the Roman army (page 257).

★ **Ein Avdat National Park:** The always-flowing stream at this park is a highlight of easy-to-navigate desert trails engineered to protect the natural environment. It is a prime ecotourism site (page 268).

★ **Avdat National Park:** Adjacent to Ein Avdat, Avdat National Park is home to one of the most famous Nabataean cities, situated along the ancient incense route (page 268).

★ **Mitzpe Ramon Observatory and Ramon Crater:** Mitzpe Ramon is the site of the largest of three massive geological craters in the Negev, as well as numerous hiking routes (page 268).

★ **Coral World Underwater Observatory:** See scores of rare, colorful tropical fish at this underwater world just a few miles outside of Eilat (page 277).

The southern half of Israel is home to the vast Negev Desert that is sparsely populated but filled with myriad significant and interesting sights.

The Negev is the largest desert in Israel, and accounts for more than half of Israel's land. It is home to the ancient city of Beer Sheva, scores of Bedouin tribes, and some of Israel's most popular ecotourism destinations.

Despite being sparsely populated, the Negev has numerous outstanding options for a range of activities such as desert hikes, camping, and off-road adventures that include riding on dirt bikes and ATVs. Some of the region's more notable ecotourism experiences include unique accommodations, like environmentally friendly, custom-designed desert huts and camel rides.

At the northeastern side of the Negev is the Dead Sea, the lowest point on earth, famed for its therapeutic waters and warm air. The Dead Sea is beloved for its mud, which you can take directly out of the sea and spread on your body. The tourism demand in the Dead Sea region means that there are a wealth of hotels, many of them luxury, that cater to guests looking to do nothing but relax and unwind.

It is also a fairly easy drive from Jerusalem, making it the perfect side trip if that is your base.

Along the western shore of the Dead Sea are the stunning ruins of Masada, believed to be a former mountaintop fortress of Herod the Great, where a group of rebel Jews took their last stand against Roman soldiers. On a clear day, you can see the expanse of the Dead Sea below.

At the southernmost tip of the Negev is Eilat, famed for its water recreation sports. It is one of the most popular vacation destinations in Israel and also one of the hottest places in the country, especially in the summer. A unique feature of Eilat is its tax-free status. It is the only place in Israel without the standard Value Added Tax (VAT) on goods and services. It is also the gateway to Petra, Jordan, just across the border.

If you have the time, energy, money, and willingness, there are many sights to see and adventures to be had in the south and Eilat.

Previous: the Ramon Crater visitors center; mosaic floor at Herod's Palace in Masada National Park.
Above: an ibex in Ein Gedi Nature Reserve.

Eilat and the Negev

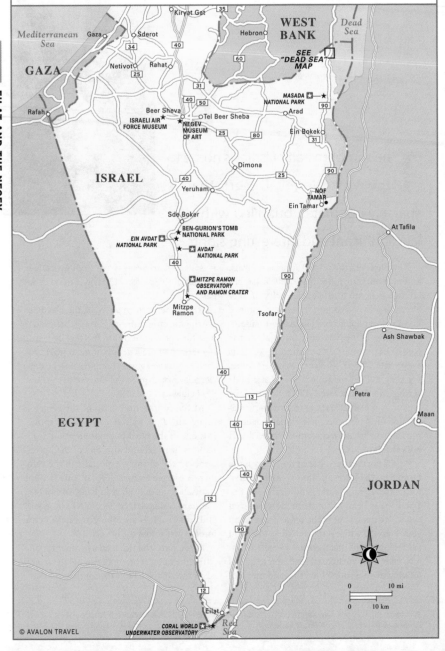

© AVALON TRAVEL

PLANNING YOUR TIME

The south is full of vast spaces of desert, punctuated by a few major destinations, including the Dead Sea, Beer Sheva, and Eilat. The minimum amount of time you should plan to spend in the south is three days, which should give you just long enough of a stay to experience the best of what the region has to offer.

Be cautious when you make any travel plans during the summer months, especially in the months of July-September. The temperature can be brutally high at times (above 105°F), and combined with the humidity in the area of the Dead Sea, it can make even the most exciting trip miserable, especially if you're not accustomed to the climate. It can also be dangerous if you don't drink enough water or avoid the sun.

You should allow at least two days for Eilat, as it is very far south, and most activities involve water sports. It is also the most logical place to jump off for a day trip to nearby Petra, Jordan, and the famed archaeological site there, for which you should allow at least one overnight stay.

The Dead Sea

The lowest point on earth, the Dead Sea draws tourists from all over the world to indulge in its rich mud and relax in its spas. The high salinity of the waters of the Dead Sea, in which nothing lives, makes it possible to easily float on the water. Surrounding the Sea are a few smaller towns and clusters of hotels and restaurants, with one large strip of mostly luxury hotels and restaurants that cater to tourists.

ORIENTATION

Once one complete body of water, the Dead Sea is now split into northern and southern basins because of the Sea's sinking water level. Some believe it is due to resource exploitation for popular health and beauty products, and others believe it is due to state exploitation of water resources. Most of the larger northern basin is within the West Bank on the western shore and within Jordan on the eastern shore. Look across the Dead Sea and you will see Jordan not far off.

In recent years, the declining water level of the Dead Sea has led to a proliferation of dangerous sinkholes, which has led to the closure of some popular free beaches. There are still plenty of options for beaches and sinkholes are closely monitored, but the area is changing.

The first destination just across the West Bank border is Ein Gedi, home to an ancient spring and waterfalls and a couple of accommodation options. The southern half of the Dead Sea is where you'll find the major grouping of hotels and activities catering to tourists in Ein Bokek and just to the south. Between Ein Gedi and Ein Bokek are various beaches and spas.

SIGHTS
★ Masada National Park

There are many mysteries surrounding **Masada National Park** (approximately one hour south of Jerusalem via Rtes. 1 and 90, tel. 03/539-6700 and 08/658-4207/8, reservation center for sound and light show tel. 08/995-9333, www.masada.org.il, www.parks.org.il, 8am-5pm daily Apr.-Sept., 8am-4pm daily Oct.-Mar., last entry one hour before closing and one hour earlier on Fri. and holiday eves, NIS30-75 depending on cable car ticket choice). Chief among them is what exactly happened to the Jewish inhabitants who were surrounded by the Roman army, besieged for months, and ultimately committed suicide to avoid capture.

One of Israel's several UNESCO World Heritage Sites, Masada is breathtaking for the view of the Dead Sea and the impossibly steep ascent that you can make by cable car or on

The Dead Sea

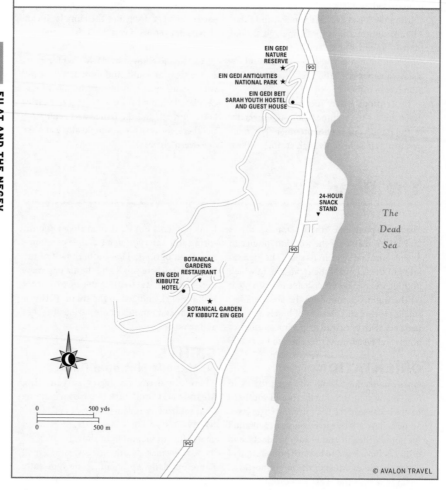

EIN GEDI NATURE RESERVE ★

EIN GEDI ANTIQUITIES NATIONAL PARK ★

EIN GEDI BEIT SARAH YOUTH HOSTEL AND GUEST HOUSE ●

90

24-HOUR SNACK STAND ▼

The Dead Sea

90

BOTANICAL GARDENS RESTAURANT ▼

EIN GEDI KIBBUTZ HOTEL ●

★ BOTANICAL GARDEN AT KIBBUTZ EIN GEDI

0   500 yds
0   500 m

90

© AVALON TRAVEL

foot. The entrance fee to the park also includes camping fees.

Masada sits at the top of a high peak above the Dead Sea. What is left today are remnants of the once-magnificent court that was originally built by King Herod. You can rent an audio guide to the site, which seems like nothing more than dusty, hot archaeological remains on top of a huge hill unless you look closely and take your time to explore. The best way to get into the spirit of Masada is with a

tour guide (inquire in advance) who can walk you through the various points and answer questions.

On a clear day, the view of the Dead Sea from Masada is incredible, and you can see it from the top of Masada or from the cable cars that take you up and down from the visitors center. You can walk up via the path on the side of the mountain, but that can be a dangerous endeavor in hot weather: People do get heat exhaustion and dehydration while on the trail. Whether you go up by cable car or trail, take water and drink continuously.

Don't miss the inventive and informative **Yigael Yadin Masada Museum** (tel. 08/658-4207/8 and 08/658-4464, museum.m@ npa.org.il, 8am-4pm Sun.-Thurs., NIS20 or combined ticket) just past the very classy gift shop. Entrance to the museum is included with the price of your ticket, and you'll get an automatically activated audio guide to accompany you through the choice, well-displayed artifacts and life-size recreations of people in scenes related to Masada. It brings the entire experience to life, and is one of the coolest museums you'll see in Israel, even though it's a bit small.

Ein Gedi Nature Reserve
About 20 minutes down the road from Masada in the direction of Jerusalem is **Ein Gedi Nature Reserve** (off Rte. 90, tel. 08/658-4285, www.parks.org.il, 8am-5pm daily Apr.-Sept., 8am-4pm daily Oct.-Mar., with additional entrance restrictions, adult NIS30, child NIS16), a charming, conveniently located reserve that is brimming with the deerlike ibex, small hyrax, and natural pools filled by water that has been flowing for about 2,000 years.

There are three main trails in, and you can take a short, relatively easy hike from the park entrance straight up to the second natural pool and swim and cool off under the waterfall. It's not deep enough for a serious swim, but it seems like heaven on a hot day. Go early in the morning before huge groups descend on the popular trails from around noon onward.

You can also see the remains of an ancient irrigation system, and there is a snack bar and souvenir shop at the entrance. But be aware that rangers patrol the area for people eating inside the reserve; you could get fined if caught eating food here.

EIN GEDI ANTIQUITIES NATIONAL PARK
Inside of the Ein Gedi Nature Reserve, just north of the main parking area, is the **Ein Gedi Antiquities National Park** (off Rte. 90, tel. 08/658-4285, www.parks.org.il, 8am-4pm Sat.-Thurs., 8am-3pm Fri., included with admission to the nature reserve) with its 1,200-year-old mosaic floor left over from the remains of an ancient Jewish synagogue from the 3rd century AD. The complex is shaded and has places to sit. The mosaic floor has mysterious inscriptions that include a warning to not reveal the local secret (likely a

the view from the main entrance to Masada National Park

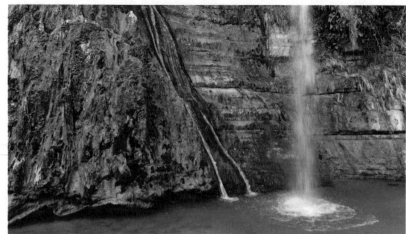
the pleasant waterfall at Ein Gedi Nature Reserve

reference to the production of a local persimmon perfume).

Qumran National Park

In 1947, a Bedouin goat herder discovered the first seven scrolls of what became known as the Dead Sea Scrolls in a cave inside of what is now **Qumran National Park** (13 miles east of Jerusalem via Hwy. 1 to Rte. 90, tel. 02/994-2235 or 02/654-1255 for guided tours, www.parks.org.il, 8am-5pm daily Apr.-Sept., 8am-4pm daily Oct.-Mar., last entry one hour before closing, adult NIS21, child NIS9). In the 1950s, 10 more caves with manuscripts were discovered. Though it took time to understand what the scrolls were, the findings rocked the worlds of archaeology, anthropology, and religion. Made by Jews between 200 BC and AD 70, the scrolls fill in important details about ancient scribal practices, traditions, and techniques of biblical interpretation.

Today you can tour the Qumran complex, the remains of an ancient city of a strict religious sect called the Qumrans, including the nearby 11 caves and underground tunnels.

Botanical Garden at Kibbutz Ein Gedi

Just inside Kibbutz Ein Gedi is the **Botanical Garden** (off Hwy. 90 alongside the Dead Sea at Tamar Regional Council, tel. 08/659-4726, www.ein-gedi.co.il, anytime, free), which makes for incredible nighttime tours with its diverse plantlife and selection of flowers that bloom after sunset. It shelters more than 1,000 varieties of flora from all over the world. People from the kibbutz actually live within the garden, and they give tours for groups and individuals.

ENTERTAINMENT AND EVENTS
Festivals

Every year the **Tamar Festival** (multiple venues, www.tamarfestival.com, Oct., NIS170-230) lasts for several days in October during the Sukkot holiday and features performances by local and international artists. Events during the day include hikes, tours, and children's activities. The festival is known for its choice lineup of activities and music featured in various venues in the south of Israel, including the Botanical Garden at Ein Gedi, the Kikar Sdom villages, and Masada. If you plan ahead and pay a bit extra, you can camp in the midst of the event.

Sports Challenges

With a lineup that includes a mountain bike marathon and moonlit running, the two-day

Veolia Desert Challenge (tel. 050/883-3004, www.desertchallenge.co.il) is for extreme sports lovers who also love the desert. The event also includes family activities, camping accommodations, and a general atmosphere of enjoying the desert through experiencing extreme sports.

The **Dead Sea Half-Marathon Race** (www.eingedi-run.co.il, Feb.) has been going strong for more than three decades. The run takes place near Ein Gedi at a time when the local temperature is more bearable and includes gorgeous views of the Dead Sea along the way.

SHOPPING

Once you are anywhere near the beaches of the Dead Sea, there are gift stores and shops everywhere people gather, mostly selling Dead Sea-related beauty and skin products, revered for their unique qualities and health benefits. The most extensive network of shopping, though, is in the area of **Ein Bokek,** just off of Route 90.

The dark side of Dead Sea products is the lack of regulations surrounding the removal and use of natural resources from the Dead Sea. The exploitation of resources from the Dead Sea has been connected to environmental problems in the area and there are lingering questions over legal claims to the land.

SPORTS AND RECREATION

The main attraction in the Dead Sea region is undoubtedly the Dead Sea itself. The lowest point on earth and filled with waters in which nothing is living, the Dead Sea is renowned for its rich mineral deposits and general health benefits.

There is a great deal of controversy surrounding the use of materials from the Dead Sea and other issues with development and exploitation of resources in the area. The Sea is slowly disappearing, and there is a major swath in its center where land is now exposed, splitting the Sea into northern and southern basins.

At many points in the Sea, you can enter the waters and rub the reputedly therapeutic mud on your body and face. Take care if you have any cuts on your body, as the salty waters will go straight into the wound and cause horrible stinging pain. Do not put your head under the water or rub the water in your eyes. If you do get water in your eyes, flush it out right away with clear water.

The major beaches of the Dead Sea are well apportioned with showers, changing rooms, snack bars, lounge chairs, and shade. The less-used beaches still often have showers, but might be lacking the mud to rub on the body.

Beaches

Just near Kibbutz Mitzpe Shalem is **Mineral Beach** (Rte. 90 near Kibbutz Mitzpe Shalem, tel. 02/994-4888, 9am-5pm Sun.-Thurs., 8am-5pm Fri.-Sat., NIS50 weekdays, NIS60 weekends and holidays) with its well-kept shores, shaded sulfur pool, plenty of mud for rubbing, and a health center that offers treatments and massages. There is also a passable cafeteria, showers, changing rooms, storage, an indoor freshwater pool, and more.

Just off Route 90, about 90 minutes south of Jerusalem, is the extremely well-developed area of **Ein Bokek** that includes two beaches with shades and chair for rent, about a dozen luxury hotels, several clinics and spas, hot springs, shopping malls, and restaurants and bars. There is also the option for free camping here.

The northernmost of the Dead Sea beaches that is closest to Jerusalem, about a 40-minute drive, is **New Kalia Beach** (tel. 02/994-2391, www.dead-sea.org.il, 8am-6pm daily Apr.-Sept., 8am-5pm daily Oct.-Mar., adult NIS40, child NIS30). The beach has a covered snack and drink bar, which plays loud music, changing rooms, showers, beach chairs, and umbrellas. It is slightly disconcerting to see the minefield warnings just a stone's throw from the beach, but there is plenty of mud and the general atmosphere is very mellow. A Bedouin tent area, camping facilities, and a Dead Sea products gift shop are also on hand.

Many people go into the Dead Sea fully clothed.

Spas and Health Resorts

Famed for its health benefits, the Dead Sea region has a wide range of spas, stretching from the Kibbutz Ein Gedi area all the way to Ein Bokek. Any hotel in the area will know of nearby spas and their reputation, but you can also try Ein Gedi **Sea of Spa** (Kibbutz Ein Gedi, tel. 08/659-4934, www.eingediseaofspa.co.il, 8am-5pm daily Oct.-Mar. and 8am-6pm Sun.-Thurs,. 8am-5pm Fri. Apr.-Sept.), with its natural hot springs, sweet water pool, natural cosmetic mud, beach, and body treatments center.

Camel Rides

En route to the Dead Sea, you'll encounter a few places that offer very brief **camel rides** for a steep fee, usually somewhere around NIS55. The camels are usually kept waiting in some kind of a parking lot or very close to the road for long periods of time, and there are little to no government regulations about the treatment and care of the animals.

FOOD

The Dead Sea area is marked by long stretches of road where there is nothing to eat, punctuated by groupings of places to get food. A couple of websites that offer listings of restaurants are www.einbokek.com and www.deadsea.co.il.

Ein Gedi

There are very few food options in the Ein Gedi area, but the **Botanical Gardens Restaurant** (Kibbutz Ein Gedi, tel. 08/659-4221, www.ein-gedi.co.il/en, 7am-10am and 6:30pm-8:30pm daily, NIS75) is a fairly nice restaurant with a huge amount of space. It feels a bit like a cafeteria and an all-you-can-eat buffet. The setting is gorgeous though, amidst the Kibbutz Ein Gedi Botanical Garden, and it is just off the hotel's lobby, where there is also a small bar and lounge area. The restaurant is kosher, but they do serve dinner on Friday night with a huge buffet.

Ein Bokek

If you find yourself in the Ein Bokek area, your best bet for finding some decent food will probably be at one of the large hotels or one of the shopping centers. If you want something on the beach, the generic beach restaurants and snack stands are easy to find.

For simple coffee, sandwiches, and salads, you can go to the local branch of **Aroma** (Petra Shopping Center, circular shopping center in the middle of Ein Bokek, tel. 08/995-4021, www.aroma.co.il/en, 8am-11pm daily,

Camel rides are easy to find near the Dead Sea.

NIS35). There isn't much atmosphere, but it is open daily and a relatively predictable experience with free wireless Internet to boot. Once you are at the shopping center, there are other options as well.

At the Leonardo Hotel Inn is the Bedouin tent restaurant and bar **Taj Mahal** (Leonardo Hotel Inn, tel. 053/809-4823, www.taj-mahal.co.il, noon-2am daily, NIS70), where you can sit on cushions and puff on a hookah. The restaurant has a fairly limited food menu, with mostly some simple steak and chicken dishes and salads, but they do have an extensive beer, wine, and alcohol list. Their schedule varies despite their published hours, especially in the off-season, so call before going to make sure they are open and serving food.

In the lobby of the Isrotel Hotel is **The Ranch House Restaurant** (Isrotel Hotel Dead Sea, off Rte. 90, tel. 08/668-9666, 7pm-11pm Sun.-Thurs., 6:30pm-11pm Sat., NIS110), an upscale establishment that serves American-style dishes, and is open mainly for dinner. The atmosphere is spacious, modern, and relaxing and their specialty is serving cuts of meat by weight.

South Dead Sea

At the very southern end of the Dead Sea are a few options for food in an area called Neot HaKikar, but most of these venues require reservations. One of them is **Secrets my Mother Told Me** (off Rte. 90 at Sodom Sq., tel. 052/899-1199), which serves breakfast, lunch, and dinner, but you must call in advance for reservations. They offer buffet-style spreads and are best for groups of four or more.

ACCOMMODATIONS

There is a wide variety of accommodations in and around the Dead Sea region, ranging from camping to five-star hotels. The fanciest hotels are grouped in and around Ein Bokek, on the southern end of the waters. This area is built up with restaurants, shops, and spas. At night, it looks a bit like Las Vegas. There are also a number of options in the area of Ein Gedi and Masada, which have about 20 minutes of road in between them. Other options are at Almog, Kalya, and Arad, which are not as close to the beaches, but still keep you in the vicinity.

Under US$100

The **Masada Guest House and Youth Hostel** (Masada at Ein Bokek, tel. 08/995-3222, www.iyha.org.il, US$98 d) is a relatively large building for a hostel that looks like it was carved out of the hillside. It has a private swimming pool (in season) and is near the entrance to Masada National Park. All 88 rooms have a private shower and bathroom, air-conditioning, and a minibar. There is also a large dining room and an Internet station available, and breakfast is included.

A charming option if you want to be in the desert but don't need to be next door to the Dead Sea is **Villa 1000** (Baraket 43 in Arad, www.zimmeril.com, US$94 d). The place is tiny, with only nine rooms, but it is set in a garden with a cookout area, there is free wireless Internet throughout, and all of the rooms are equipped for cooking. Arad is a good jumping-off point for the Dead Sea and the Negev, which are both about 30 minutes away.

US$100-150

A villa that has been converted into three separate units, **Zimmer Mantur** (Mivtza Lot 30, Arad, tel. 054/766-9308, US$125 d) has a guest garden, cookout facilities, and the rooms have balconies with views of the garden or the nearby valley. Free wireless Internet and a flat-screen TV come with the room, and

there's easy access to nearby jeep excursions in the Negev and Judean Deserts.

US$150-200

At the very southern end of the Dead Sea just next to the salt pools is **Nof Tamar** (Ein Tamar, tel. 052/886-8632, www.noftamar. co.il, US$158 d). The very tiny, three-room property has views of the Negev Desert from air-conditioned log cabin chalets that have world-class amenities including satellite TV, whirlpool bathtubs, verandas, and kitchenettes. It is about 30 minutes from Masada and an hour from Beer Sheva.

Simple but cozy, **Gil's Guest Rooms** (Neve Zohar, Ein Bokek 107, tel. 052/270-2502, www. einbokek.com/gil, US$169 d) is a viable option for accommodations if you want to be in the Ein Bokek area but want to pay a little less. There's free wireless Internet, satellite TV, and you can get breakfast and dinner on-site. It's not fancy, but the rooms are a good size and the staff is helpful in navigating around the Dead Sea area.

Just a two-minute walk from the beach, **Isrotel Gardens Hotel** (Ein Bokek, tel.

Isrotel Gardens Hotel

08/668-9090, www.gardenshotels.com, US$194 d) is a 200-room hotel with a massive, sprawling layout, spa treatments, two indoor swimming pools, an outdoor pool, and a children's pool. All of the rooms overlook the Dead Sea. The breakfast buffet is included.

Over US$200

The **Ein Gedi Hotel** (Kibbutz Ein Gedi, tel. 08/659-4222, www.ein-gedi.co.il, US$239 d) is set within a kibbutz that boasts a botanical garden and a huge outdoor swimming pool with changing rooms and showers. The hotel also has a private beach, and there is a nearby spa with mineral pools. It is a 10-minute drive from the Ein Gedi Nature Reserve and 15 minutes from Masada. All of the rooms have tea and coffee service and satellite TV. The on-site restaurant serves a huge buffet dinner on Friday night, and there is a small bar and information center with area information in the hotel's main lobby.

Daniel Dead Sea Hotel (off Rte. 90, Ein Bokek, tel. 08/668-9999, www.tamareshotels.co.il, US$302 d) is a full-fledged luxury hotel with all the trimmings in its 302 rooms with desert and Dead Sea views. The hotel also has swimming pools, a conference center, and a health club with a gym, sauna, whirlpool, and steam room. The rooms have clean, modern interiors with balconies and views of the water. Free wireless Internet use is limited to one person per room.

GETTING THERE AND AROUND

It is a world away from Jerusalem, but the Dead Sea area is remarkably easy to get to by car or bus. Once in the area, you can traverse the entire shore of the Sea along Route 90 in about 80 minutes. It is about 45 minutes to the northernmost area, Kalya, and another 30 minutes to Ein Gedi Nature Reserve, and yet another 25 minutes to the major hotel and restaurant area of Ein Bokek. From Ein Bokek you can get to the very southern end of the Dead Sea at Neot HaKikar in another 30 minutes.

Car

From Jerusalem, take Highway 1 east to Route 90 and follow the signs to the Dead Sea. You will drive for about an hour, part of the way in the West Bank, until you get to Ein Gedi, which is just over the border from the West Bank on the Israeli side. From Tel Aviv, take the same route, except add a bit more time along Highway 1. It's approximately a two-hour drive, give or take, depending on traffic.

Once you are in the area, it is very easy to get about by car. There is only one main road (Rte. 90) and everything is clearly signposted or obvious from a distance. For example, it is impossible to miss the massive grouping of hotels at Ein Bokek.

Bus

Buses go to the Dead Sea on a very regular basis from Jerusalem. **Egged** buses (www.egged.co.il, bus numbers 421, 486, 487, NIS40) is the vendor, and it takes about 90 minutes to reach Ein Gedi. The bus stops are situated along Route 90, and a good one to begin with is at the Ein Gedi Beit Sarah Youth Hostel and Guest House because it is immediately adjacent to Ein Gedi National Park.

From Tel Aviv, take off from the **Arlozorov Terminal** (bus number 421, NIS50) for the trip that takes about 2.5 hours. Watch out for other routes from Tel Aviv that require transfers.

Once you get off the bus, you'll be very close to the Ein Gedi Nature Reserve and it will be easy to get back on the bus and continue southward. Be aware that the Ein Gedi Beit Sarah Youth Hostel and Guest House won't let you in their gate if you are not a registered guest, though.

The Negev

Seemingly rather barren to the eye, the Negev is full of all kinds of wildlife that you can easily see close up, which is part of what makes it a popular destination for nature-related hikes and other activities. It is also the gateway to Eilat, the southernmost city in Israel.

ORIENTATION

The largest city in the Negev, Beer Sheva is ancient: It was founded over 3,700 years ago. Developed into a more modern city by the Ottomans and then the British, the Beer Sheva of today is a mixed city of immigrants—Jews, Arabs, and Bedouins—from dozens of countries. Home to the University of the Negev, it also makes a logical base for starting adventures in the region, particularly to Arad or Dimona (both about 40 minutes away).

About 40 minutes due south from Beer Sheva is the historic Kibbutz Sde Boker, former home of Israel's first prime minister David Ben-Gurion. The kibbutz and nearby Midreshet Sde Boker are centers for ecotourism in the region, and are a good stop on the way to see Mitzpe Ramon, Ein Avdat National Park, and the ancient Nabataean city of Avdat.

SIGHTS

Beer Sheva

Modern Beer Sheva is not the most remarkable-looking place, but it has a number of interesting and valuable stops, including a couple of good museums. Among them is the **Negev Museum of Art** (60 HaAtsmaut St., tel. 08/699-3535, www.negev-museum.org.il, 10am-4pm Mon.-Tues. and Thurs., noon-7pm Wed., 10am-2pm Fri.-Sat., NIS15) in Beer Sheva's Old City in a 1906 building that was home to the Turkish governor. The recently renovated structure has two galleries with contemporary exhibitions of photography, sculpture, prints, and paintings, and hosts live concerts in the summer.

The ancient **Tel Beer Sheba** (off the Beer Sheva-Shoket junction on Rte. 60 just south of Omer, tel. 08/646-7286, www.parks.org.il, 8am-5pm daily Apr.-Sept., 8am-4pm daily Oct.-Mar., adult NIS15, child NIS7) is most of a city that dates back to the 10th century BC. You can walk around what is left of the ancient streets and buildings, and really see the layout and imagine what it was like to live here. The Tel is considered to be

The People of the Negev

One of the most unique characteristics of the Negev is the people who live there and have lived there throughout history. In ancient times, Nabataean traders developed several cities along their profitable regional routes. Abraham made his home in the very ancient city of Beer Sheva. Others who have lived in the vast desert region throughout the ages include Arab nomads, Canaanites, Philistines, Edomites, Byzantines, Ottomans, and Jews. The ancient economy of the Negev was based largely on sheepherding, agriculture, and trade.

The modern Jewish habitation of the Negev started a century ago with about a dozen settlements. Israel's first prime minister David Ben-Gurion was a major advocate of settling in the Negev after moving to Kibbutz Sde Boker.

Among the current residents of the Negev are Arab Bedouins. As you travel through the Negev and the south of Israel, you'll notice quite a number of semipermanent Bedouin encampments or clusters of makeshift homes dotting the desert landscape. The Bedouin were once a nomadic people who have largely settled down and integrated into modern culture, but some of their nomadic tendencies endure.

of unparalleled importance in relation to the study of biblical-period urban planning and biblical history and, as such, was designated by UNESCO as a World Heritage Site. If you are here in the summer months, go as early in the morning as possible and take a hat and water. There is no shade, except for the little bit in the observation tower, which you can climb up.

The **Israeli Air Force Museum** (Hatzerim Air Force Base, Rte. 2357 about 5 miles southwest of Beer Sheva, tel. 08/990-6853, www.iaf.org.il, 8am-5pm Sun.-Thurs., 8am-1pm Sun., NIS30) exhibits Israeli aviation history, including over 140 aircraft and antiaircraft installations, among them missile launchers.

One of a kind, the **Museum of Bedouin Culture at the Joe Alon Center** (Rte. 40 to Dvira Junction, then follow signs for Joe Alon Center, www.joealon.org.il, tel. 08/991-3322, 9am-4pm Sun.-Thurs., NIS20) documents the unique aspects of Bedouin culture as it transitioned from a nomadic to modern lifestyle. It is situated in the Lahav Forest near Kibbutz Lahav, about 12 miles north of Beer Sheva. The museum is the central focus of the Joe Alon Center, inside a round building that resembles a tent. The Bedouins' story of transition is told through a series of life-size mannequins, and admission includes a cup of coffee in a Bedouin tent if you're game.

Sde Boker and Ein Avdat

Kibbutz Sde Boker and the ecotourism and historical sites close by to it make for an interesting stop as you traverse the Negev. The kibbutz has a winery and gift shop, but the main attraction is **Ben-Gurion's Hut** (Kibbutz Sde Boker, tel. 08/656-0469, www.bgh.org.il, 8:30am-4pm Sun.-Thurs., 8:30am-2pm Fri., 10am-4pm Sat. and holiday eves, last entry 30 minutes before closing, NIS10), the home of Israel's first prime minister David Ben-Gurion and his wife Paula, left just as it was when he died in 1973. The house is referred to as a hut because of its modest appearance. Ben-Gurion, who idealized the Negev as the frontier land of Israel, lived in the house with his wife when Sde Boker was just a young kibbutz. A building next to his house has an exhibit—a short historical animated film—about Ben-Gurion's connection to the Negev.

The final resting place of the prime minister and his wife can be found at **Ben-Gurion's Tomb National Park** (off Rte. 40 near Ben-Gurion College, tel. 08/655-5684, www.parks.org.il, always open, free). Their gravesites overlook a stunning desert view

Israeli Air Force plane on display in Beer Sheva

Sde Boker is an easy stop-off point to explore the desert.

that includes the Tzin Canyon and the Avdat highlands right in the midst of the Negev.

★ EIN AVDAT NATIONAL PARK

The gorgeous **Ein Avdat National Park** (off Rte. 40, tel. 08/655-5684, www.parks.org.il, 8am-5pm daily Apr.-Sept., 8am-4pm daily Oct.-Mar., last entrance one hour before closing, adult NIS29, child NIS15, combination ticket with Avdat National Park adult NIS46, child NIS24) features the Nakhal Zin canyons, springs, waterfalls, and various native plants and animals.

Ein Avdat is also home to the mysteriously ever-flowing waters of the Avdat Spring that have cut a deep, narrow canyon through the rock. For the adventurous travelers, it makes an excellent place to wade on a hot day or even take a swim.

The park features a well-designed trail that protects the natural habitat, and you can see all kinds of wildlife if you take your time and stay relatively quiet. The most commonly seen animal is the ibex, a mountain goat that is endlessly fascinating as it scales the steep desert cliffs with ease.

★ Avdat National Park

Avdat National Park (off Rte. 40, tel. 08/655-1511, www.parks.org.il, 8am-5pm daily Apr.-Sept., 8am-4pm daily Oct.-Mar., last entrance one hour before closing on Fri. and holiday eves, adult NIS27, child NIS14, combination ticket with Ein Avdat National Park adult NIS46, child NIS24) is home to one of the most famous Nabataean cities along the incense route that they used to transport incense, spices, and perfumes.

Avdat had its high point when it flourished around 30-9 BC, and it was subsequently destroyed and rebuilt, rising and falling until the Arab conquest in the 7th century AD.

Some of the most remarkable aspects of the ruins include the restored gateway on the acropolis, the Roman bathhouse and watchtower, the 4th-century churches, and caves that served as burial places, storage, and cisterns.

Avdat has a visitors center with more information about the site, including a short film about the incense route and related spices. The site is a key stop for travelers interested in understanding more about how the ancient spice route worked, its social and economic functions, and its significance regionally and globally.

★ Mitzpe Ramon Observatory and Ramon Crater

Most incredible at sunset or sunrise is the

Avdat National Park is a major attraction on the Nabataean spice route.

Mitzpe Ramon Observatory and Ramon Crater (Rte. 40, tel. 08/658-8691, www. parks.org.il, 8am-4pm Sat.-Thurs., 8am-3pm Fri. and holiday eves, one hour later in the summer, NIS44), where the largest of three massive geological craters in the Negev can be seen. The Ramon Crater Nature Reserve (Makhtesh Ramon Nature Reserve) is part of a complex that includes a visitors center with a bookstore and hiking information.

In the nature reserve are a variety of hiking trails, the more advanced trails of which can take up to three days to traverse. You can arrange hiking expeditions of all kinds through the nature reserve, and even experience Bedouin tents, rappelling, and more.

The visitors center is a good place to learn about the area and put questions to the Israel Nature Reserves Authority staff working there, as well as ask about hiring guide

The Ancient Incense Route

For seven centuries, the mysterious Nabataeans established and worked their incense trade over a network of routes that totaled more than 1,200 miles. The Nabataean incense trade route, which extended from Yemen and Oman in the Arabian Peninsula to the Mediterranean, operated from the 3rd century BC to the 4th century AD. The main trade route was from Petra, the capital city of the mighty Nabataeans in Jordan, just across the border of modern-day Israel.

The portion of the route in the Negev Desert included the four Nabataean towns of Halutsa, Mamshit, Avdat, and Shivta. The ruins of fortresses, agricultural landscapes, and advanced irrigation systems that remain are evidence of the incredible profits that were made in the trade of frankincense and other valuable incense and spices.

The water collection and irrigation systems of cisterns, reservoirs, dams, and channeling made large-scale agriculture possible in the towns along the incense route that were supported by the wealth of the incense trade. The most outstanding evidence of the water systems can be found in the vicinity of Avdat and the central Negev.

The incense route is a UNESCO World Heritage Site and considered a testimony to ancient technology and innovation used to successfully settle and support human life in the extremely harsh desert setting.

the Ramon Crater

services. There are also slide and film shows and a museum with exhibits of the area's natural habitat. Make sure to keep a map with you at all times when hiking in the area, and keep water and a hat with you. The museum's film about the crater is partially dedicated to the memory of Israel's first astronaut.

Bedouin Tents and *Khans*

Throughout the Negev you'll see extensive groups of humble, semipermanent Bedouin dwellings dotting the landscape. You can have a closer encounter with Bedouin culture by visiting a **Bedouin tent** and *khan* (roadside inn) in Sefinat Hamidbar, Khan Hashayarot, and Khan Beerotayim. The tents and *khans* (which can be good for overnight camping or a rest stop) can be found at the Mashabei Sadeh junction, near the ancient city of Avdat and the village of Ezuz. It's best to visit 10am-4pm daily. There's no formal fee, but you will be encouraged to spend money on either food or crafts and should come prepared to spend at least NIS30-40.

Along the Incense Route

Near the modern city of Dimona are the highlights of the 1,500-mile **Ancient Incense Route** that was used by merchants and traders in ancient times. A section of about 100 miles cuts through what is today known as Israel and ended at the Port of Gaza. You can visit some of the stops on the route, declared UNESCO World Heritage Sites in 2005.

At **Mamshit** (Rte. 25, about 5 miles southeast of Dimona, tel. 08/655-6478, www.parks. org.il, 8am-4pm daily Apr.-Sept., 8am-4pm daily Oct.-Mar., last entry one hour before closing, adult NIS22, child NIS10) there is a reconstructed city with streets, arched structures, mosaics, a large house, and ruins of an inn, churches, a bathhouse, rainwater collecting pools, and other structures. Mamshit was the site of the discovery of a trove of almost 11,000 silver coins. Beyond visiting the park, you can camp here overnight.

Beyond Mamshit are the sites of **Avdat,** which include the ruins of a fortress, churches, homes, a bathhouse, and a workshop. Then there was **Shivta** (tel. 08/655-5684, www. parks.org.il) and the northernmost stop of **Halutsa,** where you can find the ruins of a theater and a church.

ENTERTAINMENT AND EVENTS
Festivals

In the spring, the big show in the south is the **Zorba the Buddha Festival** (tel. 08/632-6508, www.zorba.co.il, late Mar.-Apr.), which

The Powerful and Mysterious Nabataeans

the ancient Nabataean city of Avdat, on the incense route

Much has been written and said about the empire of the ancient Nabataeans, but they, and their former capital city in Petra, Jordan, remain shrouded in an air of mystery.

The Nabataeans were master traders, builders, and experts of ancient technology for creating ingenious water systems to support and sustain desert life. Bolstered by the wealth they earned over 700 years of their hugely profitably incense trade route, they established a society and culture in the harsh desert.

Natural disasters wiped out part of the Nabataean history in their capital city of Petra, limiting definitive information about certain aspects of their culture. One thing that is known is that their traders traveled in caravans across vast distances in the deserts, transporting spices, incense, and perfumes, which were shipped out of the port at Gaza. As time passed, the way stations that grew out of their passage back and forth through the Negev Desert grew into cities where terraced agriculture and sophisticated irrigation practices helped them thrive.

The remains of the four Nabataean cities of Halutsa, Mamshit, Avdat, and Shivta are significant archaeological sites, but the most remarkable and breathtaking remnant of the Nabataeans is the ancient city of Petra in Jordan.

The Roman Empire attempted more than once to conquer the Nabataeans, and in AD 106, they finally succeeded. The caravan cities, particularly Avdat, fell into decline after the Roman conquest.

runs for four or five days and has a strong spiritual, Buddhist slant. The festival takes advantage of the desert landscape to showcase musical performances, theater, movement exhibitions, meditation, and dance. It's the kind of festival that organizers ask you to imagine sipping a cup of chai in a desert setting: complete mellowness in the heart of the desert.

For fans of indie rock music and camping in the desert, **In-D-Negev** (Mitzpe Gvulot, Rte. 234 to Ze'elim Junction, http://indnegev.

co.il, Oct., NIS90-220) is three days of music, camping, and celebrating with a general spirit of togetherness and inclusion. The festival organizers even make allowances for kids, with activities and a play area. There is usually a crowd of about 4,000 people.

SHOPPING

The best and the majority of shopping in the Negev outside of Eilat is in Beer Sheva. The most unique aspect you'll likely encounter at the **Beer Sheva Bedouin Market** (south of the David Hacham Blvd. and HaMelacha St. intersection, southwest of the Old City in Beer Sheva, 8am-4pm Thurs.) is Bedouin women completely covered in black. The majority of items for sale are racks and racks of discount clothing, as well as a few stalls for items like water pipes, toys, and candy. If you take your time, you can find some Bedouin craft items for sale, and it can be a great place to mingle with locals.

As the major metropolis for many smaller towns in the south, Beer Sheva has several strip malls that include outlet stores and a little bit of everything. There are several strip malls around town, but the biggest is collectively referred to by locals as the **Big** strip mall; it's just on the outskirts of town.

About 20 minutes northwest of Beer Sheva is the **Desert Embroidery Store and Visitor's Center** (Lakiya, off Rte. 31 north from Beer Sheva, tel. 08/651-3208, www.desert-embroidery.org, 9:30am-1:30pm Sun.-Thurs., 10am-4pm Sat., closed on Muslim holidays, call in advance), where you can buy colorful and attractive hand-embroidered items like bags, wallets, and the like. The store is run by the Association for the Improvement of Women's Status Lakiya branch. The visitors center specializes in traditional Bedouin hospitality, where you can sit on woven cushions and have a light lunch. Again, call in advance to alert them you are coming, especially if you have a large group or are planning on eating lunch here.

SPORTS AND RECREATION
National Parks and Nature Reserves

More than a park, **Timna National Park** (about 17 miles north of Eilat off Rte. 90, tel. 08/631-6756, www.parktimna.co.il, 8am-4pm Sat.-Thurs., 8am-3pm Fri. and holiday eves Sept.-June; 8am-1pm Sun.-Mon. and Wed.-Sat., 8am-1pm and 5pm-8pm Tues., with guided sunset tours by reservation, July-Aug.; park entrance: adult NIS44, child NIS39) is

an entire experience that includes hot air balloons and famed touring routes, including the incredible natural rock formations of Solomon's Pillars. There are also family activities by the lake, a restaurant and souvenir shop, and sunset and night tours.

The **Hai Bar Nature Reserve** (20 miles north of Eilat on Rte. 90, tel. 08/637-6018, www.parks.org.il, 8:30am-5pm Sun.-Thurs., 8:30am-4pm Fri.-Sat., NIS39, Predators Center only NIS25) includes a small petting zoo, an African village, and a play archaeology dig for kids. It is just under five square miles, and if you have a rental car, you can rent a tour CD and drive through the park, dodging friendly ostriches as you go. The adjacent **Predators Center** is about 7.5 square miles and home to local birds and animals of prey, including the only remaining lappet-face vultures in Israel.

Bike and Jeep Tours

The Negev is an excellent area for sporty adventures like biking tours, which can be booked through a company like **Desert Eco Tours** (tel. 052/276-5753, www.desertecotours.com). You can tour major sites in the region by bicycle on one- or two-day trips. The company also offers jeep tours, which is an excellent way to see the area, especially if you aren't used to hiking in the heat and if you can handle the bumpy terrain.

Archery

If you're up for learning something new while traveling, the **Desert Archery Park** (Mitzpe Ramon, tel. 050/534-4598, www.desertarchery.co.il, prices vary) might be of interest. You can take a hike through the desert while shooting a bow and arrow and taking in the scenery.

FOOD
Beer Sheva

A favorite standby among locals, **Saba Giabetto** (28 Rager St. Rasco Center, tel. 08/627-2829, 10am-9pm Sun.-Thurs., NIS45) is known for its homey atmosphere (Saba

Desert Ecotourism

One of the most interesting and attractive parts of touring the south of Israel is the option for experiencing what is known as desert ecotourism. In a general sense, desert ecotourism includes options for accommodations that employ sustainable practices and in many cases are built by hand to blend with the desert environment. Accommodations might also be very rough and on par with camping, including options for staying in tents with outhouses and very minimal creature comforts, as well as staying in Bedouin tent encampments.

Other aspects of desert ecotourism include farms and animal reserves that allow visitors to see desert animals up close; Bedouin arts and crafts tours; archery; and bicycling. Most aspects of desert ecotourism emphasize minimal impact on the environment but maximum exposure and experience.

A very useful website for desert ecotourism information in the south and throughout Israel is **Ecotourism Israel** (www.ecotourism-israel.com). If you are looking for guided tour options, try **Desert Eco Tours** (tel. 052/276-5753, www.desertecotours.com).

means grandfather in Hebrew), tasty sandwiches, and sassy menu with fun facts and information about the restaurant.

Serving up Middle Eastern fusion cuisine in a central location, **Arabica** (12 Hertsel St., tel. 08/627-7801, http://arabica-rest.co.il, 11:30am-last customer Sun.-Thurs., 11:30am-an hour before sunset Fri., hour after sunset-last customer Sat., NIS80) has a modern, upscale atmosphere. The menu is arranged under categories of price that start at NIS69 and go up to NIS125, and include meat and seafood dishes. It is very popular, and you might find yourself in for a long wait unless you make reservations.

Situated close to city center and hotels, **Casa do Brasil** (1 Montefiore, tel. 08/627-3330, www.casadobrasil.co.il, noon-midnight Sun.-Thurs., noon-4pm Fri., 30 minutes after sunset-last customer Sat., NIS50) is all about serving up nice, big cuts of beef in a casual, party-like atmosphere. A domestic chain with three locations, the Beer Sheva branch has a very spacious, simple interior and outdoor seating.

The cheap prices at **Metah Midbar** (Mercuz-HaNegev Building off of Yitzhak St., tel. 054/633-6020, noon-midnight Sun.-Fri., 1pm-midnight Sat., NIS35) don't come easy: a sometimes rowdy crowd of students from the nearby Ben-Gurion University campus can make for a loud atmosphere. The best

menu items include standbys like the hamburger and the chicken salad. They also have wireless Internet and outlets behind the bar, so it's a great place to stop if you want to check email or other things online.

Dimona

Dimona is a smaller town near the ancient Nabataean city of Mamshit that offers a few very simple options for food, including the typical national chains of CaféCafé and Aroma, both in Peretz Center.

A bit of a change of pace from hummus and pita, **Pizza Bachchan** (3 Herzl Blvd., tel. 08/657-0550, www.piza-pazzaz.co.il, NIS80) serves up gourmet pizza with hearty amounts of toppings. It is part of a domestic chain of pizzerias. They will deliver if you are staying at a nearby hotel. The price varies according to what kind of toppings you get, but you can generally expect to pay about NIS80 for a two-topping, medium pizza.

Mitzpe Ramon

A solid bet in the Negev for a range of dining options is Mitzpe Ramon, home of the must-see Ramon Crater.

One of the fanciest places in town, **Chez Eugène** (8/1 Har Ardon St., tel. 08/653-9595, http://mitzperamonhotel.co.il, 7pm-10pm Sun.-Thurs., noon-4pm and 7pm-10pm Fri., noon-10pm Sat., NIS90) is part of a boutique

Wineries of the Negev

It might seem surprising to hear of wineries that exist in a vast, harsh desert, but the pioneering spirit that is such a defining characteristic of the Negev and its people has made it possible.

One of the more well-established wineries in the Negev is the **Sde Boker Winery** (tel. 050/757-9212, www.sde-boker.org.il), run out of Kibbutz Sde Boker, where Israel's first prime minister and advocate of desert life, David Ben-Gurion, lived with his wife.

Another winery, **Carmey Avdat** (tel. 08/653-5177, www.carmeyavdat.com), has its vineyards in the ancient, already-existing terraces that are part of the ruins of an agricultural settlement that is about 1,500 years old. They use the annual flash floods to irrigate.

Near the Dead Sea is **Yatir Winery** (tel. 08/995-9090, www.yatirwinery.com), whose vineyards are in the largest planted forest in Israel, the Yatir. Their wines are sold at the exclusive London department store Selfridges, and they are known for their white wines.

Two others are **Boker Valley Vineyards** (tel. 052/682-2930, www.bokerfarm.com) and **Neot Semedar** (tel. 08/635-8111).

hotel with the same name. The restaurant interprets some classic dishes through the lens of local flavors and traditions, including handmade sausage, seafood dishes with cauliflower cream sauce, and coconut pudding with balsamic syrup for dessert and Negev boutique beer. The restaurant's setting in the modern Chez Eugène boutique hotel in the area known as the Spice Quarter keeps the whole experience elegant but local.

Hakatze (2 Har Ardon St., tel. 08/659-5273 or 050/756-5063, noon-8pm Mon. and Wed.-Fri., NIS40) is a simple restaurant that makes home-style Israeli food with an emphasis on grilled meats and typical Middle Eastern side dishes, including pita bread. An unusual, but nice touch is the English magazines that can be read in the back of the restaurant.

A combination coffee shop and gift shop, **Hadasa'ar** (6 Har Boker St., tel. 08/940-8473, 8am-8pm Sun.-Thurs., 8am-4pm Fri., NIS40) also sells organic groceries and operates as a semi-cooperative. It's a good place to stop off if you just want something quick and light, and maybe a souvenir for the road.

Situated inside the Ramon Inn, the **Ramon Inn Restaurant** (1 Ein Akev, tel. 08/658-8822, breakfast 7am-9am and dinner 7:30pm-9:30pm daily, NIS120 fixed price) does a huge buffet that varies by the day and includes a wide variety of dishes of local flavor (which means spicy in some cases). There's a bit of

a rush for food when the dining room doors open. You need to have a reservation if you are not a guest at the hotel, but it is guaranteed to be filling. They also serve a buffet breakfast.

Sde Boker

Situated in a fairly isolated spot, the area around Sde Boker has some phenomenal sites to visit, but very few options for restaurants. It's a good area to carry some food to go with you from Mitzpe Ramon or wherever you are coming from.

In an area where there are very few choices for something simple, the **Sde Boker Field School** (Midreshet Ben-Gurion, www.boker.org.il/english) has a decent option: a snack shop with shaded outdoor seating with an incredible view of the Negev Desert. Right next door to Kibbutz Sde Boker and not far from the Ramon Crater, it's situated in the perfect spot to just stop, have a quick bite, and move on. If you've brought snacks with you and just want a place with outdoor picnic tables and free parking, it's also convenient for that. Don't miss the view from the observation deck about 100 yards away from the picnic tables.

ACCOMMODATIONS

If you end up spending a few nights in the Negev, it's the perfect place to take advantage of some of Israel's most unique overnight stays, including desert camping and Bedouin lodging.

Under US$100

Situated near the ancient incense route, **Ras Hashita** (Meshek 85, Hatzeva, tel. 052/366-5927, US$30 d) is a very rustic and inexpensive stay in the midst of the Arava Desert. Guests put up in tents in the middle of a small complex that has space for 16 different accommodations and share an outdoor bathroom. There is also a public tent for hanging out on mats and swinging in hammocks. There is a shared kitchen, and you're allowed to cook out on the premises. Hiking trips in the desert and other excursions can be arranged from here.

Offering a truly unique place to stay, **Negev Camel Ranch** (Rte. 25, southeast of Dimona, tel. 08/655-2829, www.cameland. co.il, US$56 d) is a working farm that raises camels for riding. It's the perfect place to experience a camel desert ride and excursion into the desert. Near Mamshit, the ranch has very simple desert huts for sleeping and shared bathrooms, with towels and bedding provided. Dinner, which is only served until 7pm and is an extra US$15, is a traditional vegetarian meal that includes lentils, rice, and bread with dates and tea for dessert. You can also visit the farm and the camels for free if you're not game to stay here.

Set on the northern ridge of the Ramon Crater, **Mitzpe Ramon Youth Hostel** (4 Nahal Nikrot, Mitzpe Ramon, tel. 08/658-8443, www.iyha.org.il, US$98 d) is a typical, blandly decorated but clean hostel with a good number of rooms (almost 50), which is handy in the busy summer season when most hostels book months in advance. There are private bathrooms with showers available, and breakfast is included. If you're heading out to do some hiking, the hostel can help arrange for lunch to take, and can also assist with jeep and camel tours.

Set in Mitzpe Ramon, the very tiny **Green Backpackers** (10/6 Nahal Sirpad, tel. 08/653-2319, www.thegreenbackpackers.com, US$71 d, cash payments for in-person payment and no breakfast included with online booking) is an ecotourism hostel that caters to backpackers and is run by guides. The hostel only takes adult guests, and has free wireless Internet in common areas, a shared kitchen, and shared TV-DVD and computer station. Near the Ramon Crater and the Israel National Trail, the hostel is convenient to public transportation. You can get travel advice, maps, and rent gear here.

You'll be hard-pressed to find something as unique as the **Desert Days Eco Lodge** (off the Arava Rd. near Zukim village, tel. 052/617-0028, www.negevecolodge.com, US$99 d, often has 2-night weekend minimum during high season). Designed by Tel Aviv transplants who built the place themselves, the nine "eco-huts" in the Arava Desert look like they sprang straight up from the desert itself. Every hut mirrors and blends with the desert environment; they have solar panel-generated electricity, and used water is recycled into the desert. Huts include free wireless Internet and there is an outdoor swimming pool and a communal *khan* (roadside inn) for guests to mingle with each other and learn about the area.

US$100-150

Right in the middle of Moshav Hatzeva, **Desert Routes Inn** (Moshav Hatzeva, tel. 052/366-5927, www.shvilimbamidbar.co.il, US$134 d) is a small inn with less than a dozen rooms near the border with Jordan in the Arava Desert. The inn is the perfect combination of desert hospitality blended with modern conveniences. The cozy rooms have small but comfortable beds, and the common areas of the inn are designed with exotic, but simple touches that include woven sitting mats around huge tables, hammocks, and semi-covered outdoor patio seating. The rustic desert experience is buffered by the amenities of free wireless Internet, a hot tub, private patios with desert views, a swimming pool on the moshav, and shuttle service to and from Hatzeva Junction, where buses going to Jerusalem and Tel Aviv stop.

The **Drachim Guest House** (1 Hanasi Blvd., Dimona, tel. 08/655-6540, www.drachim.org, US$118 d) is a spacious property with 59 rooms that is something between a hotel and a hostel and just 30 minutes from the Dead Sea. Drachim's perks include a semi-Olympic indoor swimming pool, a spa, gardens, free wireless Internet, and a cafeteria where the included breakfast is served. The rooms are simple but homey, and the whole place is set up for the traveler who wants a taste of comfort and luxury without going broke.

The **Desert Olive Farm** (Ramat Negev, Sde Boker, tel. 052/558-3065, www.zimmeril.com, US$134 d) achieves the perfect combination of a desert experience with all the luxury touches that Israeli *zimmers* (rooms to rent) are known for, including whirlpool bathtubs. You can stay in a cabin, tent, or suite; note that if you stay in a tent, all of your bathroom facilities are under the stars. The farm is 20 minutes from Mitzpe Ramon, 40 minutes from Beer Sheva, and it is just absolutely gorgeous and enchanting.

The midsize **Ramon Suites Hotel** (8 Nahal Meishar St., Mitzpe Ramon, tel. 08/658-8884, www.ramonhotel.co.il, US$145 d) is basic, nice, and modern, and offers suites that have kitchenettes. The three-floor hotel has 34 rooms with free wireless Internet and the option of using a laptop for no extra charge, tea and coffee service, and spacious rooms. The highlight of Ramon Suites' location is that it's at the doorstep of the Ramon Crater Nature Reserve, and the hotel will give you a free bike to take a ride there.

US$150-200

Don't let the hot tub and nice wine selection fool you: **Boker Valley Vineyards Farm** (Rte. 40 between Tlallim and Sde Boker, tel. 08/657-3483, www.bokerfarm.com, US$172 d) is pure rustic Negev Desert accommodations. The five sweet cabins are set around the property of Negev Farms, a working wine producer with vineyards and organic olive trees. Each cabin has a refrigerator, coffee and tea service, and there is a cookout area. You can eat dinner at the farm if you arrange it in advance; it's near Avdat National Park. Neve Midbar thermal baths give discounts to guests.

Over US$200

A little piece of luxury in a desert setting, **Desert Home** (70 Ein Shaviv St., Mitzpe Ramon, tel. 052/322-9496, www.baitbamidbar.com, US$215 d) is known for its designer interior that includes bleached wood floors and carefully designed rooms painted in beautiful, calming colors. You might not need the fireplace, but the five rooms all also come with free wireless Internet, furnished balconies, a kitchenette, a satellite TV, and daily room service of the included breakfast. One last perk is the garden hot tub.

Home to a luxury hotel and one of the best restaurants in town, **Chez Eugène** (8/1 Har Ardon St., Mitzpe Ramon, tel. 08/653-9595, http://mitzperamonhotel.co.il, US$265 d) is very small with only half a dozen rooms, but it has a range of high-tech amenities including free wireless Internet, a CD and DVD player, iPod docking station, and a Playstation 3 console. Wines from the hotel's vineyards are served in the restaurant, and tours and excursions (including a night walking tour) can be organized through the concierge.

Camping

There are a variety of camping options in the Negev. Stick to designated camping areas and pay the entrance fee or you might get fined by a park ranger. The most useful website for camping information is the **Israel Nature and Parks Authority** site (www.parks.org.il). You can search parks by region, and the listings all include camping information.

GETTING THERE AND AROUND

The area of the Negev is vast and spread about with large distances in between sights and places to eat and sleep. It's possible to get around by bus and train, but there is generally very little traffic, and it also makes for fairly easy and enjoyable driving if you have a car.

Car

The main city of the Negev, Beer Sheva, is about a two-hour drive from Jerusalem, mostly along Highway 6. Though it looks circuitous on a map, the best and fastest road out of Jerusalem is immediately west and then south, rather than straight south, which will add about 20 minutes to your drive time.

From Tel Aviv, you can reach Beer Sheva in less than 90 minutes, mostly along Highway 6.

Train

The **Israel Railways** (www.rail.co.il) traverses several points in the Negev, including Beer Sheva. The trains between the south at Beer Sheva and Jerusalem take about 2.5 hours (NIS42 one-way). From Tel Aviv, it is about 80 minutes to Beer Sheva (NIS32 one-way).

Bus

By far the most convenient way to get to the Negev and to travel around in the area is by **Egged** bus (www.egged.co.il). From Jerusalem it is about two hours (bus numbers 446 and 470, NIS33 one-way) to Beer Sheva and from Tel Aviv it is about 90 minutes (bus number 370, NIS20 one-way). Once in the area, **Metrodan** buses get you around locally. They do not have a website in English, but you can find related information on a **compilation website** (www.bus.co.il).

Eilat

As far south as you can go in Israel is the resort town and diving destination of Eilat. Summer temperatures in Eilat reach well over 100°F, but in the midst of winter and early spring it is very pleasant.

Eilat has grown up around the axis of the Red Sea. Most major destinations, activities, restaurants, accommodations, and sites in Eilat are somewhere on or near the shore of the Red Sea.

If you're driving, it is almost impossible to get lost in Eilat, and it's full of massive roundabouts that make driving in a foreign country less intimidating.

SIGHTS

Eilat's main draw is its world-class diving, its beaches, and the many opulent hotel and spa options. There are a few standout places to have fun, especially if traveling with kids.

Dolphin Reef Diving Center

The **Dolphin Reef Diving Center** (Metsarim St. on South Beach, tel. 08/630-0100, www.dolphinreef.co.il, 9am-5pm Sun.-Thurs., 9am-4:30pm Fri.-Sat. and holidays, adult NIS64, child NIS44) is Israel's version of swimming with the dolphins. At the center, bottlenose dolphins can be visited from the floating piers and observation points. Guided swims are also available. Included with the entrance fee is a full day's access to the park and observation points, including beach access, but there is no lifeguard. There's an extra charge for access to the snorkeling and diving center, relaxation pools, the children's activity center, and the underwater photography center. The center also has a restaurant, and there is a bar on the beach.

★ Coral World Underwater Observatory

Hours of pure fun and enjoyment are just five miles from Eilat's city center at the **Coral World Underwater Observatory** (Rte. 90, tel. 08/636-4200, www.coralworld.com/eilat, 8:30am-5pm Sat.-Thurs., 8:30am-4pm Fri. and holidays, NIS99, including Oceanarium, child NIS89), distinguishable by the structure pointing into the sky.

Throughout the complex, which includes a cafeteria, you can look through a dozen

Eilat

To CORAL WORLD UNDERWATER OBSERVATORY,
Port of Eilat, and Red Sea Winter Jazz Festival

HATIVAT HANEGEV

YOTAM

LOS ANGELES

YERUSHALAYIM HASHLEMA

ELIOT

ARGAMAN

HATIVAT HANEGEV

ELIOT

ELIOT

ELIOT

HATMARIM AVE

ELIOT

GOLANI

Fradkin
Garden

GAN BINYAMIN

HATMARIM AVE

THE WOW
SHOW

OFARIM

RETAMIM

BLUE
HOTEL

Gan Binyamin
Central Park

HATIVAT HANEGEV

NOVA
LIKE
HOTEL

MESSI-BAR
BEATLES BAR

Sculptures
Garden

HAPALMACH STREET

40

HAARAVA

HAARAVA

Haarava
Park

40

HAARAVA

MALL
HAYAM

EILAT
AIRPORT

ASTRAL
SEASIDE
HOTEL

Ofira
Park

DURBAN

Red Sea

HAMAYIM

PROMENADE

QUEEN OF
SHEBA MALL

KAMEN STREET

THE AMERICANA
EILAT

ANTIBES

HAMAYIM

KAMPEN STREET

HAYAM

HAMAYIM

HOTEL
ZONE

Salt Desert

HAMAYIM

HERODS
BOUTIQUE

KING'S
CITY

HAYAM

To
Border Crossing
to Jordan

© AVALON TRAVEL

0
0
250 yds
250 m

the Coral World Underwater Observatory in Eilat

different windows to see bright, rare fish, including a dark room for viewing glow-in-the-dark sealife and phosphorescent fish. For an extra charge, you can go for an underwater dive in a 100-ton yellow submarine.

It's easy to spend half a day at the Observatory and Oceanarium, especially if you time your visit around daily events like the 11am shark feeding, 3pm Amazon animal feeding, a trip to the Oceanarium's simulated-motion theater, a trip up to the observatory tower where you can see the neighboring countries of Jordan and Egypt, and a visit to the café.

ENTERTAINMENT AND EVENTS
Festivals and Shows

If you are in Eilat in the dead of winter, the **Red Sea Winter Jazz Festival** (http://en.redseajazz.co.il, Jan., NIS40-150) is a combination of music, culture, and events. It spans several days and is considered one of the best festivals of its kind in all of Israel, attracting international acts and the best domestic artists. Concerts are held in three venues, one of which overlooks the Red Sea. Package deals on hotels, flights, and shows can be found on the festival website.

For a performance full of acrobatics, dance,

and lighting effects all to a soundtrack, **The WOW Show** (Royal Garden Hotel, 1 Kampen St., North Shore, tel. 08/638-6701, www.isrotel.co.il, shows run 11am-8:30pm Mon.-Sat., NIS75-110) is a fun way to spend some time. The thematic performance changes every year and sometimes includes dancing, comedians, and other performing artists.

Bars, Pubs, and Clubs

The **Three Monkeys Pub** (23 Pa'amei HaShalom St., Royal Beach Promenade, tel. 08/636-8888 or 053/809-4596, www.threemonkeyspub.co.il, 9pm-late night daily) is Eilat's oldest and most well-known sports bar and live performance venue with beach seating and a generally laid-back atmosphere. There's a huge cocktail, beer, and alcohol menu and light food options.

With its impossibly long bar and slick red-and-black interior, the **Beatles Bar** (5 Yotam, 4th Fl., tel. 077/430-1458 or 052/801-3939, shay.dvd@gmail.com, restaurant 7pm-11pm daily, dance bar 11pm-4am daily, NIS80) oozes cool. If you come earlier in the evening, you can get a burger, and if you stay late, you can dance the night away. The restaurant, which includes beach service, turns into a dance club in the wee hours.

Popular with both locals and tourists,

Messi-Bar (1 Yotam, middle floor, tel. 052/351-7336, 9:30pm-late night Tues.-Sun., minimum age 25 years) features all kinds of rock music in both English and Hebrew. The extremely casual atmosphere plays on the town's beach vibe, with sturdy, tall wooden tables and room for dancing.

SHOPPING

Eilat's special offering to shoppers is that there is no Value Added Tax (VAT) on items in stores. The selection of stores is similar to what you'll find in the rest of Israel, but they are geared toward drawing customers in for deals with special late-night sessions and an extra-soothing level of air-conditioning to escape the heat.

Shopping Malls and Centers

For everything you could possibly want to buy, Mall Hayam (1 HaPalmach, North Shore, tel. 08/634-0006, 9:30am-11:30pm Sun.-Thurs., 9am-one hour before sunset Fri.) is Eilat's biggest and Israel's most profitable mall. The mall has everything from a game center to international and domestic clothing chains to food. The multilevel mall also has a fantastic view of the Red Sea.

In close proximity to a number of hotels, the Queen of Sheba Mall (North Beach promenade near the Hilton, 10am-midnight daily) is 43,000 square feet of commerce with a view of the Eilat marina and places to grab a quick bite to eat.

Eilat's version of Rodeo Drive or a Parisian avenue is La Boulevard (5 Antiv, North Shore, tel. 08/638-6666, 9am-11pm daily), a shopping center that comes with street lamps, wood benches, air-conditioning, and cover from the sun. The products are high-end, international brands of jewelry, fashion, sporting goods, and a French-inspired bakery.

SPORTS AND RECREATION

The main sporting attraction and a major draw to the area in general is diving. Other popular water-related activities in Eilat include glass-bottom boats and the many beaches in the area.

Beaches

There are a variety of beaches in Eilat that offer something for everyone, including water sports, parties, restaurants, and nightclubs. At HaShchafim (or Herod's) Beach (north Eilat near Herod's Hotel) you can see movie screenings. HaZahav Beach (near the hotel promenade between the Isrotel Royal Beach Hotel and Dan Hotel) is synonymous with romance and has great atmosphere for just kicking back. Dolphin Reef (on Eilat-Taba Rd. after the Dead Sea Works potash plant) is the place to swim with the dolphins. Royal Beach (in front of the Royal Beach Hotel off of Pa'amei HaShalom St.) is the best bet if you want to dine on the sand.

Diving and Water Sports

Over 100 types of stony coral and 650 species of tropical fish grace the Coral Beach Nature Reserve (Coral Beach opposite the Eilat Field School, tel. 07/637-6829, www. parks.org.il, 9am-5pm daily, adult NIS35, child NIS18) at the southern end of Eilat. The centerpiece of the reserve is a 1,200-meter-long, densely populated coral reef that runs parallel to the beach.

Royal Water Sports (Shvil Hayam St., tel. 08/646-6881, www.eilat-city.net, 8:30am-7:30pm daily) is a sports club on Royal Beach with banana boats, tubing, Jet Skiing, kayaking, and paddleboats.

One of the best diving schools in the country, Aqua Sport (Mitsrayim Way, tel. 08/633-4404, www.aqua-sport.com, 9am-4pm daily) has been in business for more than four decades and can accommodate divers of every level. They also rent equipment and have showers, bathroom facilities, and Bedouin tents. Introductory dives for people ages 8-88 are offered daily.

Opposite the Coral Beach Nature Reserve is Diver's Village (Mitsrayim Way, tel. 08/637-2268, www.diversvillage.co.il), which has been operating for 20 years, rents diving and snorkeling equipment, and gives lessons. Introductory and refresher lessons are available, and there are showers and toilets, a snack bar, and three guest rooms. Introductory dives are available to kids as young as seven.

Glass-Bottom Boats

For a glimpse into the underwater world of the Red Sea without putting a toe in the water, you can ride on one of the Israel-Yam (North Shore at the marina between Caesar Hotel and Sheraton Moriah Hotel, tel. 08/633-2325, www.israel-yam.co.il, prices vary, boats depart from the marina at 10:30am, 1pm, and 3:30pm) 72-foot yachts. The boats include a sundeck, a dance floor for private parties, and a snack bar. The lowest level has a long, rectangular window for the underwater viewing floor. A two-hour ride includes a tour past the Coral Reef and the Japanese Gardens, along the Israeli-Jordanian border, and dolphin-watching on the Israeli-Egyptian border at Taba.

FOOD
Italian

With a simple atmosphere and an open kitchen, Angelina (3 Antibes on King Solomon Promenade, tel. 053/809-4348 or 08/636-3439, www.angelina-rest.co.il, 7pm-11pm Sun.-Thurs., 8pm-11pm Sat., NIS55) specializes in all manner of pizza and pasta, including a delectable zucchini, sweet potato, and feta cheese pizza pie and a spinach and gorgonzola pasta dish. The general atmosphere definitely feels like a pizzeria, but it's a nice option for a hearty Italian meal at a very affordable price, and it is right by the water with promenade seating.

Seafood

Preceded by its sterling, decades-long reputation as being one of the best seafood places in town, The Last Refuge (Turkiz St. near the underwater observatory, tel. 08/637-2437, www.rol.co.il/sites/eng/hamiflat, 12:30pm-11pm daily, NIS130) has colorful nautical interior decor and boasts a gorgeous view of the Red Sea. Some of their menu features include fish, mussels in garlic and cream, grilled lobsters, and seafood platters.

A popular spot to kick back and enjoy some atmosphere is Pago Pago (99 HaMayim, tel. 08/637-6660 or 08/633-7747, www.pagopagorest.com, 12:30pm-11:30pm daily, NIS75), situated right on the beach with a view of the Red Sea in a very sleek, modern building. The menu includes steak and seafood dishes as well as custom desserts. Try the shrimp calamari Marseille or Spanish mackerel with yogurt. The restaurant is not huge, but the dual-level layout includes a long bar and a warm atmosphere with wood flooring.

Tucked away in a discreet location is the aptly named Eddie's Hideaway (8 Eilot St., tel. 08/637-1137, http://eddies.co.il, 6pm-11:30pm Mon.-Fri., 2pm-10:30pm Sat., NIS60) is a well-known local spot that has been in business since 1979. Serving a variety of seafood and meat dishes done in the French culinary style such as shrimp, steak, and shellfish, Eddie's has a modest exterior and simple, understated interior. It makes for an excellent intimate, romantic dinner for two.

South American

If you make it a bit off the beaten path of the city center in search of a hearty meat meal, go to Little Brazil (3 Eilot St., tel. 08/637-2018, www.littlebrazil.co.il, 12:30pm-11pm daily, NIS120), an all-you-can-eat, South American Churrasco-style meat restaurant. The atmosphere is warm and friendly, and because of the location you'll get a mix of locals and tourists. But you'll also get so much meat from the roaming waiter, called a *pasador,* you won't want to eat again for days.

Cafés and Coffee Shops

In the heart of the high-end Royal Garden Hotel shops avenue, Café Boulevard (5 Antibes, tel. 08/638-6699, 8am-11pm daily, NIS45) is set up as a classic café with items on display in a case and a massive, spacious interior with small tables and sofas. Known for the quirky pictures they create in customers' latte foam, Boulevard usually features a Friday night live performance and has a decent alcohol menu.

The place to go for dessert and coffee is **Café Chocola** (6 Hatmarim Ave., tel. 08/637-2555, alonzo34@walla.com, 8am-8pm Sun.-Thurs., 8am-4pm Fri., NIS35), a French boutique bakery and patisserie that serves some of the most beautiful creations you've ever seen.

More than just a café-bakery, **Shibolym** (79 HaOrgim St., tel. 08/632-3932, www.red-seaeilat.com, 7am-9pm Sun.-Thurs., 7am-2pm Fri., NIS40) serves a range of rustic, homemade bread and pastries with homemade jams and dips. It's conveniently located in the town center, and the extra touches make their version of Israeli breakfast exceptionally delicious.

ACCOMMODATIONS

Eilat's status as a major domestic and international tourist destination means that there is a plethora of upper-end hotels and hotel chains. Many of the nicer hotels require a two-night minimum stay when booking on the weekend, and the fairly standard feature of Israeli hotels to include breakfast isn't universal in Eilat. Check in advance about included breakfast, as it might be by request only. Most hotels are grouped around the beaches and diving areas.

Under US$100

One of the most affordable places to stay in pricey Eilat is the **Sea Princess Motel** (136 Retamim St., tel. 08/910-2330, www.pninathayameilat.co.il, US$85 d), next to the Eilat Bus Station and 10 minutes to major shopping, including Mall Hayam. With about three dozen private rooms and dorm rooms that all have a TV, a fridge, and microwaves, the Sea Princess has free wireless Internet in common areas, a TV in the lobby, and a garden. The front desk is 24 hours, and you can go by foot to the nearest beach, which is about 15 minutes away.

US$100-150

Still affordable and with a few extra perks, the **Blue Hotel** (123 Ofarim St., tel. 08/632-6601, http://bluehotel.co.il, US$120 d) has a 24-hour front desk, newspaper service, and rooms with a terrace. As a guest you also have access to renting out a bicycle, a tour desk, and wireless Internet is free throughout the hotel. Recent renovations add to the general ambience of the hotel, which is very breezy and tropical. It's possible to book a package stay at the hotel for diving.

One of the coolest features of **Holitel La Playa Hotel** (3 Simtat Shfifon off of Kamen St., tel. 08/939-4455, US$145 d) is the palm tree-encircled outdoor swimming pool. The hotel, which is near Eilat Airport, is decorated in Moroccan style, and all of the rooms have a TV, sofa, and coffee and tea service. Near city center and the beach, La Playa is a larger hotel with over 200 rooms, a spa, a cinema, a library, pool tables, video games, and a mini market. When you're tired of the beach, you can order food and drinks poolside or hang out in the hotel's bar for a drink. If you book on the weekend, there is a two-night minimum stay.

The layout of **The Americana Eilat** (7 Kamen St. at North Beach, tel. 08/630-3777, www.americanahotel.co.il, US$122 d) is slightly motel-ish with three stories and rooms that open directly to the outside, but the amenities and price make it a worthwhile stay. There are a variety of types among the 140 rooms that include some with balconies and a view of the pool, kitchenettes, connecting rooms, and extra-large family rooms. The rooms are bright with comfortable, modern furnishings and include free wireless Internet, a fridge, hair dryer, and cable TV. There is also a sauna and hot tub, shaded children's pool, a supermarket, a spa club, and a restaurant and nightclub at the hotel. Not far away is the promenade and waterfront.

Tucked right into the middle of central Eilat, the **Rio Hotel** (9 Hatmarim Ave., tel. 08/630-1111, US$129 d) is a boutique establishment with a trendy, upscale interior that includes a bar, restaurant, and small pool. Very close to the airport and bus station, guests here get access to the neighborhood disco at Hotel Mega and a free glass of wine with dinner at the hotel restaurant.

US$150-200

Truly just a hop, skip, and a jump from beachfront access, **Prima Music Hotel** (Turkiz St. at Almog Beach, tel. 08/638-8555, www.prima-hotels-israel.com, US$170 d) is just five minutes from Coral Beach. The hotel's bright, tropical interior is designed on a musical theme complete with a music room with vintage records that guests can play, giving it a quirky touch. Other features include a common area sea view terrace and some rooms with a sea view, cable TV, and CD sound systems. A stay here includes a huge buffet breakfast, bicycle rentals, and the option of a dinner buffet. It's also close to scores of restaurants at Almog Beach Marina. The Olympic-size swimming pool has a view of the Red Sea and there are tennis and volleyball courts on the hotel grounds.

Trendy and very family-friendly, the **Nova Like Hotel** (6 Hativat Hanegev St., tel. 08/638-2444 reception, tel. 03/542-5555 reservations, www.atlas.co.il, US$158 d) is a recently renovated larger hotel. The rooms surround a pool and many include a balcony with a pool view. The suites with two larger hotel rooms and large studios all have a kitchenette. There's also a kids' pool, sundeck, lobby lounge and bar, bicycle rental, and live entertainment during the high season. About 10-15 minutes by foot gets you to the main Eilat beaches. Rooms include free wireless Internet and direct-dial telephones.

Boasting one of the best poolside views of the Red Sea in town, the ★ **Astral Seaside Hotel** (6 Durban St., tel. 08/636-7444, www.astralhotels.co.il, US$190 d weekdays, US$228 d weekends, hotel requires two-night stay on weekends) has a massive wooden poolside sundeck and lounge chairs. The spacious rooms are beautiful, bright, and modern and some include floor-to-ceiling windows with a terrace and sea views. The medium-size hotel also has a children's club, evening shows in high season, and in-room Swedish massages by request. There's free lobby wireless access, a synagogue, spa, lobby bar, and it's just minutes away from the sea.

The multistory **Herods Boutique** (23 Pa'amei HaShalom St., North Shore, tel. 08/638-0010 or 03/511-0000, www.herodshotels.com/en/eilat, US$193 d) has views of the lagoon and the Edom Mountains. Home to a wide variety of activities geared toward kids, the hotel's rooms include a special channel on the TV for kids, minibars, coffee and tea service, and an option for connecting doors. The interior design has slightly opulent touches, and many of the rooms have a balcony with a view. The hotel also boasts the largest conference center in Eilat as well as a swimming pool. The hotel is at the end of the promenade, but be careful when booking, as there are several hotels in Eilat with the word Herod in the title.

Equipped with its own marina, the **Vista Hotel** (17 Kamen St., North Shore, tel. 08/630-3030, www.vistaeilat.co.il, US$160 d), also near Aqaba City Center Shopping Mall, has an outdoor pool with a bar, free wireless Internet in public areas, a fitness center, a restaurant, and an indoor bar. The hotel is smallish, with about 84 rooms, but the interior layout has a very spacious, modern, clean feeling. The rooms are on the smaller side, but most of them have a cityscape or water view, and include a TV, free newspapers, a fridge, and free wireless Internet. The front desk can help with tickets and tours, business services, and currency exchange. Some cool touches are the waterfall in the pool and the arcade for kids.

An option for a more pastoral experience is **Eilot Kibbutz Country Lodging** (Kibbutz Eilot about 3 miles north of Eilat, tel. 08/635-8816, www.eilot.co.il/en, US$165 d), which allows you to be near the action of Eilat but with some peace and quiet. The hotel is small, with only 40 rooms, but offers an indoor and an outdoor pool, a garden with facilities for cookouts, rooms with balconies, and a petting zoo for kids.

Over US$200

Luxury accommodations in Eilat are big business, and the **Magic Sunrise Club Eilat** (Kibbutz Eilot, tel. 03/511-0098 or 08/630-5333, www.fattal-hotels.com, US$220 d) is a prime example of the all-inclusive options that are available. Near North Beach, Dolphin Reef, and Aqaba City Center Shopping Mall, this large hotel includes everything but free wireless Internet. There are a range of dining options, from coffee to a full restaurant, concierge service, and a 24-hour front desk. Rooms have minibars, safes, satellite TV, balconies, direct-dial phones, and some ground-floor rooms open to a broad lawn. The interior design is quite spare but very nicely done with a Spanish theme, and the rooms are very spacious. Almost everything you could need is at this hotel.

Expensive but worth every penny, the **Club Hotel Eilat** (2 Kheil HaHandasa Blvd. off of Habaz St., tel. 08/636-1666, www.clubhotels-israel.com, US$315 d) is more like an oasis compound of luxury than a hotel. The main attraction is the massive outdoor pool that includes waterslides, waterfalls, and the shade of palm trees. The hotel also has a synagogue, spa and sauna, restaurant, arcade, gym, and 40 acres of grounds. The nautical interior design of the massive, 700-room hotel almost gives the feel of being in cabins on a cruise ship. When you get tired of playing at the hotel, the beach and lagoon are within easy walking distance.

Famed for its high-quality guest service, the **Rimonim Eilat Hotel** (Tarshish St., North Shore, tel. 08/636-9369, http://english.rimonim.com, US$408 d) is literally one minute away from the Red Sea beach and right in the middle of Eilat's main shopping district. Every room has a balcony that overlooks the sea and the hotel's large outdoor pool. There is a lobby bar, restaurant, gym, and spa. The rooms are modern and designed with bright colors and extra touches like a dining bar, a large-screen TV, and sliding glass doors that lead to the balcony.

Home to the well-known nightly WOW show, the **Royal Garden Hotel** (1 Kampen St., North Shore, tel. 08/633-7010, www.isrotel.com/royal_garden, US$360 d) caters to people on family vacations with roomy suites that are decorated with wood accents and cozy interiors that feel more like home than a hotel room. The gorgeous, lagoon-like outdoor pool and water park has a snack bar, and the hotel is near the boardwalk and beach. Be warned that the hotel does not provide pool towels or have a restaurant, but every room has a kitchenette complete with utensils and a dining area.

The **U Coral Beach Club Resort** (Almog Beach, tel. 08/635-0000, www.fattal-hotels.com, US$330 d) is an all-inclusive option that has its own beach, swimming pool, and spa center. The hotel features include a bar with the option for lounging on the outdoor deck with a drink and on-site live stage performances. This 281-room hotel offers a free shuttle bus, a gift shop, a poolside bar, and rooms with all the amenities you could possibly need, decorated in a simple, modern, upscale style. Dry cleaning and laundry service, room service, babysitting, and a hair salon are also available.

INFORMATION AND SERVICES

The tourism and information services in Eilat are some of the best in Israel since it is such a popular destination.

The well-equipped and helpful **Municipal Tourism Corporation Eilat** (2 Yotam St., tel. 08/636-7890, rstourism@eilat.muni.il, 8am-5pm Sun.-Thurs.) is an operation of the City of Eilat and caters to international tourists, with a large amount of information in English.

The **city's official tourism website** (www.redseaeilat.com) is very well done with anything and everything you could want to know about Eilat. It includes listings of every kind of service imaginable.

Eilat City (www.eilat-city.net) is run by locals and a useful and easy-to-use website.

In an emergency, contact the **Eilat Tourist Police** (tel. 08/636-7209 or 106) and emergency medical services **Magen David Adom** (tel. 08/637-2333 or 101).

There are about half a dozen currency exchange locations around town, including **Money Gold** (Mall HaYam, tel. 08/634-0049, open during mall hours) and **Nawi Money Exchange** (8 Antibes St., Hilton Queen of Sheba promenade, tel. 050/388-3111, 10am-midnight Sun.-Thurs., 10am-4pm Fri.).

GETTING THERE AND AROUND

Getting to Eilat seems daunting if you are starting from Tel Aviv or Jerusalem, but once you're on the way, it's a fairly straight and uneventful (though lengthy) trip by car or bus.

Car

From Jerusalem, it is a minimum four-hour drive to Eilat. Late at night there is very little traffic and you don't have the burden of the hot sun beating down on your vehicle or fighting with the air-conditioning. The roads are not lit for most of the way, and there is a great deal of blackness as you drive through the mountainous areas near the Dead Sea and through the Negev Desert. However, every turn along the road is very clearly marked, especially in the areas where it is a two-lane highway.

From Jerusalem, follow Route 90 south as far as you can go until you reach Eilat. If you drive during the day, it's a good idea to take the whole day and incorporate a stop or two along the way at the Dead Sea.

From Tel Aviv, take Highway 6 to Route 40 south for about four hours. The route from Tel Aviv takes you past the incredible crater at Mitzpe Ramon and cuts straight through the desert with long stretches of nothing but a gas station every now and then.

Once you're in Eilat and driving about, you'll easily get the hang of navigating the plethora of enormous roundabouts that control traffic. The city is well signposted, and there is plenty of parking.

Bus

The bus trip from Jerusalem to Eilat is just under five hours on an **Egged** bus (www.egged.co.il, bus number 444, NIS80 one-way). From Tel Aviv to Eilat, it takes well over five hours (bus numbers 390 and 394, NIS80 one-way).

Once you're in Eilat, the only public transportation service in town is Egged.

Air

It is possible to reach Eilat by plane. The **Eilat Domestic Airport** (tel. 08/636-3800, www.iaa.gov.il) takes flights from Arkia, El Al, Israir, and Sun Dor airlines. The airport is small and convenient, and flying is a good option if you plan to also take in a trip to Petra, Jordan, while you're in the area. Most tour companies will pick you up directly from the airport if you arrive on a morning flight.

Petra, Jordan

Just across the border from the southernmost point in Israel is the ancient Nabataean city of Petra. Its architecture of massive colonnaded buildings is carved into the stone faces of mountains, inexpressibly exquisite.

Petra was the capital of the Nabataeans, a powerful civilization that worked the incense route that supplied the Romans. Sometimes called the lost city, as outsiders were at one time banned from entering, Petra in its current state was rediscovered by Western society about 200 years ago. In 1812 the Swiss traveler, geographer, and orientalist Johann Ludwig Burckhardt snuck into what was a closely guarded site by disguising himself as an Arab from India on his way to make a sacrifice at the tomb of the Prophet Aaron. It was his trickery that led to the Western rediscovery of the ruins of Petra.

In 1985, UNESCO declared Petra a World Heritage Site, and in a global popular vote of more than 100 million people in 2007, it was honored as one of the New Seven Wonders of the World. Much of Petra's history has been lost in the sands of time, and much of what is generally accepted about it today is taken with a grain of salt instead of as verified fact.

PLANNING YOUR TIME

Most people will tell you that you need several days to see Petra. If you have come over from Israel and are on a tight schedule, try to allow at least one overnight stay. It is possible to get a feel for Petra in one day, but time will be tight. If you cross into Jordan at Aqaba, your time will be spent getting through the border checkpoint, traveling to the site, walking in, walking around a bit, walking out, and then returning to the border. The whole process takes about 12 hours and is the quickest possible version of a trip to Petra if you are coming directly from Eilat on the Israeli side.

There are plenty of very affordable accommodations in the immediate area within walking distance to Petra. In addition, a two-day entry ticket to Petra costs about US$5 more than the rather expensive single-entry ticket.

Previous: tourists visiting the ancient ruins of Petra; traditional sand art in bottles. **Above:** a Bedouin man riding his camel.

Look for ★ to find recommended
sights, activities, dining, and lodging.

Highlights

★ **Wadi Rum:** This expanse of desert in Jordan is full of unusual rock formations. Mountains of sandstone and granite rise as high as 5,500 feet (page 292).

★ **Roman Theater:** This Roman-style theater is a wonder of ancient architecture (page 295).

★ **Byzantine Church:** Built on top of other ruins, the Byzantine Church in Petra has 70 square meters of mosaic floors (page 296).

★ **Great Temple:** Petra's largest freestanding structure, the Great Temple underwent extensive excavation work carried out by students from the Joukowsky Institute at Brown University (page 296).

★ **The Al-Deir Monastery:** Up 800 rock-cut steps above Petra's amphitheater is this monastery and its unique, massive urn (page 297).

Petra, Jordan

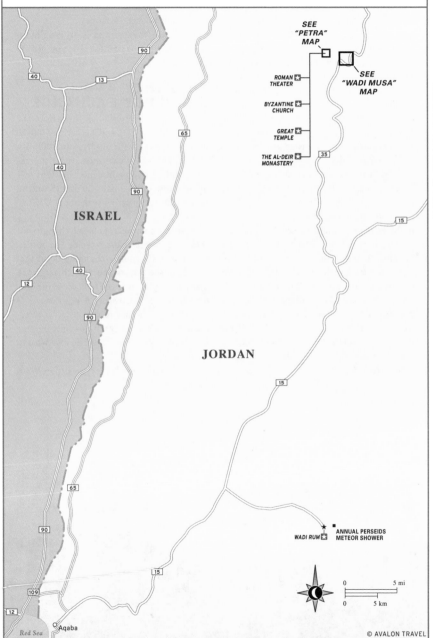

SEE "PETRA" MAP

SEE "WADI MUSA" MAP

ROMAN THEATER

BYZANTINE CHURCH

GREAT TEMPLE

THE AL-DEIR MONASTERY

ISRAEL

JORDAN

WADI RUM

ANNUAL PERSEIDS METEOR SHOWER

Red Sea

Aqaba

0   5 mi
0   5 km

© AVALON TRAVEL

VISAS, PASSPORTS, AND ENTRANCE FEES

There are three land border crossings from Israel into Jordan in the north, center, and south of the country. The two most convenient and relevant for travelers to Petra are the Allenby/King Hussein Bridge Border Crossing and the border crossing at Eilat-Aqaba. Visas are issued on the spot at the Eilat crossing, and you don't need to provide photographs.

If you cross at the Allenby/King Hussein Bridge, you need to pay for your visa (about JD16) in advance at the Jordanian embassy in Tel Aviv. You will need two photographs, and you'll get the visa within 24 hours.

If you enter Jordan by air, you will need to pay for a single-entry Jordanian visa (about JD20), which you can do at the airport, usually in the same place where you change money.

If you cross from Eilat to Aqaba by sea or land, through the port or at the crossing from Israel, your visa should be free for one month for most nationalities, including Americans and Canadians. The only fee you might be charged is an exit fee of JD5 for overland exits back into Israel. Aqaba is a Special Economic Zone Area (SEZA) set up for free trade, which is why the visa requirements are different.

When heading to Aqaba, do not pay tour guides on the Israeli side of the border who tell you to give them cash for a visa, as they may simply pocket the money.

Make sure that your passport is valid for at least six months past the date you plan to leave Jordan.

CURRENCY AND CURRENCY EXCHANGE

The official currency of Jordan is the Jordanian dinar (JD), and it is divided into 10 dirham, 100 qirsh (or piasters), or 1000 fils. Half dinar and 1 dinar coins are most common, and bills come in denominations of 1 dinar, 5 dinars, 10 dinars, 20 dinars, and 50 dinars. JD1 is typically worth about US$1.40 or NIS5.50.

If you are coming from Israel, change your shekels to dinars before crossing the border, or at one of the money-changing desks that are along the way as you pass through the many stops that you need to make at the border (Wadi Araba Crossing/South Border). If you are trying to pay in shekels after entering Jordan, it will really put a damper on your trip, as most people will have no idea what to charge you.

You can also get by very easily in Wadi

Welcome to Jordan.

The Shrine of Aaron

At the very top of Mount Aaron (Jabal Haroun) in Petra is the modest, white-domed Shrine of Aaron. The shrine commemorates the death of Aaron, the elder brother of Moses, and was constructed by the Egyptian Mameluk Sultan in the 13th century.

The highest point in Petra, the shrine is perched on part of the Sharah mountain range. According to tradition, the location of the shrine is the place where Aaron died.

Since antiquity, other religious structures have been built here. According to tradition, a 10-year-old Muhammad visited Aaron's shrine. The site was closely guarded by Bedouins to keep away non-Muslims for a long time, but now it is a site of pilgrimage for Jews, Christians, and Muslims. Aaron is considered a prophet in all three religions.

It is a long hike up a rugged mountain to the site. If you go, plan ahead, set out early in the morning, and take water and protection from the sun.

PETRA, JORDAN

Musa and Petra with U.S. currency, but don't expect change and keep the conversion rates in mind when getting prices.

HISTORY

Dating back to prehistoric times, Petra was at one time at a key crossroad point between Arabia, Egypt, and Syria-Phoenicia. It is widely believed to have been built and inhabited by the powerful Nabataean incense route traders, who used it as their capital city. The Byzantines, Romans, and Crusaders were also residents and contributed to the construction of different buildings and the city layout.

The structures of Petra are partially constructed and partially carved out of the rose-colored rock in the midst of a series of cavernous gorges and rocky mountain peaks. The color of the stone is where Petra gets its nickname of the "rose city."

One of the most famous archaeological sites in the world and an outstanding example of a blending of Hellenistic architecture and Eastern traditions, Petra is in a part of the world that suffered numerous earthquakes.

One of the most fascinating aspects of Petra's history is how much of it remains a mystery. On a guided trip through Petra, you may hear your guide refer to this uncertainty with the standard line that, "85 percent of Petra's history is unknown." Though the unknown is a bit frustrating as a visitor, the mystery makes it all the more enchanting and exciting. It's a place where your imagination about the ancient world can run wild.

ORIENTATION

Petra is between the Dead Sea and the Red Sea in Jordan. If you set out from Petra from the southernmost border entry on the Israel side at Eilat (there are three border entries), you will find yourself in Aqaba, Jordan. From Aqaba, you can take a taxi, bus, or tour bus to Petra. It takes about two hours including one or two short stops.

About halfway along the way to Petra from the south, you will pass by Wadi Rum, a desert landscape that has been immortalized in Western films and is a popular ecotourism destination.

In Wadi Rum and along the way to Petra you will see very unusual rock formations, including bright bands of colorful mineral deposits etched into the stone landscape in beautiful colors.

Once you arrive, you will find yourself in an Arab village called Wadi Musa, immediately adjacent to the archaeological site of Petra. Wadi Musa is home to about 99 percent of Petra's restaurants, accommodations, and services. The large Jordanian city of Amman is about 3.5 hours to the north.

Sights

The road from the border of Egypt at Aqaba, which most tour groups and guides use as a rally point for excursions to Petra, is marked by the stark distinction of almost nothing but desert for about two hours, except for Wadi Rum. Once you get to Wadi Musa, the main site is Petra.

★ WADI RUM

On the way to Petra is the incredible and unique landscape of the **Wadi Rum Protected Area** (Rte. 15 between Aqaba and Petra, www.wadirum.jo, JD5, under 12 free), the location where much of the 1962 classic by David Lean, *Lawrence of Arabia,* was filmed. *Transformers II* and part of one of the *Star Wars* movies were also filmed here.

Wadi Rum is a 720-square-kilometer expanse of desert that is full of unusual rock formations and mountains of sandstone and granite that rise to the heights of 5,500 feet in some areas and are often compared to the

Petra

THE AL-DEIR MONASTERY

WINGED LION TEMPLE

BASIN RESTAURANT

THE CARDO

GREAT TEMPLE

BYZANTINE CHURCH

SOUVENIRS

ROMAN THEATER

SAND CASTLE BAZAAR

PETRA BY NIGHT SHOW

THE TREASURY

CAMEL RIDES

HIGH PLACE OF SACRIFICE

To Wadi Musa and Petra Main Gate

THE SIQ

0   200 yds
0   200 m

© AVALON TRAVEL

Wadi Musa

To Al-Beidha and Little Petra

To Beit Zaman Hotel and Resort

LA MAISON

PETRA MOON HOTEL

BEIT ZAMAN HOTEL AND RESORT

SILK ROAD RESTAURANT

TURKISH BATH

VISITOR'S CENTER

VISITOR'S CENTER SHOPS

ROCKY MOUNTAIN HOTEL

PETRA MAIN GATE

AL-WADI

HORSEBACK RENTAL

SHAHEED ROUNDABOUT

AL RASHID HOTEL

35

OBELISK TOMB

To Petra

0   250 yds

0   250 m

35

35

© AVALON TRAVEL

surface of the moon. Visiting Wadi Rum is strictly controlled. The safest and easiest thing to do is hire a travel guide through a hotel in Aqaba who can take you to Wadi Rum.

Another option is to go to Wadi Rum's **Visitors' Centre** (one hour northeast of Aqaba on Rte. 15, turn right at sign, tel. 03/209-0600), which has posted prices for hiring a local Bedouin guide who can escort you in a 4x4 vehicle or by camel. It's also possible to hire a guide for a campout in a Bedouin tent. Don't forget water, a hat with a brim, and sunscreen.

The Visitors' Centre is part of a complex of buildings that includes an interpretation center, crafts shops, a ticket office, and a restaurant. Within Wadi Rum there is a range of natural sites to see, including ancient rock paintings, historical points of interest, and dramatic places to view the sunrise or sunset from atop desert sand dunes.

PETRA

The ancient site of **Petra** (www.visitpetra.jo, 6am-6pm daily Apr.-Oct., 6am-4pm daily Nov.-Mar., 7am-4pm daily during the month of Ramadan, JD50-90 for one day, JD55 for two days) is next to the Arab village of Wadi Musa. The **Visitor Center** can sell you tickets, arrange for guides, and give you

The Nabataean Capital

Petra is believed to be the capital city of the Arab tribe of the Nabataeans, who made their first appearance around the 6th century BC, just east of Jordan in the desert. Originating from the southeast of the Arabian Peninsula, they gradually expanded their territory and by the 2nd century BC had established a more organized society.

Highly independent and apt at dodging military conquest, the Nabataeans were influenced by Hellenistic culture, as can be seen in the remnants of their art and architecture. The Greek historian Herodotus refers to the Nabataeans in 312 BC and their capital city of Petra.

Petra has a long history of conquest. It was sacked in 312 BC by the army of King Antigonus. On their retreat, though, the army was destroyed in the desert after taking a massive haul of treasure from the city. Around 63 BC, King Aretas III somehow managed to prevent a Roman military conquest of Petra. After Julius Caesar's assassination and the ensuing chaos in 44 BC, Petra had to begin paying tribute to Rome. Failure to pay resulted in two invasions, one by Herod the Great, who gained control of part of their territory and lucrative trade routes.

After the death of the final Nabataean ruler, Rabbel II, Rome annexed Petra and redesigned parts of it in the Roman style. During Roman rule, it's believed that Petra's population grew to about 25,000. But over time and with shifts in trade routes, the Nabataeans profited less and less from trade and eventually abandoned Petra around the 4th century AD. Not much is known about the exact reasons Petra was abandoned, but very few possessions were left behind, suggesting a well-organized, planned departure.

background information. It is located at the end of a row of small shops just before the entrance to Petra and downhill from the tourist bus parking lots. The entry ticket is JD40 more if you are not staying overnight in Petra.

Ticket prices differ based on whether you are a foreigner or a local, the length of the stay, and the number of times you plan on entering. It is almost impossible to see the site adequately in one day. It is expensive to enter Petra, but quite affordable to add an extra day or two to the base ticket price for multiple entries.

Wear the most comfortable shoes you own, and be prepared for a mini-hike in and out of the site, which takes at least an hour each way. Once you are inside, you will have plenty of opportunities to climb up into buildings and explore different ruins. There are horse-drawn carriages that can take you in and out of the first main canyon.

Obelisk Tomb

Just between the *siq* (main passage) and the main entrance to Petra is the mysterious **Obelisk Tomb,** situated next to huge rocks

with strange curves. The beautiful tomb is Egyptian with Nabataean and Egyptian inscriptions.

The *Siq*

The main passage into Petra is called the *siq,* which means cleft, and it is an almost 4,000-foot-long canyon cut through the mountains that leads to the breathtaking first view of Petra.

Along the way, there are all kinds of details worth stopping to take in, including notches for votives that might have been ceremonial, paving stones, and the waterway system that lines both sides of the floor of the *siq.* This is where Harrison Ford rode his horse in a memorable scene in *Indiana Jones and the Last Crusade.*

The Treasury (Al-Khazneh)

The first dramatic view in Petra is the breathtaking **Treasury.** It's both impossible to miss and difficult to drag yourself away from. Known to locals as Al-Khazneh, its colonnaded facade is a towering 130 feet, with depictions of mythological figures carved into the stone.

The most famous and most photographed of Petra's many sites, the treasury is thought to house something valuable, money perhaps, in the urn at the top of the structure, and people have been trying to dislodge it for years to see if it really contains riches. Why archaeologists haven't attempted to simply inspect the urn is a complicated question.

★ Roman Theater

With an estimated capacity of 3,000-7,000 people, the **Roman Theater** is impossible to miss.

The theater dates back to around 9 BC to AD 40 and was restored in the past decade. Built during the reign of King Aretas IV, its capacity is believed to indicate that at one time the population of Petra was about 24,000 people, based on the Roman-style building practices of making one seat for every family.

You can climb up and get a view into the amphitheater from close up, where you'll also get a better perspective of the semicircular structure and the strange feature in the back of some previously existing tombs cut into during construction of the theater. It makes a great spot for a photograph, as you'll find yourself dwarfed by your surroundings.

Royal Tombs

There are several hundred elaborate tombs with intricate carvings in the rock throughout Petra. Many are empty and you can walk inside them (they are very cave-like). Just opposite the amphitheater, you'll see the **Royal Tombs** above ground level with columns cut into the rock wall face. A Byzantine inscription states that one of the tombs was the final resting place of King Malichus II until it was converted into a church in AD 447.

In the immediate vicinity is the ceremonial Palace Tomb, likely used as a place to hold funerals or feasts, and the Tomb of Sextus Florentius, the Roman governor of Arabia who loved the desert region so much that he wanted to be buried here.

The Cardo

Though devastated by a major earthquake in AD 363, Petra's main street (originally Nabataean but reconstructed by the Romans around the early 1st century BC when it was a Roman outpost) still has some of its original marble stones and inscriptions. One inscription from AD 114 attests to the restoration of the cardo after Rome annexed the Nabataean Kingdom.

Petra's massive Roman Theater

The Roman **cardo,** or main thoroughfare, a typical feature of cities conquered by Rome, served as the major street for commerce and ceremonial processions. As you walk, notice small patches of road underfoot that are easy to trip over.

★ Byzantine Church

Probably built over earlier ruins of Petra is the **Byzantine Church,** notable for its remarkably-intact 70 square meters of mosaic floors. Pictures in the mosaics include depictions of mythological figures and the four seasons. The church and the mosaics are still in the process of being excavated and preserved.

In 1993, the famed Petra Scrolls were discovered in the Byzantine Church. The collection of 152 papyrus scrolls date back to the 6th century AD (confounding because this was after Petra is believed to have already started to decline).

The scrolls represent the largest collection of written material from antiquity to have ever been found in Jordan. They were studied by a team from the United States and a team from Finland. They contain a great deal of information about the region in the Byzantine era,

agricultural practices, property and estate practices, tax records, and details about how residents of Petra lived in tight proximity to one another.

★ Great Temple

So much is unknown about the Nabataeans, and this includes who exactly they worshipped. The **Great Temple** is a perfect example of this. The largest freestanding structure in Petra, it recently underwent extensive excavation work carried out by students from the Joukowsky Institute at Brown University. The institute has a detailed, extensive, and interactive map of the excavation on its website (www.brown.edu/Departments/Joukowsky_Institute/Petra).

The temple is also known as the Temple of Dushara, after the god who some believe was worshipped here. It is generally agreed that it was probably the main place of worship in Nabataean Petra. Complete with its own theater, the entire site is about 92 by 131 feet and features crafted limestone and a complex system of tunnels. Important to the Nabataeans during the 1st century BC, it was probably also used by the Byzantines.

the mosaic floor of the Byzantine Church

The massive, complex structure sits on a slightly elevated position with stairs leading up to it and is rectangular in shape with major upper and lower sections. It is one of the most important archaeological and architectural structures in Petra. The Brown University map gives a very complete picture of what used to exist here.

High Place of Sacrifice

A popular early-morning hike is up to the **High Place of Sacrifice** (take the steps to the left just near the amphitheater and go to the right at the top of the stairs), which takes about 90 minutes each way. The site is at the top of the ridge, where you can see how animals were sacrificed in two large depressions with drains for their blood. An altar, obelisks, and the ruins of a building that was probably used by priests are just before where the path leads down to a stone fountain. If you continue walking, you'll see a few more complexes and the ruins of tombs, halls, and an ancient garbage dump.

★ The Al-Deir Monastery

In a location that requires a bit of a hike to get to is the **Al-Deir Monastery** (up a flight of 800 rock-cut steps above the amphitheater). It takes about 90 minutes one way. The path, though it has so many steps, is not too steep and is relatively easy to follow. You'll know you're on the right track when you see a sign to the Lion Tomb.

The monastery stands 164 feet wide and 147 feet tall, and the inner walls are marked with the symbols of crosses.

The highlight of Al-Deir is the crowning urn, which you can walk around the top of by going up some steps. The view of the surrounding landscape from the rim of the urn is fantastic.

Petra Nabataean Museum

Opened in 1994, the **Petra Nabataean Museum** (tel. 03/215-6060, www.nabatea. net, 9am-4pm daily, free with Petra entrance) houses over 600 artifacts that have been discovered in Petra over the years. The three main exhibition halls include a depiction of Nabataean history, specific exhibitions in the area, and a collection of Neolithic artifacts, Nabataean pottery, bronze statues, jewelry, coins, and ornaments.

the Al-Deir Monastery

Petra Archaeological Museum

The older and smaller of two museums in Petra is the **Petra Archaeological Museum** (tel. 03/215-6060, 9am-4pm daily, free with Petra entrance) in an ancient Nabataean cave on the slope of Al-Habis. Opened in 1963, it has a main hall and two side rooms with finds from regional excavations that date to the Edomite, Nabataean, Roman, and Byzantine periods.

Entertainment and Events

Throughout the year Petra has some unusual entertainment offerings tailored around its sights. Neighboring modern-day Wadi Musa is a small Arab village that offers very little in the way of any kind of entertainment, other than eating out.

PETRA BY NIGHT SHOW

Petra shuts down early, but you can experience it by candlelight during the **Petra by Night Show** (8:30pm Mon., Wed.-Thurs., JD17, under 12 free). During the two-hour show, you can see the *siq* and the Treasury lit up with flickering light and listen to the ancient sounds of a Bedouin shepherd's flute for a soundtrack while local guides tell stories. On full moons, you can also get a guided night tour, but you must check with the visitors center and reserve in advance.

ANNUAL PERSEIDS METEOR SHOWER

The **Annual Perseids Meteor Shower** (Aug., peak nights are Aug. 12-13) is an incredible natural phenomena that is best seen from Wadi Rum because of the total lack of city lights and noise. At its peak, there are about 50-80 meteors per hour. Many tour companies have outings that you can join to see the showers.

Petra by Night in the light of hundreds of candles

Three Cups of Coffee: The Bedouin Coffee Ceremony

coffee, Bedouin style

If you get a chance to take part in a traditional Bedouin coffee ceremony while you're in Jordan, keep in mind that there will be three cups of (very strong) coffee. The Bedouin consider coffee to be a sacred beverage that is a symbol of wealth and hospitality.

The coffee ceremony is called a *jaha*, and can be extremely lengthy. Traditionally, it starts at dawn in a Bedouin tent, where water is boiled over coals, and the crushed arabica beans and cardamom are added to the water and left to steep.

When you finally get down to drinking the coffee, there will be three cups. The first cup of coffee is for the soul, the second cup of coffee is for the sword, and the third cup of coffee is in honor of your status as a guest. Another interpretation is that the three cups symbolize hospitality, welcome, and cheer. Asking for a fourth cup of coffee could be considered greedy (and bad for your blood pressure).

During the coffee ceremony, there is usually singing and the rattling of cups and thumping of a long wooden post. The singing was part of the Bedouin tradition in the past during long desert crossings.

Shopping

Entering Petra is extremely cheap for Jordanians, which is part of the reason that you will see a huge number of locals, including young kids, selling all kinds of things from camel and donkey rides to carriage rides with horses, to cheap necklaces and postcards. Look closely at the animals before you buy a ride on one of them: Many are not well cared for and some even have repeated injuries from the makeshift gear they are wearing.

GIFTS AND SOUVENIRS

There is no shortage of places to buy cheap, low-end gifts and souvenirs in Petra and the surrounding area. There are many shops just before the entrance to the site that sell all

souvenir shops at the entrance to Petra

kinds of items and even more vendors inside of Petra with makeshift stands selling everything from books about Petra to bottles of artistically arranged sand.

Feel free to bargain with vendors, as they will start with a high price, but don't try to go lower than a third of the original price.

Sand Castle Bazaar

Near the entrance to Petra is the well-established **Sand Castle Bazaar** (tel. 079/570-5064, http://petrasandcastle.com, 6:30am-5pm Sat.-Thurs.), which sells antiques, stone mosaic art panels, oil lamps, carpets, jewelry, silver, ceramics, and sand bottles. The bazaar has a second location near the Silk Road Hotel in Wadi Musa that ships items worldwide.

Ladies of the Queen Noor Foundation

A silver workshop and large souvenir store with a small coffee stand can be found at the popular pit stop at the **Ladies of the Queen Noor Foundation** (road just outside of Wadi Musa, 9am-6pm Mon.-Sat.). The store has a silver craft workshop with the option to have a necklace custom-made (which you need to wait a few days for).

Nabataean Pottery

Another enduring Nabataean treasure is their distinctive red clay pottery, which can be divided into two groups: coarser common wares and the more famous eggshell-thin wares embellished with black designs that ranged from very small saucers to trays about three feet across. Their pottery-making skills are believed to have been handed down to them from the Edomites.

The production source of Nabataean pottery was near Petra, and included oil lamps (thousands have been found throughout Petra), incense and perfume bottles (found throughout their former empire), and beautiful, thin serving dishes and platters.

Pottery kilns were discovered in the ash-Sharah Mountains northeast of Petra in 1979, and at least a dozen kilns and portions of numerous on-site workshops have been found since then. At least one kiln was discovered in Wadi Musa as well.

Excellent examples of fine Nabataean pottery can be seen in the museum at Masada and at museums in Petra and throughout Jordan. The kilns can be seen in the Petra Archaeological Museum.

Wadi Musa

The modern village adjacent to Petra has basic amenities, as well as several shops selling souvenirs. Another specialty of shops in Wadi Musa is heavy silver antique necklaces.

Local Crafts

Just next to the visitors center at the entrance to Petra are two crafts shops that sell many locally handmade products that support local women's organizations. One shop is run for the benefit of the **Rural Women of Jordan** and the other is for the **Ladies' Working Circle of Wadi Musa** (both shop hours are generally the same as Petra). Beyond the more common embroidered items, both shops also sell jewelry boxes with inlaid mother-of-pearl, sand bottles, pottery, metalwork, and woven pillows.

Sports and Recreation

Petra's options for recreation are mostly related to outdoor sports, and there are some great hikes. If you are confident on horseback you can take a ride through the *siq* to enter the main site. If you want to opt for something more luxurious, take in a spa or Turkish bath.

HIKING

There are several good hikes in Petra that range from 30 minutes to 90 minutes. One of the best trails is just at the entrance to Petra at the end of the *siq*, just **above the Treasury.** There are several stops along the trail which is about 90 minutes one way if you walk to the end.

You can also set out on the trail that starts out near the amphitheater, just to the left and leads to the lion tombs, the sacrificial altars, and Al-Deir Monastery.

If you are not an experienced hiker, it might be advisable to hire a guide in advance to lead you through this part of Petra, though getting lost is unlikely. Try to set out early in the morning, by at least 8am.

A couple of good choices are **Petra Moon Tours** (based in Wadi Musa, tel. 03/215-6665 or 079/617-0666, www.petramoon.com) and **Bedouin Lifestyle** (Wadi Rum, tel. 077/913-1803, www.bedouinlifestyle.com).

a speedy carriage ride through the *siq*

PETRA, JORDAN
SPORTS AND RECREATION

HORSEBACK RIDING

At the entrance to Petra you will see several horses waiting to be taken for a **horseback ride** (included with price of the Petra entrance fee). If you are an animal lover, though, you might be turned off about using your money to support the apparent exploitation of the horses and other animals you'll see in Petra. Many of them are not well cared for and have injuries acquired from being made to work in the tourism trade.

If you find a horse that you are satisfied is well cared for, riding around the area could be a very enjoyable experience and add to the atmosphere of being in such an ancient location. It is recommended only for experienced riders, as the road is quite rocky.

HORSE-DRAWN CARRIAGES

At first glance, the **horse-drawn carriages** (JD25) of Petra look charming and innocent. But they fly up and down the *siq* at breakneck speed. Though they give weary tourists a way to get in and out of the site more quickly, it is not a smooth ride. Most of the passengers look more terrified than enchanted when seen in passing. If you do take a carriage in or out of Petra, just remember that they will go at a fairly quick pace, and you won't be able to stop once you start.

CAMEL RIDES

At the entrance to Petra, in front of the Treasury, and throughout Petra, you will see camels being hired out for **camel rides** (JD20). It's more of a short stroll or a chance to stand and pose for a picture than a ride, but the novelty of it is hard to resist, even if the price is a bit steep.

DONKEY RIDES

Also tempting, especially if you are getting a bit weary of walking around the loose, easy-to-stumble-over rocks, are **donkey rides** (JD15), which are usually rented out by young boys. You might get a little donkey-and-boy shadow following you about until you cave in and buy a ride. Here again, look closely at the condition of the donkeys: Many of them have heavy chains across their noses for a harness, which cuts into the skin of the animal, causing multilayered injuries.

Camels wait for riders in front of the Treasury.

TURKISH BATHS

For some relaxation, the **Salome Turkish Bath** (Wadi Musa, tel. 03/215-7342, www.salometurkishbath.com) is a family-owned and run operation that offers a steam room session, exfoliation, and massage. A treatment can be followed with herbal tea. Ask for transportation to and from your hotel when calling to make a reservation, as it is included with their services.

Food

If you eliminate the dozens of area hotels from the equation, Wadi Musa still has a nice range of at least 30 restaurants and eateries to choose from. Most of them are in the village center, and many are within easy walking distance of Petra.

ARABIC AND TRADITIONAL BEDOUIN

A popular spot for a bite to eat, the **Red Cave** (near Petra Main Gate, tel. 03/215-7799 or 077/771-5223, 9am-11pm daily, JD10) is a slightly more expensive option among a field of tourist-centric choices. But they serve up very generous portions of Bedouin dishes, including *gallayah,* and have indoor and outdoor seating (in the shade). It is very easy to spot with its red sign that hangs over the sidewalk and one the many stops to eat near Petra's main gate. They also have a wide selection of vegetarian dishes, including soups and stews.

Some of the most impeccable service and best coffee you will find in Wadi Musa are to be had at the ★ **Silk Road Restaurant** (Silk Road Hotel, tel. 03/215-7222, www.petrasilkroad.com, 8am-9pm daily, JD10 for buffet). The buffet here has a tasty, wide variety of salads and traditional, typical Arabic dishes. The hotel also has a traditional indoor-outdoor Bedouin-style café that is very small but beautifully decorated with Bedouin tapestries. It makes a perfect spot for a quiet coffee or tea and a light snack.

It has a fairly typical setting (aside from the tables around the fountain) and fairly typical prices, but the **Al Arabi** restaurant (at the Shaheed roundabout, tel. 03/215-7661, yhamadeen@link.net.jo, 6am-midnight daily, JD5) has some seriously delicious dishes and is very centrally located. For JD2 you can get a milk and fruit smoothie to go with the spicy Arabic food they serve.

BUFFET

One of the best buffets in town with the standard strong Turkish coffee, **Petra Zaman** (Main St., tel. 079/553-6391, http://petrazamanrestaurant.weebly.com, 9am-11pm daily, JD3) serves a variety of salads and vegetarian dishes in their homey, central restaurant. They specialize in the regional favorite chicken and rice *maglubeh* dish, which comes in a pot and is flipped onto your plate upside-down when served.

The **Basin Restaurant** (Petra near the monastery, tel. 03/215-6266, 11:30am-3pm daily, JD17 for lunch buffet) is about one mile past the Treasury in Petra and run by the Crowne Plaza Hotel group. It is the most upscale option inside of the antiquities sites of Petra; you will see several other snack shops along the way. The restaurant serves a fairly large buffet, which includes several dessert options, and the typical offerings of hummus, salads, and some meat dishes. The patio seating is shaded and the restaurant has a great view of Petra, but they cater to groups and the prices are on the high end for Petra.

Bedouin Cuisine

a serving of *fatteh*

Traditionally cooked on an open fire, Bedouin food has a unique style that is worth sampling while you're in Petra. There are plenty of opportunities to try different Bedouin food, which is typically eaten with the hands, including dipping rolled-up rice balls into sauce.

There are a few styles of bread that come with Bedouin meals: the more standard pita; the thin, crepe-like **shraak** cooked on a domed pan over a fire; and **taboon,** usually thicker and made from darker flour.

Mansaf is a favorite dish usually reserved for special occasions or for special guests made of stewed lamb meat over rice with yogurt and pine nuts.

Maglubeh, which translates to "upside down," is a mixture of chicken, potatoes, peppers, vegetables, and rice stacked and layered in one pot and then flipped upside down onto a plate after it is cooked. It is usually eaten family-style. Several restaurants in Petra serve *maglubeh.*

Fatteh, easy to find and simple, is a delicious dish made from bread and yogurt, which some-times includes hummus, and is served with chopped raw onions and olive oil.

INTERNATIONAL FUSION

Serving everything from pizza and pasta to hearty omelets and Bedouin food, ★ **Al-Wadi** (Shaheed roundabout, tel. 077/633-1431 or 079/530-0135, mashalehl@yahoo.com, 7am-10:30pm daily, JD4) is a popular choice for people who are not sure what they are in the mood to eat. The atmosphere is quaint, though the interior is a bit dark, with Bedouin-style touches. Try the lamb casserole if you are in the mood for some local home cooking.

Accommodations

As a tourist destination, Petra's adjacent village of Wadi Musa offers a variety of accommodations from lower-end to luxury, but the large majority of the approximately three dozen hotels in the area cost under US$100.

UNDER US$100

Surprisingly upscale and modern for the price, the **Petra Moon Hotel** (Petra Visitor Center St., tel. 03/215-6220, www.petramoonhotel.com, US$85 d) is a mere 100 yards from Petra. The rooms are spacious and have pretty, modern, art deco touches, such as purple walls next to black and white furnishings, and private balconies. The rooms have satellite TV, a DVD player, telephone, bathrobes and a bathtub, extra-long beds, a CD player, minibar, and tea service. The five-storey hotel also has a roof garden with an outdoor pool, buffet breakfast in the restaurant, and a small grocery store. You can set up a horseback ride through the concierge desk when you tire of hiking through Petra.

Centrally and conveniently located, **Amra Palace Hotel** (just up from the Shaheed roundabout next to Cleopatra Hotel, tel. 03/215-7070, www.amrapalace.com, US$57 d) is also in walking distance to Petra and has a warm, modern exterior and interior with huge beds and a small sitting area in the rooms. The hotel's high points include an indoor pool, a spa, flat-screen satellite TVs, wake-up service, and a terrace for drinks that overlooks the garden. The restaurant offerings in the hotel differ a bit by the season, but in the summer they include an outdoor Bedouin restaurant serving traditional barbecued meat.

The smaller 76-room **La Maison Hotel** (off Tourist St. behind Moevenpick Hotel, tel. 03/215-6401, www.lamaisonhotel.com.jo, US$30 d) has renovated rooms with mountain views, free wireless Internet, satellite TV, and minibars. The furnishings are spare and include only the basics with white tile flooring,

giving the general environment a slightly sterile feeling. But the recent renovation means everything that you do have in the rooms is top-notch and in very new condition including a minibar, air-conditioning, and safe deposit box. There is also a lobby lounge bar that serves food. It is just a five-minute walk to Petra.

Known for its superfriendly staff, the **Al Rashid Hotel** (Main St. at the Shaheed roundabout, tel. 03/215-6800, rashid@joinnet.com.jo, US$50 d) is right near Wadi Musa's main offerings for shopping. The recently renovated rooms have free wireless Internet and are decorated very simply, but all include a private bathroom. The very small 28-room hotel serves lunch and dinner in its restaurant. It is about half a mile from Petra.

For a completely different experience than what you could find in a hotel, ★ **The Rock Camp** (Beidha Little Petra, about 9 miles north of Petra, tel. 06/567-9050, www.therockpetra.com, US$76 d) offers luxury Bedouin tent accommodations in the desert. While you're at the Rock Camp, you can try out henna tattoos or play dress up in Bedouin clothing. Meals are served in a large common tent and around a campfire. All of the tents are set up with beds and traditional fittings for bedding and flooring, and there are common bathrooms. The staff (available 24 hours) will also help you arrange outings in the area if you're interested.

A 10-minute walk to Wadi Musa's center, the ★ **Rocky Mountain Hotel** (Main St., tel. 03/215-7393 or 03/215-5100, rockymountainhotel@yahoo.com, US$43 d) has some of the most fantastic views in town from its Bedouin tapestry-decorated dining room and is one of the more attractive budget hotels in town.

The small hotel is popular for its rooftop terrace where you can dine on request, private bathrooms, free wireless Internet (as well as a lobby computer), and shuttle service to Petra. During the day, you can buy a lunch box or light snack and drink. The rooms are decorated with nice, comfy touches like fluffy, bright throw rugs and extrathick blankets for the cold desert nights.

US$100-150

The **Marriott Petra** (Taybeh Rd., outside of Wadi Musa, tel. 03/215-6407, www.marriott. com/hotels, $US 120 d) is one of the few high-end luxury accommodations in the area just a 10-minute drive from Wadi Musa. Most of the hotel's rooms have views of Petra or Petra Valley. When you're not hiking in the hot and dust, you can stay in the hotel and luxuriate in the outdoor pool, sauna, or Turkish bath, or eat in the hotel restaurant. There's no need to hire a taxi to drive you to Petra: The hotel has free shuttles to take you. The rooms are nice and spacious; they include huge windows for the panoramic views and comfortable touches like couches.

The **Moevenpick Resort Petra** (Tourism St., next to the Visitors Center, tel. 03/215-7111, www.moevenpick-hotels.com, US$130 d) is five-star, large resort hotel (and part of a regional luxury chain) with 183 rooms that features a ton of outdoor access without leaving the hotel grounds. About as close as you can get to the entrance of Petra, the hotel features balconies for every room, a rooftop terrace, and two restaurants. The rooms themselves are pure luxury. Recently renovated, they all come with satellite TV, free wireless Internet, a desk, and every amenity you could need. The hotel also has a tea room, a plush lobby bar, and a fitness center. The beautiful stone lobby has a massive arched colonnaded courtyard for sitting and relaxing with a tea or coffee.

US$150-200

Featuring the unique touch of 19th-century-style furniture and housed in a stone building that evokes a bygone era, the ★ **Beit Zaman Hotel and Resort** (Al Nawafleh St., tel. 03/215-7401, www.beit-zaman.com, US$190 d) is a medium-size hotel with both an indoor and outdoor pool.

The rooms succeed at combining local flavor with world-class luxury, including locally crafted tapestries on the walls and beds, some rooms with Arab-style architecture and arched doorways, minibar, safe, and private bathroom. The hotel's restaurant serves Arabic food, and you can arrange for outdoor excursions with the hotel staff. A small downside is that the hotel charges for their shuttle to Petra, which is two miles away.

Information and Services

ONLINE RESOURCES AND TOURISM BOARDS

There are several very useful websites if you plan on doing any research about Petra and the surrounding area prior to or during your trip here.

For local information, try the **Petra Development and Tourism Regional Authority** website (28 Wadi Musa, tel. 03/215-7093, www.visitpetra.jo), which has good general information about a wide range of things from currency rates to background information.

The website for the village of **Wadi Rum** (www.wadirum.jo) is also a good source for information about locals in the area and has a listing of tourism-related services.

For national information, the **Jordan Ministry of Tourism and Antiquities** (tel. 06/460-3360, www.tourism.jo) has tourism videos and statistics.

The official site of the **Jordan Tourism Board** (tel. 06/567-8294, www.visitjordan. com) is robust and has great photos and essential information.

Finally, the **Royal Society for the**

Conservation of Nature (www.rscn.org.jo) provides information about nature conservation and research, ecotourism, community projects, and handicrafts throughout Jordan.

For general background, **Nabatea.net** (nabataea.net) isn't the most modern website, but it has quite a few external links and more information about the Nabataeans than you will need.

PRIVATE TOUR COMPANIES

There are quite a few tour companies that operate in Petra. If you are coming from Israel and pay a company there for services, don't be surprised if you are passed off to a gauntlet of different companies and guides before you actually reach your destination.

To make arrangements directly with a company that works in Jordan, there are several good options. One of the most popular and experienced at working with English speakers is **Petra Moon Tours** (based in Wadi Musa, tel. 03/215-6665 or 079/617-0666, www.petramoon.com). They offer a very wide variety of tours, including archaeological, experiential, participatory, and alternative. They also host an annual two-week writing workshop in Petra in June.

Run by two Bedouin guides who are lifelong residents of Wadi Rum, **Bedouin Lifestyle** (tel. 077/913-1803, www.bedouinlifestyle.

com) specializes in tours that expose visitors to Bedouin customs and traditions, including hiking, camel rides, camping under the stars, and jeep rides through the desert.

Run by a Jordanian family and in operation since 1994, **Jordan Travel** (tel. 03/215-4666, www.jordantours-travel.com) provides customized, private tours of sites all throughout Jordan.

The U.S.-based **Insider's Petra** (toll-free U.S. tel. 855/928-2538, www.insiderspetra.com) is an alternative for making tour arrangements in advance without the guesswork of dealing with someone in another country. The company can arrange individual and group travel experiences, and the founder and president is an American based in the United States.

VISITORS CENTER

The Petra **Visitors Center** (outside of Petra Main Gate, tel. 03/215-6029, 6:30am-5pm Sat.-Thurs.) provides a variety of information about the site. Ask before entering if the price of a horse ride through the *siq* is still included in the admission fee (it was at time of publication).

Through the visitors center, you can also arrange to hire a **Bedouin guide** (about JD50) for the entire day or for a half day. A **Jordanian guide** (JD9-57) can also be arranged.

Transportation

Getting to Petra is relatively simple, but getting around is a bit harder. No vehicles are allowed inside the actual archaeological site, and the village of Wadi Musa is a bit isolated.

ENTERING AND EXITING JORDAN

Transportation options to and from Wadi Musa are limited, as many people arrive and leave with large tour buses. The unofficial

public transportation stop is the Shaheed roundabout; just ask anybody and they will be able to point you in the right direction.

Air

Jordan has more than one airport, but the most common entry point is the Amman Airport, officially known as the **Queen Alia International Airport** (airport-authority.com/AMM). There are flights between Amman and Tel Aviv on a regular basis.

Car

Aqaba is about a 10-minute drive from the Eilat border crossing and Wadi Musa is about two hours from Aqaba. If you are driving from Amman, it is about 3.5 hours.

After you cross into Aqaba, if you are driving yourself to Petra, you can visit one of the two **Hertz** locations (Alnahda St. and Aqaba Airport, tel. 03/201-6206, www.hertz.com, 8am-1pm and 4pm-9pm daily, Aqaba airport closes at 7pm, US$88 d).

Bus

If you are interested in getting to Amman, you can take the **JETT** bus (www.jett.com.jo), which is a big white vehicle that looks just like a tourist bus (rather than a public bus). The bus leaves from Wadi Musa once a day at 5pm and costs JD11. There are several stops in Aqaba where buses depart about half a dozen times a day (8am-6:30pm).

Border Control

Don't be surprised by the incredibly complex, circuitous route that you will need to take through border control when you are coming from Eilat and crossing into Aqaba. You will have your passport checked and stamped several times. Just follow the general flow of traffic or ask any one of the guards standing about if you are unsure about which window to stop at next.

The border opens at 8am, and it is best to be there before it opens to bypass the lines of people as much as possible.

GETTING AROUND

Once you are in Wadi Musa, if you need to drive anywhere it is easy and relatively cheap to take a taxi. If you do have a car, you won't be at much risk of getting lost. It is a fairly desolate area, and Petra and Wadi Musa are the only attractions for miles around.

Background

The Landscape

You will often hear Israelis say that theirs is a small country, and it's true. The total area of the State of Israel is 8,630 miles, comprised mostly of landmass. At its widest it is 85 miles across and from the northernmost point to the southernmost point it is 290 miles.

GEOGRAPHY

Israel's western coast runs along the Mediterranean Sea, and elsewhere Israel is bordered by several other countries, not all of which can be characterized as friendly. In the north, its neighbors are Lebanon and Syria; on the east is the Hashemite Kingdom of Jordan; and Egypt is in the south.

The West Bank, a landmass of about 2,270 square miles, sits between Israel and Jordan; some refer to it as Judea and Samaria and others as the Palestinian Territories. To characterize the West Bank as part of Israel is a grave misnomer. The West Bank's three distinct divisions fall under the categories of A, B, and C: Palestinian Authority-controlled, joint Palestinian Authority and Israeli-controlled, and Israeli-controlled, respectively. About 60 percent of the West Bank is Area B or C, and there are 400,000 Israelis living there, including those who are residents of East Jerusalem.

The number of Arab residents of the West Bank is a matter of huge debate, but is usually cited as somewhere between 2.6 million and 2.7 million. Part of the dispute over accurate census numbers is due to inclusion of populations from East Jerusalem and Gaza. The majority (over 60 percent) of the country's 8.46 million people live in either the metropolitan Tel Aviv area or Jerusalem.

As for the West Bank's landscape, a major feature in the summer and autumn months is the silvery-green olive trees. The terraced hillsides and fertile valleys have been farmed for generations. The gorgeous landscape of the West Bank is filled with rocky, rolling hills.

Distances in Israel are strikingly small, but the changes in weather and landscape can be drastic. In one hour, you can go from the cool, breezy mountains of Jerusalem to the flat, humid seaside town of Tel Aviv. The coastal plain of the north and its bordering rich farmland, with chalk and sandstone cliffs, is home to deepwater ports.

A number of mountain ranges run from north to south through the landscape. In the perpetually green north, the volcanic eruption-created basalt Golan Heights tower over the Hula Valley. In the Galilee, where some elevations go as high as 4,000 feet above sea level, the hills are mostly dolomite and soft limestone.

Between Israel and the West Bank in the north is the Jezreel Valley, another fertile valley that is heavily cultivated.

Along the eastern side of Israel, part of the Syrian-African Rift that split the crust of the earth millions of years ago, are the Jordan Valley and the Arava. The land ranges from semiarid in the south to fertile in the north.

The south of Israel is home to the Negev Desert, and although it accounts for about half of the country's landmass, it is the least inhabited. The extremely arid south is made up of low sandstone hills and plains with a huge number of canyons amid the sandstone landscape that are prone to flash flooding in the winter. Campaigns to make the desert green with tree plantings have gained in popularity and practice, but the region is still largely desert.

A bit farther south, the Negev is characterized by barren stone peaks and plateaus littered with rocks. Here you will find three

---

erosive craters that are so huge that they are tourist attractions. The largest, Ramon Crater, is about 5 miles across at its widest, about 24 miles long, and about 1,600 feet deep.

At the very south of Israel is Eilat and the Red Sea, where gray and red granite and sandstone form the base of the landscape.

SEAS AND RIVERS

One of the most significant bodies of water in the region is the Sea of Galilee. At 695 feet below sea level and between the hills of the Galilee and the Golan Heights, it is the most important source of water in Israel and home to several significant historic and religious sites.

The Sea of Galilee feeds the Jordan River and has a circumference of only about 30 miles. On the southern shore in the town of Tiberias, an electronic meter displays the Sea's water level, a number of national interest. In early 2013, following weeks of heavy rain, the sea level was higher than it had been in several years and ended a seven-year drought. In 2016, the sea suffered one of its worst years on record, though, prompting the announcement of another drought.

Coming from the southern mouth of the Sea of Galilee, the Jordan River runs for about 186 miles, descending 2,300 feet from north to south through the Syrian-African Rift that split the crust of the earth millions of years ago. The river is fed by tributaries from Mount Hermon and empties into the Dead Sea, the lowest point on Earth. The Jordan Valley ranges from fertile in the north to semiarid in the south.

The Dead Sea sits at 1,300 feet below sea level on the southern end of the Jordan Valley. Its waters have the highest level of salinity and density of any body of water in the world, and are famed for their rich mineral deposits (and mud), which include table and industrial salt, bromine, magnesium, and potash.

Since 1960, the water level of the Dead Sea has dropped by more than 35 feet, partially caused by massive water diversion projects conducted by Israel and Jordan. The water diversion projects have reduced the amount of incoming water to the Dead Sea by 75 percent. In 2015, so many sinkholes had appeared in the land and sea from the lack of water that some public beaches and at least one hotel were closed for safety. Sinkholes continue to be a danger in the area.

South of the Dead Sea, which has separated into an upper section and a lower section over time, is the Arava, also part of the Syrian-African Rift and Israel's savanna region. The

the Sea of Galilee

Arava continues to Israel's Red Sea outlet: the Gulf of Eilat, a subtropical region and home to some of the most remarkable coral reefs and unusual marinelife in the world.

CLIMATE

The climate in Israel and the West Bank vary widely from temperate to tropical to alpine. There are two distinct seasons, though two additional very brief transitions are often evident in between those.

Between November to May is the rainy season, or winter. Though it does not rain constantly, rainfall and lower temperatures (about 31°F at the lowest in some areas) do predominate.

From June through October, there is little to no rainfall, and the temperature rises steadily to a daily low of 66°F in some areas before starting its decline in late September. The average high throughout the country during the dry season ranges 84-104°F. The months of July and August are the most brutally punishing in terms of heat.

The variance in climate is marked by mild coastal winters, cooler summers in elevated regions (such as Jerusalem), and almost year-round semidesert conditions in the Negev.

ENVIRONMENTAL ISSUES
Drought and Flash Floods

One of the major environmental issues in the region is drought. The mean annual rainfall is a mere 8 inches in the south and about 28 inches in the north.

In the winter months, the rainfall that does come can sometimes cause flash floods, particularly in the south with its canyons of bone-dry rock. On occasion, a person or an animal will get swept away by one of these flash floods that seem to come out of nowhere, though that is rare.

Heat Waves

The punishing heat of the summer months (particularly during July and August) becomes more pronounced during a prolonged heat wave when the temperature can reach 95-105°F and higher, even in typically temperate Jerusalem. The greatest risk during heat waves to humans is suffering from dehydration or heatstroke, of which some of the symptoms are dizziness, nausea, confusion, blurred vision, and vomiting. Left untreated, dehydration and heatstroke can lead to complications that can cause death. It is imperative to drink plenty of water while in the region and to protect yourself from the sun, even when there is no heat wave.

Sandstorms

On rare occasion the air in Tel Aviv and elsewhere will be filled with a very fine, yellow dust, typically at the end of a heat wave. It is not exactly a sandstorm, but it turns the air yellow and leaves a layer of dust on everything, including your skin. Sand in the air at the end of a heat wave typically indicates that the heat wave is about to break and is usually followed by a brief rainfall that turns things a bit muddy.

History

The histories of the regions of Israel, the West Bank, and Petra are long, winding, complex, and interconnected. In modern times, differing claims and versions of historical events are very much part of conversations and actions taken related to the land and political stances on important issues. In other words, the history of this region is very much alive and well and plays an active role in dictating the future.

ANCIENT CIVILIZATION

Canaan is the area generally defined as Palestine in historical and biblical literature, sculpture of young King David at the Tower of David Museum citadel in Jerusalem

and the most significant literary texts on regional history are the Old Testament, the Ras Shamra texts, and the Amarna Letters, dispatches from the 14th century BC from Palestinian and Syrian governors to their Egyptian rulers.

The history and culture of the region has been influenced by a number of cultures, including Egyptian, Mycenaean, Cretan, Hurrian, Byzantine, Mesopotamian, Greek, Roman, and British. It is believed that the Canaanites were the first people to have used an alphabet, based on an archaeological discovery of a language that is widely recognized as a parent language to the Greek and Latin alphabets.

Around the time of the Early Iron Age, approximately 1250 BC, the Israelites came into Canaan after their exodus from Egypt and 40 years of wandering in the desert. In the next century, the Philistines invaded and established a strong hold over the region through a series of city-states, but it was broken under King David's leadership. King David also managed to capture Jerusalem from the Canaanites. The 10th century marked the beginning of the land being known as Israel.

Around the time of King David (about 1000-960 BC), the various tribes of Israel were consolidated into a united kingdom. King David made the Canaanite city of Jerusalem his capital and according to tradition, moved the Ark of the Covenant there, which was believed to contain the living presence of God. Around the time of 960-920 BC, David's son, Solomon, carried out the wish of his deceased father to build a great temple to house the Ark. The period of Solomon's rule is associated with the peak of Israelite grandeur; King Solomon oversaw the building of the First Temple, which was later destroyed. He also managed to forge treaties with neighboring kingdoms, including Egypt and Sheba, and create other important building projects in addition to the Temple.

The Kingdom of Israel was guided by strong, spiritual, monotheistic beliefs in one all-powerful God (Yahweh), the Lord Creator of the

and is known today as Israel and the West Bank (also called Judea and Samaria or Palestine). The names of Canaan and Canaanites for its inhabitants appear in Egyptian and Phoenician writings from approximately the 15th century BC and in the Old Testament of the Bible. The earliest human inhabitants of coastal Canaan go back to Paleolithic and Mesolithic times. Evidence of human settlements has been found in Jericho dating back to 8000 BC.

Israelites conquered Palestine around the late 2nd century BC or earlier, but there were others before them. The Egyptians, the Hyksos, and the Hurrians also invaded. During the Late Bronze Age, about 1550-1200 BC, the Egyptians were the main dominating power in the region, despite challenges from the Hittites and the Hapiru, who some believe were the original Hebrews.

Most archaeological excavations of the area have been conducted since the 20th century,

Universe. That belief was often used by rulers to help unify the kingdom and its people.

Around 920 BC, Solomon died, and the kingdom splintered into north and south halves. Israel was in the north with its capital Samaria, and the Kingdom of Judah was in the south with its capital Jerusalem. A period of frequent instability and lack of unity between the north and south followed, and by 721 BC, the Neo-Assyrian Empire became the new ruling force, expelling people to make room for its own settlements. In 587 BC, Jerusalem was sacked by the Babylonian king Nebuchadnezzar II. The Temple was destroyed, and the ruling class and skilled craftsmen were deported to Babylon.

The deportation by the Neo-Assyrians and Babylonians of the people of the Kingdom of Israel was the end of the existence of the nation of Israel until the modern state's creation in 1948. It also marked the beginning of the Jewish Diaspora and the start of the development of a religious framework in Judaism outside of the land of Israel. Connections between the ancient state and the modern state, including the name, remain an oft-debated and emotionally charged issue.

EARLY HISTORY

After the destruction of the First Temple, between 538-142 BC, there were several waves of tens of thousands of Jews who were allowed to return to Israel. They had varying degrees of self-rule over a period of about four centuries under Persian and Hellenistic authority.

Construction of a Second Temple on the site of the first one began in 521 BC and was finished in 516, during a period when Jerusalem's city walls were refortified.

Around 37 BC, Herod the Great was appointed king of Judea by the Romans and he launched a massive construction campaign, the evidence of which can be seen today in Caesarea, Masada, Jerusalem, and Herodium. Herod remodeled and renewed the Temple to a state of grandeur, but his efforts to appease the subjects to his rule failed to win their loyalty.

After a relatively brief period rule by the Hasmonean dynasty of Seleucids, the Romans came into power around 40 BC, and Israel became a Roman province. It was not long after this that Jesus appeared in Jerusalem and other areas in what is now Israel and the West Bank. According to tradition, he performed many miracles in Jerusalem, spread his teachings, and while standing atop the Mount of Olives, wept over the coming destruction of the holy city. Jerusalem is also where Jesus was crucified, buried, and said to have risen from the dead.

By AD 66, ongoing violence and anger against Roman rule and oppression had erupted into full-scale revolt. By AD 70, Jerusalem, including the Second Temple, had been razed to the ground by the Romans. The account by the well-known contemporary historian Josephus Flavius tells that hundreds of thousands of Jews died in the siege on Jerusalem and throughout Israel, including in the siege on the last stand of Jewish revolutionaries at Masada. Thousands more were sold into slavery.

Several hundred years later after generations of Roman rule and the declaration of Christianity as the official religion of the Roman kingdom around AD 325, Helena, mother of Constantine the Great, came to the Holy Land to begin construction of some of the world's first churches.

Under Helena's supervision, construction commenced on the Church of the Nativity (where Jesus is said to have been born), the Chapel of the Apostles on the Mount of Olives (where Jesus is said to have ascended to heaven), the Church of the Holy Sepulchre (where Jesus is said to have been crucified, buried, and resurrected), and another structure near Hebron.

During the 7th century, Jerusalem was the object of military conquest multiple times. It was sacked and claimed first by the Persians, then taken back by the Byzantines, and finally by the Islamic Empire. Around 690, under the rule of the Islamic Empire, the Dome of the Rock was built on the Temple Mount at the site of the First and Second Temples. According to Islamic

ancient Roman ruins at Caesarea

tradition, the site is where Prophet Muhammad ascended to heaven. The region would remain under Islamic rule until about 1099.

Between the 8th and 9th centuries, the seventh of a series of historically massive and powerful earthquakes struck the region, destroying Tiberias, Beit She'an, Hippos, and Pella.

Between 1099 and 1291, the Crusaders and their multiple campaigns to reclaim the Holy Land dominated the region, until the ancient city of Akko fell to the Egyptians and the Crusader kingdom of Jerusalem was ended. The land was under Mamluk rule until 1516 when the Ottomans took over and ruled until 1917.

MODERN HISTORY

Near the end of the 400 years of Ottoman rule, in 1860 the first neighborhood was built outside the Old City walls of Jerusalem, and the First Aliya, a large-scale immigration of Jews, came to Israel. The Second Aliya came between 1904 and 1914. Both groups were mainly from Russia and Poland. By 1909, the first modern, all-Jewish city of Tel Aviv had been founded, and by 1917, British conquest had seized power from the Ottomans with the promise of a "Jewish national home in Palestine" by Foreign Minister Balfour.

The years between 1918 and 1948 were marked by British rule, and more groups

of Aliya from Europe. In 1922, the British granted the Mandate for Palestine, with 75 percent of the area going to Transjordan (modern-day Jordan) and 25 percent designated for Jews. In this period, major universities were established in Haifa (Technion) and Jerusalem (Hebrew University).

During the British Mandate prior to World War II, there were several instances of significant violence and fighting between Arabs, who had been living in the region for centuries, and Jews. By 1947, the United Nations proposed the establishment of both Arab and Jewish states in the land of Israel.

MODERN WARS

Achieving the seemingly elusive peace between Arabs and Jews in the region has been an incredibly long and drawn-out process that started before Israel was ever officially a state. In May 1948, the British Mandate ended and the State of Israel was established.

The day after the state was formally declared, five Arab countries invaded Israel, marking the beginning of the War of Independence which lasted until 1949, when armistice agreements were signed with Egypt, Jordan, Syria, and Lebanon. Jerusalem was divided into east and west with East Jerusalem under Jordanian rule and West Jerusalem under Israeli rule. In 1948-1952, there were massive waves of immigration from European and Arab countries.

In 1967, the Six-Day War reunited Jerusalem's east and west sides of the city, though the east side is now technically part of the West Bank. The Six-Day War was followed by the Egyptian War of Attrition (1968-1970) and the Yom Kippur War (1973). Following the Camp David Accords, the Israel-Egypt Peace Treaty was signed, normalizing relations between the two countries.

After peace with Egypt and Jordan, internal domestic violence erupted in 1987 in Israel-administered areas with the First Intifada, followed by the Gulf War (1991). On the verge of a domestic peace agreement in 1995, then Prime Minister Yitzhak Rabin was assassinated in Tel Aviv. By 2000, the Second Intifada erupted, followed by years of violent internal regional instability.

In 2005, the highly controversial Gaza Disengagement Plan was carried out under the leadership of Prime Minister Ariel Sharon (who had a stroke and went into a coma almost immediately afterward), whereby Israel unilaterally withdrew all Jewish settlements in Gaza. Subsequently falling under the rule of the terrorist organization Hamas, Gaza has become a hotbed of violence and the center of destruction when fighting breaks out between Hamas and Israel.

Government and Economy

GOVERNMENT

There are two governments in the region, one for Israel and one for the West Bank: the government of the State of Israel and the Palestinian Authority. If and when there is an agreement made about a two-state solution for the region, it will be made between these two bodies. However, the major power in the region, politically, economically, legally, and militarily, is Israel.

Symbolism

The flag of the State of Israel is designed based on the Jewish prayer shawl with the blue star of David in the center. Israel's official emblem is a menorah flanked by olive branches that represent Israel's desire for peace. The national anthem, *Hatikvah*, was penned by Jewish poet Naphtali Herz Imber in 1878, and the words express the hope of the Jewish people to live as a free and sovereign people in the land of Israel.

The flag used to represent the State of Palestine is a tricolor flag with three equal horizontal stripes of black, white, and green, with a sideways triangle of red on the left. It is based on a variety of different flags, including the one used during the 1916 Arab revolt.

Israeli Government Organization

The Israeli government is a parliamentary democracy, with free elections, a prime minister, and a president. The system is based on the concept of a division of powers between the legislative, executive, and judicial branches.

POLITICAL PARTIES AND ELECTIONS

Israel's unicameral parliament is called the Knesset, and functions in plenary sessions through 15 standing committees and 120 members. The Knesset generally runs for terms of four years, and its makeup is determined after general elections. Both Hebrew and Arabic are officially recognized languages of the Knesset, though debates on issues are conducted in Hebrew with simultaneous translation if a member wishes to speak Arabic.

The party with the most power in the Knesset following the 2015 elections is Likud, the party of Prime Minister Benjamin "Bibi" Netanyahu.

Israeli citizens are eligible to vote from age 18, and they vote for a political party to represent them in the Knesset, not for individuals. There are a wide range of political parties that run for seats in the Knesset representing a broad range of beliefs and positions on the issues.

Election Day in Israel is a national holiday, and if a voter is outside of their polling district, free transportation is provided to them. Polling stations are provided for military personnel, prisoners, hospital patients, merchant sailors, and Israelis on official work abroad.

ALLIANCES AND ENEMIES

Israel's political situation is characterized largely by a range of staunch advocates and lukewarm alliances. Immediately in Israel's neighborhood, Egypt and Jordan are border countries that have generally good relations with Israel. Relations with Turkey blow hot and cold, and Israel is not on good terms with Syria, Lebanon, or Iran.

The positions of western countries vary, but the United States is Israel's single greatest ally in the world. Other countries like Australia and Canada are basically supportive, but there is a great deal of political activism over the plight of Palestinians that originates in the west. The United Kingdom is on good terms with Israel, but its public discourse regularly challenges Israel's settlement policies in the West Bank and its human rights record vis-à-vis Arab residents of the West Bank and Israel.

JUDICIAL AND PENAL SYSTEMS

Israel's judiciary system is independent. Judges are appointed by the president after being recommended by a committee of Supreme Court judges, public figures, and members of the bar. Judicial appointments are permanent until mandatory retirement at age 70.

There are several types of courts, including special courts (such as traffic, labor, juvenile), religious courts, magistrates' court, district court, and the Supreme Court.

ISRAELI MILITARY

The Israeli Defense Force (IDF) has been tested in battle through several generations since the establishment of the State of Israel in 1948, and has fought in six major wars and numerous smaller ones. The highest-level public officials and politicians were often individuals who distinguished themselves during military service and in war.

Service in the IDF is compulsory for all eligible men and women at the age of 18. The male term of service is three years, while women serve for two years, and deferments can be made for students or new immigrants. Reserve duty obligations continue for men until age 51, and every soldier serves in a reserve unit that they are called to work for at least once a year. Ultraorthodox members of society are exempt from military service.

Palestinian Authority Government Organization

The Palestinian National Authority, also called the Palestinian Authority (PA), was established as an interim self-governing authority following the Oslo accords in 2003. The PA governs parts of the West Bank. It used to also govern Gaza, which is now under the control of Hamas.

The PA embodies many of the characteristics of a state, including a legislative and executive body, and a semi-independent judiciary.

Leadership includes a president, cabinet, and a prime minister.

PALESTINIAN AUTHORITY MILITARY

The Palestinian Authority military patrols certain areas of the West Bank, including some parts of Bethlehem, Hebron, Ramallah, and some checkpoints. They are largely a peacekeeping force.

ECONOMY

The Israeli economy was started virtually from scratch almost 70 years ago (officially) and has weathered crises and deprivation of various kinds. The modern free-market economy is bolstered by R&D, high-tech industries, nanotechnology, solar energy, irrigation innovation, agriculture, and a thriving start-up scene admired internationally.

Exports and Imports

In the past 30 years, significant free trade agreements have been made with the United States, the European Union, and a number of countries in Latin America. Israel's export of goods and services is about $80 billion annually.

Israel has struggled to balance its hefty trade deficit, which has been the price for its rapid economic growth. The somewhat limited domestic market and small economy mean that Israel must rely on expansion of exports, particularly industrial exports.

Most imports, about 85 percent, are production inputs and fuel, largely from Europe, followed by the Americas, then Asia, and other countries. Most exports of goods go to the United States, Europe, and Asia. Excluding the export of diamonds, Israel's exports to the United States exceed its imports, but its overall imports exceed its exports.

Almost two-thirds of Israel's annual trade deficits have been covered through unilateral transfers, including foreign pensions, money brought in by immigrants, and hefty donations from overseas Jewish fundraising organizations that have gone straight into the coffers of health, education, and social service organizations and institutions. Grants from generous foreign governments, particularly the United States, have also bolstered the economy.

Agriculture

Scarce natural resources, particularly water and arable land, define Israel's production system in its agricultural sector. Aggressive innovation and ongoing cooperation between researchers, farmers, and agricultural industries drive the growth in agricultural production. The development and application of new methods across the board have fostered a sophisticated modern agricultural industry in a country where more than half of the land is desert.

The dogged innovation of the Israeli agricultural industry and its close cooperation with the R&D world have fostered a marketable international agribusiness export sector with agro-technology solutions. Particularly valuable to the outside and developing world have been innovations in regard to water.

The wide variety of creative solutions developed in response to extremely limited water resources include desalinization plants and drip agriculture.

Most of the country's food and flowers are produced domestically and supplemented by imports that mainly include grain, oilseeds, meat, coffee, cocoa, and sugar. Israel exports heavily to Europe during the winter, sending fruits, vegetables, and flowers.

Industry

Israel has overcome the small size of its country and its lack of raw materials and natural resources by focusing on its highly qualified workforce, R&D centers, and scientific institutes. The country's modern industry is centered around the manufacturing of products with added value. Today, over a quarter of the industrial workforce works in high-tech manufacturing.

Much of Israel's modern manufacturing base was developed straight out of 19th-century workshops that produced farming implements and processed agricultural products. When entrepreneurs and engineers with years of experience immigrated to Israel in the 1930s, they were followed by an increased demand for industrial products during World War II.

Most of the industrial output from Israel centered around traditional products like food processing, furniture, chemicals, plastics, and other items, until the 1970s. This output was followed by a period marked by arms embargoes, which forced industrialization to focus on developing and manufacturing arms for self-defense. Massive investment in the arms industry and aviation gave life to new technologies that would later be the foundation of Israel's high-tech industries. These include medical devices, telecommunications, computer software and hardware, and more.

Two waves of human resources in the 1980s and 1990s bolstered the fledgling high-tech industries: first, the return of Israelis who had been working in Silicon Valley to open development centers for multinationals including Intel, Microsoft, and IBM; second, the huge wave of technicians, scientists, medical workers, and engineers who fled the former Soviet Union in the 1990s after its fall.

Another ace in the hole in Israel's industrial sector is the diamond industry. The country's reputation as a high-quality source for diamond manufacturing and trading has made it a leader in the industry. Tel Aviv's famed diamond district is just one of the ways that the country showcases its cutting-edge technologies, competitive prices, and high yield of polished diamonds from the rough. The Israel Diamond Exchange is the largest diamond trading floor in the world, and diamond exports are in the neighborhood of about $10 billion a year. Most imports are sent to the United States, Hong Kong, Belgium, and Switzerland.

Entrepreneurship and Invention

Israel has earned a reputation for being a hotbed of entrepreneurship, innovation, and invention, bolstered in part by the publication of a book called *Start-up Nation: The Story of Israel's Economic Miracle*, which details the numerous ways in which the country has repeatedly innovated and invented its way into the 21st century.

The premise of the book is based on the fact that despite being a young country with a population of just over 8.4 million and surrounded by enemies, Israel is home to more start-up companies than Japan, China, India, Korea, Canada and the United Kingdom combined.

Distribution of Wealth

In 2011, massive, long-term public protests over Israel's distribution of wealth broke out throughout the country, centered mostly in Tel Aviv. The protests evolved into weeks-long encampments, mostly of young people, who demanded a more equitable distribution of economic wealth and a more equitable distribution of economic burden in their society.

Between 2005 and 2007, Israel had a millionaire boom, producing more millionaires per capita than any country in the world. The current estimated net worth of Israel's 500 richest people is in the neighborhood of US$140 billion (the country's GDP is about US$306 billion).

One of the most serious issues in the debate about the distribution of wealth stems from the perceived affordability of housing among the middle and lower class. The purchase of second homes in Tel Aviv and Jerusalem by wealthy foreigners is seen as having a major impact on housing prices. In the past eight years, housing prices in some neighborhoods in Israel have risen by 25 percent. Settlements and apartment prices in the West Bank, on the other hand, remain extremely affordable.

Tourism

Israel's most frequently visited cities, Jerusalem and Tel Aviv, continue to work hard to become international tourist destinations. With the gradual stabilizing of the internal security of Israel has come a stabilized tourism base. Since 2010, the average number of visitors to the country has been about three million people per year. Most visitors come from Europe, and about a quarter are from the United States. Since 2015, the numbers of tourists to some cities has dropped by as much as 40 percent, in large part due to spates of violence and conflict.

An average of about 30 percent of people visit Israel on a pilgrimage, while others

a group of visitors in Jerusalem

come for leisure, to visit family, or on business. The vast majority of all tourists (about 80 percent), no matter why they are visiting the country, include Jerusalem as a destination. About 65 percent include Tel Aviv as a destination, about 45 percent go to the Dead Sea, and about 20 percent go to Tiberias and the Sea of Galilee.

People and Culture

DEMOGRAPHY

When the State of Israel was established, the country's population was about 806,000. Today it is more than 8.4 million. About 75 percent of residents are Jewish, over 20 percent are Arab, and all other groups make up just over 4 percent of the population. Over 70 percent of the total Jewish population was born in Israel; a native-born Jewish Israeli is known as a *sabra*.

Israel has 14 cities with over 100,000 residents; the 6 cities of Jerusalem, Tel Aviv-Yafo, Haifa, Rishon LeTsiyon, Petah Tikva, and Ashdod all have over 200,000 residents.

Israel has had periods of massive, concentrated immigration tied to world events. In 1990 alone, after the fall of the Soviet Union, more than 199,000 immigrants came to Israel, and another 176,000 in 1991. In the past few years, however, there has been an average of 16,500 immigrants to the country per year.

Israel suffers severely on the international stage from problems related to religious and ethnic tensions between the Jewish majority and Arab minority, which impacts its ability to attract a larger number of tourists and immigrants. Though daily life in major cities such as Tel Aviv, Jerusalem, and elsewhere is largely peaceful and various ethnicities and religions peacefully coexist, violence does erupt on a fairly regular basis. With the rule of neighboring Gaza in the hands of Hamas, the greatest domestic threat comes from attacks that originate in Gaza, such as rocket attacks. In recent years, isolated acts of violence carried out by individuals have also been on the rise, particularly beginning in 2015.

The West Bank, with its complex and multilayered governance and distribution of security between the Palestinian Authority and Israel, is also sometimes the source of religious and ethnic tension, protests, and violence.

Jews

As an ethnic group, Jews constitute about 75 percent of the population of Israel. Of those, about 72 percent are Israel-born and about 19 percent are European or American-born. About 9 percent were born in Africa and Asia.

Arabs

The Arab population of Israel stands at about 23 percent and includes those who are Muslim, Christian, and Jewish. Bedouin and Druze peoples fall under the category of the Arab population.

RELIGION

Though Israel is officially a Jewish state, for all intents and purposes residents of Israel enjoy religious freedom to practice whatever faith they choose.

Those who are registered with the government as practicing Judaism comprise about 58 percent of the population, non-Arab Christians are about 2 percent, and those not classified by religion are almost 5 percent. Of Israel's Arab population, 84 percent (about 20 percent of the population) are practicing Muslims, and almost 8 percent are Arab Christians. Another 9 percent are Druze.

Judaism

More than 58 percent of the people of Israel identify themselves as practicing the religion of Judaism, an ancient monotheistic faith with varying degrees of orthodoxy. The degree of orthodoxy of the Diaspora of people who practice Judaism around the world varies. The same is true in Israel, with pockets of people practicing orthodox, ultraorthodox, and reform Judaism, to name a few.

Particularly in Jerusalem but also throughout Israel and the West Bank, religious individuals can be somewhat identified by their dress. The men wear long, black coats and large black hats, and the women dress in long skirts and dresses with their arms and legs covered, and their heads covered with a hat, scarf, or wig.

On the day of worship on Friday, religious services are performed in synagogues. The more religious synagogues separate men and women into different worship areas. The holiest site in the holiest city to Jews is the Western Wall in Jerusalem (also known as the Kotel). It is the last remaining piece of the outer wall of the courtyard of the great temple that was twice built and destroyed on that spot in history.

reading the Torah in Jerusalem

Christianity

The Christian community in Israel, which is about 2 percent of the population, represents a wide variety of different sects from all over the world. There are Greek Orthodox, Russian Orthodox, Catholic, and others. Though they are only a small part of the population overall in the country, the Roman Catholic Church owns a large portion of land in Jerusalem.

Islam

About 20 percent of Israel's population practices the religion of Islam; they are known as Muslims. The Islamic religion, in general, is fairly strict and generally forbids drinking alcohol. Friday is the day of prayer for Muslims, which makes it a difficult day to visit the Old City, as Al Aqsa Mosque (the third holiest site in Islam) becomes very crowded.

Religious services are performed in mosques, which can often be distinguished by the nearby minaret (tower) from which the call to prayer is broadcast five times a day. In terms of dress, Muslim women (especially in more conservative areas like Nablus) dress in a very covered-up manner with headscarves, long sleeves, and covered legs. In some cases women's faces and hands are also covered.

LANGUAGE

Israel has two official languages: Hebrew and Arabic. But English is a compulsory second language taught throughout much of the secondary level education system, so the majority of Hebrew speakers and many Arabic speakers also speak and understand English at least at a conversational level.

Almost all signs, menus, transportation tables, and tourist information are written in English.

THE ARTS

The arts in Israel are a well-developed and robust part of society. In addition to the many skills and traditions that generations of immigrants have brought with them from their original countries, the indigenous arts, crafts, and culture play a significant role.

ornate mosque gate in Jerusalem

Literature

Israel's literary culture is dominated by Hebrew-speaking authors, but in recent years the Arabic-speaking community has also made significant breakthroughs and contributions.

An ongoing issue in Israel's literary community is the slow death that independent booksellers are suffering due to the existence of a couple of major national chains. These chains are often accused of selling books at much less than their value, angering both authors and independent booksellers, who cannot compete with the prices. In recent years, many independent booksellers have been forced into closing.

Despite the challenges to independent sellers, you can still find a variety of different types of bookstores in major cities that sell material in various languages including Hebrew, Arabic, French, and English. Major periodicals in English, Arabic, French, and sometimes Russian are also sold at national chain stores and smaller shops.

Jerusalem hosts a renowned international literature conference every year, but it is sometimes overshadowed by authors who choose to publicly boycott attending on the grounds of concerns over Israel's presence in the West Bank and its position on issues related to the Arab population. The largest Arab city of Ramallah also hosts an annual Literary Festival.

Visual Arts

The thriving visual arts scene in Israel is supported by the large number of museums, from the Israel Museum in Jerusalem to the Tel Aviv Museum of Art, to scores of venues of all sizes. Modern visual art in Israel shows international influences and the meeting of East and West, and reflects the influences of the land, traditions, and cultures.

Visual artists in Israel are engaged in a wide range of disciplines, including painting, photography, and sculpture. Part of what makes Israeli visual art unique is its emphasis and reflections on the local landscape, domestic social issues, and politics.

Music and Dance

The thriving dance scene in Israel has developed mainly in the Jewish folk dance genre and artistic dance centered around stage productions. The major influence of European dance began in the 1920s, and has developed to a highly professional level through a number of companies and ensembles. Dance in Israel is influenced by the region's various social, cultural, and religious backgrounds.

There are currently over a dozen major professional dance companies in Israel, mostly in Tel Aviv, that perform domestically and internationally. There are also dance groups based in Ramallah.

The annual Israel Festival is the country's major multidisciplinary arts festival, held over a period of a few weeks in Jerusalem.

The music scene in Israel is just as vibrant as other places in the world, if not more. The country's offerings start with the world-class classical music of the Israeli Philharmonic Orchestra and the New Israeli Opera. The country's music scene has been enhanced by waves of European immigrants who brought along skills and influences from the best traditions in the world. The variations of music genres range from Arabic and Hebrew pop to Middle Eastern jazz, rock, and mainstream American music.

the Youth Wing at the Israel Museum in Jerusalem

Essentials

Transportation

GETTING THERE

There are a variety of ways to get to Israel and the West Bank, though most visitors arrive by air through the international airport in Tel Aviv.

Air

Tel Aviv's **Ben Gurion International Airport** (tel. 03/975-2386, www.iaa.gov.il) is a massive, modern airport with flights to and from almost everywhere in the world. It is about a 15-minute drive from Tel Aviv and about one hour from Jerusalem. Once at the airport, you can easily get to your destination by hotel shuttle, train, taxi, *sherut* (share taxi), or bus.

During the Jewish Sabbath—late Friday afternoon until Saturday night—things slow down considerably. The airport is still open, but certain airlines might not operate (such as Israel's El Al) and public transportation to and from the airport doesn't operate. Yom Kippur, when almost nobody drives and all public transportation shuts down, would present problems.

Jordan's international airport, **Queen Alia International Airport** (airport-authority. com/AMM) has flights between Amman and Tel Aviv on a regular basis. You can also fly into Amman and get to the West Bank by vehicle through one of the border crossings.

Boat

Some people traveling by boat end up visiting Israel while on their way somewhere else, such as cruise ship passengers who stay for 1-2 days and longer, and some are ferry passengers who are traveling with cars. Both types of passengers go through the international **Port of Haifa** (www.haifaport.co.il). The port includes a large terminal with a wide variety of passenger facilities, including a waiting area, a duty-free shop, a souvenir shop, a cafeteria, a VAT (Value Added Tax) reimbursement counter and currency exchange, a Ministry of Interior services office, and other travel-related services.

Typical customs and immigrations procedures apply for passengers who want to exit the port and enter Israel. There is long- and short-term parking next to the passenger terminal. People on foot can walk about 10 minutes to the port's exit and take a taxicab to wherever they are going in Haifa.

Land

From **Jordan** (www.visitjordan.com) there are three land border crossings into Israel from the north, center, and south. The central and southern border crossings are the most convenient and frequently used, while the northernmost crossing is isolated from major cities and attractions.

The **Wadi Araba Crossing/South Border** (6:30am-8pm Sun.-Thurs., 8am-8pm Fri.-Sat.) connects the resort towns of Eilat in Israel and Aqaba in Jordan. Visas are issued on the spot at the Eilat crossing, and you don't need to provide photographs.

The **Allenby/King Hussein Bridge** is in the southern Jordan Valley (8am-8pm for entering Jordan, 8am-2pm for leaving Jordan Sun.-Thurs., 8am-1pm Fri.-Sat.). Private cars and tour buses are not allowed to cross, so you have to change vehicles when crossing the border. If coming from Israel, pay for your visa in advance (about JD16) at the Jordanian embassy in Tel Aviv, and you will need two photographs. You will receive a visa within 24 hours.

Ben Gurion International Airport in Tel Aviv

Americans and Canadians coming from Jordan into Israel do not need to apply for a visa in advance. They will be issued a visa at the crossing. There will usually be an exit fee of JD10 when coming from Jordan into Israel. Always travel with a passport that is valid for at least six months beyond your dates of travel.

GETTING AROUND

It is fairly easy to get around Israel because of the excellent bus systems that exist nationally and within the large cities. You can basically get almost anywhere you want by bus, including areas in the West Bank near Jewish settlements. The various train systems are less convenient because of their somewhat limited routes and slow pace, but they do offer a good option for transportation.

Train

The national train system, the **Israel Railways** (www.rail.co.il), is a fairly convenient way to get around many parts of Israel, particularly useful for north to south routes. Just be aware that the railway system is also plagued by ongoing issues that include labor strikes and problems with keeping to the timetable. Daily and multi-journey tickets are available, and kids under the age of five travel for free.

The station stops in Jerusalem are quite far off the beaten path, on the outskirts of town near the zoo and the Malha Mall. Just to get to and from the Jerusalem train station to the city center, you will need to take a taxi, bus, or car. The station stops in Tel Aviv are numerous, convenient, and centrally located.

If you go by train from the airport, you can be in Tel Aviv's city center in about 10 minutes and in Jerusalem in about 2.5 hours (the route from the airport to Jerusalem is abnormally long). There are several train lines that leave every 20-30 minutes from the airport.

Train etiquette at crowded stops when passengers are boarding and disembarking is somewhat nonexistent. Basically, be prepared to shove your way on or off the train or risk getting stuck.

Light-Rail (Jerusalem Only)

Though Haifa and Tel Aviv are in the process of establishing a light-rail train, currently the only city that has a functioning **light-rail** is Jerusalem (tel. 073/210-0601 or *3686 from any local phone, www.citypass.co.il, 5:30am-midnight Sun.-Thurs., 5:30am-3pm Fri. and holiday eves, 7pm-midnight Sat., NIS5.9 for a single ride, or multi-ride on Rav Kav Card). Tourists get a discounted public transportation ticket, but there is not an extensive network of stops throughout the city. All tickets are valid for continued use for 90 minutes from the time they were purchased.

The route of Jerusalem's light-rail is fairly limited, but there are plans to expand it. It is roughly along the old border between East and West Jerusalem, and it is convenient if you want to get somewhere in East Jerusalem. It has stops next to the *shuk*, city center, Mount Herzl, and Yad Vashem.

Subway (Haifa Only)

The only subway in Israel is the six-station Haifa subway, the **Carmelit** (http://carmelithaifa.com, 6am-midnight Sun.-Thurs., 6am-3pm Fri., after sunset-midnight Sat., single ticket about NIS7). It is most useful for going between the lower city, Wadi Nisnas, and straight up the mountain until Hanassi Boulevard. You can buy a single, daily, or 10-ride ticket.

Bus

The main bus company that essentially comprises the national bus system of long-distance routes in Israel runs the green and white **Egged** (www.egged.co.il/Eng) buses. They can get you almost anywhere you want to go, including to some areas in the West Bank.

Overall information about buses in Israel is online (http://bus.co.il).

You can pay cash for your bus ticket (about NIS7 within the city) while boarding the bus and do not need to wait at the ticket window if you are traveling from the central bus station. If you know you'll be making a return trip (say between Jerusalem and Tel Aviv), buy your ticket on the bus and you will get a small discount. Central bus stations in major cities such as Tel Aviv, Jerusalem, and Beer Sheva display route information in English and Hebrew on monitors in the station.

You can also buy a Rav Kav Card for 10 or 20 rides, also good for transfers, and each ride will be at a small discount.

Once you are on the bus, depending on where you are going, there are a few things to be aware of. First of all, the safety rules are fairly loose, and when seats are sold out on a long-distance bus, you can sit or stand in the aisle or the stairwell at the back of the bus. Eating and drinking are allowed, but if traveling with Jewish orthodox passengers (distinguishable by their black hats, black coats, beards, and white shirts), it is advisable to avoid sitting next to them.

The public transportation depot at the Tel Aviv airport is on the second floor near Gates

bus in Tel Aviv

21 and 23. Buses go from there to the Egged station at nearby Airport City, and then you can transfer to regular Egged bus lines. The buses from Airport City to the airport are free. The Egged buses will get you to south Tel Aviv's Central Bus Station.

You can also go between Jerusalem's Central Bus Station and the airport by Egged bus. It takes about one hour in normal traffic. Try to avoid making the trip on a Friday afternoon, as traffic will typically be the worst at that time.

The Tel Aviv, Jerusalem, and Beer Sheva central bus stations have tons of taxis available for hire, as do many of the smaller city bus stations.

In Tel Aviv, the city bus line, **Dan** (tel. 03/639-4444, www.dan.co.il/english) operates a series of very convenient lines throughout the city, and they have detailed information on their English-language website. They shut down on the weekend.

In Jerusalem, the bus system is extremely convenient, and the buses are frequent. There is a discounted public transportation ticket for tourists for public buses, operated by Egged. There is also a double-decker city tour bus that you can hop on and off all day long at major sights after buying a 24- or 48-hour ticket. The one-stop shop for Jerusalem transportation information, including the buses, is **Jerusalem Transportation** (www.jet.gov.il). A one-way ticket is about NIS7 and cannot be used for transfers.

Though there have been efforts in recent years to have some buses operate during the weekend in Tel Aviv, at the time of publication the only city in the entire country of Israel with buses that operate on the weekend (with partial service) is Haifa. The closest thing to public transportation that is available in other cities on the weekend is the *sherut* (share taxis), which are more expensive and less convenient.

Other bus operators work throughout the country. In the center of the country, bus operators include **Superbus** (www.superbus.co.il), as well as **Kavim** (www.kavim-t.co.il).

Kavim also operates in the north. Other operators in the north include **Nazareth Buses** (www.ntt-buses.com) and **Golan Bus** (www.golanbus.co.il). In the south, the major bus operator is **Metropoline** (www.metropoline.com). Many of these bus operators do not have English websites available.

Taxi and Share Taxi

Throughout Israel, **taxicabs** are everywhere, but most cost 25 percent more on weekends and between 9pm-5am. One good option if you want to order a cab to come and pick you up (which will cost about NIS5 extra) is to ask any hotel front desk for the name of a taxi company. A company that operates nationally and is recommended by the Municipality of Jerusalem is **Rehavia Taxi** (Taxi Stand at 3 Agron St. in Jerusalem, tel. 02/625-4444 or 02/622-2444).

Sherut **(share taxis)** are an option in most parts of the country, and especially for travel between Tel Aviv and Jerusalem. On the weekend, they are your best (and almost only) option. A *sherut* from Jerusalem to Tel Aviv is about NIS35 or less, and leaves from the base of Tolerance Square seven days a week. The *sherut* from Tel Aviv leaves from the Central Bus Station (106 Levinski St.), just east of Neve Tzedek and Florentin. Keep in mind that a *sherut* will only depart when all of the seats are full. Depending on how you time it, you might be waiting for 20-30 minutes for the taxi to fill up. While you're riding in the *sherut,* if you need to get out somewhere, it's perfectly acceptable to ask the driver to let you out as soon as possible; drivers stop upon request at the first chance they have to pull over.

Car

Americans in Israel are allowed to drive with their foreign license for up to one year after arriving in the country. There are quite a number of rental car companies that operate throughout Israel, the most prevalent of which are **Hertz** (19 King David St. in Jerusalem, tel. 02/623-1351, www.hertz.co.il) and **Budget** (23 King David St. in Jerusalem, tel. 03/935-0015), offering a wide variety of options; car rentals run about US$45 day after mandatory insurance is added. The largest domestic car rental company in Israel is Eldan (114 HaYarkon St. in Tel Aviv, tel. 03/527-1166, www.eldan.co.il); Shlomo Sixt (122 HaYarkon St. in Tel Aviv, tel. 03/524-4935, www.shlomo.co.il) is another good option. The central area for car rental offices in Jerusalem is on King David Street, just across from the King David Hotel, near Mamilla shopping center. In Tel Aviv, there is a stretch of car rental companies right on the promenade to the beach around 114 HaYarkon Street.

The parking system throughout Israel is uniform and has strict rules, but there are many unspoken exceptions, especially during the weekend when parking rules are suspended. For instance, you might see cars parked on the sidewalk, or facing the wrong direction when parked along the street.

Red and white stripes mean no parking; blue and white stripes signify paid parking by a street meter (a machine that sometimes only takes cash); and gray means free. Other paid parking in certain neighborhoods or small lots will have a yellow and black sign with hours of paid parking where you must buy a ticket and leave it on your car dash with the date stamp showing. Paid parking costs approximately NIS10 for 90 minutes.

If you are going to be driving on a daily basis for an extended period of time, Yellow gas stations sell an automatic pay in advance meter that you leave on the side of your vehicle. The meter costs NIS100 and you can pay for time on it as you go. If you have a smartphone, you may be able to install the Pango app which you can use to pay for parking.

Driving yourself is fairly straightforward, as 99 percent of the road signs are posted in English, Hebrew, and Arabic. Don't panic if you think you're on the right road but don't see signs, or see signs for something with a different spelling. It is not uncommon to have no signage to a certain place until the last minute, or for signage names to change in their spelling of the place. The best thing to do is stop and ask for directions. But be prepared to stop more than once because when people give directions in Israel they typically tell you to go to a certain point and then ask someone else.

If you drive into Tel Aviv, take Highway 1 coming from the direction of Jerusalem, and Highway 2 when coming from the direction of Haifa. You will merge onto Highway 20, also known as Ayalon Highway, which runs through the center of Tel Aviv; about half a dozen exits on the Ayalon get you into different parts of the city.

If you drive into Jerusalem, take Highway 1 and just follow the signs. There are several exits to Jerusalem, some of which will take you far into the outskirts and hills of town. Try to keep as close to City Center as possible, as that is where most hotels are, and where you will have the best luck getting your bearings. Driving within the city of Jerusalem can be extremely complicated and confusing, so take your time, and if you think you are lost, don't hesitate to stop.

TIPS FOR DRIVING

The key to driving while you're in the Middle East is to stay calm and focused, which will help you navigate the tricky road rules. The general guidelines are to keep moving, don't be afraid to improvise (especially in Jerusalem), and don't be afraid to honk your horn. Particularly for Americans, honking can be taken as rude, but it is an important mode of communication in the Middle East, where the roads are often older and narrower.

Some roads were built during times when they were used by donkey carts and horses, so they aren't quite wide enough for cars. Other roads were built up the side of mountains as cities grew over hundreds of years and are extremely steep. Take your time and have a GPS with you wherever you go.

There is no right turn on red, and you probably won't get a ticket if you park on the side of the street facing the wrong way.

CHECKPOINTS

There are checkpoints posted in various locations between Israel and the West Bank, inside the West Bank at the edge of Israel-controlled territory, at the Tel Aviv airport, and at Gaza. Sometimes officers at a checkpoint will ask you to open your trunk, so know where that release is located and be ready to open it. If you are stopped at the airport, you might be asked a series of questions. Don't panic if you are questioned. It is typically related to whatever the current security situation is and not you personally. There are also security checkpoints going into most major buildings where you will need to open your bag for inspection.

GAS CONVERSION

The price of 95 octane gas in the government-regulated system at gas stations throughout Israel fluctuates, but is about NIS6 per liter. At full-service gas stations, it costs 0.18 more per liter. The price of gas is updated by the government once a month and published in all daily newspapers.

Air

At Israel's domestic airport, **Dov Hoz** (www.iaa.gov.il), you can catch flights to the popular southern tourist city of Eilat and the **Eilat Domestic Airport** (tel. 08/636-3800, www.iaa.gov.il), which takes flights from Arkia, El Al, Israir, and Sun Dor airlines. It is small and convenient, and a good option if you plan to also take in a trip to Petra, Jordan, while you're in the area. Most tour companies will pick you up directly from the airport.

Hitchhiking

Hitchhiking for a ride in Israel and the West Bank is fairly common, but carries the same risks as hitchhiking anywhere else. The regional signal for someone seeking a ride is to point their index finger at the ground in front of them. Especially on the weekend or on Friday afternoons, you will see more hitchhikers than usual.

If you are driving and see a soldier hitchhiking, understand that it is against military regulations for soldiers to hitchhike and they could face time in the brig if they are caught taking a ride.

the checkpoint at Hebron

Visas and Officialdom

Israeli bureaucracy is infamous, but getting into Israel from one of the many countries that they have a visa waiver program with is fairly easy.

VISAS AND PASSPORTS

If you have a passport that is valid for a minimum of six months after your date of exit from the country and you are coming from a visa waiver country, you do not have to arrange for a visa in advance to enter Israel. You will be automatically granted a three-month tourist visa upon entering Israel and there is no fee. The countries that have a visa waiver program with Israel include the United States, the United Kingdom, Australia, Canada, New Zealand, South Africa, and others.

The same six-month rule for passports applies to entering Jordan. If you plan to visit Arab countries (aside from Jordan) for the duration of your passport, ask for your visa stamp to Israel to be put on a separate piece of paper. It is not an uncommon request, as a passport with a stamp from Israel might make it very difficult or impossible to gain entry into many Arab countries.

Visas to Jordan are usually good for one month and can be obtained from the **Jordanian embassy in Tel Aviv** (14 Abba Hillel St., in the Tel Aviv suburb of Ramat Gan, tel. 03/751-7752), in your home country, or at the Wadi Araba Crossing/South Border. Aqaba is a special economic zone and there should be no visa fee for Americans.

ISRAELI EMBASSIES AND CONSULATES ABROAD

Israel maintains embassies and consulates all over the world. In the United States, there are Consulate General offices of Israel in New York, Atlanta, Boston, Houston, Chicago, Miami, Philadelphia, San Francisco, and Los Angeles, as well as the Israeli Embassy in Washington, D.C.

FOREIGN EMBASSIES AND CONSULATES IN ISRAEL

Though Jerusalem is Israel's capital city and the seat of its federal government, countries with diplomatic relations with Israel maintain their embassies in Tel Aviv. The reason for this is related to Jerusalem's complicated international legal status. If a foreign government established its embassy in Jerusalem (instead of the consulates there now), it might be seen as an indication of the recognition of Jerusalem as the capital city of Israel. It would also seriously complicate matters in the event that an independent Palestinian state was established. For that reason, embassies of foreign governments, including the United States, are located in Tel Aviv.

There are two locations for the **Consulate of the United States in Jerusalem** (main consulate at 18 Agron Rd., and consular services at 14 David Flusser St., tel. 02/630-4000 or 02/622-7230 for emergencies and during nonbusiness hours, http://jerusalem.usconsulate.gov). The consulate in East Jerusalem essentially straddles the east-west "border" of the city. Appointments are mandatory for all visits to the consulate.

The **U.S. Embassy in Tel Aviv** (71 HaYarkon St., tel. 03/519-7475 or 03/519-7575 for emergencies and during nonbusiness hours, http://israel.usembassy.gov) has a useful email alert system that tells American citizens of serious security threats and advises areas not to travel in during times of violence and unrest in the region. Before traveling to Israel, you can register with the consulate or embassy for alerts.

TAXES

The Israeli taxing system uses what they call a Value Added Tax (VAT) of more than 16 percent for the purchase of goods and services. VAT is included in the price of many items (such as restaurants). However, if you purchase a more expensive item as a gift or souvenir while in the country (minimum NIS400), ask for tax refund forms. You will be eligible to get the VAT back when going through customs. Note that non-Israeli citizens or people who are not residents of Israel are not required to pay VAT for items like hotels and car rentals.

CUSTOMS

The standard fare of items are prohibited for import by Israeli customs, including weapons and drugs. They also restrict the import of games of chance, pornographic material, plants and soil, and pets. You can bring up to US$200 worth of tax-free gifts into Israel, 250 grams of cigarettes, and one bottle of liquor. You can convert up to US$3,000 in cash at the airport when you leave.

Be particularly careful about buying any kind of antiquities or archaeological artifacts and then transporting them out of the country; you must have a certificate that identifies the object in question. If you buy from a licensed antiquities dealer, they will provide you with such a certificate.

MEDICAL REQUIREMENTS

Inoculations and vaccinations are not required for entry to Israel and Jordan.

POLITICAL AFFILIATIONS AND AGENDAS

If you enter Israel with a specific intention or action that relates to a political agenda (particularly one that would be seen as against the state), you might be prevented from entering the country. This usually applies to large groups with a high profile, but you might be questioned by customs about the purpose of your trip to Israel.

POLICE

In some areas of Israel, there are **Tourist Police** (tel. 03/516-5382) who specifically work to serve tourists with any criminal matter (such as theft) or an emergency. There are tourist police offices in Tel Aviv near the beach, on the corner of Herbert Samuel and Geula Streets. You can also call the tourist police if you have an emergency.

Recreation

Though it is a small country, the options for outdoor recreation in Israel are staggering. In addition to a wide variety of archaeological sites that have national parks around them and serve the dual purpose of hiking spots and sightseeing locations, there are nature reserves and options for hiking, biking, diving, camping, swimming, and many other sports.

The recreation opportunities in the West Bank are much less developed, but if you're an experienced hiker, you can find your way to some really nice spots and walk among groves of olive and lemon trees. Many groups organize hikes through social media, which is a great way to participate in a guided hike for a reasonable price with a group.

Petra and Jordan in general are home to vast expanses of desert that offer the unique experiences that can only be found there, and have a fairly well-developed tourism industry.

NATIONAL PARKS AND NATURE RESERVES

The **Israel Nature and Parks Authority** (3 Am Ve'Olamo St., Jerusalem, tel. 02/500-5444 or dial *3639 in-country, www.parks.

org.il, for information and tour reservations email moked@npa.org.il) maintains parks and nature reserves all over the country that vary widely in price. Many of these include archaeological sites. The least expensive are about NIS5 and the most expensive are about NIS50.

Jordan also has a nice national parks system, though it is recommended to travel with a tour guide or go on a guided outing. The most highly recommended of Jordan's national park experiences is **Wadi Rum** (Rte. 15 between Aqaba and Petra, www.wadirum.jo), which is on the way to Petra from the border crossing at Eilat-Aqaba.

HIKING

Hiking in Israel, the West Bank, and Jordan is a very popular pastime and favorite family outing, particularly in the warmer dry season. Depending on the area you go hiking in, there are a few things to be aware of. Always bring water, sunscreen, and a hat, even if you are accustomed to being in a warm climate. If you get dehydrated or get sunstroke, the symptoms might not appear until you are in a dangerous condition. Experienced hikers will tell you that if you are drinking enough water, you should be looking for a restroom about every 90 minutes or so.

Along many hiking routes, there are places to swim that include streams, waterfalls, springs, and ancient cisterns (artificially constructed cave-like structures that were once used to gather water from the rainfall). It is culturally acceptable to swim in these areas, though you will always want to have some kind of swimwear or clothes you don't mind getting wet.

If you go for a hike in an area where you think there might be swimming, take some kind of shoes that you can wear while in the water, as the bottoms of water springs are often very rocky.

The biggest and most well-marked hike is the **Israel National Trail** (www.israelnationaltrail.com), a 620-mile route that stretches from the Red Sea to Israel's border with Lebanon. The National Trail passes through many cities, including Tel Aviv, Haifa, and Netanya. It is possible to follow the trail for any portion you want.

BICYCLING

One of the best and least-advertised features of the boutique hotel industry is that they often offer **free bicycle rentals** to guests. The phrase bicycle rental is a misnomer that you might see on hotel websites; there is

biking along a Tel Aviv beach

visitors hiking in Ein Gedi

typically no fee involved. You can just borrow a bike for free for the day. This custom is particularly common among the boutique hotels in Israel's north coast, in the south, and in Eilat. Ask your hotel when booking if they let guests borrow bikes for free.

In Tel Aviv, the green bicycles of the **Tel-O-Fun** (www.tel-o-fun.co.il/en, NIS20 for a couple of hours) bike rental system can be found throughout the city, and you can pick up and drop off a bike at any Tel-O-Fun location. The first half-hour of usage is free, and there is no law in Tel Aviv that requires bicyclists to wear a helmet.

SWIMMING

There are scores of places throughout Israel to swim that include the Mediterranean Sea, public pools, hotel pools (sometimes even if you are not staying there you can use them for a fee), springs and related streams, cisterns, the Sea of Galilee, the Dead Sea, and the Red Sea. In the hot summer month of August in Jerusalem, you might even see fully clothed ultraorthodox families swimming in the public fountains in the parks.

There are sometimes restrictions on swimming with separated male and female times and areas when the pools are visited by orthodox Jews. If a pool has designated hours

for male and female swimming, it will be listed on the schedule, but it is always best to ask. Some beaches, particularly along the Mediterranean, have designated male and female hours, or designated male and female beaches.

DIVING

The hottest diving spots in the region are in the **Red Sea,** with its world-renowned coral reef, year-round warm temperatures, and well-developed tourism industry that is able to cater to the needs of visitors.

COOKING OUT

In general, as with many other things in this region, the rules about cooking out are fairly loose. Basically, you can cook out almost anywhere you want to (within reason).

If you happen to be in Israel during the **Yom Ha'atzmaut** holiday (National Independence Day, around May 14, corresponding to the Jewish calendar), you will see cooking out like you have probably never witnessed. Most businesses shut down and people go out in droves to find any piece of ground they can to cook out on. Even the pristine grass on the grounds of the national rose garden next to the Israeli Knesset is fair game for setting up a small grill and starting a fire.

If you pass by one of the large (or small) parks in any city, you will see a cloud of smoke hovering above it from the cookout frenzy.

If you want to take part, it is easy to buy a small grill (NIS20) prior to the holiday at most grocery stores and small convenience stores.

Food

The food in Israel and Jordan is basically a combination of a Mediterranean and Middle Eastern diet that emphasizes fruits, vegetables, whole grains, and non-processed foods, with a few common threads that can be found almost everywhere you go.

HUMMUS AND FALAFEL

Two of the most famous and favorite food dishes are hummus and falafel. Hummus is a sort of paste that is generally made from chickpeas, olive oil, and tahini. Hummus can be used as a dip on pita or on the side of your plate with main dishes, or as a sort of dressing on top of dishes like salad. It is also commonly used in shwarma sandwiches.

Falafel are deep-fried balls of mashed chickpeas that have been blended with onions and herbs. They can be bought from street vendors, in the *shuk,* and from small shops that specialize in falafel. Falafel is commonly

served stuffed inside of a pita sandwich with lettuce, tomatoes, pickles, and tahini (a commonly served paste of sesame seeds and olive oil). It makes a filling and sometimes very cheap meal if you are not buying it in a tourist area.

SHWARMA

The many shops that sell shwarma are distinguishable by the large chunk of lamb meat cooking on a spit in a prominent location. The meat is cut directly off of the spit and typically served in a pita sandwich. You can usually tell if a shwarma shop is good by how juicy the meat is. If customers are not coming to eat frequently, the meat might look a bit dried out.

BEDOUIN

Bedouin food, which can be found throughout the region but particularly in the south of Israel and in Jordan, is traditionally cooked

a typical breakfast of the Galilee region

on an open fire and eaten with the hands. Common Bedouin meals include the more standard pita; the thin, crepe-like *shraak* pita that is cooked on a domed pan over a fire; and *taboon,* which is usually thicker and made from darker flour. Other typical Bedouin ingredients and dishes focus on lamb meat, rice, and yogurt.

DRUZE

Arab people of Syrian descent, the Druze are known for their delicious dishes that include many typical facets of Middle Eastern food, such as pita, hummus, vegetables, and lamb and chicken dishes. Druze stew, a delicious combination of meat, potatoes, and vegetables, is worth trying when you're in the region.

KOSHER AND NONKOSHER

Some areas of Israel have a multilayered system of following the religious dietary laws of being kosher. The level to which the restaurant follows kosher regulations determines the type of certificate it will display. Kosher certifications are always posted in public view and are often advertised on websites.

Particularly in Jerusalem, most restaurants

are kosher, so they will either serve milk or meat, but not both. At a kosher restaurant that serves meat, for example, you will not be able to get a latte or ice cream for dessert. They might serve milk-substitute dishes, though, so it is always worth asking.

The production of kosher food is overseen by a rabbi who certifies the food as being kosher according to Jewish law. The level of supervision and adherence to religious dietary law determines the differing types of kosher certification. The three levels from least restricted to most restricted are kosher, glatt kosher, and mehadrin kosher.

Some hotels cater to religious Jewish customers and adhere to kosher religious laws. These establishments will basically not serve a hot meal on Friday night (unless it was cooked hours earlier and kept warm somehow) or on Saturday until nighttime. Restaurants that keep kosher close on Friday in the late afternoon (depending on the time of the year, around 3 or 4pm). Some will not open again until Sunday morning, but many open later in the evening on Saturday night after the Sabbath has ended, generally around 9pm, and then stay open later than usual.

Accommodations

There are several different types of accommodation options when traveling throughout Israel, the West Bank, and Jordan. Options range from five-star resorts to extremely casual accommodations, such as renting a room in someone's home.

GUESTHOUSES (ZIMMERS)

The fairly ubiquitous and lovely option of a *zimmer* (also spelled *tsimmer*) is one of the best ways to experience regional hospitality, food, and culture. A *zimmer* is typically family owned and operated and set up as a series of private cabins or bungalows spread across

the *zimmer* grounds and centered around a main building where meals and sometimes recreation can be found.

There are two main categories of *zimmers:* luxury and luxury-rustic. The luxury-level *zimmers* include amenities such as a large, flat-screen TV and a whirlpool hot tub. The rustic *zimmers* usually won't include any kind of a TV and will emphasize a more natural, country experience. *Zimmer* cabins often have private porches, but ask in advance about bathing accommodations, because the bathtub (and sometimes the toilet) are often placed in a prominent spot in your room and not inside a closed-off bathroom.

While the north of Israel, in the Galilee and Golan Heights, is full of *zimmers,* they can be found throughout Israel. The website for **Rural Tourism in Israel** (www.zimmeril. com) is an invaluable resource, as many *zimmers* don't maintain their own website, social media pages, or even have an email address and can only be reached by telephone.

Some *zimmers* are located in moshavs, which are basically cooperative neighborhoods that are sometimes a bit off the beaten path.

GUEST ROOMS

Arranging for a guest room is a tricky matter, and you probably need to be in the country already or have a trusted go-between like a tour guide to make arrangements. Particularly in the West Bank, you can inquire at the shops that cater to tourists (especially in Bethlehem) if they know of any houses in town that rent rooms out.

BUDGET, MID-RANGE, BOUTIQUE, AND HIGH-END HOTELS

The range of hotels in Israel, the West Bank, and Jordan is just as broad as any other region that caters to tourists, but the main thing to be aware of is the size of rooms, even in higher-end hotels, are often on the smaller side, more in accordance with European standards. Budget hotels and mid-range hotels will often be a bit sparse in the furnishings and will have tile floors (not carpeting), but they usually have free wireless Internet. High-end and luxury hotels, in turn, will usually charge for Internet access, but have every amenity you can imagine, down to the smallest detail.

There are a couple of common features for the majority of hotels in the region. One is that breakfast is included with the rate of your room. In some cases, you can upgrade your room rate to have all meals included. Once in a blue moon, the standard breakfast-included practice is not kept at a hotel, so it is always best to ask in advance.

The included breakfast is typically served around 7am-9am, but always ask in advance. It includes hot and cold drinks, salads, eggs, toast, and more. If you try to take food out of the breakfast area, hotel staff will charge you extra.

The general practice for room service in mid-range hotels and up is that you can often get at least hot and cold drinks delivered to your room.

HOSTELS

The hostel system in Israel is surprisingly well-developed and the best of the hostels book extremely far in advance, sometimes as far as six months. Hostel options in Jerusalem include places to stay in the Old City as well as near City Center. The **Israel Youth Hostel Association (IYHA)** (tel. 059/951-0511, www. iyha.org.il/eng) has English-speaking hotline representatives and a very easy-to-use booking website for hostels throughout the region. Though the hostel listing is not comprehensive, it includes hostels that are sanctioned members of the IYHA.

FIELD SCHOOLS

The **Society for Protection of Nature in Israel** (tel. 03/638-8653, www.natureisrael.org) is more than just a resource for nature activities in Israel. They also maintain a group of affordable, hostel-like accommodations throughout Israel that are called field schools. Many field schools are located near major tourist destinations and offer an excellent alternative to a more expensive hotel. The organization's emphasis on nature preservation also means that field school staff are knowledgeable about outdoor activities in the region where they are located.

KIBBUTZIM

There are a number of kibbutzim in Israel that generate part of their economy from operating luxury, resort-like hotels or more mid-range accommodations. When you stay at one of these kibbutz hotels (Ramat Rachel on the outskirts of Jerusalem is a good example), you will typically have access to certain kibbutz amenities, including a swimming pool, playgrounds, and the like.

CAMPING

You will be hard-pressed to find a clearinghouse of published information in English about camping in Israel, the West Bank, and Jordan. Though there are many, many excellent camping sites throughout the area, and particularly in Israel, information about campsites, costs, and regulations is generally only published in Hebrew.

The two best resources to check for camping information are the **Israel National Parks** (tel. 02/500-5444 or dial *3639 incountry, www.parks.org.il) and the **Society** for Protection of Nature in Israel (tel. 03/638-8688, www.natureisrael.org).

ARAB AND BEDOUIN GUEST ENCAMPMENTS

Throughout the south of Israel, the Negev, in the Golan Heights, and in Petra, you can experience Arab and Bedouin culture by visiting a **Bedouin tent.** The easiest areas to find these are in the Negev at Sefinat Hamidbar, Khan Hashayarot, and Khan Beerotayim, as well as at the Mashabei Sadeh junction, near the ancient city of Avdat and the village of Ezuz. Surrounding Petra and near Petra are also excellent places to find Bedouin tent encampments, in which you can stay overnight.

Conduct and Customs

The general rule with conduct and customs in Israel, the West Bank, and Jordan balances on two ends of the spectrum: live and let live or extremely strict. In general, the more religious the area you are in (Jewish, Muslim, or Christian), the more strictly the conservative conduct and religious customs are adhered to. This includes everything from clothing to food, and it particularly applies to women.

ETIQUETTE

There are a few things to keep in mind when navigating the general regional etiquette of the Middle East. One is that you will likely encounter at least one person who is unwilling to shake your hand for religious reasons, again, particularly if you are a woman.

Also in a general sense, people are more direct, less prone to effected pleasantries, and often more willing to get involved in other people's personal affairs (including giving unsolicited advice or directions). This directness and familiar approach to communicating takes some getting used to.

CONVERSATION

When talking with people, it is advisable to speak up and be as direct and decisive as possible. If you know what you want or what you are after in a conversation or interaction, you're likely to get better results than if you hesitate or are timid about what you're saying. Don't be alarmed or intimidated if someone speaks to you in a loud voice that sounds like yelling. It is just conversation.

In Israel, the common greeting is "shalom," which means peace. In Arabic, it is "as-salaam alaikum," which means peace be upon you. If you say nothing else in the native languages, try these two phrases out.

CLOTHING

Before you travel to any area, check in advance what the customs regarding clothing are. In some towns in the West Bank, women don't show their bare arms and legs and a man in shorts would stick out. In the ultraorthodox areas of certain towns in Israel, people also dress extremely conservatively. It's not advisable to walk through these areas in shorts and a tank top on a hot summer day. In Jerusalem,

A sign in Capernaum asks visitors to adhere to certain rules.

there have been cases of women being accosted and even physically attacked for dressing in a manner that is considered immodest by the religious.

Jerusalem is more conservative, while Tel Aviv is a bit wild.

Religious Sites

Most religious sites have signage to explain the site's expectations. Depending on the site, this can include covering your head, taking off your hat, covering your shoulders, having covered legs, keeping your cell phone off, refraining from flash photography, refraining from photography completely, keeping your speaking voice low, no public displays of affection, and on and on.

DINING

When you go out to eat, you can stay as long as you want. It is the rare waiter who will approach you in any eating establishment to ask if you want the check, unless the restaurant is

extremely busy. The custom is to let customers sit as long as they want until they are ready to leave. The waiter might continue to come back and ask if you want more of something, but they will not prompt you to leave.

The one exception to this is the preemptive measure some places will take during Shabbat (particularly in Jerusalem) if you come in without a reservation. The customary approach is to explain that you don't have a reservation, to which the host or hostess might say they have a table for you but it is reserved for a group that is arriving in a certain amount of time. That is your cue to understand that you can sit and eat, but you must leave within the allotted time.

SHABBAT (SABBATH)

The Jewish Shabbat (or Sabbath) starts on Friday at sundown and ends on Saturday night after three stars are out in the sky (when it is fully dark). Depending on how religious someone is, Shabbat can involve restrictions on using motorized transport, electricity, and working. Taxicabs still operate, but their fees are higher than normal. The one exception to public transportation shutdowns is in Haifa, where some public buses run on a limited schedule throughout Shabbat.

In Israel, Shabbat is the weekend for everyone (except Muslims and most Arabs) whether they are religious or not. All government offices and services stop, including public transportation. One exception to a major shutdown is East Jerusalem, which is predominately Arab, and where everything continues to hum along as normal. Arab areas shut down on Friday afternoon, which is their major prayer time during the week. Also, any restaurant that is kosher is closed. In Jerusalem, that means that all but about 15 restaurants shut down for more than 24 hours.

RAMADAN

The holy month of Ramadan is generally from early July to early August; the exact dates vary slightly every year. Ramadan involves fasting from morning until evening, when a large meal is eaten. It is the one time of the year during which it would be quite inconvenient to visit a predominately Arab area, as many things close or operate on a special schedule.

Travel Tips

WHEN TO GO

You will generally want to avoid traveling to Israel, Jordan, and the West Bank during major religious holidays. Jewish, Muslim, and Christian calendars are available online, but the biggest holidays are Passover and Easter, Hanukkah, Sukkot, Ramadan, and Christmas. Hotel rates will be higher during these times, and many venues will be closed in certain areas.

The month of August is not an advisable time to visit Jerusalem. It is a time of year when many children are not in camp, day care, or school, and it is also a major holiday for the ultraorthodox community. Jerusalem becomes extraordinarily crowded (including the museums, roads, and restaurants) during this time.

SHOPPING AND BARGAINING

There are a few unique aspects to shopping in the region. One is that if you are in Tel Aviv or Jerusalem, there are numerous Israeli designers who design and make wonderful clothes, shoes, bags, and other accessories. These are unique, domestically produced items that are largely sold only in Israel. They are typically extremely well made, durable, and attractive. Made in Israel products are sold everywhere from large shopping malls to small boutique stores on the street.

One of the worst types of places to shop is in tourist areas. The prices, quality, and selection are often worse than elsewhere, and vendors will often try to convince you that something is antique or much more valuable than what they are selling it for. The upside, however, is that if you have the stamina, you can drive a pretty hard bargain with shopkeepers, particularly in Jerusalem's Old City shops. Shop owners might chase you after you start walking away in refusal of a price they offered, shouting out an even lower price. The general rule of thumb is not to expect to negotiate the price down by more than a third.

When buying antiquities of any kind, always get the certificate of authenticity from the seller, as grave robbers and antiquities thieves are a major regional problem. If an antique item you bought is discovered by customs, you will not be able to leave the country without a certificate from the seller.

If someone bought you a present while you are in the country, don't leave it wrapped; be prepared to have it scanned for bombing materials by the Israeli security personnel at the airport if you mention you are carrying a gift someone gave you.

TIPPING

It is customary to tip about 15 percent to service personnel, including waiters and bellhops, but it is not customary to tip taxi drivers. In restaurants, you will often see a note on your receipt which says Service is Not Included, which means that they want your money.

OPPORTUNITIES FOR STUDY AND EMPLOYMENT

There are many work and study opportunities in Israel, but unless you plan on staying long-term, most of the work opportunities are voluntary and unpaid. There are several types of programs that you can participate in, including internships and fellowships, touring and experiential activities, volunteering programs, Hebrew language programs, Arabic language programs, academic programs, Jewish studies programs, and activist-based travel (similar to volunteer experiences).

ACCESS FOR TRAVELERS WITH DISABILITIES

Israel is pretty well-equipped for travelers with disabilities, but the older sections of cities, such as Jerusalem's Old City, are less so.

The West Bank and Jordan are not really set up to serve travelers with disabilities, though some of the nicer hotels do make certain accommodations.

TRAVELING WITH CHILDREN

Though it might seem like a tricky area to travel with children, nothing could be further from the truth. As long as adequate preparations are made for sun protection and hydration, it is very easy to travel in the region with a child. The general culture in this part of the world is centered on family life (including extended families), and people are accustomed to families that have at least 3-7 children.

For this reason, it is easy to be accommodated for your needs with children in hotels, restaurants, and in tourist destinations. One caveat to this is that the public safety standards are not as strict as North Americans are accustomed to, so it's best to be a bit more alert about what's going on around you. Most hotels will have very nice cribs (some charge a bit extra, but not all) that you can use in your hotel room. Ask for the crib in advance, and it will be set up in your room on arrival.

The general regional atmosphere in regard to children is accepting also in restaurants, where something like a crying baby likely won't cause any of the customers to even bat an eye. The typical sounds and actions of babies and children are so familiar in the culture that you can usually expect a very understanding and helpful reaction when traveling with children.

WOMEN TRAVELING ALONE

It can be a bit tricky for a woman to travel solo in certain parts of Israel, and in the West Bank and Jordan. The best way to keep a low profile is to dress conservatively. There aren't any real dangers for a woman traveling alone in this region, but it is also not that common, and it is a male-dominated society with widely varying expectations about the role women play.

SENIOR TRAVELERS

The most important thing for senior travelers to keep in mind while traveling in the region is to be cautious about the potential dangers of the Middle East sun. In the hottest summer months, it's advisable to conduct outdoor activities before 10:30am and after 3pm. When it's hottest, always drink plenty of water and wear a hat and sunscreen.

GAY AND LESBIAN TRAVELERS

The main place in the region where gay and lesbian people are openly accepted is Tel Aviv and its immediate suburbs. The city caters to gay and lesbian travelers so openly that its municipal website has a special section for gay and lesbian travel.

In much more conservative Jerusalem, there are some gay bars and clubs, but in day-to-day life, gays and lesbians are very much under the radar. Jerusalem is a city where you will seldom see anybody, gay or straight, making public displays of affection.

Health and Safety

MEDICAL CARE IN ISRAEL

Israel's health care facilities are modern, world-class operations, and if you need medical service, you can go to one of its many hospitals. Dial 101 from any phone at any time if you have an emergency (most people speak English). Some cities also have pharmacies and drugstores that operate 24 hours a day.

VACCINATIONS

You do not need vaccinations to enter Israel or Jordan, but it is best to travel with valid health insurance. You can get travel insurance for your trip, which will protect you in the case of any major mishaps.

You will see signs posted from the Israeli Ministry of Health reminding people to drink water and to carry it with you and drink it regularly (even if you're not thirsty) to avoid dehydration and heatstroke. Tap water is perfectly safe to drink in all parts of Israel.

BOMB SHELTERS AND ALARMS

Many houses, buildings, and hotels have bomb shelters. If you don't know where a bomb shelter is, the next safest place is in a stairwell as far from windows as possible.

The sound of a wailing bomb alarm is unmistakable and could go off at any time of day or night. From the time you hear the sound of the alarm, you will have about two minutes to get to a bomb shelter or safety before impact.

Israel's highly sophisticated Iron Dome system (partly funded by the U.S. government) has been tested plenty in recent years, and it is very effective at intercepting and detonating incoming rockets while they are still in the air. Most of them never hit the ground.

Don't be tempted to pet or feed the stray cats.

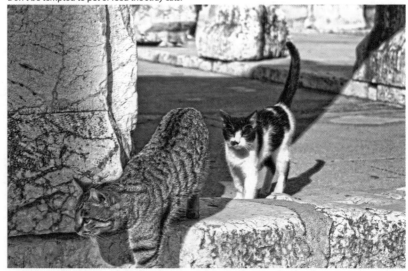

CONTACT LENSES AND GLASSES

If you wear contacts lenses or glasses, note your prescription level in advance, as you will be able to easily buy contacts or glasses in any drugstore, optometrist shop, or glasses store once you are in the country. There is no doctor's prescription required.

STRAY CATS

You might notice a large number of stray cats wandering around different cities, particularly in areas where there are more people. Most of these cats are not only strays, they were born on the streets and might carry disease. Don't pet stray cats or try to feed them.

Information and Services

MONEY
Israel

The Israeli currency is the New Israeli Shekel (NIS or shekel), and it is divided into 100 Agorot. The most current exchange rates are available from the **Bank of Israel** (tel. 02/655-2211, www.bankisrael.gov.il). The U.S. dollar generally hovers around an exchange rate US$1 to NIS4. Major tourist areas have currency exchange services.

Israeli banks are open Sunday-Thursday about 9am-noon, then close for a few hours, and open again about 2pm-5pm. Cash can be withdrawn from ATMs 24 hours a day.

Non-Israeli citizens can get a VAT (Value Added Tax) refund if they don't have an Israeli passport and are visiting Israel as a tourist. The goods should have been bought in a store included in the VAT refund program and the purchase amount in one tax invoice including VAT must exceed NIS400.

The West Bank

You can pay for goods and services in the West Bank using U.S. dollars or Israeli shekels, though it is best to use shekels.

Jordan

The official currency of Jordan is the Jordanian dinar (JD), and it is divided into 10 dirham, 100 qirsh (or piasters), or 1,000 fils. Half dinar and 1 dinar coins are most common, and bills come in 1 dinar, 5 dinars, 10 dinars, 20 dinars, and 50 dinars denominations. JD1 is typically worth about US$1.40 or NIS5.20.

If you are coming from Israel, change your shekels to Jordanian dinars before crossing the border, or at one of the money-changing desks that are along the way as you pass through the many stops that you need to make it through the border (Eilat-Aqaba border crossing). If you are trying to pay in shekels after entering Jordan, it will really put a damper on your trip, as most people will have no idea what to charge you.

Traveler's Checks and Credit Cards

It's possible to pay for goods and services with traveler's checks in Israel, but it might be a bit inconvenient. A good bet is to change traveler's checks to cash as needed. Major credit cards are accepted almost everywhere.

CONSULATES

Israel's designation of Jerusalem as its national capital is a matter of some dispute in the international arena. In diplomatic terms, this translates to foreign embassies being located in Tel Aviv and some foreign consulates being located in Jerusalem. Only some countries with an embassy in Tel Aviv also have a consulate in Jerusalem.

The **U.S. Consulate General** (18 Agron St. and 14 David Flusser Rd., tel. 02/622-7230, http://jerusalem.usconsulate.gov, jerusalem-visa@state.gov for non-immigrant visa questions) has two buildings. The one for consular services is located between the neighborhoods of German Colony and Bak'a and the Sherover-Haas Promenade.

The U.K. Consulate General (19 Nashashibi St. in Sheikh Jarrah, tel. 02/541-4100, http://ukinjerusalem.fco.gov.uk, britain.jerusalem@fco.gov.uk) is in East Jerusalem.

The Embassy of Canada (3/5 Nirim St., Tel Aviv, tel. 03/636-3300, www.canadain-ternational.gc.ca/israel, taviv@international.gc.ca) is in Tel Aviv. Canada does not maintain a consulate in Jerusalem.

The Embassy of Australia (Discount Bank Tower, Level 28, 23 Yehuda Halevi St., Tel Aviv, tel. 03/693-5000, www.israel.embassy.gov.au) is in Tel Aviv. Australia does not maintain a consulate in Jerusalem.

COMMUNICATIONS AND MEDIA
Internet Access
One of the best features of Israel is the fact that you get free wireless Internet almost everywhere you go. Most restaurants, cafés, and coffee shops have free wireless Internet, so as long as you have a computer you can get Internet access. Internet cafés are much less common, but most large luxury hotels with business centers will agree to let you use their business center computers for a small fee.

Printed and Online News
There are several major newspapers in English, Arabic, Hebrew, and Russian that are distributed throughout Israel and the West Bank. Those published in English and Hebrew include the *Jerusalem Post, Ha'aretz,* and *Yedioth Ahronoth* (known online as Ynet), among others. The *International New York Times* is published only in English, and the *Jerusalem Report* is an English-only magazine sold in bookstores and on newsstands.

Arabic publications include *al-Sennara* and *al-Ittihad,* among others.

MAPS AND TOURIST INFORMATION
Maps
Israel's Ministry of Tourism (goisrael.com) has online maps of major cities and pilgrimage sites as PDF files that can be easily printed. Eye on Israel (www.eyeonisrael.com) has interactive maps of Israel and major cities, including tourist sites, hotels, geographical information, and a historical atlas. Hard copy maps, including city maps, road maps, touring maps, and hiking maps are available for online purchase on the Ministry of Housing and Construction's website (www.gov.il).

Tourism Offices
There are tourist offices located throughout Israel in major cities, including in Tel Aviv (Ben-Gurion International Airport, tel. 03/975-4260, doritk@tourism.gov.il, open 24 hours a day), Jerusalem (Jaffa Gate, tel. 02/628-0403, orenm@tourism.gov.il, 8:30am-5pm Sat.-Thurs., 8:30am-1pm Fri.), Nazareth (58 Casanova St., tel. 04/675-0555, ronnye@tourism.gov.il, 8:30am-5pm Mon.-Fri., 9am-1pm Sat.), Eilat (8 Beit Hagesher St., tel. 08/630-9111, eilatinfo@tourism.gov.il, 8:30am-5pm Sun.-Thurs., 8am-1pm Sat.), and Haifa (48 Ben-Gurion St., www.tour-haifa.co.il/eng, 9am-5pm Sun.-Thurs., 9am-1pm Fri., 10am-3pm Sat.).

WEIGHTS AND MEASURES
The Israeli system of weights and measures is based on the metric system. The most common conversions include 1 kilogram (2.2 pounds), 1 meter (1.1 yards), 1 liter (1 quart), 1 dunnam (0.22 acres), and 1 kilometer (about 0.6 miles).

ELECTRICITY
Similar to most European systems, Asia, and the Middle East in general, Israel uses a 220V system (220V-240V) at 50 Hz. European visitors shouldn't have any trouble, except for a possible converter for the unique Israeli

outlet system of a type H plug that has two flat prongs that form a V and one vertical grounding prong on the bottom. You can buy a converter for an American plug at any electronics store for about NIS4.

Visitors from the United States will need to make a few adjustments because they use 110V appliances, and also visitors need to be aware that Israel's 50 Hz system might cause some problems with appliances (such as analog clocks), even with a transformer. Don't plug your 110V directly into an Israeli outlet,

and be careful with bringing a hair dryer from the United States.

TIME ZONES

Israel, the West Bank, and Jordan all operate three hours ahead of Greenwich Mean Time (GMT+3), but only Israel and the West Bank also operate on daylight saving time. They switch to daylight saving time on the last Friday before April 2 and switch back on the last Sunday before Yom Kippur (about late Sept.-Oct.) every year.

Resources

Hebrew Phrasebook

PRONUNCIATION

Hebrew is, for the most part, a straightforward language that is logical and doesn't have very many exceptions.

Consonants

Aleph	Ah-lehf
Bet	BEHT
Gimel	GEE-mel
Dalet	DAH-let
Hey	Hay
Vav	Vahv
Zayin	ZAIN
Khet	het
Tet	TEHT
Yud	YOOD
Kaf	KAHF
Lamed	LAH-med
Mem	Mehm
Nun	NOON
Samech	Sah-Mekh
Ayin	Ah-yeen
Pe	PEH
Tsadi	SAH-di
Quf	KOOF
Resh	Rehsh
Shin	SHEEN
Tav	TAHV

Accent

Through the ages, as the Jewish population spread throughout the world, different accents developed. Most people who speak Hebrew today speak what is known as modern Hebrew, which is the Hebrew that is used in Israel. The variance in pronunciations is seen primarily during religious ceremonies, especially when reading from the Torah.

COMMON PHRASES

Hello, good-bye, or peace *Shalom*
Good morning *Boker tov*
Good evening *Erev tov*
See you soon *L'hitra'ot*
What's up? *Ma nishma?*
Yes *Ken*
No *Lo*
Thank you *Toda*
Excuse me/I'm sorry *Slicha*
Please/You're welcome *Bevakasha*
What is your name? (male/female) *Eich korim lecha/lach?*
My name is… *Shmi…*
How are you? (male/female) *Ma shlomcha/shlomech?*
Fine, OK *B'seder*
Not good *Lo tov*
Excellent *Metzuyan*
I'm tired (male/female) *Ani ayef/ayefa*

BASIC, COURTEOUS, AND RELIGIOUS EXPRESSIONS

Please excuse me *Slicha bevakasha*
Just a minute *Shneeyah*
Just hold on a minute *Shneeyah rega*
No thank you *Lo toda*
Thanks to God *Toda le-El*
Happy holiday *Hag sahmeah*

EATING AND SHOPPING

Do you have...? (male/female) Yesh lecha/lach...?
How much? Kama zeh oleh?
I want... (male/female) Ani rotzeh/rotzah...
I don't want... (male/female) Ani lo rotzeh/rotzah...
Money Kesef
Change (literally, "leftovers") Odef
Waiter/waitress Meltzar/meltzarit (though you will always just say Slicha)
Water Mayim
Coffee Kafeh
Latte Kafeh Afuh
Tea Tay

GETTING AROUND

I'm going to...(male/female) Ani nose'a l'.../Ani nosa'at l'...
There is... Yesh...
There is no... Ain...
Do you know where...is? (male/female) Aht yoda'at eifoh nimtza...?/Ata yodea eifoh nimtza...?
Wait/Just a moment Rega
Restaurant Mis'adah
Bathroom (services) Sherutim
Post office (mail) Do'ar
Street Rechov
Boulevard Sderot
Market Shuk
Museum Muzion
Synagogue Beit knesset
Church Knaissia
Central bus station Tachana merkazit
Taxi (regular) Monit
Shared taxi Sherut
Automobile Mechonit
Train Rakevet
Bus Otoboos
Hotel Malon
Hostel Akhsaniya
Room Cheder
Beach Chof
Grocery store Makolet
What is this?/What is the reason for this? Mah zeh?

Food Okhel
Right Yemina
Left Smola
Straight Yashar

AT THE BORDER AND AT CHECKPOINTS

Passport Darkon
Open (your trunk) Leef to ach
Are you American? Ahtah Amerikai?

EMERGENCIES

Do you speak English? (male/female) Ata medaber Anglit?/Aaht medaberet Anglit?
I don't speak Hebrew (male/female) Ani lo medaber Ivrit/Ani lo medaberet Ivrit
Police Mishtara
Doctor Rofe
Hospital Beit cholim
Passport Darkon

USEFUL QUESTIONS

Who Mi
What Mah
When Matai
Where Eh-fo
Why Lama
What is this? Mah zeh?
How Eich
How much does it cost? Kamah zeh oleh?
Where are the restrooms? Eifo hasherutim?
What time is it? Mah hasha'ah?
What happened? Mah karah?

NUMBERS

One Achat
Two Shtayim
Three Shalosh
Four Arba
Five Chamesh
Six Shesh
Seven Sheva
Eight Shmone
Nine Tesha

Ten *Eser*
Eleven *Achat esrey*
Twelve *Shtem esrey*
Thirteen *Shlosh esrey*
Fourteen *Arba esrey*
Fifteen *Chamesh esrey*
Sixteen *Shesh esrey*
Seventeen *Shva esrey*
Eighteen *Shmoneh esrey*
Nineteen *Tsha esrey*
Twenty *Esrim*
Thirty *Shloshim*
Forty *Arbaim*
Fifty *Chamishim*
Sixty *Shishim*
Seventy *Shivim*
Eighty *Shmonim*
Ninety *Tishim*
One hundred *Mea*
Two hundred *Mataim*
Three hundred *Shlosh meot*
Four hundred *Arba meot*
Five hundred *Chamesh meot*
Six hundred *Shesh meot*
Seven hundred *Shva meot*

Eight hundred *Shmone meot*
Nine hundred *Tsha meot*
One thousand *Elef*
Two thousand *Alpayeem*
Three thousand *Shloshet alafim*

DAYS OF THE WEEK

Sunday *Yom rishon*
Monday *Yom shenee*
Tuesday *Yom shlishi*
Wednesday *Yom revi'i*
Thursday *Yom chamishi*
Friday *Yom shishi*
Saturday (Sabbath) *Shabbat*

TIMES

Hour, time *Sha'a*
Day *Yom*
Week *Shavua*
Month *Chodesh*
Year *Shana*
Today *Ha'yom*
Yesterday *Etmol*
Tomorrow *Machar*

Arabic Phrasebook

BASIC PHRASES

Hello, nice to meet you *Marhaba ana
saeed b-mareftak*
Do you speak English? *Hal tatakallam al
ingliyziyya?*
Do you understand English? *Hal tafham
al ingliyziyya?*
Yes *Na-am*
No *Laa*
I understand *Fahamt*
I do not understand *Laa afham*
Please repeat *Aiyd law samaht*
Good morning *Sabaah il-khair*
Good evening *Masa il-khair*
Good night *Tisibh ala khair*

Hello *Marhaba*
Hello (response) *Ahlan*
Goodbye *Ma-a is-salaama*
How are you? (male/female) *Kayf
haalak/haalik?*
Fine *Bikhair*

ASKING FOR HELP

I don't speak Arabic *Ana laa atahadith
al-arabiya*
Please speak more slowly *Laww samaht
tahadith ala mahil*
Where is the bathroom? *Ayn il-
hammaam?*
I'm sorry *Ana aasiff*

Suggested Reading

MODERN HISTORY AND CURRENT AFFAIRS

There are numerous books about the current affairs and modern history of Israel and the region, but a few stand out. Also, once you are in Israel, look for the fairly robust selections in the English sections of bookstores that have titles by regional authors.

Carter, Jimmy. *Palestine: Peace Not Apartheid.* Simon and Schuster, 2006. A controversial look by former president Carter on how to bring peace to Israel and justice to Palestine.

Cohen, Rich. *Israel is Real: An Obsessive Quest to Understand the Jewish Nation and Its History.* Picador, 2009. An entertaining yet scholarly look at the history of the Jewish people from the time of the destruction of the Second Temple through the modern era.

Oz, Amos. *How to Cure a Fanatic.* Princeton University Press, 2010. Amos Oz is a beloved Israeli author and also internationally acclaimed. His pair of essays are about how to settle the question of real estate to bring peace to the Israeli-Palestinian relationship.

Senor, Dan, and Saul Singer. *Start-up Nation: The Story of Israel's Economic Miracle.* Twelve, 2009. A comprehensive and illuminating look at how Israel, a country of just over seven million people and limited resources, manages to produce more start-ups than more stable and well-developed countries like Japan, Canada, and the United Kingdom.

Zertal, Idith, and Akiva Eldar. *Lords of the Land: The War for Israel's Settlements in the Occupied Territories, 1967-2007.* Nation Books, 2009. The tragic yet gripping story of Jewish settlement in the West Bank and Gaza Strip and how it has impacted every facet of modern Israeli life, as told by a professor (Zertal) and a leading journalist (Eldar).

HISTORICAL CHRONICLES

Among the mountains of historical chronicles that have been published, there are several that are must-reads.

Collins, Larry, and Dominique LaPierre. *O Jerusalem!* Simon and Schuster, 1972. The extremely thick book is an account of the bitter 1948 dispute between the Arabs and Jews over Jerusalem and emphasizes prominent individuals and the British in the process.

Flavius, Josephus, and William Whiston (translation). *The Wars of the Jews.* Digireads.com, 2010. One of the most frequently referenced historians of his time, Flavius Josephus was a Jewish historian and Roman citizen who wrote detailed (and some say questionable) accounts of the events of his time in AD 75.

Oren, Michael. *Six Days of War: June 1967 and the Making of the Modern Middle East.* Presidio Press/Random House, 2002. This international best-seller by the U.S. ambassador to Israel details six days of the definitive Arab-Israeli battle in June 1967 and its lingering impact on the peace process and the world.

Suha, Sabbagh. *Palestinian Women of Gaza and the West Bank.* Indiana University Press, 1998. A collection of insider perspective essays on the roles of women in Gaza and the West Bank and their approach to dealing with issues of gender, feminism, and politics.

LITERATURE

The literary scene in Israel and the West Bank is robust, but there are a few voices who dominate the industry.

Grossman, David. *Someone to Run With.* Farrar, Straus and Giroux, 2000. The fictional story of life and love on the streets of Jerusalem, told from the perspective of a 16-year-old boy.

Oz, Amos. *Scenes from Village Life.* Houghton Mifflin Harcourt, 2011. A collection of essays set in a bygone era in a fictitious pioneer village.

FOOD

A great selection of books on food in the region can be found at local bookstores.

El-Haddad, Laila, and Maggie Schmitt. *The Gaza Kitchen: A Palestinian Culinary Journey.* Just World Books, 2013. Full of rich illustrations, this book explores the culinary heritage of people living in Gaza and the West Bank, using recipes from their kitchens.

Ottolenghi, Yotam, and Sami Tamimi. *Jerusalem: A Cookbook.* Ten Speed Press, 2012. Jerusalem locals Ottolenghi and Tamimi explore the cuisine of their home city with its varied cultural and religious influences.

TRAVEL AND EXPLORATION

Insider guides to the region are largely published in Hebrew, and there are a few specialized guides to specific regional travel experiences.

Saar, Jacob. *Israel National Trail and the Jerusalem Trail (Hike the Land of Israel).* Gefen, 2011. A full guide to the Israel National Trail and the Jerusalem Trail and the hiking experiences they present, including maps and tips for the trail.

Szepsi, Stefan. *Walking Palestine: 25 Journeys into the West Bank.* Interlink Books, 2012. An alternative look at how to skip the politics of the West Bank and just experience its natural beauty through beginner walks and more advanced hikes, including information for local guides, restaurants, and accommodations.

POLITICAL

The plethora of political books related to Israel and the West Bank is astounding, but you can start with some classics, old and new.

Said, Edward. *Orientalism.* Vintage Books, 1979. From one of the region's most noted critics and authors comes an examination of how the West observes Arabs.

Shehadeh, Raja, and Penny Johnson. *Shifting Sands: The Unraveling of the Old Order in the Middle East.* Profile, 2015. A collection of essays edited by Shehadeh and Johnson about the shifting power paradigm in the Middle East.

Yousef, Mosab Hassan, and Ron Brackin. *Son of Hamas: A Gripping Account of Terror, Betrayal, Political Intrigue, and Unthinkable Choices.* Tyndale, 2010. A controversial, real-life account from the eldest son of a founding member of Hamas.

THE HOLOCAUST

The number of books written on the Holocaust is almost countless, and titles continue to be published every year.

Range, Peter Ross. *1924: The Year That Made Hitler.* Hachette Book Group, 2016. The dark story of Hitler's life in the year 1924 and how it shaped the monster that he would become.

Safdie, Moshe. *Yad Vashem: Moshe Safdie— The Architecture of Memory.* Lars Mueller Publishers, 2006. Israel's most famous and prolific architect examines his painstakingly designed project: the Yad Vashem Holocaust memorial in Jerusalem.

Suggested Viewing

MODERN CULTURE AND CURRENT AFFAIRS

The Israeli movie industry is very active and films often become nominees for Academy Awards. Following are a few selections.

Binisty, Thierry. *A Bottle in the Gaza Sea.* 100 minutes, 2011, Hebrew and Arabic subtitled in English. Two teenagers, a Jewish girl in Israel and an Arab boy in Gaza, change the course of their lives after becoming pen pals.

Burshtein, Rama. *Fill the Void.* 90 minutes, 2012, Hebrew and French subtitled in English. A young orthodox woman is pressured into marriage with a widower.

Yedaya, Keren. *Jaffa.* 106 minutes, 2009, Hebrew and Arabic subtitled in English. A look at the intersecting lives of Jews and Arabs in Tel Aviv's Jaffa.

Internet Resources

There are a good number of websites with useful information about Israel, the West Bank, and Jordan in English. Some websites are slow to update or are missing information, so it's always a good idea to cross-reference information. The following is a selection of the best, most relevant, and most useful.

JERUSALEM

GoJerusalem.com
www.gojerusalem.com
A private venture dubbed simply GoJerusalem.com contains helpful, descriptive, and fairly up-to-date listings on hotels, tours, and sightseeing, though much of the information has been republished on iTravelJerusalem.

iTravelJerusalem
www.itraveljerusalem.com
The official tourism website of the city of Jerusalem was launched in 2012 and has current information on food, accommodations, sightseeing, and events.

The Municipality of the City of Jerusalem
www.jerusalem.muni.il
The Municipality of the City of Jerusalem website has basic information about the city and some resources for visitors.

GOVERNMENT

Israeli Government
www.gov.il
The Israeli government portal is a good jumping-off point for any branch of the Israeli government online.

Israeli Ministry of Foreign Affairs
www.mfa.gov.il
The official site for the Israeli Ministry of Foreign Affairs has domestic facts, issues, statistics, and foreign government relations information.

TOURISM AND CITIES

City of Haifa
www.tour-haifa.co.il/eng
The City of Haifa's official tourism website is a good resource for navigating the city.

City of Tel Aviv
www.tel-aviv.gov.il
The City of Tel Aviv's official website also has useful information, maps, and tips.

Eye on Israel
www.eyeonisrael.com
The private enterprise Eye on Israel offers interactive maps of Israel and its major cities, including tourist sites, hotels, geographical information, and a historical atlas.

Israeli Ministry of Tourism
www.goisrael.com
The official Israeli Ministry of Tourism website has online maps of major cities and pilgrimage sites as PDF files that can be easily printed.

Tel Aviv Tourism Board
www.visit-tel-aviv.com
The Tel Aviv Tourism Board's official website has every kind of information you could possibly need to enjoy the city by day or night.

PARKS AND RECREATION

Israel Nature and Parks Authority
www.parks.org.il
The official website of the Israel Nature and Parks Authority contains a comprehensive listing of the names, locations, admission fees, descriptions, and contact information for national parks and nature reserves throughout Israel (if you can get the spelling of the park right).

Israel National Trail
www.israelnationaltrail.com
A useful guide to the Israel National Trail, with maps, information, and guidelines to taking the hike.

FOOD

Tel Aviv Food
http://telavivfood.wordpress.com
An extremely useful blog with amateur but very detailed reviews of a range of Tel Aviv restaurants, this blog is run by a team of local Tel Aviv foodies with a distinctive fork-rating system and tons of photographs.

ACCOMMODATIONS

Israel Youth Hostel Association (IYHA)
www.iyha.org.il/eng
The official website of the Israel Youth Hostel Association (IYHA) is easy to use and allows you to check the availability of youth hostels in Israel by region.

Zimmeril.com
www.zimmeril.com
Though not an official site for *zimmers,* this site has a fairly comprehensive listing of Israel's *zimmers* (guesthouses) throughout the country, including their contact information, which can be very hard to find otherwise.

TRANSPORTATION

Dan Buses
www.dan.co.il
The official website of the Tel Aviv city bus line Dan has route and ticketing information.

Egged
www.egged.co.il/Eng
The official website of Israel's national bus company Egged, which also operates throughout Jerusalem, has route and ticket information, but you need to dig a bit to get the right bus number.

Israel Railways
www.rail.co.il/EN
The official website of Israel's national train system has convenient and easy to use listings of times and prices for rail tickets.

Jerusalem Light-Rail
www.citypass.co.il
Jerusalem's official light-rail website has

schedule, ticketing, a route map, and news updates for passengers.

Tel-O-Fun Bikes
www.tel-o-fun.co.il/en
Tel Aviv's citywide bicycle rental website for the green Tel-O-Fun Bikes has detailed instructions and payment and usage information for bike rentals.

WEST BANK
This Week in Palestine
www.thisweekinpalestine.com
The website of the weekly publication *This Week in Palestine* is a useful guide for events and things happening in the West Bank.

Travel Palestine
http://travelpalestine.ps
The official tourism website for the West Bank is not as robust or user-friendly as it could be, but it is one of the few online resources of its kind available in English.

Visit Palestine
www.visitpalestine.ps/en
Another tourism website called Visit Palestine is more detailed and comprehensive than Travel Palestine site, and it's very easy to use.

JORDAN
Jordan Ministry of Tourism and Antiquities
www.tourism.jo
The official website of the Jordan Ministry of Tourism and Antiquities is particularly useful for background and historical information.

Jordan Tourism Board
www.visitjordan.com
The official tourism website of Jordan has the basic information you might need before visiting.

Petra Development and Tourism Regional Authority
www.visitpetra.jo
The official website of the Petra Development and Tourism Regional Authority has good general information about a wide range of things from currency rates to background information.

Wadi Rum
www.wadirum.jo
Petra's neighboring village Wadi Rum has a website that is a good resource for local information on restaurants, hotels, and resources.

Index

List of Maps

Photo Credits

Title Page: Petra by Night Show © Joseph Calev | Dreamstime.com; page 4: flamingoes in Eilat © Dafna Tal/www.goisrael.com; page 5: (top) souvenir shop in Hebron © Genevieve Belmaker, (bottom) bread cart in Jerusalem © VanderWolfImages | Dreamstime.com; page 6 (top left) © Alexandr Makarenko | Dreamstime.com, (top right) © Milesfoto | Dreamstime.com, (bottom) © Noam Chen/www.goisrael.com; page 7 (top) Maria Barski/123rf.com, (bottom left) © Rafael Ben-ari | Dreamstime.com, (bottom right) © Israel Ministry of Tourism; page 8 © Dana Friedlander/www.goisrael.com; page 9 (top) © Rafael Ben-ari | Dreamstime.com, (bottom left) © Rafael Ben-ari | Dreamstime.com, (bottom right) © Rndmst | Dreamstime.com; page 10 © Rafael Ben-ari | Dreamstime.com; page 11 © Israel Ministry of Tourism; page 12 © Rndmst | Dreamstime.com; page 13 © Nataliya Pylayeva | Dreamstime.com; page 14 © Evgeniy Fesenko | Dreamstime.com; page 15 © Rafael Ben-ari | Dreamstime.com; page 16 © Rafael Ben-ari | Dreamstime.com; page 17 (left) © Mira Agron | Dreamstime.com, (right) © Serbysh | Dreamstime.com; page 18 © Rafael Ben-ari | Dreamstime.com; page 19 © Itamar Grinberg/www.goisrael.com; page 20 © Moreno Soppelsa | Dreamstime.com; page 21 (top) © Genevieve Belmaker, (bottom) © Rafael Ben-ari | Dreamstime.com; page 22 © Inna Felker | Dreamstime.com; page 23 © 2016 National Photo Collection/Mark Neyman; page 24 © Rafal Kubiak | Dreamstime.com; page 25 © Evan Spiler | Dreamstime.com; page 26 © Nina J. Grant; page 27 © Dana Friedlander/www.goisrael.com; page 29 © Inna Felker | Dreamstime.com; pages 30-31 the Mount of Olives © Israel Ministry of Tourism; page 31 prayer in the women's section of the Western Wall © Mira Agron | Dreamstime.com; page 32 © Wiltding | Dreamstime.com; page 33 (top) © Eunika Sopotnicka/123rf.com, (bottom) © Kyrylo Glivin/123rf.com; page 35 © Rafael Ben-Ari/123rf.com; page 44 © rndms/123rf.com; page 45 © Noam Chen/www.goisrael.com; page 46 © 2016 National Photo Collection/Moshe Milner; page 47 © 2016 National Photo Collection/Mark Neyman; page 48 © 2016 National Photo Collection/Amos Ben Gershom; page 51 © Genevieve Belmaker; page 52 © Genevieve Belmaker; page 54 © Andrey Shevchenko | Dreamstime.com; page 55 © 2016 National Photo Collection/Moshe Milner; page 56 © Jacek Sopotnicki | Dreamstime.com; page 58 © 2016 National Photo Collection/Mark Neyman; page 60 © 2016 National Photo Collection/Amos Ben Gershom; page 62 © www.goisrael.com; pages 65-79 © Genevieve Belmaker; page 86 © Grand Café; page 88 © Noam Chen/www.goisrael.com; page 89 © Waldorf Astoria; page 97 © Genevieve Belmaker; page 99 © Dr. L Ereshefsky; page 101 © Alexandr Makarenko | Dreamstime.com; page 103 (top) © Dmitry Pistrov/123rf.com, (bottom) © liorpt/123rf.com; page 105 © Heike Jestram/123rf.com; page 109 © Dana Friedlander/www.goisrael.com; page 112 © Dana Friedlander/www.goisrael.com; page 113 © rndms/123rf.com; pages 114-118 © Dana Friedlander/www.goisrael.com; page 119 © Israel Ministry of Tourism; page 124 © Rafael Ben-Ari/123rf.com; page 125 © Eldad Carin/123rf.com; page 127-131 © Dana Friedlander/www.goisrael.com; page 132 © flik47/123rf.com; page 133-135 © Dana Friedlander/www.goisrael.com; page 148 © Rafael Ben-ari | Dreamstime.com; page 150 (top) © Rafael Ben-Ari/123rf.com, (bottom) © liorpt/123rf.com; page 151 © Mikhail Kusayev/123rf.com; page 155 © Itamar Grinberg/Israel Ministry of Tourism; pages 158-159 © Genevieve Belmaker; page 161 © Irina Opachevsky/123rf.com; pages 163-164 © Genevieve Belmaker; page 167 © 1926 Hotel; page 171 © Irina Opachevsky | Dreamstime.com; page 173 © Hitmans | Dreamstime.com; page 174 © Maurizio Giovanni Bersanelli/123rf.com; page 175 © Efendi Hotel/Assaf Pinchuk; page 177 © alex postovski/123rf.com; page 180 © vvvita/123rf.com; 181 © Israel Ministry of Tourism; page 183 © Genevieve Belmaker; page 186 © Rafael Ben-Ari/123rf.com; page 189 (top) © ella/123rf.com, (bottom) © Leonid Pilnik/123rf.com; page 191 © Itamar Grinberg/Israel Ministry of Tourism; page 197 © Zvonimir Atletic/123rf.com; page 198 © Itamar Grinberg/Israel Ministry of Tourism; page 199 © Israel Ministry of Tourism; page 200 © Irina Opachevsky | Dreamstime.com; page 206 © Israel Ministry of Tourism; page 208 © Mordagan/Israel Ministry of Tourism;

Also Available

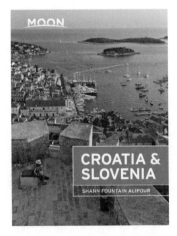

MAP SYMBOLS

▦ Expressway	○ City/Town	✈ Airport	⚐ Golf Course	
▦ Primary Road	◉ State Capital	✈ Airfield	🅿 Parking Area	
▦ Secondary Road	⊛ National Capital	▲ Mountain	⬟ Archaeological Site	
⋯ Unpaved Road	★ Point of Interest	✦ Unique Natural Feature	⛪ Church	
── Feature Trail	• Accommodation		⛽ Gas Station	
┄┄ Other Trail	▼ Restaurant/Bar	🕊 Waterfall		
⋯ Ferry	■ Other Location	♠ Park	〰 Glacier	
▦ Pedestrian Walkway		⬧ Trailhead	Mangrove	
▥ Stairs	∧ Campground	⛷ Skiing Area	Reef	
			Swamp	

CONVERSION TABLES

°C = (°F - 32) / 1.8
°F = (°C x 1.8) + 32
1 inch = 2.54 centimeters (cm)
1 foot = 0.304 meters (m)
1 yard = 0.914 meters
1 mile = 1.6093 kilometers (km)
1 km = 0.6214 miles
1 fathom = 1.8288 m
1 chain = 20.1168 m
1 furlong = 201.168 m
1 acre = 0.4047 hectares
1 sq km = 100 hectares
1 sq mile = 2.59 square km
1 ounce = 28.35 grams
1 pound = 0.4536 kilograms
1 short ton = 0.90718 metric ton
1 short ton = 2,000 pounds
1 long ton = 1.016 metric tons
1 long ton = 2,240 pounds
1 metric ton = 1,000 kilograms
1 quart = 0.94635 liters
1 US gallon = 3.7854 liters
1 Imperial gallon = 4.5459 liters
1 nautical mile = 1.852 km

MOON ISRAEL & THE WEST BANK

Avalon Travel
A Hachette Book Group company
1700 Fourth Street
Berkeley, CA 94710, USA
www.moon.com

Editor and Series Manager: Kathryn Ettinger
Copy Editor: Ashley Benning
Graphics Coordinator: Elizabeth Jang
Production Coordinator: Elizabeth Jang
Cover Design: Faceout Studios, Charles Brock
Interior Design: Domini Dragoone
Moon Logo: Tim McGrath
Map Editor: Albert Angulo
Cartographers: Brian Shotwell, Albert Angulo,
    Stephanie Poulain
Indexer: Deana Shields

ISBN-13: 978-1-63121-361-8
ISSN: 2473-8387

Printing History
1st Edition — November 2016
5 4 3 2 1

Text © 2016 by Genevieve Belmaker.
Maps © 2016 by Avalon Travel.
All rights reserved.

Front cover photo: a camel and rider near Dormition
    Abbey in Jerusalem © Mark Pearson / Alamy

Back cover photo: colorful souvenirs for sale
    © Amilevin | Dreamstime.com

Printed in Canada by Friesens

KEEPING CURRENT

If you have a favorite gem you'd like to see included in the next edition, or
see anything that needs updating, clarification, or correction, please drop
us a line. Send your comments via email to feedback@moon.com, or use the
address above.